Post-Olympism?

Global Sport Cultures

Eds. Gary Armstrong, *Brunel University*, Richard Giulianotti, *University of Aberdeen*, and David Andrews, *The University of Maryland*

From the Olympics and the World Cup to extreme sports and kabaddi, the social significance of sport at both global and local levels has become increasingly clear in recent years. The contested nature of identity is widely addressed in the social sciences, but sport as a particularly revealing site of such contestation, in both industrializing and post-industrial nations, has been less fruitfully explored. Further, sport and sporting corporations are increasingly powerful players in the world economy. Sport is now central to the social and technological development of mass media, notably in telecommunications and digital television. It is also a crucial medium through which specific populations and political elites communicate and interact with each other on a global stage.

Berg Publishers are pleased to announce a new book series that will examine and evaluate the role of sport in the contemporary world. Truly global in scope, the series seeks to adopt a grounded, constructively critical stance towards prior work within sport studies and to answer such questions as:

- How are sports experienced and practised at the everyday level within local settings?
- How do specific cultures construct and negotiate forms of social stratification (such as gender, class, ethnicity) within sporting contexts?
- What is the impact of mediation and corporate globalisation upon local sports cultures?

Determinedly interdisciplinary, the series will nevertheless privilege anthropological, historical and sociological approaches, but will consider submissions from cultural studies, economics, geography, human kinetics, international relations, law, philosophy and political science. The series is particularly committed to research that draws upon primary source materials or ethnographic fieldwork.

Books already published in the series:

Fear and Loathing in World Football, *edited by Gary Armstrong and Richard Giulianotti*

Mud, Sweat and Beers: A Cultural History of Sport and Alcohol, *by Tony Collins and Wray Vamplew*

Sport and Postcolonialism, *edited by John Bale and Mike Cronin*

Football in France: A Social History, *by Geoff Hare*

GLOBAL SPORT CULTURES

Post-Olympism?
Questioning Sport in the Twenty-first Century

Edited by
John Bale and Mette Krogh Christensen

Oxford • New York

First published in 2004 by
Berg
Editorial offices:
1st Floor, Angel Court, 81 St Clements Street, Oxford OX4 1AW, UK
175 Fifth Avenue, New York, NY 10010, USA

Berg is the imprint of Oxford International Publishers Ltd.

Library of Congress Cataloging-in-Publication Data
A catalogue record for this book is available from the Library of Congress.

British Library Cataloguing-in-Publication Data
A catalogue record for this book is available from the British Library.

ISBN   1 85973 714 5 (Cloth)
       1 85973 719 6 (Paper)

Typeset by JS Typesetting Ltd, Wellingborough, Northants
Printed in the United Kingdom by Biddles Ltd, King's Lynn

www.bergpublishers.com

Contents

Contents

Acknowledgements

The chapters in this book were originally presented as papers at a conference (bearing the same title as the book) held in Aarhus, Denmark, in September 2002. The conference was organized by the Department of Sports Science and the Centre for Cultural Research at Aarhus University and we must thank colleagues for collaborating in this project. We therefore acknowledge the support of Jens-Ole Jensen, Jens Behrend Christensen, Thorsten Hansen, Ole Høiris and Ulla Rasmussen. Ulla's secretarial and general organizational skills were soon recognized as being second to none.

For help in funding the conference we must thank the Department of Sports Science and the Faculty of Science at Aarhus University, the Danish Sports Federation, the Danish Ministry of Culture and Team Denmark. Without the support of these organizations, the production of this interdisciplinary and international collection would have been impossible.

We are extremely grateful to our authors for submitting their chapters (more or less) on time and for providing excellent manuscripts which required the minimum of editing. At Berg we would like to thank Kathryn Earle, Anne Hobbs, Jenny Howell and Felicity Howlett for their patience, help and support in transforming what started off as a set of conference papers into a coherent text.

John Bale
Mette Krogh Christensen

Notes on Contributors

John Bale teaches and researches at Aarhus University, Denmark and Keele University, UK. He has been a visiting professor at the University of Jyväskylä, Finland, the University of Western Ontario, Canada, and the University of Queensland, Australia. His most recent books are *Imagined Olympians* (University of Minnesota Press, 2002) and *Running Cultures* (Frank Cass, 2004). He has also edited (with Mike Cronin) *Sport and Postcolonialism* (Berg, 2003).

Douglas Booth is a professor at Waikato University, New Zealand and teaches courses on the history of sport. He is the author of *The Race Game: Sport and Politics in South Africa* (1998) and *Australian Beach Cultures: The History of Sun, Sand and Surf* (2001). Professor Booth is currently undertaking research into knowledge and methods in the history of sport.

Douglas Brown is an assistant professor in the Faculty of Kinesiology at the University of Calgary. His research is both historical and ethnographic. He attempts to reorient the critical eyes of researchers and students on the physical experience of movement rather than merely the spectating experience. In the past, he has examined the aesthetic imperative that Pierre de Coubertin envisioned for modern sport and the Olympic Games. He also studies the culture of mountaineering in the Canadian Rocky Mountains.

Susan Brownell was a nationally ranked athlete in the US before winning a gold medal in the heptathlon at the 1986 Chinese National College Games, while studying at Beijing University. Her experiences are recounted in her book *Training the Body for China: Sports in the Moral Order of the People's Republic* (1995). She is an associate professor and Chair of the Department of Anthropology at the University of Missouri, St Louis.

Ben Carrington teaches sociology and cultural studies at the University of Brighton, England. He has edited (with Ian McDonald) *'Race', Sport and British Society* (Taylor and Francis, 2001).

Richard Cashman is an Associate Professor in History and Director of the Centre for Olympic Studies at the University of New South Wales and is also the

President of the Australian Society for Sports History. His special interests are Australian and Asian sports history, including colonization and decolonization, the Olympic Games and mega-events. Some recent books include *Sport in the National Imagination: Australian Sport in the Federation Decades* (2002) and *Staging the Olympics: The Event and its Impact* (1999), edited with Anthony Hughes.

Mette Krogh Christensen teaches and researches at the Department of Sport Science, Aarhus University, Denmark. Her research interests lie in the fields of life histories of physical education teachers and sports participants and in educational aspects of sports. She has published several books and academic papers.

Søren Damkjær studied at Dartmouth College, University of Copenhagen, the Sorbonne and Moscow State University. He is associate professor of Cultural Sociology and Sports Sciences at the University of Copenhagen. His present research interests comprise general sociology, the sociology and philosophy of the body, philosophy (in particular, aesthetics) and the theory of movement and dance.

Henning Eichberg is a cultural sociologist and historian. He is research fellow at the Research Institute of Sport, Culture and Civil Society (IFO) in Gerlev, Denmark. His fields of study are the history and cultural sociology of body culture and sport; the cultural ecology of movement, the history of early modern military technology; Indonesian studies and studies in democracy, ethnic minorities and national identity.

John Hoberman is a professor of Germanic languages at the University of Texas at Austin. He is author of several books on various aspects of sports. These include *Sport and Political Ideology* (1984), *Mortal Engines* (1992) and *Darwin's Athletes* (1997). He is a visiting professor at the University of Southern Denmark at Odense.

Arnd Krüger is a professor of sport science and head of the Sport and Society Section at George-August Universität in Göttingen. He is the author of more than twenty books. He has served three terms as Dean of the Social Science Faculty of his university. His most recent publications include *The Nazi Olympics* (edited with William Murray, University of Illinois Press, 2003). He is also a former Olympian and has served as president of the European Committee for the History of Sports.

Helen Jefferson Lenskyj is a professor at the Ontario Institute for Studies in Education, University of Toronto. As a sport sociologist, she has specialized in gender and sexuality issues since 1980, and in Olympic industry critiques since 1992. Her two most recent books are *Inside the Olympic Industry: Power, Politics and Activism* (SUNY, 2000) and *The Best Olympics Ever? Social Impacts of Sydney 2000* (SUNY, 2002).

Sigmund Loland is professor of sport philosophy at the Norwegian University for Sport and Physical Education in Oslo. His research interests include ethics of sport, epistemological issues in sport and sport science, sport and ecology, and the history of ideas of sport. His latest book is *Fair Play in Sport – A Moral Norm System* (Routledge, 2002).

Verner Møller is associate professor at the Institute of Sport Science and Clinical Biomecanics in the Faculty of Health Sciences at the University of Southern Denmark. He has edited and written books on sports, health and doping and has co-edited (with John Nauright) the anthology *The Essence of Sport* (2003). His main field of research is body culture, health, drugs and elite sports.

Synthia Sydnor is an associate professor at the University of Illinois where she has appointments in kinesiology, criticism and interpretive theory, cultural studies and interpretive research and the John Henry Newman Institute of Catholic Thought. She has been a National Endowment for the Humanities fellow, book review editor of the *Journal of Sport History* and is currently an assistant editor of *Journal of Sport and Social Issues*.

Alan Tomlinson is professor of sport and leisure studies at the University of Brighton, UK, where he leads the Sport and Leisure Cultures research group and heads the Chelsea School Research Centre. He studied humanities and sociology at the University of Kent, took master's and doctoral degrees at the University of Sussex, has written many articles, and authored or edited more than thirty books/volumes, on the social history and sociology of sport, popular culture, leisure and consumption.

Kevin B. Wamsley is a sport historian at the University of Western Ontario, where he is Director of the International Centre for Olympic Studies. He has published in the areas of Canadian Sport History and on the Olympic Games, particularly in the areas of politics and gender. He is also co-editor of *OLYMPIKA: The International Journal of Olympic Studies*.

Introduction: Post-Olympism?

John Bale and Mette Krogh Christensen

This book raises questions about the nature and future of achievement sport in the twenty-first century by focusing specifically on sport's high altar, the Olympic Games. The Olympics has become achievement sport *in extremis*. In this book we seek to look *beyond* Olympism, hence our title, *Post-Olympism?* (note the all-important question mark). We take 'post-Olympism' both literally and metaphorically. Some chapters *do* look towards the future, offering suggestive scenarios, but others look back (to the future?) to past Olympic events in order to evaluate their post-Olympic-ness, or to explore the effects that the Games have had on the places and spaces they have previously occupied. Additionally, several chapters reappraise the ways in which the Olympics has been conventionally written and researched.

A vast amount has been written about the modern Olympic Games. A bibliography of written works about the subject would turn out to be a tome in itself. Representations of the Olympics range across a huge spectrum – from statistical gazetteers to sensitive biographies of Olympic heroes; from staid histories to sensational exposés; and from status quo reviews to neo-marxist critiques. The Olympics has been read as *the* global event where, by using the global currency of sports, lasting friendships are forged. The Games have also been interpreted as a modern version of 'bread and circuses' where athletes and spectators are duped by rampant commercialization (Brohm, 1978). Given the many and varied ways of representing the Olympics, it is hardly surprising that the interdisciplinary array of authors, whose writings feature in the following chapters, do not nail their flags to any single or particular philosophical mast. Some chapters support the Olympic ideal in principle but all are broadly critical, their critiques coming from various disciplinary, philosophical and ideological sources. More important, perhaps, is that each chapter has something thought-provoking to say about the Olympic Games as we enter the third millennium of their existence in modern form. And as befitting a *post*-Olympic book we also feel that it asks some new questions.

The prefix 'post', applied in recent decades to (at least) modernism, feminism and colonialism, is ambiguous. Several of this book's authors seek, in their respective chapters, to define what they understand by 'post-Olympism'. Drawing on a categorization of forms of postmodernism proposed by geographer Michael Dear (2000), 'post-Olympism' can first be understood as a time period, an era or *epoch*. For example, post-Olympism could be applied to the problematical period following the (re)formulation of the Olympic Games in the final decade of the nineteenth century – an example of a break with precedent. It could also be used to describe a time in the future when some kinds of body cultural practice will post-date what we today know as the Olympics. Additionally, it could be seen as the time period following *each* Olympic Games in which their legacies are explored and evaluated. Furthermore, an age of post-Olympism might be read as a time when the ideals of Olympism, as adumbrated by Pierre de Coubertin, appeared to have been changed in some way – corrupted, exploited or ignored, for example.

Second, post-Olympism can be interpreted as a *type* or *style*. Are late-modern Olympics something fundamentally different from those of the early twentieth century? Are they more predictable, more standardized, more kitsch-like? It could be argued that since, say, 1936, the Olympics has been driven by different ideologies from those perceived by the founding fathers of Olympism, William Penny Brookes and Pierre de Coubertin, or that recent Olympic Games have become kitsch and commercial, bland and banal forms of what preceded them. Post-Olympism as a process could clearly be linked to the processes of colonialism and postcolonialism. After all, Olympism has been a prosletyzing religion, a movement that its modern founder wished to diffuse to all parts of the world. In many senses Olympism formed part of the colonial project, something that we are forcefully reminded of by several authors in this book. Additionally, the post-Olympic might be read as privileging aesthetics over results.

A third way of reading post-Olympism is as a *method* by which the Olympic Games can be explored, interpreted, written and researched. The Olympics has been studied and written (that is, re-presented) by scholars from a variety of academic disciplines (with, we suggest, historians leading the way), as well as by journalists and enthusiasts, propagandists and apologists. However, following the 'linguistic turn' in the humanities and social sciences, explorations of *how* the Olympics has been written and might be represented, seem long overdue. Indeed, we regard this as our starting point in ordering the contents of this book, recognizing that our knowledge of the Olympics is overwhelmingly the result of how the Games are explored and mediated. True, John MacAloon (1992) has questioned the ways in which the Olympics is represented, stressing the need for much more ethnographic work in Olympic research, but little has been done that examines the actual writing of the Games. There is a case for exploring the rhetorical modes that serve to transform the multi-sensual experiences of competing and spectating at the world's major sports event into representations that we consume in mediated form.

Writing the Games

Several chapters in *Post-Olympism?* focus on issues of textual (and to a lesser extent, visual) representation and in Chapter 1 Douglas Booth makes an important start in this direction by scrutinizing the writing of the Olympics. Drawing on literary theory and revisionist historians, Booth examines several styles of tackling the writing of the Games, and deconstructs the different approaches they take. Driving home the significance of the way the Olympics is *written*, he self-consciously adopts the textual tactic of refusing to privilege the 'Olympic Games' as a proper noun. Elsewhere, Booth and Tatz (2000) explain this textually subversive move – their lack of 'veneration of capital letters':

> The ancient Olympic games were held at Olympia, hence the use of upper case as a place name. The modern versions of these super sports festivals bear no resemblance to the ancient version or to the place called Olympia – thus the small 'o'. There may well be – or rather, there may well have been – a case for talking about a *philosophy* of olympism, but that gives it no greater claim to a capital letter than liberalism, humanitarianism, authoritarianism, fascism or utopianism. (Booth and Tatz 2000, p. xv)

Drawing on the work of Benedict Anderson (1983, p. 5), we can argue that Olympism-with-a- capital-O has a tendency to deny its status as an ideology and instead, to hypostatize it, to present it as something substantial or unchanging. As has been noted, 'there is no immutable code of Olympism' – what is acceptable has been modified over time and is interpreted differently from place to place (Tomlinson and Whannel, 1984, p. ix). While we have not insisted that all authors adopt Booth's textual ploy, his intervention into the conventional writing of the very word 'Olympic' does illustrate the problem of re-presenting the Olympics. We are dependent mainly on written work for our knowledge and senses of the Games, and of what they are. Booth's way of writing the 'olympics' is no trendy textual trick. In his own way he shows that words do matter. Thinking beyond the transparency of writing might be said to mark the first step in scripting post-Olympism.

Booth's historiography is followed by Arnd Krüger's interrogation of the record of the 1936 Olympics. Krüger's implication, in Chapter 2, is that the Berlin 'Games' were, in a sense, illustrative of a postmodern condition (perhaps several postmodern conditions), a theme exemplified in later chapters which meld post-Olympism with postmodernism (see Damkjær's wide-ranging Chapter 14). Krüger stresses the impossibility of obtaining anything but an opaque image of the Olympics. Since 1936 (if not before), the writing of the Olympics has been postmodern in the sense that it is impossible to record 'the truth' of the Games. At the same time, the 'Nazi Olympics', and subsequent Games, can be read as simulations of what the Olympics might (be intended to) be. They are rather like Baudrillard's view of the first Gulf War: they did not take place. It is the gloss, the cosmetic and the aesthetic that are important (see chapters 13 to 15 by Møller, Damkjær and Wamsley respectively). What we see and read are flickering images of the Olympics. Other chapters that focus (at least tangentially) on *writing* are exemplified by those by Brown (Chapter 6) with his impressionistic and collage-type style, Tomlinson (Chapter 9) with his experiential encounter (fieldwork, ethnography) with the landscape of the Sydney Olympics, and Sydnor (Chapter 10) with her 'thought exercise'.

Additionally, in writing the Olympics it has been rare to read the various, traditionally muted, 'voices' from individuals and nations historically beyond the full embrace of the modern Olympic movement, though a notable exception is the stunning compilation of materials relating to the 1936 Olympics by Reinhard Rürup (1996). Susan Brownell, Henning Eichberg and Ben Carrington, in Chapters 3 through 5, provide a voice for muted groups such as Chinese Olympic leaders, indigenous Australian athletes and those from tropical Africa respectively. Furthermore, Brown, in Chapter 6, represents the voice of the non-elite sportsperson who utilizes a former Olympic facility. And Helen Lenskyj (Chapter 8) recognizes the voices of those who oppose the presence of such Olympic facilities in their back yards. The chapters noted above, and others in this book, are post-Olympic in the sense that they tend to write *beyond* the canon of Olympic studies.

A Global Currency

The Olympic Games can be read as one of the few cultural forms that bond (to a degree, at least) the world's peoples together. The universal nature of the rules and records of sport make the Olympics a global phenomenon *par excellence*. But the Games can, at the same time, be seen as divisive, racist, elitist, homophobic and sexist. While the Games can be read as sources of urban and regional regeneration, they can also be seen as contributing to environmental degradation. From 1896 onwards, the Olympics has presented a wide range of problems. Critiques of the Games have come from a variety of sources. De Coubertin himself was enraged by the so-called 'Anthropology days' of the St Louis Olympics in 1904, which featured native peoples ('savages' in the parlance of the Olympic report) who were made to compete in Olympic events such as sprinting, jumping and throwing (Goksøyr, 1990). It was predicted by certain members of the committee who organized these events that the 'savage' would out-perform the athletes who had competed in the same events at the St Louis Games. To their disappointment, the Ainus, Patagonians, native Americans and Turks achieved quantified performances far slower, lower and weaker than those of the Olympians. This was hardly surprising, given that they had never encountered such body-cultural practices before. The Olympics were revealed as a forum where racial rhetoric reared its head.

Racism was repeated more crudely in 1936. The Berlin Olympics, the subject of Arnd Krüger's Chapter 2, witnessed the German attempt to ban Jews from the national team (Guttmann, 1992). Jews were read by the Nazis as unathletic, incapable of sporting performances, incompatible with Olympian athleticism, cowardly and lacking in 'sufficient courage for athletic contests' (quoted in Rigauer, 1981, p. 96). Additionally, Hitler made it clear that if he had his own way, black athletes would be excluded from subsequent Olympics. They were regarded as naturally superior because of their animal likeness and hence provided unfair competition. The Olympics survived the Nazi Olympics, in no small part because of the way Berlin had been 'normalized' for the occasion. In Riefenstahl's film *Olympia*, Hitler and Berlin were respectively seen as a polite sports fan and as being sanitized and safe. And after all, as Krüger points out, what was the difference between people gathering to enjoy the Olympics from those tourists who journeyed to the Bavarian Alps?

The spectre of 'race' has far from disappeared from Olympic discourse. As late as 1944, a writer in a Swedish encyclopedia noted that it was highly unlikely that blacks would ever make athletes of Olympic standard (Goksøyr, 1990). A decade later, however, Ernst Jokl and his Finnish associates (Jokl et al. 1956) were able to demonstrate, in their so-called 'anthropological' study of the 1952 Olympics in Helsinki, that the widespread success of African athletes was likely – a prediction that turned out to be remarkably prescient. Nevertheless, Olympic rhetoric, particularly that fuelled by the popular press, continues to racialize the Olympic record. The Olympics is both written and performed through a Eurocentric lens and the theme of Eurocentricism works as a central motif in several of the chapters that follow.

In 1936 the Olympic movement faced the problem that the host nation had adopted human rights policies that, on the face of it, contravened the norms of other western nations. On the other hand, as Krüger shows, many members of other participating nations were both anti-black and antisemitic, not least the United States. And in 2008, the Olympic Games are scheduled for Beijing. Susan Brownell's Chapter 3 invites comparison with some of Krüger's observations preceding it. She not only makes space the voice of the 'other' – a senior figure in Chinese Olympism – but also asks important post-Olympic questions: what can China do for Olympism and what can Olympism do for

China? Does the acceptance of Beijing as a host city mirror that of Berlin in the mid-1930s?

'Race' continues to feature in the Olympics, despite the rhetorics of 'racial equality' and 'multiculturalism'. Olympians from Africa and Asia continue to be stereotyped. In Chapter 4 Henning Eichberg explores the imbrication of ethnicity and identity. He asks to whom the individually driven athlete can relate and offers a number of sources for identification. One dimension that harks back to Coubertin's notion of 'sporting geographies' is the various possible allegiances that Olympic athletes may possess. It seems clear that a 'postcolonial condition' is emerging in which the nation-state is increasingly a sort of 'leaking container' (Taylor, 1994). By this we mean that Olympic athletes can no longer be said to 'represent' the nation for which they nominally compete. Here, a prime example is Wilson Kipketer, the Kenyan-Dane 800 metres runner, but there are many others: for example, Zola Budd, the South African-British distance runner, and the American-Dominican 400 metres hurdler, Felix Sanchez. Such athletes, at least, share their identity between their nations of upbringing and the ones for which they wear their athletic uniform; but they may also share it with the nationality of their coach, their place of residence, or the shoe companies who sponsor them. In such situations, the Olympics as an inter*national* event becomes meaningless. John Hoberman's notion (in Chapter 11) of the 'denationalization' of global competition is illuminated in such cases. Added to this, Eichberg teases out different levels of identity, contrasting tribe with nation, indigenous Australian with adopted Dane.

Coubertin favoured 'national' as opposed to 'nation-state' representation in the Olympics and saw the Games as a 'sporting geography' rather than a 'political geography'. In other words, he felt that the Olympics were bigger than politics. Although this has proved to be an illusion, there have been occasions when nations rather than states have competed, Finland (literally) distancing itself from Russia in 1912, for example. Identity in the Olympics, therefore, *has* been represented in sporting rather than national terms. And Eichberg echoes Coubertin in his speculation about future Olympics having representatives of, say, Quebec, Wales or Brittany (for example). An alternative promise, of course, is of Adidas versus Nike or one pharmaceutical firm against another (again note Hoberman's allusions to sportive nationalisms in Chapter 11).

Historical aspects of 'race' and the continued presence of 'racial' characterization in the Sydney Olympics are explored much more explicitly by Ben Carrington, in Chapter 5. He addresses the Olympics as an example of global cultural space in which supranational (cosmopolitan) modes of identity formation have, in principle, been made possible. Cosmopolitanism can indeed be seen to be a characteristic of the kind of mobile sports-workers of the twenty-first century, noted earlier, but tends to be applied only to an elite of sports persons. Carrington demonstrates, however, that while the Olympics appears to offer public spaces where a new, humanistic politics may be forged, the narratives of nationalism and exceptionalism render the project problematic. He pleads for Olympic Games which downplay nationalism and where 'failures' can be read as achievements; where racial stereotypes disappear in a world of a cosmopolitanism as ethics.

Criticism of and opposition to the Olympics have been commonplace during the twentieth century. Coubertin himself strongly contested the holding of the Games in St Louis. He also criticized the layout of the London Games in 1908, describing the White City Stadium as soulless and sombre. On the other hand, the Paris Games, held in the Bois de Boulogne (and seen by many observers as a farce), was read by Coubertin as delightful with grass and trees in abundance (Coubertin, 2000). Opposition to the Berlin Games was widespread. Controversy also followed the Munich Games in 1972 when the question was raised about whether the Olympics should have finished earlier than planned, following the assassination in the Olympic village of Israeli athletes by Arab terrorists. The English novelist Alan Sillitoe (1975) observed that

> The resumption of these so-called games in such indecent haste only emphasised their true spirit – that of a host country unwilling to give up its financial investments; and of athletes who are in the grip of their physical investment at the expense of all human feeling. (Sillitoe, 1975, p. 88)

Here Sillitoe raises fundamental ethical questions about the priorities of the Olympics – and of Olympic athletes. Such ethical critiques are mirrored in the neo-marxist view of the Olympics, reflected, for example, in the writing of Jean-Marie Brohm (1978); and Lenskyj in Chapter 8 and Møller in Chapter 13 review crises of various kinds at other Olympic Games.

After the Event

The Olympic Games leave many legacies, some of which remain for decades, even centuries. Others are short lived. Additionally, drawing on the language of welfare economics the Olympics generate both positive and negative externalities (or spillover effects). The benefits a city of region might gain from the Olympics are said to be various infrastructural provisions such as highways, sports facilities and iconic architecture. The dis-benefits of such mega-events include residential dislocation and the continued payments of high taxes long after the Games have finished. A substantial literature exists on these topics (Lenskyj, 2002; Roche, 2000).

Of special interest to Douglas Brown (Chapter 6) is the use to which Olympic facilities were put in Calgary, following the 1988 Winter Olympics. He focuses specifically on the Calgary Olympic Oval speed skating facility. He traces his feelings about using this 'Olympian' facility and how it has impacted on his daily life. He records the imbrication of his role as a scholar, studying a facility, and his love of skating. Brown's chapter straddles methodology, description, interpretation and theory. The Oval is not simply a former Olympic facility; it is an arena of post-Olympic experiences, a place for hanging-out, a place for mixing and mingling with skating's stars, a fragmentation of Oval space between top-class and hobbyist skaters. To Brown's regret, however, he acknowledges that surveillance and control has replaced the more chaotic and 'free-for-all' ambience that he had previously experienced. A post-Olympic facility seemed to have reverted to some of its former 'Olympian' characteristics.

It is possible to identify several threats to the future of the Olympics. In Chapter 7 Richard Cashman draws attention to the emergence of various other single and multi-sport mega-events that act in economic competition with the Olympics. He also alludes to the proliferation of new sports and the desire of several nations and regions to make the Games less Eurocentric. Recognizing, as other authors have, the Eurocentric character of the Olympics, Cashman foresees a further reinvention of the Olympics, that is by accommodating aspects of the changing global sports system. For example, the Games should replace some Western sports with those from say Asia, in order to correct the Eurocentric dominance that currently typifies the Olympics. The sports that might form appropriate candidates for discontinuation are those that are capital-intensive, events such as yachting, equestrianism, some field events such as pole-vaulting and certain winter-sport activities which most countries of the world cannot realistically expect to adopt to any degree. A more fundamental philosophical shift, that would encourage broader participation, is explored by Loland in Chapter 12.

Another scenario for the future is painted by Helen Lenskyj in Chapter 8. For much of Olympic history, the voices of those who consume more of the Olympics than they would freely choose (i.e. have the Games forced upon them) have been highly muted. However, as Lenskyj shows, there has long been opposition to various aspects of the Games, opposition that has, in several cases, been highly successful. Lenskyj identifies a large number of opponents of Olympism in the various forms in which it is manifested, not only by NIMBYism (not in my back yard) but also by anti-globalization. She notes that much opposition to the Olympics is played down in national and local media. The Olympics, however, can be seen as a site where post-Olympism meets anti-globalization. The visibility of anti-globalization movements, allied to anti-Olympic movements, is unlikely to diminish. In the future, the Olympics, a forum that puts on display the products of repressive sports-goods producers on the one hand and those of globalized multinational corporations on the other, will also be a focus for radical protests, marches, riots and confrontations. Contrasting with Lenskyj's chapter is the one following it, Alan Tomlinson's Chapter 9. In many ways he takes a more positive approach yet recognizes that the metaphors of the theme park and the freak show are far from inappropriate, when applied to the Sydney games. Working as a fan, flâneur and social scientist, his keen eye records not only the sanitization and Americanization of the modern Olympics but also its fun and family outings. He suggests that the future of the games lie in fantasy and fun, mirroring Sydnor's sentiments in Chapter 10.

Citius, Altius, Fortius

From the early 1890s, De Coubertin was applying the Olympic slogan, 'citius, altius, fortius', 'faster, higher, stronger' (Young, 1996, p. 108). From the start, speed was put first. In Olympic sport speed has been privileged, slowness denigrated. Slow performers such as the skier, Eddie ('the eagle') Edwards, the British ski-jumper, and the swimmer, Eric ('the eel') Moussambani, from Equatorial Guinea, provide the Olympic media with figures of fun and the sustenance of stereotypes, the popular press rarely recognizing their subversive (or heroic) qualities. The promise of a world record is part of the attraction of the Olympics; a slowly run (or swum) race is seen as an under-achievement, unworthy of the Olympian heights athletes are supposed to achieve. Speed is seen as the essence of modern sport. The continuous improvement of world records has been achieved, in part, by the greater number of sports participants than previously. Technology has no doubt contributed. The cinder track has given way to the synthetic; the river to the swimming pool (Bale, 1985); the amphetamine to the steroid, the 'natural athlete' to the cyborg (Cole, 1998). Olympic records have been constantly improved.

The notion of speed is central to Synthia Sydnor's Chapter 10 in which she delights in speculating about various transcendent, aesthetic and electronic scenarios for an Olympic future. Just as the top athletes have been speeding up, so too has the transmission of the Olympics over time and space. Sydnor draws on contemporary allusions to a 'speeding up' of society at large, often thought to have resulted in 'time–space compression' (Harvey, 1989). Speed, time, space and acceleration, Sydnor points out, 'are central issues in the ontology of post-sport'. Yet she sees the futurescape of Olympism as one including a strengthened link between aesthetics and sport, a subject taken up by Møller and Damkjær in Chapters 13 and 14 respectively. Sydnor pushes the simulation metaphor into the world of hyper-reality, a world where young people can instantaneously engage with cyber-sport, where many of the 'traditional' Olympic activities such as art and sculpture are revived in electronic forms; 'glorious collabourations', 'drenched with sacramentalism', where athletes, scholars, street people and filmmakers collide, but not in any antagonistic way.

To be sure, the Olympics has been a spectacle of speed. The statistics show that the 1896 (men's – there were no women's events) 100 metres final was won in 12.0 seconds while the winning time in 2000 was 9.87 – over 20 metres' difference. At the global scale, results in sports have been getting faster. Space is being compressed by time. On the other hand, the balance of speed has shifted between continents during the life-cycle of the modern Games. In the 1920s and 1930s Japanese athletes were major forces in swimming events. Today swimming tends to be dominated by Australians and Americans. On the running track, Finns dominated the middle distances before the Second World War whereas today, in these events, it is Africans, notably but not exclusively from Kenya and Ethiopia, who win the medals. Indeed, in countries like Britain, Olympic athletes in some events are 'slowing down'. It is unlikely that the Olympic performances by British runners like Sebastian Coe, Steve Ovett and Steve Cram will be matched (both in absolute and relative terms) in the foreseeable future. And the best-ever Olympic results from many countries in the world have always been relatively slow.

Slowness is implicit in the scenario painted by Sigmund Loland in Chapter 12. If Sydnor melds hi-tech with a kind of new-ageism and medieval sacramentalism, Loland encourages us to consider a less specialized and less vulnerable, but more sustainable, world of sport. While acknowledging that highly specialized sports, such as the 100 metres sprint, possess great beauty, he also argues that body-cultural activities that require the fine-tuning of a limited number of qualities, make participants in such activities vulnerable to various forms of manipulation. He therefore advocates the introduction of activities that require a greater variety of skills, hence reducing the extreme specialization that he sees polluting elite sports people.

Post-Olympism and Postmodernism

The Olympic Games, despite the 'green' rhetoric that usually surrounds them, are still seen by some as environmental pollutants. But the pollution of the body has, of course, been also recorded in sensational stories from the running track, the swimming pool, the weight-lifting arena and the cycling circuit. The Olympics has become a high-profile site for 'doping'. This is nothing particularly new. Evidence of what is today termed 'substance-abuse' being found in the Olympics has been documented for the best part of a century (Hoberman, 1992; Møller, 2003). The widespread use of amphetamine among Olympic athletes in the 1950s and 1960s has also been highlighted (e.g. Pirie, 1961, pp. 28–9). The popularity of the Olympics, however, does not seem to have been affected by numerous doping scandals. This and, for example, the kitsch style of the opening and closing ceremonies, suggest a postmodern condition of the Olympics.

The similarity between post-Olympism and postmodernism is difficult to ignore. We have already alluded to such a linkage in our earlier discussion of representation and implicit in the chapters by Brown, Sydnor, Hoberman, Tomlinson and Loland are different kinds of postmodernisms, i.e. time–space compression, the ambiguity of 'representation' (in its various guises), the centrality of the simulation, and a sort of 'back to the future' Olympism respectively. Postmodernism and deconstruction are, to some observers, similar or even synonymous. In Chapter 13 Verner Møller raises an important question about the future of the Olympic lying in aesthetics. He arrives at this through a deconstruction that centres on the apparent contradiction that while the Olympics are increasingly being exposed to scandals – not only doping – of various kinds, public interest is far from lagging and, if television spectatorship is anything to go by, is increasing. It has also been noted that among the most popular of the Olympic events is the opening ceremony, an event devoid of any sport at all. Møller argues that the continued interest in the Games is not because of sport per se but as a result of its aesthetic qualities (see also Møller, 2003). In other words, surface appearance and image rather than sports skills and results are what is important in the Games' survival (see also Bernstein, 2002). This is a conclusion with far-ranging (post-Olympic) implications. It is contested vigorously in Chapter 14 by Søren Damkjær. In a detailed exploration of the varied forms and contexts of aesthetics in sports, he also outlines what a postmodern Olympics would look like. He then concludes by arguing for the 'impossibility' of post-Olympism on the grounds that the 'hard sports' such as track and field are totally prepared to sacrifice aesthetics for results while those 'soft sports' such as ice-dance have become reduced mirror images of the hard variety, with the emphasis being ultimately placed on scores. He implies that to rid the Olympics of winners and losers would not make the Games post-Olympics but non-Olympic.

These two chapters provide a background for continued debate about whether aesthetics will replace competitive sport as a magnet for Olympic spectatorship. At this point we would suggest that more empirical work needs to be undertaken into the ideas raised by these questions, resurrecting, perhaps, MacAloon's plea for ethnographic and anthropological studies of the Olympic Games.

Have the Olympic Games run their course? This is the question addressed by Kevin Wamsley in the final chapter. To return to our introductory paragraphs, it is impossible to discuss 'the Olympic Games' as static, unchanging cultural phenomena. Perhaps 'olympic games' is, after all, the correct spelling. And perhaps, as Wamsley's 'social critique' observes, the biggest problem with Olympism is the Olympic Games. While the early Games were often *associated with* international, capitalistic and imperialistic expositions, the Olympics came to *assume* these very characteristics themselves, plus Orwellian 'doublespeak'.

The title of this book ends with a question mark. We provide the chapters that follow in the hopeful form of a dialogue. That is, questions are raised to which we hope readers feel provoked to respond.

Post-Øolympism? Questioning Øolympic Historiography

Douglas Booth

Ambiguity accompanied initial scholarly analyses and popular uses of the prefix 'post'. But by the early 1990s a consensus had emerged among social theorists that 'post' connoted a condition of reflection that involved dissection, especially of modernity; hence postmodernism (Kumar, 1995, pp. 66–7). Added to olympism, the prefix 'post' thus implies an occasion for critically reflecting on the modern olympic movement and games (see Kevin Wamsley's contribution to this book, Chapter 15). Consistent with this notion of post-olympism, this chapter questions olympic historiography. Two conditions make pertinent such an analysis of a field that attracts many social historians of sport. First, the juxtaposition of radically different histories of the olympics raises questions about the interpretation of the historical record. Why do olympic scholars, for example Maurice Roche (2000), Helen Lenskyj (2000) and Robert Barney, Stephen Wenn and Scott Martyn (2002), produce such diverse histories? Second, interrogating olympic historiography seems relevant in the context of new questions, new methods and new theories associated with the cultural turn in social history and the emergence of deconstructionist history.

This chapter comprises two sections. The first investigates the general nature of historical knowledge with specific reference to olympic history, and follows a framework developed by Alun Munslow (1997) who discerns three basic models of historical inquiry: reconstruction, construction and deconstruction. Reconstructionism, and to a lesser degree constructionism, dominate olympic history. Reconstructionists and constructionists privilege empirical methods, accept historical evidence as proof that they can recover the past, and insist that their forms of representation are transparent enough to ensure the objectivity of their observations. The key difference between reconstructionists and constructionists is the extent to which they engage *a priori* knowledge. The latter willingly embrace the concepts and theories of others as tools to propose and explain relationships between events; reconstructionists oppose theory on the grounds that it subjects historians to 'predetermined explanatory schemes' and reduces them to 'tailoring evidence' (Elton, 1991, p. 27). Sceptical of objective empirical history, deconstructionists view history 'as a constituted narrative' devoid of 'moral or intellectual certainty' (Munslow, 1997, pp. 14, 15). Slow to penetrate olympic history, deconstructionism nonetheless poses some major challenges for reconstructionism which places inordinate confidence in the cognitive power of narratives that are held to emanate naturally from historical facts.

The second section examines more explicit applications of historical knowledge in sport history under the heading 'explanatory paradigms'. An 'interactive structure of workable questions and the factual statements which are adduced to answer them' (Fischer, 1970, p. xv), an explanatory paradigm carries quite specific philosophical assumptions and constitutes the framework used by historians to orientate their arguments. Olympic history comprises seven basic explanatory paradigms: traditional narrative, advocacy, contextual, comparative, causal, social change and linguistic.

Models of Olympic History

Historians disagree about much: the objectives of history, the meaning of facts, the construction of facts, methods of procedure, the role of theory, the basis of theory, the form of presentation. But they also agree that history is an evidence-based discipline, and that evidence imposes limits on interpretation. The philosophical and epistemological agreements and disagreements within olympic history are examined below using Munslow's three models of historical inquiry. Olympic history supports mainly reconstructionists and a number of constructionists; deconstructionists are largely absent. Each group conceptualizes history around a different set of objectives, epistemology and mode of presentation.

Reconstruction

Operating under the assumption that they can discover the past as it actually happened, reconstructionists promote history as a realist epistemology in which knowledge derives from empirical evidence and forensic research into primary sources. Forensic research means interrogating, collaborating and contextualizing sources to verify them as real and true. Reconstructionists maintain that history exists independently of the historian and that the past can be approached objectively without ideological contamination. 'The historian is permitted only one attitude, that of impartial observer, unmoved equally by admiration or repugnance', say reconstructionists, who insist that real historians are obliged to 'simply relate the facts' and to avoid dictating readers' responses (Stanford, 1994, p. 91). Disdainful of ideological intrusions, reconstructionists are particularly vigilant of colleagues who mesh ideology with sources: this amounts to subjectivity and distorts history. Pierre-Yves Boulongne (2000) accuses 'feminist leagues', 'radical political groups' and the 'sporting-counter-society' of misconstruing Pierre de Coubertin, the founder of the International Olympic Committee (IOC), by ignoring his encouragement of women and girls whom he wanted to partake in physical activity. These 'malicious detractors', Boulongne rails, 'abbreviate quotations' and remove evidence from its historical context.

Narrative is the medium of presentation in reconstructionism. Reconstructonists assume a close correspondence between the language in their sources and the past, and maintain that narratives are essentially transparent. In evaluating good representations of olympic history, reconstructionists gauge the structure, unity and coherence of the narrative. They place maximum emphasis on the narrative as a whole process and the way it informs the structure of the argument, although reconstructionists also assess relationships between individual statements and sources. Cross-examination of evidence involves interrogation of language to ascertain the tone and accuracy of sources, and to clarify what particular sources say and what they leave out. More specifically, interrogation entails questions about word usage, figures of speech and stylistic cadence and the way that these articulate ideas and sympathies (Gottschalk, 1969, pp. 149–50). Reconstructionists maintain a strong vigilance over style and rhetoric in their sources and especially in colleagues' texts. Style has 'enormous evidential value, both in getting and in giving evidence'; rhetoric is a 'mechanical trick' associated with propaganda, poetics and oratory (Gay, 1974, p. 3; see also Gottschalk, 1969, pp. 17–19). Yet, for all their talk about careful scrutiny of colleagues' language, reconstructionists rarely take their evaluations beyond banal observations about grace of expression and clarity of writing.

Construction

Like reconstructionists, constructionists believe that empirical evidence provides the ultimate source of knowledge about the past. In this sense reconstructionism and constructionism are evidence-based, objectivist-inspired models in which historians aspire to build accurate, independent and truthful reconstructions of the past. Both also distinguish history from fiction and value judgements: history means discovering and recording what actually happened in the past. Where these models diverge is with respect to acceptance of *a priori* knowledge, particularly theory and theoretical concepts (Struna, 1996, p. 252). Real historical phenomena, according to conservative reconstructionists, are unique configurations and one-off occurrences: history consists of the 'stories of . . . individual lives or happenings, all seemingly individual and unrepeatable' (Postan, 1971, p. 62). A form of methodological individualism emphasizing human actions and intentions, or what sociologists call agency (Lukes, 1973), conservative reconstructionism casts theory into the realm of speculation. Theory, argues Geoffrey Elton (1991, pp. 15, 19) 'infuses predestined meaning' into history. In short, theory is antithetical to the objectives and practices of conservative reconstructionism.

John MacAloon illustrates the conservative reconstructionist's wariness of theoretical concepts in his biography of de Coubertin. MacAloon relegates concepts well behind historical facts and detail. Although MacAloon (1981, pp. xiii, 17) employs concepts borrowed from cultural theory, sociology and psychology, he asserts that these are purely 'strategic recourses' in the 'absence' of primary sources. MacAloon's suspicion of concepts also appears later in the text where he dismisses different classifications of de Coubertin as 'enlightened reactionary' and 'bourgeois liberal'. 'There is little to recommend one shorthand over the other', MacAloon writes, 'like most men', de Coubertin 'possessed . . . views which do not easily amalgamate under simple labels' (1981, p. 312, 142n).

Not all reconstructionists are so averse to theory; not all reconstructionists consider the investigation of unique events as the 'litmus test' of historical knowledge. They acknowledge that historians also discern patterns of behaviour across time, societies and social groups, and that they categorize different forms of human action and place them into general moulds. Such approaches compel historians to think 'in terms of abstraction' and theory (Munslow, 1997, pp. 22–3; see also Tosh, 1991, pp. 154–5). For example, collective identities such as nationalities, social classes, amateurs, olympians, and volunteers are invaluable and indispensable historical abstractions.

Constructionists deem theory integral to historical research. Summing up the constructionist viewpoint, the German economic historian Werner Sombart (1929, p. 3) argued that 'the writer of history who desires to be more than a mere antiquarian must have a thorough *theoretical* training in those fields of inquiry with which his work is concerned'. While not denying that historians require an intimate and technical knowledge of their sources, Sombart deemed these skills elementary. Constructionists consider theory fundamental to history for three reasons. First, the range and volume of evidence bearing on many historical problems is so large that historians cannot avoid selection, and theory is a critical tool. It provides frameworks and principles for selecting evidence and thus steers practitioners away from contradictions in their explanations. Second, theory brings to the fore interrelations between the components of human experiences at given times and in so doing enriches historical accounts. Third, as already mentioned, identifying historical patterns invariably involves some form of abstract thinking and connections to theoretical explanations and interpretations. Responding to the common charge levelled by conservative reconstructionists that theory predetermines history, constructionists counter that theories enhance understanding and that no one can 'approach their evidence innocent of presupposition' (Munslow, 1997, pp. 23, 40).

Where do olympic historians sit in this debate between reconstructionists and constructionists over theory? The reconstructionist position holds minimal sway but this does not mean that olympic historians have embraced 'complex social science constructionism'. Olympic historians have not employed the historical record to construct formal theories of the modern olympics or olympism, nor have they used it to apply, test or confirm theories. On the other hand, many olympic historians utilize 'organizing concepts', as distinct from full-fledged theories, to 'fine focus' their interpretations of the evidence. Perhaps better recognized as classes of objects (e.g. amateur sports), general notions (e.g. amateurism, professionalization, commercialization), themes (e.g. sporting ideologies, nationalism, international relations), periods (e.g. age of fascism, era of the boycott, Cold War) and constellations of interrelated traits (e.g. modernity, tradition, globalization), concepts abound in olympic history. However, these are descriptive labels that do not in themselves explain how something came about or changed. Nonetheless, by merely identifying recurrent features and patterns, concepts expose new realms of observation, enabling historians to move past the 'single instance' and to 'transcend immediate perceptions' (Burke, 1992, p. 29; Denzin, 1989, p. 13).

The range of concepts in olympic history raises the question, where do they come from? Like MacAloon, most olympic historians simply appropriate concepts from outside the field. John Hoberman (1995) is one exception. His concept of idealistic internationalism derives from a comparison of four international organizations: the Red Cross, the Esperanto movement, the Scouting movement, and the olympic movement. By examining 'analogies between historical instances' and 'compar[ing the] actions and sentiments' of the agents who create international movements, Hoberman's approach is consistent with historian Arthur Stinchcombe's (1978, pp. 17, 22) advice for inventing a 'profound concept'. Yet, it is not clear how far Hoberman wants to extend the analogies between idealistic international movements. Only the olympic movement appears as a twentieth-century idealistic internationalism. The Red Cross, formed in 1863, hardly rates a mention, even in discussions of nineteenth-century internationalism; the Esperanto and Scouting movements receive scant attention in the interwar age of fascism and completely disappear from the discussion relating to the post-Second World War era. Indeed, idealistic internationalism becomes increasingly irrelevant to Hoberman's argument. Stinchcombe (1978) and the social science methodologist Norman Denzin (1989) regard concepts as the major units of theory: concepts define the shape and content of theory, especially when linked together. The fact that Hoberman (1995) makes no attempt to link idealistic internationalism to other concepts and thus develop a full-fledged theory is reflected in the title of his article: '*Toward a Theory of Olympic Internationalism*'.

Deconstruction

Deconstructionist historians are highly sceptical of the claims to truth made by objective empirical history and they view history as a constituted narrative devoid of moral or intellectual certainty. Deconstructionists argue that historical understanding involves unavoidable relativism (the belief that there are no overarching rules or procedures for precisely measuring bodies of knowledge, conceptual schemes or theories, and that without fixed benchmarks the only outcome can be difference and uncertainty: Munslow, 1997, p. 188). Thus, deconstructionists do not promote the single interpretation associated with *the* history, e.g. *the* history of women olympians. Rather, they examine different perspectives within *the* history, e.g. successful women olympians, women excluded from the olympics, black female olympians, Islamic female olympians and so forth. In this sense, deconstructionists acknowledge that each group has its own unique perspective and faces its own struggles and, moreover, that every group is subjected to internal pressures and tensions. Proceeding from the premise that nothing written can be read as meaning, deconstructionist historians delve into the production of sources and texts with a sharp eye on the intentions of the author. While many reconstructionists believe that their interrogations of, or conversations with, sources is tantamount to deconstruction, deconstructionists disagree. According to deconstructionists, historians necessarily impose themselves on the reconstruction process and any notion that they can isolate themselves is erroneous (Munslow, 1997, p. 118). In this sense, deconstructionism poses major challenges for reconstructionism which places inordinate confidence in the cognitive power of narratives.

As we shall see, deconstructionism shares with post-olympism common ideas about critical reflection. But deconstructionism has yet to colonize olympic history. I am not aware of any olympic historians who have embraced the primary assumptions of deconstructionist history that language 'constitutes the content of history' and that it provides the 'concepts and categories deployed to order and explain historical evidence' (Munslow, 1997, p. 181). The closest olympic history comes to deconstructionism is Douglas Brown's (2001) discourse analysis of Pierre de Coubertin's *Revue Olympique*. Epistemologically acceptable to reconstructionists, Brown's work is discussed at the end of the following section, which examines the more explicit applications of historical knowledge in olympic history.

Explanatory Paradigms

More specific than a model, yet less prescriptive than a method, an explanatory paradigm is an 'interactive structure of workable questions and the factual statements which are adduced to answer them' (Fischer, 1970, p. xv). Olympic historians structure their arguments, or frame their questions and answers, within seven distinct explanatory paradigms: traditional narrative, advocacy, contextual, comparative, causal, social change and linguistic. Of course, most historians embrace two or three paradigms, although the philosophical assumptions in any one piece of work will determine the combination and range of paradigms. Generally speaking, the traditional narrative, advocacy and contextual explanatory paradigms fall within the ambit of reconstructionism, the comparative, causal and social change paradigms align with constructionism, and the linguistic paradigm sides with deconstructionism. As explained, the contextual, comparative and causal paradigms can also support the philosophies of both reconstructionism and constructionism.

Traditional Narrative Paradigm

The subject of vigorous debate, historians nonetheless agree that at the heart of narrative lies 'some sense of story' (Berkhofer, 1995, p. 37) and that it is the overwhelmingly dominant form of representing the past. Conservative reconstructionists assume a high degree of correspondence between narrative and the past, and promote the view that a narrative is simply the medium of their histories, the shape and structure of which closely resemble actual events in the past. In other words, reconstructionists hold that narrative language is mimetic or referential, that is, unproblematic or, at the very least, adequate to the job of describing the past. Reconstructionists believe that an historical explanation materializes 'naturally from the archival raw data, its meaning offered as interpretation in the form of a story related explicitly, impersonally, transparently, and without resort to any of the devices used by writers of literary narratives, viz., imagery or figurative language' (Munslow, 1997, p. 10).

The reconstructionist assumption that a narrative is merely the form by which historians present the past as a collation of discovered facts is apparent in numerous olympic histories (e.g. Howell and Howell, 1988; Gordon, 1994; Martin and Gynn, 2000). Barney, Wenn and Martyn's (2002) history of commercialism in the olympic movement continues this approach. Catalogues of facts buttress their history. Dates, times and places, acronyms of sporting, corporate, media and marketing organizations, and the names of olympic and corporate officials, CEOs and administrators pour forth, flooding the pages. At first glance, this narrative of olympic commercialism is a technical, pristine recovery of the past. But one soon finds the authors intruding in both the sources and the narrative. Barney et al. (2002) admit selecting their sources. Their primary sources are official IOC documents, specifically selected to aid the investigation of commercialism 'from the perspective of the IOC, rather than . . . from the perspective of television networks, corporate sponsors, and media' (Barney et al., 2002, p. xiv). And just as historians make decisions about which sources to use, so too they make decisions about how to organize and write their material. Barney et al. are no exception. The extent to which they impose themselves on their commercialization narrative can be discerned by deconstructing their work using Hayden White's (1973) literary model of historical explanation. Like other social historians, historians of sport and the olympics have mostly ignored White's work. The work of Murray Phillips (2003) is one important exception

White's model consists of three surface tiers – emplotment, argument and ideological implication – which sit atop a deep structure of tropes. The surface tiers and the deep structure each consist of four forms (see Table 1.1). Barney *et al.* (2002) occupy a very specific place in White's model.

Barney *et al.* (*BWM* in Table 1.1) employ a metonymic trope. Metonymy reduces wholes (e.g. the commercialization of the olympic movement and its fulfilment of the philosophy of olympism) to component parts (e.g. the IOC, media, corporations, marketing companies). Barney et al. prioritize these parts and place the IOC at the crest. With respect to emplotment, Barney et al.'s narrative of the history of commercialization follows a romantic plot. Unsporting-like disputes, excesses, corruption and commercial tawdriness all appear in their narrative, but the success of the Sydney 2000 olympics is proof writ large of the benefits deriving from commercialization. Barney et al. present a formist argument: they emphasize the unique, atomistic and dispersive character of events and people. In so doing they 'graphically . . . represent vivid individual events from which it is possible to make significant generalizations' (Munslow,

Table 1.1 *Locating Barney, Wenn and Martyn (2002) in White's Literary Model of Historical Explanation*

Trope	Emplotment	Argument	Ideological implication
Metaphor	Romantic (*BWM*)	Formist (*BWM*)	Anarchist
Metonymy (*BWM*)	Tragic	Mechanistic	Radical
Synecdoche	Comic	Organicist	Conservative
Irony	Satirical	Contextualist	Liberal (*BWM*)

1997, p. 158). Among their examples are Avery Brundage's fanatical opposition to commercialism, Lord Killanin's pondering about, and embracement of, commercialism, and Juan Antonio Samaranch's whole-hearted endorsement and determination to control the process.

Barney et al. (2002, p. xiv) maintain that their 'sources permit us to tell the tale truthfully and objectively' and they declare that the IOC has neither 'sponsored' nor 'endorsed' their history. But these claims do not render their narrative free from ideology. On the contrary, within the framework of White's model, the trio present a liberal moral ideology. Liberalism is typically optimistic about change, does not consider structural change necessary, and views change through the analogy of adjustments or fine tunings of a mechanism (White, 1973, p. 24). This is particularly evident in Barney et al.'s conception of the desirability of olympic commercialism. Ultimately, they present commercialism as a process of introducing and incorporating host cities and global corporations into olympic ideals. They believe this is a worthy goal that can unite and energize entire communities as well as foster identity and improve the morale of citizens.

From a deconstructionist perspective it is not the facts of IOC commercialism that determine how Barney et al. construct their narrative. Instead, they bring a set of ontological and epistemological beliefs to the facts that they use to create a history, rather than to discover the past as it actually was. Barney et al. are not unique in this respect: according to White (1973), all historians create history.

As well as traditional narratives, olympic history supports advocacy as a paradigmatic form of reconstructionism. Advocates make a virtue of their forensic interrogation of sources.

Advocacy Paradigm

Reconstructionists charge advocates with undermining the objectivity of history and destroying the credibility of the historian as a 'neutral, or disinterested, judge' whose 'conclusions . . . display . . . judicial qualities of balance and evenhandedness' (Novick, 1988, p. 2). But as Robert Berkhofer (1995, p. 165) reminds us, 'there is a difference between arguing *for* a point of view' and 'arguing *from* a point of view' (emphasis added) and by definition all historians are advocates for particular cases, stances or interpretations. Factual arguments are rife in olympic history. Did Edwin Flack represent Australia or the London Athletic Club at the 1896 olympic games in Athens (Booth and Tatz, 2000, pp. 81–2; Young, 1996, p. 141)? Did British athletes compete in the 1904 olympic games in St Louis (Gordon, 1994, pp. xxiii–xxvi)? Did Dorando Pietri or Pietri Dorando represent Italy in the 1908 olympic games (Barney, 2000)? In this chapter the term advocate refers exclusively to those historians whose basic objective is to debunk myths associated with the olympic games. The best example is arguably David Young (1984), who exposes the myth that ancient Greek Olympians were amateurs.

Advocates combine two methods: forensic interrogation of the evidence, and examination of the motives and interests of myth builders. After scouring the literature, Young (1984, p. 7) reports he cannot find a shred of evidence to support the case that the ancient Greeks had a concept even vaguely similar to amateurism. Young then proceeds to identify the key propagators of the amateur myth as a band of second-rate classical scholars (Paul Shorey, John Mahaffy, Percy Gardner, E. N. Gardiner, H. A. Harris) and a coterie of olympic officials (Caspar Whitney (member of the IOC and president of the United States Olympic Committee), Pierre de Coubertin, Avery Brundage). With the exception of Gardner, whom Young (1984, p. x) describes as a 'true Victorian Englishman', these men 'adulated' Victorian aristocracy and indeed '*wished* that they were Victorian aristocrats' (Young, 1984, pp. x, 35). As such they subscribed to class exclusive amateur sport and looked to the olympic games as a bastion for, in Whitney's words, the 'more refined elements' (Young, 1984, pp. 26–7). In this context, ancient Greece became a 'precept for the athletic system which they themselves preferred' (Young, 1984, p. 8).

What criteria should historians use to assess the neutrality or objectivity of advocates? Dennis Smith (1991, p. 163) classifies advocates according to how they handle the relationship between involvement (the capacity to empathize with and evoke the situation of particular participants in specific historical situations) and detachment (the capacity to observe processes and relationships objectively, discounting political/moral commitments and emotion-laden responses). On this basis Smith (1991, p. 165) distinguishes four categories of advocate: judges, partisan eyewitnesses, expert witnesses and leading counsels.

Avoiding theory and trying to 'give coherence to as much empirical complexity as possible', judges 'achieve a creative balance between involvement and detach-ment, each complementing the other'. Young is a first-rate judge. While praising the modern olympic movement as 'one of the world's greatest institutions', Young (1984, p. ix) believes that it will not reach its potential as the world's 'greatest hope' unless we understand the truth of its history. Usually involved with a particular viewpoint, the partisan eyewitness might 'achieve detachment' although they find it difficult. Bruce Kidd exemplifies the partisan eyewitness in his advocacy for Toronto as an olympic host (Kidd, 1992) and for olympic education (Kidd, 1996). In contrast to the partisan eyewitness, the expert witness is genuinely free from involvement and achieves a high degree of detachment. Whether such a scholar exists in olympic history is doubtful. Lastly, leading counsels express a high degree of involvement and shun notions of detachment. Leading counsels identify strongly with the interests of specific groups they research. Unabashed defenders of the olympics (e.g. Lucas, 1980; Howell, 1994) and staunch critics (e.g. Booth and Tatz, 1994; Lenskyj, 2000, 2002) qualify as leading counsels. Interestingly, Hoberman (1995, p. 2) attributes the 'stagnation' of olympic history to 'seemingly endless debates' between leading counsels.

Contextual Paradigm

Nothing is more fundamental in the lexicon and methodology of history than context (Struna, 1996, pp. 262–4). 'Although historians may differ among themselves about what constitutes a proper context in any given case', observes Berkhofer (1995, p. 31), 'they do not question the basic desirability of finding one as the appropriate background for understanding past ideas, behaviours and institutions'.

Despite the importance of contextualization, 'historians rarely discuss what [this] involves' or 'the larger implications . . . for the profession or its audience' (Berkhofer, 1995, p. 32). The general consensus is contextualization establishes patterns that share relationships beyond a temporal juxtaposition. Philosopher William Walsh (1974) elaborates. Historians, he says

> initially confront what looks like a largely unconnected mass of material, and . . . then go on to show that sense can be made of it by revealing certain pervasive themes or developments. In specifying what was going on at the time, [historians] both sum up individual events and tell us how to take them. Or . . . they pick out what [is] significant in the events they relate, [that is], what points beyond itself and connects with other happenings as phases in a continuous process. (Walsh, 1974, p. 136; see also Struna, 1986)

Historians may agree that temporal contiguity meets the criteria for contextualization, however contextual relationships are not necessarily well integrated. On the contrary, the contextualist 'impulse is not to integrate all the events and trends that might be identified in the whole historical field, but rather to link them together in a chain of provisional and restricted characterizations of finite provinces of manifestly "significant" occurrence' (White, 1973, pp. 18–19).

Arthur Marwick (1998) delineates contextual relationships using a model comprising four principal components:

1. **Major forces and constraints**
   - *structural* (geographical, demographic, economic and technological),
   - *ideological* (what is believed and is possible to be believed, existing political and social philosophies), and
   - *institutional* (systems of government, justice, policing and voting, educational, religious and working-class organizations, and the family).

2. **Events** (Great Depression, Second World War).
3. **Human agencies** (politicians, presidents, prime ministers, protest movements).
4. **Convergences and contingencies** (interrelationships between events and human agencies that generate unforeseen events and circumstances).

Allen Guttmann's *The Olympics* (1992) and Alfred Senn's *Power, Politics, and the Olympic Games* (1999) illustrate Marwick's model. Both scholars endeavour to understand the olympic movement within the context of twentieth-century nationalism and international political relations. Nationalism and international politics provided ideological forces in the forms of fascism, the Cold War and decolonization; all sharpened the olympic games as surrogate war. International political crises invariably spilled over into the games. The Soviet invasion of Hungary in 1956 precipitated a bloody torrid encounter when the two countries met in a water polo match in the Melbourne olympics. Apartheid and the Soviet invasion of Afghanistan precipitated boycotts. Human agents, particularly presidents de Coubertin, Brundage and Samaranch, loom large in Guttmann's and Senn's histories. Likewise, events and human agents have frequently converged to generate new, unforseen circumstances. For example, in the 1980s the end of the Cold War, the commercial success of the 1984 Los Angeles games, and a politically ambitious president of the IOC converged to contribute to a renewed interest in hosting the games.

Marwick's model, however, does not inform historians about which forces, which events, which agents, or which convergences they should privilege. In other words, historians working in the contextualist paradigm cannot avoid judgements. Guttmann (1992) and Senn (1999), for example, deem political philosophy the most relevant ideological context; Douglas Brown (2001) by contrast privileges the social philosophy of modernist aesthetics. Contextualization is vulnerable to 'losing touch with the dramatological', that is, the various 'ritualistic and theatrical features which contribute to the charisma, aura and popular attraction' of the event (Roche, 2000, pp. 12, 20) and there is nothing inherent in Marwick's model to ameliorate this tendency. Guttmann (1992) and Senn (1999) ignore the dramatological. Guttmann's brief discussions of athletic performances capture some of the spectacle nature of different games but, ironically, these accounts fail to contextualize the cultural practice of sport.

Reconstructionists and constructionists both utilize the contextual paradigm. However, they conceptualize it differently. Reconstructionists stress the 'non-repetitive elements' and the 'individuality of the overall network of relationships'; constructionists deem contextualization a matter of theory. The reconstructionist perspective prevails in olympic history. This has particular relevance for the next explanatory paradigm: comparison. As Robert Berkhofer (1995) explains, where contextualism renders the unit of study and its context unique, comparative history practically becomes an oxymoron.

Comparitive Paradigm

Comparisons involving allusions to another case in order to illustrate or highlight aspects of a particular case abound in olympic history. Comparisons include instances of similar or different kinds and they range across space, time, practices, ideologies, institutions, groups and individuals. Comparing traditional Western and popular East European perceptions of the olympic movement, James Riordan (1993) identifies two competing sets of ideas (see Table 1.2).

Historical research is not conducive to comparative approaches that require primary sources from different regions, spanning long time periods, or which demand high competence in more than one language. In practice, historical competence and expertise is typically confined to precise time periods and geographical regions that become smaller as the number of sources escalates. Comparing the costs and benefits of economic and non-economic factors over the eight summer olympic games held since 1972, Holger Preuss (2000) confronted an array of methodological obstacles: changing economic contexts, shifting political climates, different organizing committees and governments pursuing different motives and financing models, and speaking different languages, incompatible accounting systems, and diverse urban geographies.

Table 1.2 *Comparative Perceptions of the Olympic Movement*

Traditional Western perceptions	*Popular East European perceptions*
Non-political	Political, ideological
Amateur, voluntary	State shamateurism, coercion
Independent clubs, amateur federations, University sponsorship	Security/armed forces
Universal, autonomous	Soviet Russian hegemony
Fair play, open participation	Win at all costs, drug abuse, child exploitation
Sport for all, self-financing	Distorted priorities in national income dispensation

Source: Riordan (1993, p. 34).

Notwithstanding a plethora of comparisons, Hoberman is the only olympic historian I am aware of to use comparison as a means to formulate a concept. However, not even Hoberman uses his concept of idealistic internationalism to construct a causal historical explanation. Edward Carr (1990, pp. 104–5; see also Struna, 1996, pp. 256, 258–9) may have placed causation at the heart of the historical enterprise, but olympic historians have generally shied from the causal paradigm.

Causal Paradigm

As with the contextualization and comparative explanatory paradigms, conservative reconstructionists and constructionists conceptualize causation differently. The former assume direct relationships between causes and effects. For example:

- if event *B* (e.g. the intensification of competition between cities to host the olympic games)
- happened immediately after event *A* (e.g. the 1984 Los Angeles games)
- then *B* must have happened because of *A* (i.e. the profit that Los Angeles returned from the games – as a result of maximizing income from television, sponsorship and merchandizing – 'embolden[ed] other candidate cities' to follow suit: Hill, 1996, p. 158).

Here a set of purely fortuitous or contingent (and agent driven) factors transformed international perspectives about hosting the games. When Tehran withdrew its bid to host the 1984 games, the IOC had only one candidate city: Los Angeles. And the Los Angeles organizing committee exploited this situation to impose its commercial interests and demands on the IOC. Indeed, interest in hosting the games had been in decline since the 1970s with three cities bidding for 1976, two for 1980 (and 1988) and just one for 1984. Following Los Angeles six cities bid to host 1992, five for 2000 and eleven for 2004 (Roche, 2000, p. 136).

Most reconstructionists, and certainly constructionists, regard contingent factors as superficial and search for the causes of phenomena elsewhere. Many olympic historians allude to social structures but structural causation tends to play second fiddle to contextualization particularly ideological forces (e.g. amateurism, fascism), institutional systems (e.g. state sponsored sport, college sport), events (e.g. First and Second World Wars) and human agents (e.g. de Coubertin, Brundage). In large part this stems from the failure of olympic historians to adequately deal with the concept of structure.

Often used to describe simple patterns identified by observation, in social history implicit assumptions usually underpin the term structure:

first, that the phenomenon under inspection can be analyzed as a series of component units of a specified type (e.g. roles, classes, value-commitments, genders, societies); second, that these units are related to each other in quite definite ways; third, that the relationships between units connect together to give the phenomenon under observation a characteristic pattern which needs to be understood as a totality; and fourth, that the pattern of relationships is relatively stable and enduring over time. (Waters, 1994, p. 92)

These four assumptions appear in Maurice Roche's (2000) analysis of modern mega-events as components of the structure of modernity.

International mega-events, such as expos and sports tournaments, are integral to the functioning of modernity. They offered early moderns an opportunity to review their lives and relationships in a world that promised to satisfy their needs for identity but which, under the impetus of industrialization, scientization, militarization and state violence, threatened their very social and individual existence *per se* (Roche, 2000, pp. 218–20). Contemporary mega-events offer late-moderns 'cultural resources' to help them adapt to 'incessant technological and organisational change' in the labour force, '"information overload" . . . and the chaos of "choice" in consumer markets', and an increasingly plural and complex cultural and political life (Roche, 2000, pp. 220–1). The olympics has contributed to the 'development and promulgation' of ideas about national collective identity, the 'inclusion' of different groups in the traditions and destinies of specific nations, and an understanding of the 'obligations and rights of participation' associated with national life (Roche, 2000, p. 198). Olympic games provide moderns with 'enduring motivations and special opportunities to participate in collective projects' that, *inter alia*, 'structure social space and time, display the dramatic and symbolic possibilities of organised and effective social action, and reaffirm the embodied agency of people as individual actors' (Roche, 2000, p. 222). Lastly, the allure of positive international images and status (Roche, 2000, p. 152) consolidated mega-events as permanent features of modernity, with producers largely oblivious to fears about high costs and public debt. Competition to host olympic games existed from before the First World War and continued into the 1920s (two cities bid for 1904, three for 1908, four for the cancelled games of 1916 and six for 1924). Interest declined in the 1930s and 1940s during which the IOC aligned itself with fascism, but new mega-sporting events such as workers' games, women's olympics and Empire games (Commonwealth games from 1952) filled the void. Interest in hosting the olympics games returned after the Second World War with seven and nine cities bidding for the 1952 and 1956 games respectively. Similarly, while threats of boycotts and exorbitant costs appear to have put a brake on hosting the olympics in the late 1970s and early 1980s, that pressure did not extend to other mega-sporting events, as the goodwill games, gay games and fresh interest in the football world cup testify.

The central issue here is that structural analyses lead to quite different conclusions to contingent analyses where the focus is on agents and agency. Roche's structural analysis challenges MacAloon's investment in de Coubertin as *the* agent of *the* mega-sporting event. Seen through Roche's lens, MacAloon's (1981, p. xii) claim that 'it is impossible to understand the origins *or* the persistent "structure" of the Olympics without understanding [de Coubertin]' is significantly less compelling. On the other hand, although structural analysis would undoubtedly sharpen some olympic history, it is susceptible to reductionism, the glossing over of complexity. This is true, for example, with respect to Roche's (2000) discussion of the institutionalization of international public culture.

Social Change Paradigm

Olympic historians, like other social historians, 'spend most of their time explaining change – or its absence' (Tosh, 1991, pp. 154–5). Questions about increasing commercialization, the appropriation of the games as a tool of national identity, and the integration of women and racial and ethnic minorities, occupy many olympic historians. In social history the very breadth of these questions typically 'invites the application of theory' (Tosh, 1991, p. 154). Yet, as previously noted, olympic historians have generally shied from theory, neither constructing it nor employing it as a heuristic device. In dealing with social change, the vast majority of olympic historians draw upon contextualization, emphasizing new social forces, events and agents but, as noted earlier, they typically conceptualize social forces such as the economy and technology as vague sets of conditions rather than determining structures.

Dennis Phillips' history of *Australian Women at the Olympic Games* (1992) illustrates olympic history's approach to social change. Phillips contextualizes the increasing number of women selected in Australian olympic teams during the twentieth century against broader social changes with particular credence given to the growing independence of women precipitated by their movement into the workforce after the two world wars. The 'experience' of the Second World War, for example, 'had the effect of challenging some of society's more inflexible political and social assumptions. For women, the postwar world held out at least the possibility of substantial change in some of the fixed notions about their "proper place" in society' (Phillips, 1992, p. 51).

Like many other olympic historians working in the social change paradigm, Phillips details the lives of individual agents, in particular the struggles waged by female olympians against societal norms and family pressures. Triple gold medallist Shirley Strickland left home at 12 to attend boarding school. While still at school, she participated in a wide variety of sports but her main interests were academic. Intelligent and capable, she was determined to go to university. Refused admission to engineering when the faculty told her that there were no female toilets in the building, she took an honours degree in nuclear physics at the University of Western Australia. (Phillips, 1992, p. 54)

In her own words, Strickland 'felt the need for both physical and mental challenges. A teacher once had told me about the Greek ideal of harmony and balance and I wanted to test my capabilities. I liked the challenge of seeing how far I could go' (cited in Phillips, 1992, p. 54). Such detail earns peer respect. Referring to MacAloon's biography of de Coubertin, anthropologist Victor Turner praises the olympic scholar for his 'alertness to the refractory details of individual life and the particular history in which it is embedded' (MacAloon, 1981, backflap).

Linguistic Paradigm

Since the mid-1980s social historians have shown a growing interest in cultural aspects of sport, that is, how different groups employ symbols, language, texts and the like to create traditions, embody values, propagate ideas and nurture institutions. Such is the attention to culture that one can legitimately talk about a cultural turn. Within the cultural turn much scholarship focuses on language that is integral to the constitution, transmission, representation and trans-formation of cultural life. Social and cultural historians increasingly understand language as giving meaning to social life, acknowledging its power to build communities, to demarcate social, political and cultural struggles, to simultaneously connect and disconnect individuals and groups, to construct genders, to sell goods, propositions and ideologies (Hunt, 1989, p. 17).

Deconstructionist history also rests on the pillar of language. Deconstructionist historians examine the form and structure of narratives and search for what they claim are the power relations inherent in narratives. They pose questions such as who's speaking? and who's speaking for whom? Although language issues arise in all three models of historical inquiry, within deconstructionism they assume a peculiar epistemological slant. Whereas reconstructionists regard language as a generally transparent medium and recognize a close correspondence between the language found in sources/texts and past reality, deconstructionists question the degree to which language corresponds to the social world in the past and the present. Deconstructionist historians are far more sensitive to the persuasive, deceptive, manipulative and controlling nature of language than reconstructionists. Whereas reconstructionists typically present their histories as omniscient narrators of coherent, unified stories, deconstructionists prefer fragmenting and differentiating what they charge are the spurious unities in reconstructionist narratives. Thus, deconstructionists devote more attention to the form and narrative structure of their sources and texts, that is, to the *meaning of the message*. By contrast the principal issue of language for reconstructionists is the *mode of the medium* – that is whether the historian presents their work in a clear and lucid manner (Carrard, 1992).

Logically, epistemological aspects of language should occupy centre stage of the cultural turn in social history. Lynn Hunt (1989, p. 20) establishes the connection when she notes that 'as historians learn to analyze their subjects' representations of their worlds, they inevitably begin to reflect on the nature of their own efforts to represent history; the practice of history is, after all, a process of text creating and of "seeing", that is, giving form to subjects'. And this, in a nutshell, is the essence of the deconstructionist project. In olympic studies, sport sociologists are incorporating language analysis into their work (e.g. McKay et al., 2000; Tomlinson, 2000b; Atkinson and Young, 2002), but their historian colleagues appear resigned to contextualizing the olympics within international politics and commerce, and are largely blind to recent shifts and trends. Lamenting on the cultural turn's failure to penetrate olympic history, Douglas Brown (2001, p. 78) refers to a 'reluctance to acknowledge or consider' sport as culture. With respect to deconstructionism, it appears their reconstructionist proclivities convince olympic historians that the decon-structionist project is either an unsubstantiated attack on the reliability of historical evidence or a metaphysical epistemological issue that belongs in the realm of philosophy far out of reach of the traditional craft of history.

Brown (2001) is the only olympic historian I am aware of to pick up on the cultural turn and make language the subject of study. Beginning with the observation that de Coubertin considered sport a form of culture, Brown (2001) analyses the discourse in early editions of *Revue Olympique*, the official organ of the IOC. Following Michel Foucault (1972, 1977, 1981a) the term discourse embraces a specific sense of language in which its use determines consciousness, and ultimately being, by virtue of facilitating, or excluding from consideration, certain ways of thinking about experiences and by framing behaviour. In this sense, linguistic structures are said to shape social structures and cultural practices, such as sport and the olympics, and therefore to constitute history. Such a concept stands in marked contrast to earlier theories that held language as essentially corresponding to, or unproblematically representing, reality (Tosh, 1991, pp. 87, 89; Munslow, 1997, p. 122). Foucault's later historical projects (e.g. 1981b) connected the deployment of power to the body (Gordon, 1980) and focused on 'the body as produced by and existing in discourse', and the body as '*the* link between daily practices on the one hand and the large scale organization of power on the other' (Shilling, 1993, p. 75). Brown's study also includes the body.

Unlike other olympic historians who dismiss the *Revue Olympique* as 'little more than a clearinghouse' for de Coubertin's 'esoteric writing projects' (Brown, 2001, p. 81), Brown (2001, p. 79) locates it 'firmly within the dominant [modernist] discourse of aesthetics, art and culture'. The journal

> bound sport to aesthetic concepts such as the autonomy or disinterestedness of beauty, the intellectual enlightenment and the universality of beauty and truth. In de Coubertin's theory, sport and physical activity belonged to the realm of high culture. These were forms of culture that could lead to higher insights about the human condition; they could illuminate universal truths. In effect, the *Revue Olympique* aligned sport with the central tenets of aesthetic modernism. (Brown, 2001, p. 101)

At least one editorial in *Revue Olympique* criticized men who sought 'public recognition for their beautiful athletic physiques' as 'ultimately "abnormal, monstrous, and dangerous to society"' (Brown, 2001, p. 92). Such condemnation, says Brown, 'though amusing', articulated 'several important concepts associated with the discourse of modernism' that appeared frequently in the journal.

> Of particular importance is the effort to distinguish the relationship between aesthetic perception, the experience of pleasure derived from one's own physical beauty, and the social value of pleasure derived from exploiting that beauty for external gain. The *Revue Olympique* could only condone pleasure derived from one's physical beauty if it were free from external reward, or appreciated in a purely disinterested (aesthetic) way. The idea of a disinterested experience of physical pleasure seems to parallel the amateur sport ethos that promoted the disinterested pleasure of competition and winning. (Brown, 2001, p. 92)

Thus, as Brown (2001, p. 92) concludes, 'a concept that derives from the discourse of aesthetics was influencing the public's knowledge of sport in two ways'.

The experience of sport history in the 1990s suggests that olympic historians will likely accommodate epistemologically non-threatening forms of the linguistic paradigm (Parratt, 1998, p. 13) such as the type of discourse analysis undertaken by Brown (2001). In fact, Foucauldian discourse analysis has become almost orthodox among sport historians examining the policing of female physicality (e.g. Vertinsky, 1994; Cahn, 1995). On the other hand, it remains doubtful whether reconstructionist-orientated olympic historians are prepared to accommodate deconstructionist history and its demands for practitioners to critically engage their own work and the broader discipline.

Conclusion

Olympic historians have overwhelmingly framed their questions with a view to debunking myths and contextualizing olympic events within international politics and, more recently, global commerce. Operating within these explanatory paradigms, olympic historians have produced valuable and insightful work. Still, much remains to be done. In their gravitation towards the exceptional – whether in the forms of leaders (de Coubertin, Brundage, Samaranch), athletes (Jim Thorpe, 'Babe' Didrikson Zaharias, Jesse Owens, Muhammad Ali) or events (Berlin 1936, Munich 1972) – olympic historians have failed to either contextualize the olympics within broader structural social change or to see ordinary olympic participants – spectators, volunteers, non-medalling athletes – much less give them form or a voice. The way television portrays the olympics, through a dominant official lens, and particularly in its celebration of sporting hierarchies and stars, no doubt contributes to this limited historical focus that ignores competing perspectives and narratives (MacAloon, 1984). The diffusion into olympic history of the cultural turn, and the accompanying linguistic explanatory paradigm, may help rectify some historical omissions. But one should not anticipate olympic historians readily connecting the linguistic paradigm to epistemological assumptions about language or reflecting on their own representations of history. Evidence for the lack of reflexivity exists in the continued uses of 'Olympism' and 'Olympics', and even 'Olympic Games'. Whatever the justification for describing olympism as a philosophy, it has no greater claim to a capital letter, and the veneration implied, than liberalism, humanitarianism, authoritarianism, utopianism or fascism. Similarly, the olympic games are an arbitrary collection of sports – athletics, gymnastics, swimming, weightlifting – none of which carries reverential capital letters. When confronted with such issues historians typically consign them to the realm of metaphysics, arguing that they have no place in the traditional craft of history. This is precisely the issue: just as the concept of post-olympism raises important questions about the values and contributions of the olympic movement, as well as the sources of its power and how it decorates itself (Roche, 2000, p. 194), so deconstructionist history questions the basic goals and methods of history as an academic discipline. Can olympic historians continue ignoring these disciplinary signposts in the twenty-first century?

'What's the Difference between Propaganda for Tourism or for a Political Regime?'

Was the 1936 Olympics the first Postmodern Spectacle?

Arnd Krüger

Perspective

Postmodernism has taught us that the perspective of the author has to be taken into consideration. When I finished my doctoral dissertation on the 1936 Olympics and its impact on foreign public opinion in 1971 at the History Department of the University of Cologne (Krüger, 1972), I approached the German Federal Institute for Sport Science (Bundesinstitut für Sportwissenschaft) for a printing subsidy for what I (and my faculty) thought was a pretty good manuscript. The sub-section head of the Institute in charge of such applications contacted me and recommended that I should cut out everything that I had written – on the basis of archival sources – about how the Nazis staged the Games, and instead concentrate entirely on the foreign public opinion. Under these conditions I would get half of my book printed by a decent publisher.

Maybe 27-year-old PhDs should shy away from questioning the wisdom of an agent of the federal government; but I did not only think that it was a scandal. I also recognized the name of the expert who wanted to perpetuate Nazi propaganda about how well the German sport authorities organized the Games in the true spirit of Olympism, when, in reality it was the Nazi government that had its way in staging a gigantic propaganda show. This sub-section head of a federal government agency had written his own PhD thesis on the 1936 Olympics as a staff member of the then German Propaganda Minister in 1938 and had continued his career after the war in various federal ministries. With the help of my local (Liberal) Member of Parliament the question was solved and my thesis was printed in full by a prominent publisher, with a subsidy by the Bundesinstitut. So only thirty-six years after the Berlin Olympic Games the first German book was published that looked at the archival evidence of how the Nazis staged the biggest propaganda stunt the world had seen in sport.[1]

An Olympian myself, I had easy access to many of the Olympic participants of the 'Nazi Games'. The more of them I interviewed, the more I learned that the 1936 Olympics are many different things to many different people – just like the current Games. The hype and the professionalism were the same for the athletes who were promoted for their success – or disregarded if they failed. Are the 'Nazi Olympics' as iridescent as you expect postmodern events to be? Can everybody read into them what fits one's own imagination? Was the influence of Goebbels' ministry and that of foreign newspapers so strong that even today we are only looking at images of images?

Introduction

What do we know about the 1936 Olympics? Of course, many of us have seen Leni Riefenstahl's *Olympia* (Graham, 1986). We have read Richard Mandell's (1971) *Nazi Olympics*. German readers have also read Carl Diem's reports about the 1936 Olympic Games and there are many books about the Olympic Games written during the Nazi regime and after (Alkemeyer, 1966; Teichler, 1976; Hart-Davis, 1986; Rürup, 1996). Postmodernism has taught us that we should be careful about an 'endlessly reduplicated hallucinatory veil of images [which] effaces the distinction between appearance and reality' (Featherstone, 1995, p. 44). Is it possible to know the reality about the Olympic Games of 1936 if all we have are images of images? Bill Murray and I have edited a book containing chapters about the view of the *Nazi Olympics* from eleven different countries. If those views are compared it is questionable whether one is really dealing with the same event (Krüger and Murray, 2003). Whatever was discussed about sport and/or Nazism at the time in that particular country has maintained its influence until today. The national perspective, medals won or lost, the prospect about the next Games, the roles of the Workers' Sport movement (Krüger and Riordan, 1996), of the Jewish community, or of emigrants: all these perspectives were fed by pictures from the German Propaganda Ministry and by journalists who were sent to the Games. If you look at it from a global perspective you have a kaleidoscope of distinct ideas about the very same events.

> Postmodernity features a commodification of information and a transcendence of the print era . . . it is based on and fed by signs, images, spectacles . . . Thanks to technology, mass media interpret, produce and distribute images and therefore revolutionize ways of knowing and apprehending reality . . . In fact, mass media are so present in societies of reproduction that they tend to become reality. (Rail, 1998, p. 150)

Of course, nobody regards postmodernity as having started in 1936. But let us test the hypothesis that Goebbels' Propaganda Ministry was capable of deceiving the world and that today we still have a hard time distinguishing between fact and fiction. We assume that the production and commodification of culture for an open market are partially responsible for postmodern conditions. In that time it was not the market but the Nazi Propaganda Ministry produced and distributed powerful images, its staff continued to protect these images years after the Games were over. Nazi mass media were so present in societies of reproduction that their images tend to become reality.

The most impressive book about the Nazi Games remains Richard Mandell's masterpiece, *The Nazi Olympics*, in which he tells the story as reported by the *New York Times*. Typical for postmodernism is the copy of the copy. What, then, were the original Games? As the postmodernist would ask, were there any original Games? There was complete censorship of all photographs and newsreels. The Riefenstahl movie *Olympia* – in spite of being over five hours long in its two parts – used only a small proportion of the footage produced for the movie, to assure a perfect corporate identity for the Games. This was not opposed, as the photo rights belonged to the organizers. Indeed, the 1928 Amsterdam Games were the first to make use of this. The Nazis did not sell the rights like the previous organizers but used them exclusively for their photo crews, providing 'beautiful' pre-selected photos to the international press for free. This makes it difficult to come visually to the core of the Games (if there was one) as we have only those official pictures from inside the arenas that the Nazis want us to have.

Olympic Games under a Dictatorship

The Olympic Games of 1936 were the first to take place in a country run by a dictatorship. It is not known whether the IOC would have given the Games to Berlin and approved of Garmisch-Partenkirchen had it known at the time of the decision, by circular mail in 1931, that the Nazis would gain power in Germany eighteen months later. The only other serious contender to stage the Games was Barcelona, in the Catalonia province of Spain. The IOC had accepted its application at the time of Primo de Rivera's dictatorship (1923–31) – and had not objected to the Spanish dictator at the time of application. Why did Barcelona have to wait until 1992 to get the Games? Was it simply Germany's turn to stage them? Was it the Spanish dictatorship? Was it the turmoil in the streets of Barcelona when the IOC met there in April 1931? Was the Spanish government in Madrid not one hundred per cent behind the application of Barcelona, the capital of Catalonia, which was demanding independence from centralist Spain (Krüger, 1999a)? Berlin seemed to be less risky for the development of the Olympic Games. The other applicants had been Rome, Helsinki,

Nuremberg (at the time, more than one city per country could apply), Frankfurt, Dublin, Cologne, Budapest, Alexandria and Buenos Aires.

Rome, the representative of the only clear-cut fascist country at the time, was not seriously considered. Does that make the IOC anti-fascist at the time? Germany had shown that it was capable of staging huge sport festivals at the highest international standards while at the same time Spain stood for political and organizational chaos. Was this enough to convince a clear majority that in 1936 it ought to be Germany? The German representatives on the IOC were well connected while the Italians did not have much support. Berlin had already received the 1916 Games that were cancelled due to the First World War. Nor should it be overlooked that Germany had been the number two nation in the Olympics of 1928 in Amsterdam; Italy was fifth and Spain only twenty-fourth in the unofficial medal table. Germany was also capable of staging the Olympic Winter Games, which would have been difficult in Spain. So, giving the Games to Berlin in 1931 was a reasonable thing to do and the IOC majority of forty-three to sixteen (Berlin versus Barcelona) showed this clearly (Krüger, 1994).

The German sport authorities used their plans for 1916 at first and demanded only 6 million Reichsmark (RM) (£300,000 or US$1.5 million) from the German government to get ready for the Games, an amount they would later pay back from ticket sales. When the Games were fully assured for Nazi Germany, the Hitler government was completely behind the Games, building a new stadium instead of remodelling an old one, providing in excess of 100 million RM. Money no longer mattered for the Olympics. To assure a perfect Games with minimal interference from abroad there was complete postal censorship in and out of Berlin at the times of the Games, eliminating for example, the letters that were sent to Olympic athletes from organizations that had tried to ensure a boycott of the Olympics. Athletes, coaches and administrators were spied upon and were thoroughly supervised by the secret police. Although later Olympics also had strong security measures, the Nazi government was not only concerned about security but also intent on assuring a positive image abroad, monitoring extensively the foreign press reactions and acting rapidly if the positive image of Germany and the Olympics seemed to be endangered. Now that the *Circular Orders* of the Propaganda Ministry concerning the Olympics have been identified,[2] the degree of influence that could be taken under dictatorial conditions become highly visible (Bohrmann, 1993). Can there be free sport in an unfree society? Today, there is a commodification of information in a market society; at that time the government coerced German journalists to report what they were told. If you did not cooperate as a German journalist you lost your job – if not worse.

Olympic Education and the Peace Mission of the IOC

After Germany had broken the Munich accord and its army marched into Czechoslovakia in 1939, the IOC decided to give the Olympic Winter Games of 1940 yet another time to Garmisch-Partenkirchen and Nazi Germany – rather than calling the Games off after Japan (Sapporo) had given them back. St Moritz and Oslo, which had also applied for the 1940 Games, demanded so many changes in Olympic rules, using the opportunity to blackmail the IOC that they were no serious contenders (Bernett, 1980). For the IOC it was the question of calling the Games off or give them to Nazi Germany, a flagrant aggressor. The IOC preferred the aggressor over calling the Games off – so maybe the IOC would have given the Olympic Games of 1936 to Germany even if the Nazis had been in power at the times of the decision (Krüger, 1982). From the correspondences of a number of IOC members it becomes obvious that they were anti-Semites. Mussolini used sports to modernize Italy and many IOC members were very enthusiastic about fascism. This is the period when for a short time (1930–1) Augusto Turati, Secretary General of the Italian Fascist Party, was an IOC member (Gori, 2003).

Pierre de Coubertin, the founder of the modern Olympics movement, was asked in a press interview after the Berlin Olympics in Nazi Germany what he thought about them. Coubertin's response was correctly summarized by the interviewer: 'What's the difference between propaganda for tourism – like in the Los Angeles Olympics of 1932 – or for a political regime? The most important thing is that the Olympic movement made a successful step forward' (Krüger, 1999b). Isn't that what postmodernism is about? You don't care any more about the metanarrative of olympism – in this case of peace, international understanding, the brotherhood of humankind, humanistic ideals – or fascism. What is left over is the show for the sake of the show, with little distinction between high culture and low culture (Strinati, 1994; Krüger, 1996a).

The Historical Perspective

When looking at the 1936 Olympics, we should put it into proper historical perspective. When the Games of 1904 took place in St Louis, Missouri, racial segregation there was much more visibly present than in Nazi Germany in 1936. When African American athletes from the American South wanted to qualify for the US Olympic team in 1936, they had to travel to the North because in the South they could not compete together with white athletes. When the track and field team of Ohio State University, for which the hero of the Berlin Olympics, Jesse Owens, competed, travelled to the South, their multiple world record holder had to stay home (Owens, 1970; Baker, 1986). Nobody had ever suggested that the Olympic Games should not be held in the US or that the US be excluded from the Olympic Games. Non-intervention in internal affairs was the general policy of sport organizations until 1968, when South Africa was banned due to its Apartheid Laws.

At the IOC meeting during the Los Angeles Olympic Games in 1932, some IOC members were worried that, in case Hitler was in power in Germany in 1936, the Games would bar Jewish and/or non-white athletes due to the blatant racism for which the Nazis stood. 'Aryan' Games also raised the question about the emerging Asian nations taking part in the Olympic Games since 1912 (Nakamura, 2003).[3] Nobody seemed to be worried about the potential political situation in Germany. The pogroms could not really be foreseen in August 1932, and even if they could have, the IOC members were concerned only with the sporting side of the Games and very little with the political climate in the organizing country.

IOC member Karl Ritter von Halt, PhD, president of the German Track and Field Federation, volunteered to ask Hitler. Ritter von Halt, who had received a personal knighthood for bravery at the end of the First World War, personally knew some of the Bavarian military men around Hitler very well and so had no difficulty in talking with the future German Führer for an hour. Hitler confirmed that he would honour any obligation, be a good host and would not care which foreign country would send which athletes. Although this was in direct contradiction of the Party newspaper, *Völkischer Beobachter*, that had demanded the exclusion of Negroes, the IOC was happy, as fiddling around with the site of the Games would have been difficult in late 1932 – and an intervention in the way Germany would select its team was no more considered the duty of the IOC than to influence the US about how it would provide equal chances for its African American athletes. Until the very end of the war, the German racial laws were applied only to German citizens and citizens of occupied territories. Jews with a passport of a neutral country had nothing to fear in Germany. Germany respected international law in this respect – just as much as it expected that neutral countries would respect international law in relation to German citizens.

Much of the later discussion about the Olympic Games of 1936 refers to them out of context. We should not overlook the fact that most of these men on the IOC knew each other, not just from their involvement in Olympic matters but from their respective sports. Carl Diem, the main organizer of the 1936 Olympic Summer Games, had been a founding member of the International Amateur Athletics Federation (IAAF), the strongest sports governing body in Olympic Sports. He had served on its executive board for a long period of time and knew very well those responsible for international track and field. These included Sigfrid Edström, vice-president of the IOC as of 1937 and president of the IAAF, and Avery Brundage, president of the American Olympic Committee,[4] so crucial in the battle for international participation in the 1936 Olympics (Guttmann, 1984). Ritter von Halt, president of the Organizing Committee of the Olympic Winter Games and of German track and field, knew the two of them even better. Olympic Games take place every four years, but there was an annual track and field circuit in Europe that comprised the major track meets in Scandinavia and Germany. Even at the time when Germany was barred from the Olympic Games, individual American and Scandinavian athletes toured the German track circuit (Holmäng, 1992). The Nazi period was not much different in this respect. The only problem athletes and functionaries had when making money on the circuit was that their financial gain could not be paid out in dollars, but in transatlantic boat tickets and valuable merchandise.

The Amateur Athletic Union (AAU), as the responsible federation for US track and field, drew some of its income from the money their athletes received in meets in Europe over the summer. They had participated in international track meets in Nazi Germany from 1933 to 1935 and could not see why the Olympic Games would be any different. Winter sports in Europe were such an international affair that, when the US Olympic Committee finally decided that an American team should go to Garmisch-Partenkirchen, the majority of the American team was already in Europe competing.

According to Cashmore (2000), the hallmarks of postmodernity in sport are characterized by a rejection of 'all-encompassing theories, grand narratives, or ideologies'. The fact that 'knowledge is always indeterminate and truth is contingent on the particular circumstances of time and space', a 'variety and plurality' which 'are preferred over uniformity and singularity', 'work (or production) which was once regarded as the nexus of social life has been supplanted by consumption'. If we take this as the basis for the 1936 Olympics we see that we have doubts what Olympism (the metanarrative) stands for; we see that the years prior to 1936 have to be considered and not the much more brutal Nazi years thereafter.

Maybe we should give the IOC the benefit of the doubt. The IOC gave the Olympic Games of 1936 to Germany and it provided only an 'Olympic pause' in the brutality toward German Jewish citizens. It gave the Olympic Games of 1980 to the Soviet Union without much result concerning the human rights situation inside the country. It provided the Olympic Games of 1988 to dictatorial South Korea hoping for the best – and it helped speed up the process of democratization in that country. Now, the Olympic Games of 2008 are given to China, which occupies illegally more space than Germany did in 1936 and has more political prisoners than Germany. Just as much as the IOC had hoped in 1933 that the Olympic Games would help improve the situation, so the IOC – and we? – are hoping the same for 2008.

General Sherrill and the Change of Policy

In June 1933 the IOC was to meet in Vienna for its thirty-second session, thirty of the sixty-four members attending. Realistically, this would have been the last chance to transfer the Olympic Games from Germany to another country. But there was no immediate alternative contender. A later withdrawal would have made staging the Games difficult. The *New York Times* (1933a) published an interview with Carl Diem, who expressed a 'mixture of shock and incredulity' that the Americans were thinking of a boycott or the possibility that the Games might be relocated. Diem insisted that there was not the slightest hint of discrimination in Germany, but the *New York Times* was not to be put off and followed the interview with its own pointed political comments. These would not be its last. Indeed it was in the political rather than the sporting columns of the US press that the issue was pursued (*New York Times*, 1933b). Political commentators were not restrained by some of the sporting realities, such as the logistics of running a major sports event, precisely the same mentality that had President Jimmy Carter four decades later assuming that the venue for the Games could be shifted at short notice (Hoberman, 1986; Vinokur, 1988; Hulme, 1990).

Under pressure concerning the attitude he held in regard to the upcoming IOC meeting in Vienna, particularly from organs of Jewish opinion, Avery Brundage assured all who wanted to know that he would not allow the Games to be held in a country that violated Olympic rules. Lewald was already hard at work using his deep knowledge of American sport to influence Brundage, assuring him that 'there will not be the slightest discrimination' (*New York Times*, 1933c).

The precise nature of the 'Olympic rules' was widely discussed in the American press. While it was agreed that the Germans would be good hosts and would not interfere in the selection of the athletes in visiting teams, the issue of Jews in Germany could not so easily be dismissed. In an Associated Press interview, the newly appointed *Reichssportführer* protested that this was an internal German affair. 'German sports are for Aryans . . . German youth leadership is for Aryans and not for Jews' (*New York Times*, 1933d). Besides, to be part of the German team you did not only have to show a decent 'performance', but the contenders had to show 'their general and moral fitness for representing Germany' (*New York Times*, 1933e). All this time, the Jewish tennis star, Dr Daniel Prenn, had been excluded from the German Davis Cup team, to become a *cause célèbre* in the British press (*The Times*, 18 April 1933, p. 5). Many German sports organizations had taken over the rules of the *Deutsche Turnerbund* to require a test of 'Aryan' descent and of *völkisch* knowledge as a prerequisite for participation on any German international team.

It was thought that the IOC would take the right decision in Vienna when it met at its annual session. No one was arguing that the decision was too important to be left to a sporting body. Formally, the IOC does not have members of particular countries, but members to represent the IOC in particular countries. The three US members were Colonel William May Garland (1866–1948), a Los Angeles businessman and president of the Organizing Committee of the Olympic Games of 1932 (Lucas, 1982), Commodore Ernest Lee Jahncke (1877–1960), a former Assistant Secretary for the Navy under President Hoover (Lucas, 1991) and Brigadier General Charles H. Sherrill (1867–1936), a former ambassador of the United States in Argentina and Turkey. In sporting circles Sherrill had the best reputation as he had a lifelong involvement in sports, first as a top class sprinter for Yale, many times Ivy League champion and one of the inventors of the crouch start. He was also a sympathizer with fascism, as can be seen from his writing. Before going to Vienna, Sherrill telegraphed the *Jewish Congress* that had lobbied against Olympic Games in Berlin: 'Rest assured that I will stoutly maintain the American principle that all citizens are equal under all laws' (*New York Times*, 1933f).

On 5 June 1933 the Olympic Games in Berlin made the front page headlines of the *New York Times* for the first time. What was discussed mainly on the sports pages and in some of the specialist press, had reached the scope of a potential sensation: 'Sherrill demands equality for Jews in the Olympics' (*New York Times*, 1933g).

In the correspondence between members prior to the Vienna meeting, Baillet-Latour told German members that he was against 'German Games' (Krüger, 1994),[5] and even the pro-Nazi president of the IAAF and IOC vice-president Sigfrid Edström (Krüger, 1978) came to the conclusion in a letter to Baillet-Latour: 'Now Mr. Hitler can make up his mind whether he wants the Olympic Games or not'.[6] For Baillet-Latour, it was not important where the Olympic Games of 1936 took place so long as they took place. For this reason he wanted to take a decision for a different city than Berlin if the German chancellor or one of his ministers did not come up with a declaration to assure all members that the principles of the Olympics be honoured.[7]

The Vienna meeting came up with the face-saving device that pleased Sherrill so much. The Germans had to produce an unambiguously worded communiqué about the non-exclusion of German Jews, but Sherrill still celebrated what he saw as a victory, and this was how it was reported in the front pages of the press: 'Reich keeps Games – giving way on Jews' (*New York Times*, 1933h); 'Germany keeps Olympics by pledging equality to Jews'. Sherrill gave lengthy interviews about his role in the negotiations, and said of his German colleagues: 'I do not know how they did it – but they did it' (*New York Herald Tribune*, 1933). The *New York Times* (1933h) celebrated the victory as a 'great surprise . . . and the opinion has been expressed that a real blow had been struck in the cause of racial freedom at least in the realm of sports.' In a leading article the *New York Times* (1933i) followed it up the next day: 'Nazi leaders are always speaking of the necessity of combating a world propaganda directed against them. Let them be assured that there is no more effective way of combating anti-Hitler propaganda then the avowal of error and the promise of amendments as in the Olympic case.'

Sherrill's efforts to get a Jew on the German team had been shown to be mere eyewash, however. Hitler's true feelings were revealed two years later in a conversation with Sherrill, on 24 August 1935, when he insisted that he would rather replace the international Olympic Games with 'purely German Olympics' than permit foreign nations to decide who should be on the German team.[8] He would not interfere with the selection process in other countries either and the IOC should not interfere in German matters.[9] Sherrill was shocked as this contradicted the Vienna Accord. He immediately sent an urgent letter to the IOC president Baillet-Latour.[10]

> I am of course entirely willing to tell you everything said by the *Führer* on the subject, but cannot risk putting it in a letter [sent from Germany]. Entirely confidentially, and not to be repeated by you to any of our colleagues (especially not the Germans!), I urge you to talk personally with the *Führer*, and show him the *Ministerium des Inneren* June 1933 letter you received in Vienna from Berlin about exclusion of German Jews from the German 1936 team. You are in for the greatest shock of your entire life! It will be a trying test for even your remarkable tact and savoir faire; and the sooner you meet the situation, the better the hope for your success, instead of a destructive explosion.[11]

The historical facts are relatively clear: Germany did not have any Jews on its 1936 Olympic team. By autumn 1935 the *Nuremberg Racial Laws* clearly defined what constituted a 'Jew' in Germany. Only two 'Half-Jews' were permitted on the team: Rudi Ball on the hockey team in the Winter Games, and Helene Mayer as a foil fencer in the Summer Games.

According to Jardine (1993), postmodernity is characterized by taking 'truth' and 'falsehood' out of their opposition. If we 'are to avoid the repetitious violence of moralistic thinking' we have to reformulate a new approach to 'truth', 'no one can tell the truth – at least not all of it', and 'henceforth, "truth" can only be thought through that which subverts it.' Much of what we know about the 1936 Olympics comes from newspaper reports, official communiqués and

Bulletins. What took place behind the scenes was not visible at the time, as the newspapers wanted to represent only what they considered useful for their point of view. By being in the news even false facts acquire their own momentum which have carried a distorted view of factuality until today. Finally, we know a great deal about the consumers of the spectacle of the Olympic Games, about how the spectacle was produced for consumption – but what do we know about the athletes and their daily grind to qualify and get ready for the Games?

Hans Fritsch

Hans Fritsch (1911–87) was the flag bearer of the German Olympic team in Berlin. For many, this blond giant, decathlon man, German record-holder in the double discus and double javelin (in both cases you throw with the right and with the left arm and the performances are added up so it is a sign of a perfectly built body to do equally well with left and right) was the icon of the ideal Nazi. Before the Games he was one of the favourites in the discus throw, but carrying around the flag in the opening ceremony did not help his performance and he did not make the Olympic final. For many, Hans Fritsch was the perfect symbol of Nazism, big, strong, blond, blue eyed, a second lieutenant of the air force. After the war he was often projected as a symbol of Nazism – the Nazi flag bearer.

Hans Fritsch was a 'state-amateur', a professional athlete of sorts. When graduating from high school he was already a track star. He joined the police force to be able to train twice a day. When the Nazis came to power and broke the Treaty of Versailles, building up an air force, a navy and increasing the size of the German army, Hans Fritsch joined the air force as he (like many other policemen) was offered a promotion of one rank and equal training conditions. All went well until he started to march into the Olympic Stadium – out of step. As an athlete he had never really learned to march as a military person was supposed to. When the Games were over, he had not won a medal and was sent to Brunswick to start serious flight training. His athletic career was reduced to true amateur status. Eventually he became a captain in the air force, a highly decorated fighter pilot in the war. Shot down over Sicily, he then became a pilots' instructor.

At the end of the war, when Germany no longer had any planes, Hans Fritsch was part of the chief of staff of the 25th Army which was built up of remainders of all sorts of troops and was supposed to defend Oldenburg down to the last man. The 25th Army marched out in the open to surrender on a field outside the city, against explicit orders from Berlin. Hans Fritsch was the interpreter of the capitulation. When the British commander recognized Captain Fritsch as the flag bearer of the Olympics, he was hired as the British interpreter. He later became cultural representative of the British Occupation Forces in the small German state of Oldenburg. If Germany had participated in the 1948 Olympics, Hans Fritsch would still have represented Germany in the discus throw.

Hans Fritsch never was a member of the Nazi Party. He was later reactivated to help build up the air force of the federal republic and retired as a colonel. He became the founding member of the German section of 'Olympians International' and was responsible, against much ill will from many sport functionaries, for honouring Olympians who had died in the war, no matter whether as soldiers, by bombs or in German concentration camps.

What then is left over of this symbol of Nazism? Helene Meyer, the German (half-)Jewish athlete who won the Olympic silver medal in foil fencing, wrote in Hans's scrap book: 'It is the man which makes the difference'. Is that what we can learn from the Nazi Olympics (Krüger, 2000)? Even one of the central icons of Nazism at the Nazi Olympics turned out anything but Nazi, an athlete who could have been part of any other major Olympic team.

Official Propaganda

Germany assured the greatest public relations effort that had been involved in a sporting event. While the Los Angeles Games of 1932 had already broken all records by contacting 3,400 sport administrators and newspapers with its English language newsletters, the German propaganda only started with the Los Angeles addresses. By October 1934 the propaganda committee was providing 24,000 copies of its newsletter worldwide to 2,030 German and 5,120 foreign addresses. This included 615 German and 3,075 foreign newspapers and journals (Organisationskomitee, 1937, vol. 1, pp. 92f). In February 1935 the travel offices of the German Railways abroad started to advertise the Olympic Games as the best place for a holiday in 1936. In April 1935, the press service was enlarged and was now translated and printed in fourteen languages (the original five, i.e. German, English, French, Spanish and Italian, plus Dutch, Danish, Norwegian, Swedish, Finnish, Polish, Hungarian, Czech and Portuguese). In total, thirty-three of these press service bulletins were printed (ibid.). From June 1935 Olympic placards were distributed complete with logo in nineteen languages and a total press run of 156,000 copies. The Olympic rings and the Olympic bell with Hitler's appeal to the youth of the world established the sponsor's name. In September 1935, leaflets were distributed in fourteen languages and a press run of 2.4 million. Photographs of superb quality were sent out worldwide. The ten days of the torch run from Olympia to Berlin received the full attention of every aspect of the German media. As well as spreading the good word, the committee countered the bad.[12] Press conferences stressed the peace message of the Games to which the host nation fully adhered.

In terms of participating journalists, these were by far the most successful games until 1964 when more radio and television journalists went to the Olympics and 1968 when for the first time the print press had more staff at the Games (Moragas Spà, 1995). In Berlin 700 foreign journalists from 593 foreign media (including 55 German speakers), 1,000 German journalists from 225 different media, 15 wire services with 150 journalists, 41 foreign radio stations present (from 41 countries), 450 radio technicians and 15,950 photos officially taken by German photographers for selection for the Berlin Olympics alone (Lyberg, 1996).

The Berlin Olympics were also the first to be directly televised to some Berlin city centre television sets. With such a large number of journalists it is not surprising that many different visions about the Games have been circulated. The Berlin Olympics reached an estimated 300 million radio listeners and was thus the media event that had the highest direct coverage of the world thus far.

> Postmodernism as a term represents one attempt to come to terms with the predominance of the mass media in contemporary societies. The fact that postmodernism refers to the increasing importance of mass media definitions of reality – that reality is what the media say it is, namely a question of images and surfaces – is related quite simply to the rise of modern forms of mass communication and the associated proliferation of popular culture signs. (Strinati, 1994)

The Nazi Olympics was the media event with the most journalists the world had seen thus far. A high degree of professionalism and technology went into the staging of the Games to a global audience. The mass media defined what reality was, independent of a core message and thus produced a proto-postmodernist spectacle.

The Olympic Torch Relay

Torch relays are shown on ancient vases from Greek antiquity. Carl Diem, who had been the organizer of road relays in Germany, had the idea of such a relay as a propaganda stunt to raise the interest for the Games in the last days before the opening and at the same time demonstrate the connection of the ancient games with the modern ones.

Anything that had to do with the image of the Games or cost money had to be approved by the responsible minister. This in Germany has been the interior minister ever since this decision was taken in 1914. Although Carl Diem (as general secretary) and Theodor Lewald (as president of the Organizing Committee) insisted that they were fully in charge of the Games, they had signed a statement that they would pretend such an independence only internationally to avoid negative foreign reaction, but in reality they would do as told (Krüger, 1975a; Pfeiffer and Krüger, 1995). As the Reich paid for the substantial deficit, they had no chance but to accept.

The torch relay was approved by a civil servant of the Propaganda Ministry, Haegert, in charge of foreign propaganda. Does anybody remember today that the torch relay was a Nazi propaganda show? The idea to connect with the Ancient Games was such a useful stunt that none of following Games would miss such an opportunity. What does this invented tradition (Hobsbawm and Ranger, 1983) mean for this feature of the 1936 Games? Syndy Sydnor (1989) has shown that the later use of the torch relay can be seen as a postmodern symbol as the actual purpose has long been forgotten. If we look closer at the re-creation and use of the relay by the propaganda minister we see that it is an invented tradition that even at the time of its first use in 1936 had a different meaning for different people.

Coubertin's Political Economy

Coubertin spent a lot of time and thought on the beautification of the Games. Here we are at the heart of the political economy of John Ruskin as Coubertin followed the lead of this English philosopher (Boulongne, 1975). For Ruskin things had to be beautiful to have a more unique sales value (Krüger, 1996b, 1996c, 1999c). He created the English Arts and Craft movement to convince the artisan that he is better off when he produces unique and beautiful things, rather than mass production in a factory. To what extent did Coubertin know and accept Ruskin, not only as an aesthetician but also as a political economist? Coubertin at least mentioned that he had read Ruskin and not just about him (Coubertin, 1911). He resented that Ruskin did not include eurythmics in his *Gesamtkunstwerk* which, for Coubertin, included the expression through movement: Diem included such rhythmical dances in the show programme of the Berlin Games. For Coubertin the French styles of previous epochs best represented such unity of form, colour, and style. He therefore discussed whether things should not be all done in the styles of Louis XV or XVI (Coubertin, 1911).

But as far as Ruskin goes, Coubertin is with him. The Arts and Crafts movement which Ruskin organized in England has often been used as being synonymous for putting decorations on everything; this is the basis of Coubertin's thinking. Coubertin spent a lot of time considering the decorations in the sport stadia, with flags, garlands, emblems and the use of the actual sporting implements. He pondered how this sort of decoration could best be achieved not only in the opening and closing ceremonies, but also throughout the Games. It is in this context that he invented the Olympic flag, which was shown for the first time at the celebration of the twentieth anniversary of the Olympic movement in 1914 and flown for the first time at the Olympic Games of 1920 in Antwerp (Coubertin, 1931). He discussed the best form of trophies, assuming that the sporting implement itself would be a good trophy if properly adorned. But he accepted that what is correct for a foil or discus does not work for a canoe or skiffs (Coubertin, 1911). For others at the time trophies were viewed as part of the question of amateurism, which put emphasis on the financial value of the price (Coubertin, 1902). Coubertin, however, was concerned, just like Ruskin, with the beauty, as by this the value would come by itself.

He also considered how best to build the stadium to have the Games set in the most splendid environment. How should you construct the grandstands and terraces to ensure the best view – and have the most aesthetic ensemble? In this context he even used *se ruskinianiser* as an intransitive verb, so familiar had he become with Ruskin's concepts. What does he mean with the verb: the eye accustoms itself to the constant beautification of things to avoid straight lines (like many stadia are) and put matters in the proper proportions and colours, to beautify so as to increase its value (Coubertin, 1902).

Coubertin was also aware of the fact that what is a proper decoration in one country may not be so proper for another. Coubertin who had travelled a great deal through many countries discussed his experiences in a transcultural context. He used as one of the examples the flower and reef decorations in Greece and said that to him as a Frenchman they made the impression of a funeral and recommended that one should find styles that are generally acceptable. For the same reason he did not like cypresses in the stadium as they made it look like a funeral home (Coubertin, 1902). Looking at the fine national differences, Coubertin was searching keenly for international understanding (Coubertin, 1898).

Coubertin was thinking about night meets under floodlights, events in the light of lanterns (all in the same colour), about fireworks (not to be done during the competitions as that would draw the attention away from the athletes), the use of electrically illuminated flowers, Bengalis fires, torches. All these light effects were used by Coubertin as a means of decoration in which he invested a lot of thought (Coubertin, 1911). Finally, he proposed marches, ceremonies like the Olympic oath,[13] and the unity of sight and sound – and no more than one speaker, trying to keep the verbal part that could not be integrated into action as short as possible (Coubertin, 1911).

The organizers of the Olympic Games have followed Coubertin's lead and have attempted to make the Olympic Games something special, more than the mere assembly of many world championships. The sporting event should be in a unity of the athlete with the spectator, with the surroundings, the decoration, the landscape etc. Coubertin attempted such a noble *Gesamtkunstwerk* (Coubertin, 1911).

Coubertin's political economy is based on John Ruskin. Today, when we look at the commercial value of the Games we see that the beautification and the corporate identity of the Games which were started by Coubertin make a big difference. It is not just the super world championships. Olympic Games are special for most sports. Coubertin's political economy is seldom dealt with, as it is assumed that he was so amateur that he was not concerned about money. Yet for the 1914 Olympic Congress he enlisted the Pommerey Champagne company as major sponsor, well knowing that the congress would be successful if people had enough excellent champagne (Krüger, 1997). In an economic sense Coubertin was probably right that the Olympics should stay away from political interpretations and just look how the product is improved (Wynsberghe and Ritchie, 1998).

The organizers of the 1936 Olympics tried to create such a *Gesamtkunstwerk* in the sense of Coubertin and Ruskin. In these Games everybody can interpret his or her own vision of sport – the very essence of postmodernism.

Brohm versus Bernett

Jean-Marie Brohm, French sport historian and sociologist, and Hajo Bernett, German sport historian and expert on the Nazi period, had a major argument at the Fiftieth Anniversary Conference of the Berlin Games. For Bernett (and many others) the Nazis had perverted the noble Olympic spirit when they staged the Olympics in the spirit of Nazism (Bernett, 1985). Brohm on the other hand insisted that the Olympics have been 'proto-fascist' from the beginning, and, therefore, they could be staged to perfection only in a fascist country. So, for him the Nazis did not pervert the Games but created a perfect Games (Brohm, 1986). To create ranking orders of people purely on the basis of physical characteristics, to enjoy the victory of the strong and despise the losers are typical traits of fascism – and of many sport fans. The question has been raised and discussed whether it is fascistic to enjoy the defeat of your opponents (Tännsjö, 2000).

In the context of postmodernism the discussion between Brohm and Bernett has yet another significance: it shows that we do not know much about Olympism, the core of the Olympic Games. What did the Olympic Games stand for when, at the time, the IOC praised Nazism? A postmodernist would ask whether the Olympic Games have any core at all. Amateurism, something much cherished by IOC president Avery Brundage, was not taken all that seriously by the founder of the IOC. Commercialism, much scorned by current critics of the Olympic movement, has its origin in the political economy and Ruskin-based acts of Coubertin (Krüger, 1996b). Whether we are sceptical about Olympic ideology or about the usage of that ideology at a particular Games just shows that one of the major traits of postmodernism had reached the Olympic Games of 1936: Olympism was commodified and did not have any definite mutually accepted core. The 'Nazi Olympics' question any metanarrative Olympism has ever stood for (Lyotard, 1984).

Conclusion

The Nazis produced a gigantic propaganda show to convince the world that all was well in Germany, yet at the same time they were preparing for war and the Holocaust. It should not be overlooked that anti-Semitism was not only a German phenomenon at the time and that appeasement was the international policy of most nations in that period – judging from hindsight of the Second World War and the Holocaust does not meet the historical reality of 1936. The German sport movement had a long history of counteracting the exclusionist policy of the German anti-Semites so the IOC had good reason to believe that it was helping in the progress of Germany's road towards political stability when staging the Games of 1936 in Nazi Germany (Krüger, 2001).

But the IOC also transferred the Olympic Winter Games of 1940 to Germany, indicating that maybe the IOC was not even concerned about the political situation in the country. After the Second World War the decision of giving the Olympic Games of 1980 to Moscow and those of 2008 to Peking also indicates that the IOC's optimism, that the presence of the Olympics does make a difference to a country, still plays a dominating role. Having Games in countries that wrongfully occupy other nations and have an abundance of political prisoners is not really in accordance with what people think the Olympics stands for. Maybe in 1936, the storm troopers were closer to the truth when they cried out 'Once the Olympics are through we'll beat up the Jew' (Krüger, 1999d).

Just as thousands of Nazi public relations and propaganda experts have tried to influence us to see only the good side of the Games, so a 'Holocaust industry' wants us to see only the bad side. Many of the arguments that were exchanged in the newspapers at the time are still discussed today. The Nazi Olympics showed how difficult it is to get to the actual core of a matter (if there is one) once the mass media get hold of an event. If Coubertin was right, that it does not matter why you advertise the Games as long as you advertise them well and stage them in a grandiose manner, then maybe we should forget, with Coubertin, the good and the bad sides and just look at the beautiful side, and what the Berlin Olympics did for the progress of the Olympic idea. In that sense the Nazi Olympics might be considered a postmodern event.

3

China and Olympism

Susan Brownell

What Comes after the -Isms? Postmodernism, Postcolonialism, and Post-Olympism (but not Post-Nationalism)

In July 2002, I met with the IOC member in China and elder statesman of Chinese sports, He Zhenliang, in Beijing. In 1979, Mr He became the first IOC member in the People's Republic of China (PRC) after nearly thirty years of negotiating with the IOC over its recognition of Taiwan as a representative of China. After discussing a number of other issues, we had a few spare minutes, so I told him that I was writing a paper on 'post-Olympism' *(hou Aolinpike zhuyi*, a word I invented to translate the theme of this book) where I planned to discuss the future influence of the 2008 Beijing Olympic Games on Olympism. I asked him how he would address this question. He replied that although he had not used the label of post-Olympism, he had devoted much thought to an issue that might fit the description. He believed that the future of the Olympic movement lies in cultural diversification. If the Olympic movement is to remain a vital force, then it must become truly multicultural so that it embraces the national cultures of the world outside of the West. He further noted that this would mean that more non-Western and developing nations should host the Olympic Games in the future, and that this would be much more likely if the new president, Jacques Rogge, reversed the past policy of growth so that the Games were of a size that would be manageable for those nations that are not among the world's wealthiest. Therefore, a very important moment in the course of the Olympic movement would occur at the next IOC session, where it would be seen whether a policy change would carry through. In the half-year since that conversation, results have been mixed: it was proposed that some sports be deleted from the programme, but it was proposed that others be added, and it is not yet clear whether any of the proposed deletions will take place. Still, it does appear that there will be resistance to expansion under Rogge, and perhaps that is a start.

I want to take Mr He's ideas as a starting point for my contribution to this volume, not only because I learned something from him, but also because I realized that he saw the question of post-Olympism from a different standpoint from myself. His viewpoint represented a non-Western voice, more specifically a Chinese voice, which is typically under-represented in academic debates about the future of the Olympic Games. If I had not had this conversation with Mr He, I probably would have framed this chapter differently, by asking whether Olympism as an ideal has any future in view of the moral crises that have continuously threatened the Games, and the frequent failure of the Games to live up to the ideals set for them. I would have spent a fair portion of this chapter on the topic that has most occupied the interested observers in China and abroad: will the Olympic Games change China?

Instead, I want to pursue a different line of inquiry and spend more time on the question: will China change Olympism? Because my conversation with Mr He made me think about the fact that Olympism as an ideal emerged and was firmly embedded in the ideologies of nineteenth- and twentieth-century modernism and colonialism. If we are now leaving these behind and entering an era of *post*modernism and *post*colonialism, then we need to abandon the modernist and colonialist assumptions in Olympism in order to arrive at a '*post*-Olympism'. It is modernist and colonialist for the Western media and IOC members to fixate on whether the Olympic Games will propel China toward a more Western-style democracy. It is also modernist for Chinese people to fixate on whether the Games will propel Beijing into the ranks of the world's modern cities, and China into the ranks of the world economic and political superpowers. I am not saying that these are not worthwhile questions, but my point is that they are old questions; they are not post-Olympic questions. If we are to conduct a discussion in the spirit of post-Olympism, then we need to shift our point of reference.

What was modernism? It was a faith in the forces of technological and social modernization, which assumed that the inevitable course of history was for societies to move from primitive to intermediate to advanced, to use the terminology of the great modernization theorist, sociologist Talcott Parsons. In Parsons's scheme, China was an 'intermediate' society (Parsons, 1966). Modernism tended to assume that there was only one kind of social organization and one kind of religious and cultural worldview that were conducive to modernization. In China, for example, modernization theorists considered the strength of the family and collectivist thinking to be an obstacle to modernization, as was the Buddhist religious tradition.

What was colonialism? It was a faith that the West could propel the rest of the world toward its own model of civilization, a model that was used to justify often brutal imperialist expansion, relying on imposed divisions of race, gender, and class, and free and slave labour (Stoler and Cooper, 1997). That colonialist attitudes still exist within the Olympic movement was revealed in the gaffe committed by Toronto's mayor, Mel Lastman, when he was asked if he would travel to Africa to support Toronto's bid for the 2008 Olympic Games. He was reported to have said, 'What the hell do I want to go to a place like Mombasa [for]? . . . I just see myself in a pot of boiling water with all these natives dancing around me' (Roughton, 2001).

What was Olympism? It was a faith that the force of an ideal could propel the modernized nations of the globe toward world peace. This was a Western ideal that traced its roots to some rather unusual, local ideas in ancient Greece that linked sport, competition and culture. These notions were still unique when they were reinvented according to the modernist vision at the turn of the nineteenth century. The Eurocentrism of the leaders of the IOC led them to assume that their values of fair play, pursuit of excellence and citius, altius, fortius were universally understood – which they were not – and they often assumed that the spread of these values would benefit the world, and that this dissemination would be a one-way process in which the light of Western civilization would be fired up in the dark corners of the world. Over time, Olympism has also seemed to entail a faith in growth and the notion that bigger is better – increasing numbers of nations, sometimes participating at a moral cost because of the ideology of 'amoral universalism' (Hoberman, 1986, p. 2). It was more corporate sponsorship, more media coverage, more sports events, and more elaborate opening and closing ceremonies, each Games supposed to outdo the last. As Sigmund Loland phrases it, 'enough was not enough' (see Chapter 12).

So what follows after the -isms of modernism, colonialism and Olympism? What would a post-Olympism look like, if it left modernism and colonialism behind? We can imagine it would entail a recognition that the world is multicultural and likely to stay that way; that the Olympic movement is a dialogue between cultures, not a one-way conversation dominated by the West; that Olympism will inevitably be changed by this dialogue; that bigger is not always better; that modernity takes many shapes and forms. We should understand that this is not an idealist process in which ungrounded ideas slowly supplant each other, but rather all of this will take place through hard-fought battles on the ground between real people pursuing their political goals. As Hoberman (1986) reminded us, this will involve hard work on the part of many different people: no matter what the media pundits might say, a single 7 foot 5 inch Chinese basketball player cannot bring about world peace for us simply by stepping onto a basketball court in the US.[1]

With this introduction, let me proceed to address the substantive issues surrounding the topic of China and Olympism. Will Olympism change China? Will China change Olympism? Will Beijing 2008 move Olympism toward a

Table 3.1 *Representation in the IOC Structure by Region of the World*

Region	IOC Members		IOC Executive Board		Numbers of NOCs		IF Headquarter Locations	
Europe	57	45%	9	60%	48*	24%	51	81%
Western	*46*	*36%*	*8*	*53%*	*26*	*14%*	*50*	*79%*
Eastern	*11*	*9%*	*1*	*6.7%*	*21*	*11%*	*1*	*2%*
Asia	18	14%	1	6.7%	27	14%	4	6%
Africa	17	13%	1	6.7%	53	27%	0	0%
Middle East	8*	6%	1	6.7%	15	8%	0	0%
South/Central America	16	13%	1	6.7%	40	20%	0	0%
North America	7	5%	1	6.7%	2	1%	8	13%
Oceania	5	4%	1	6.7%	14	7%	0	0%
Total	128	100%	15	100%	199	100%	63	100%

Note: *The NOC of Israel is officially classified as European by the IOC and is counted there; however, the Israeli IOC member was counted under the Middle East by this author. Figures current as of April 2002, taken from the *2002 Olympic Movement Directory* (Lausanne: International Olympic Committee).

more multicultural post-Olympism? Let me start with an analysis of the concrete power structures that underlie Olympism at the start of the twenty-first century, before I return to the realm of ideas at the end of this chapter.

Table 3.1 shows the regional variation in the global distribution of representation in the IOC structure. In 2002, the IOC consisted of 128 members. Numerically, Western Europe dominates the IOC membership with 36 per cent of the total members, and when Eastern Europe is included, Europe possesses 45 per cent of the IOC members. This is in part because of Western Europe's central role in the history of the IOC, and in part because of its numerical domination of the Winter Olympic Games.

The Power of the Host City

The major source of power of the IOC is the power to award an Olympic Games to a city. The hosting of an Olympic Games by a city and nation is also arguably the major point at which historical transformation, and in particular the movement or lack of movement toward greater diversity, takes place. In their 106-year history, the Summer Olympic Games have only twice been held outside of the West (Europe and its former colonies in North America and Oceania). It is amusing for me to note Richard Cashman's observation in Chapter 7 that the 'Asia-Pacific' region has been awarded nine Games and has held seven, because while Australians might argue that the Asia-Pacific constitutes a world region, in China the focal region has been Asia, and the points of reference have been the Games held in Japan and South Korea, China's Asian rivals. In the Chinese literature it is rare to see the Australian games lumped in with the Asian games. In 1964 they were held in Asia for the first time, in Tokyo. This move to Asia had been delayed for twenty-four years by the Second World War: Tokyo had been awarded the 1940 Olympic Games, but they were cancelled due to Japan's invasion of parts of East Asia and the onset of what was ultimately to be a world war. In 1988 the Games were held in Seoul, South Korea. And of course they will be held in Beijing, China, in 2008. They have never been held on the African continent or in the Middle East; they have been held only once in Central America (Mexico City, 1968), but never on the South American continent.

History shows that the Asian Olympic Games were pivotal points for the move toward diversification. There are only two sports on the Olympic programme with origins that clearly lie outside of the West. Judo was added to the programme for the Tokyo Olympics, and taekwondo was added for the Seoul Olympics. In 2008, Beijing hopes to add wushu (martial arts), but this has been vetoed by the IOC, at least for the time being. Japan's hosting of the 1964 Olympic Games had a tremendous impact in the Far East and in the rest of the world. Developing nations looked at Tokyo as an example and an inspiration: if Japan did it, then they could, too. In that sense it was an extremely important breakthrough. The event had a particularly strong effect on Japan's closest Far Eastern neighbours and rivals – South Korea and the PRC. On the one hand, it gave them hope in the possibility of hosting their own Olympic Games. On the other hand, the fierce sense of rivalry made it seem imperative that they should do so, as a kind of evening of scores. For if Japan could host an Olympic Games in 1964, nineteen years after 'losing' the Second World War, then justice and reason should mean that those nations who suffered so greatly under the Japanese occupation, and who were supposedly the 'winners' of the war, should also be awarded this honour and the global recognition that goes with it. When Beijing hosts the 2008 Olympic Games, it is likely that this effect will be felt again. Developing nations and non-Western nations will again feel that if China can do it, then they can too.

Japan's presence as the strongest Asian sports power was reinforced by the 1964 Games, and it was extremely influential in IOC policies toward Asian nations, particularly toward the sticky problem of the China–Taiwan conflict. Once Japan got its foot in the door, it opened it up a crack for China. China had withdrawn from the 1956 Melbourne Olympic Games after seven years of conflict over the IOC's recognition of a team from Taiwan, which claimed to represent all of China, and then in 1959 it withdrew from the IOC altogether. In 1964 the PRC was not represented in the IOC nor the Olympic Games, as well as the United Nations and other world organizations. By the 1970s the global political structure was changing, and some progress was being made toward the resolution of the conflict. During all of this time the Japanese IOC members and sports leaders had been acting as mediators between China, Taiwan and the IOC. As recounted in the biography of Mr He (Liang, 2000, pp. 77–9), in 1972 the impetus first came from the Council of Asian National Olympic Committees, one of whose vice-presidents was Japanese. The inclusion of China in the 1974 Asian Games was first raised in 1972 by the host nation, Iran. The Japanese Olympic Committee next took up China's cause, and called for the IOC to recognize the PRC. In 1973 Japan sent a delegation to China to discuss the problem, one of whose members was the Japanese IOC member Seiji Takata. It was not until 1979 that China finally regained its seat in the IOC after years of tricky negotiations; this occurred at the IOC meeting in Nagoya, Japan. While these negotiations never split clearly along regional lines, it seems that if China had not had the support of Asian nations with some degree of influence in the IOC, it would not have happened. China's withdrawal from the IOC in 1956 had followed a period of seven years in which China had looked for the support of its socialist 'Big Brother', the Soviet Union, but was repeatedly disappointed by the Soviet Union's tendency to put its own agenda ahead of the Chinese. The IOC president, American Avery Brundage, was China's main obstacle within the IOC, and he was able to circumvent the few Western Europeans who supported China's cause. Of course, the next IOC president, Irishman Lord Killanin, finally presided over China's re-inclusion in the IOC, although this process took longer than it might have if he had pushed a 'revolution' instead of an 'evolution'. In sum, the impetus for China's rejoining the IOC came from Asia, first from the power that Iran had as host of the Asian Games, then from Japan's influence as the Asian sports power and past host of an Olympic Games. Hosting regional and Olympic Games gives a nation some degree of negotiating power, thus constituting a crucial moment when cultural diversification can occur. When Beijing hosts the Games in 2008, the world will see the effects of a process of diversification that began half a century earlier. This also shows the very slow pace at which such transformations occur in world organizations.

The hosting of Olympic Games has also afforded opportunities for citizens of the host nation to move upward in the IOC power structure. One reason is that cities that have hosted Olympic Games are allotted a second member of the IOC, a system that helps maintains Western Europe's domination of the IOC through its dominance of the Winter Games. Perhaps more importantly, the long bidding and hosting process brings IOC members and administrative staff into close contact with members of the host nation, and they gain experience and expertise. If they are skilful politicians, they begin to form alliances within the IOC. Since in many ways the IOC operates according to personalized patron–client relationships, rather than abstract bureaucratic principles, these alliances are of utmost importance.

One example is the rise to power of South Korea's Kim Un Yong. He had served as the president of the World Taekwondo Federation since 1973, and in 1986 became president of the General Association of International Sports Federations (GAISF). He was the vice-president of the Seoul Olympic Organizing Committee and was in charge of the television rights negotiations. He was co-opted as an IOC member in 1986, was elected to its executive board in 1988, and became chairman of the IOC Radio and TV Commission in 1989 (Larson and Park, 1993, pp. 74–5, 185). Due to the phenomenal importance of television rights in Olympic finances, these positions meant he was very influential. In 1992 he was elected as an IOC vice-president. In 2001 he launched a bid for the presidency of the IOC, and although he was defeated by Jacques Rogge, his surprisingly strong candidacy put him two votes ahead of Canadian Dick Pound, who for many years had been labelled as Samaranch's chosen successor.

He Zhenliang

The restoration of China's seat in the IOC in 1979 also opened the door for the rise to power of He Zhenliang, who became the first member of the IOC in the People's Republic of China. He was elected to the executive board of the IOC in 1985, and was elected vice-president in 1989. In 1993 he led Beijing's first bid for the 2000 Olympic Games, which Beijing lost by two votes to Sydney. Finally he was behind Beijing's successful bid for the 2008 Olympic Games in July, 2001. He became very influential within the IOC, and due to him China's influence in the IOC arguably surpassed that of Japan. He was an advocate for non-Western nations, particularly Asian nations, within the IOC. His wife, journalist Liang Lijuan, wrote a biography entitled *He Zhenliang and Olympism*, which contains a section entitled 'Opposing Eurocentrism'. The following account is from that book, which I have translated into English:

> European sports developed comparatively early, and the majority of previous Olympic Games were held by European nations. The IOC was founded in Europe, its headquarters are in Europe, and European members outnumber those of other nations. Therefore it is unavoidable that inside the IOC there exists a certain degree of Eurocentrism. Zhenliang experienced this problem early on in his dealings with the IOC. After being co-opted as a member, Zhenliang established that he would fight for the dissemination and globalization of the Olympic Movement. When he became a member of the executive board, he was in an even better position to do this. He first requested that the IOC consider the numerous developing nations in thinking about offering sports events and allocating revenue. It should also be said, Zhenliang realized that inside the executive board there were those who paid attention to this problem,

including Samaranch. Nevertheless, perhaps because old habits die hard, their way of thinking often unconsciously expressed Eurocentrism. When things were clearly inappropriate, Zhenliang expressed his feelings. (Liang, 2000, p. 281)

This section of the book describes a number of examples of Mr He's fight against Eurocentrism. In 1991 the executive board discussed the programme for the opening ceremonies put forth by the Barcelona Olympic Organizing Committee, which included a display of the flag of the European Union. He made a speech pointing out that 'the Olympic Games are the world's games, not Europe's games', and he argued that the only flags that could be displayed were Olympic flags and those of the host nation and various participating teams (Liang, 2000, pp. 281–2).

Mr He also, in repeated communications with Samaranch, advocated the addition of several Asian members to the IOC, such as Singapore's Ser Miang Ng, China's Lü Shengrong (president of the international badminton federation, and a woman), and Chinese athlete Deng Yaping (several times world table tennis champion, appointed to the Athletes Commission). He also argued for a revision of the criteria for the distribution of revenues from the lucrative programme of corporate sponsorships, so that they were shared more equally between the wealthy developed nations and the developing nations, and the US did not receive an excessively large portion (Liang, 2000, pp. 283–5).

The stories in this section of *He Zhenliang and Olympism* reinforce the point made previously: diversity results from real work and struggle. These are just a few examples of the kinds of battles that have been fought, and must continue to be fought, if Olympism is to change, and if China is to play a role in changing it.

Will Olympism Change China?

Let me now briefly touch upon the question of whether Olympism will change China, before returning to the question that is my main interest here.

The bid process itself puts the host city under a great deal of pressure to conform to Western standards and this pressure only intensifies if the city is awarded the Games. To begin, all documents must be in the two official languages of the IOC, English and French, which puts a heavy burden on a nation such as China, in which the lingua franca is neither. The 2008 candidature file was a very detailed document requiring the bid city to respond to seventeen categories of questions about its economic and political structures and its social and cultural traditions. It also required the submission of thirty signed covenants or guarantees by the relevant authorities. One noteworthy example was the immigration and customs guarantee, which stated that 'nothwithstanding any regulations in your country to the contrary', all holders of the Olympic identity card will be authorized temporary entrance into the country, and will be allowed to import and export goods for the IOC free of all customs duties.[2] This was in violation of China's constitution, customs and censorship laws, and caused much stress among the members of the Beijing Organizing Bid Committee (BOBICO). As related to myself and John MacAloon during a meeting with the committee in January 2001, they finally decided to present the problem to the top leadership, the State Council, saying, 'Look, this is what the IOC requires. If we bid for the Games we must do it right. Do we bid or not?' And the answer came back: bid. This again illustrates that on the surface the Olympic Games might appear as a harmonious meeting of world cultures, but beneath the surface this meeting of cultures involves at every turn difficult discussions and concessions. These must be motivated by a strong desire on the part of the host nation to take part in this process.

In 1993, during Beijing's first bid for the 2000 Olympic Games, the US Congress issued resolutions opposing the bid on the grounds of China's human rights record. Although such action was threatened before the decision in 2001 on the host city for the 2008 Games, it did not come to pass. Still, it is clear that China's human rights record was the major point of contention in the Western media and among Western politicians, and it is to be expected that it will remain a strong point of contention through 2008. In 1993, with the attention surrounding China's bid for the 2000 Games and its application to enter the World Trade Organization, at least six major political dissidents were released from prison, including democracy activist Wei Jingsheng and Roman Catholic bishop, Wang Milu. During the bid process in 2001, multiple petitions were sent to Chinese leaders, the IOC, multiple national governments, and human rights groups. Fax machines and email inboxes were flooded with messages, many of them concerning Tibet and the religious sect Falun Gong, to the point that some had to be shut down. During both bids, there were both crackdowns and releases, and it is likely that this cycle will reoccur as the 2008 Games approach. Between crackdowns and releases, will any change result? Leading up to 2008, Beijing will be placed under a media microscope that will make coverage of Gorbachev's visit and the demonstrations in Tian An Men Square in 1989 pale by comparison. Then, several hundred journalists were present in Beijing; for the 2008 Games, the IOC estimated that it would request accreditation for 17,000 members of the media. Some of the most important guarantees demanded by the IOC are in regard to support for the media. In addition, the number of unaccredited media who show up and report on events outside of the official venues may well be twice that. In sum, there could well be 40,000 members of the world's media swarming around all of the nooks and crannies in Beijing. Journalists being what they are, we can be sure that they will not all be looking for whitewashed stories. There will be no way for the Chinese government to control what they see and say. Dissidents and critics will gain more media attention than they would otherwise have had, and will have a platform from which to make their voices heard. A look at the headlines that surrounded Beijing's bid in 2001 reveals the depth of the hostility in the Western media: 'China Doesn't Deserve the Olympics', 'What human-rights violations? Beijing still front-runner for 2008 Games', 'Unwelcome Bid from Beijing', 'Olympics Tied Up in Chinese Puzzle', and others. Of course, there were also positive headlines, but the point is that China will endure intense worldwide scrutiny, which will be contentious at times and painful for many Chinese people. However, it is the contention and debate beneath the harmonious surface of the Olympic Games where the real work of intercultural understanding takes place.

When Beijingers ask whether the Olympics will change China, however, this is not what they have in mind. They are more concerned with whether their standard of living will improve. One of the areas in which there will be a tremendous transformation is in the physical environment of the city. A 'Green Olympics' is one of the three main themes of the bid (along with the 'Science and Technology Olympics' and the 'Civilized Olympics'). Beijing pledged US$12 billion between 1998 and 2007 to improve the transportation infrastructure, clean up the air and water, build parks, reforest land around the city and beautify the city (Pan, 2001). This is nine times the estimated cost of the Games themselves. In a 1993 Internet poll of 26,000 readers, *China News Digest* found that 95 per cent of the respondents approved of Beijing hosting the Games, but only 70 per cent felt it would improve their quality of life (*China News Digest*, 1993). This is significant because *China News Digest* was founded in the wake of the 1989 student protests, is banned in China and its worldwide readership tends to be critical of the Chinese government. In 2001, the IOC commissioned a Gallup poll because of doubts about the results of Chinese-commissioned polls: this poll showed a 94 per cent approval rate among Beijing residents. These are doubtless the highest approval rates that any host city has ever had. Clearly, Beijing residents have a high level of confidence in the promises of the Games. Yet their hopes and dreams do not occupy the prominent place in the Western imagination that is occupied by the question of human rights. The changes that the West hopes will be brought to China by the Games are not exactly the same changes that the Chinese themselves hope for.

So I would like to reiterate the point made above: the question of whether Olympism will change China often veils modernist and colonialist fantasies. This kind of attitude is also found among the Western IOC members who supported

Beijing's bid. An example is Dick Pound of Canada, who said, 'My decision [to vote for Beijing in the 2000 Games rather than Sydney] was over whether the Olympics could do something for a country that's never had them. Can we open it up? It wasn't because there was anything in it for the IOC' (Byers, 2000).

Will China Change Olympism?

In its bid for the 2008 Games, the Beijing Organizing Bid Committee proposed three themes for the games: humanism, science and technology, and environmentalism. The concept of a 'humanistic' or 'civilized' Olympics is particularly important to a consideration of multiculturalism within Olympism. In its presentation to the IOC membership, BOBICO argued that a central characteristic of Chinese culture is its *renwen*. This word is difficult to translate in this context, although it is normally the translation for the academic word 'humanities'. It is formed from the characters for *ren*, 'human', and *wen*, 'writing, literary pursuits, culture'. BOBICO initially translated it as a 'civilized' Olympics. The meaning of the concept was encapsulated in a heading in *Beijing 2008*, a book that tells the story of Beijing's bid: 'Civilized Olympics: With Humankind as the Root, Emphasize the Spread of Universal Love' (Ma and Qin, 2001, p. 35). The book further recounts that when BOBICO sought the advice of international experts on how to promote its bid, they were told that they should emphasize the 5,000-year-old cultural history of the Chinese people and 'use the appeal of culture to attract the world'. They felt that, indeed, this formed a large part of Beijing's successful bid:

> Beijing's success demonstrates that deep and detailed information about Chinese culture can be taken in by the different peoples of the world. If the Chinese nation truly opens up her broad bosom to embrace people from all corners of the world, then Chinese culture will now and in the future produce an even greater influence on global development. (Ma and Qin, 2001, p. 32)

Beijing's most important cultural goal is to display China's humanistic characteristics to the world. Mr He told me that he hoped this would be China's main contribution to Olympism. In the formal bid presentation in Moscow, announcer Yang Lan spent four minutes on the topic of 'Olympism and Culture' and among other things she outlined how Chinese culture could enrich Olympic culture. She emphasized that for 3,000 years Beijing has been a meeting place for the people of the world, since it was first founded as a city in 1045 BC (Ma and Qin, 2001, p. 33).

Beijing 2008 describes Chinese humanism as follows: unlike other traditions, which either emphasize nature over humankind (Greece) or humans transcending nature (India, Hebrew), Chinese culture is characterized by the notion 'respect the spirits but keep them at a distance', valuing human life and emphasizing action in the world. Humankind occupies a high position in this world as the 'most intelligent of the ten thousand animals' and there is a 'worship of heaven and humankind' in which humans and heaven are equals. However, this valuation of humankind does not value individualism and the development of individual freedom, but rather emphasizes that individuals are parts of groups, with a duty to the clan and the nation. The result is an understanding of humans that emphasizes clan and collectivism. The book further observes that in its one-hundred-year history, Olympism has also taken humankind as its foundation, which enabled the Olympic Idea to engage with the different national cultures of the world. When the 'five-circle flag' waves over the 3,000-year-old Beijing, it will mark perhaps the greatest contact and cooperation between Eastern and Western cultures of all time. It will also reveal the appeal of Eastern culture to the entire globe. This will be an Olympics unlike any other because it will truly propel the Olympic movement to become a transcultural, transethnic, transnational, global cultural system (Ma and Qin, 2001, p. 36).

Because they are the 'Other' within the Olympic movement, Mr He, the bid committee and sports scholars were forced to think deeply about how to express a multicultural voice within the Olympic movement. Their ideas about humanism and East–West cultural difference are the latest expressions of a long conversation with the West that began in the early 1900s. One of the important early figures was Irving Babbitt, a professor of French literature at Harvard, whose work influenced two of his Chinese students. Best known in the West for books on Rousseau, college teaching of literature and humanities, and modern French criticism, he was best known in China for two articles comparing humanistic education in China and the West, which were translated into Chinese. One was published in the inaugural issue of *Critical Review* in 1922 with a cover depicting portraits of Socrates and Confucius back to back. In it, he called on Chinese youth to pursue a 'humanistic internationalism' that blended the essential Greek background of the West with the essential Confucian background of the East, and he called for a Confucian revival in China (Liu, 1995, p. 248). His ideas were utilized by an intellectual faction known as the National Essence School, usually regarded as conservatives who wished to maintain the 'humanistic essence' (*renwen zhuyi*) of traditional Chinese culture against the onslaught of Westernization advocated by the New Culture Movement in the second and third decades of the twentieth century (Liu, 1995, p. 251). In 1922, one of the proponents of this view argued, 'the authentic culture of the West, and our own national essence may very well benefit and help reinvent each other' (Liu, 1995, p. 254). It is clear why this way of thinking would be useful in the twenty-first century for Chinese trying to make sense of the encounter of East and West that is embodied in the 2008 Beijing Olympic Games: this event, which is characterized as having roots in ancient Greece – the originating point of Western civilization – will take place in Beijing, the heart of Eastern civilization. This symbolic construction of the Beijing Olympic Games as a meeting of the essences of Eastern and Western civilization resonates both with intellectual traditions within China, and with the Western essentialist intellectual traditions that have dominated the Olympic movement itself. Now, as in the early decades of the twentieth century, this is way of looking at China–West relations that downplays conflict and tension (Liu, 1995, p. 254).

The concept of humanism continued to play an important role in literary, philosophical and ultimately political debates throughout the Communist era, which saw a repudiation of Western humanism in favour of a Marxist focus on human nature as determined by class. China is a nation, somewhat like France (and rather unlike the US), in which intellectuals carry on high-level philosophical debates in public media, which are considered to have a significant influence on political trends and social life. At the beginning of the reform era, the intellectual discussion of humanism surfaced as part of the repudiation of the calamitous years of the Cultural Revolution (1966–76). In 1979–80 a spate of essays argued for humanism as a defence against 'feudal' thinking and personality cults such as the disastrous Mao cult that had just come to an end; against bureaucratism and elite privilege; and against the oppressive, dehumanizing impact of such a political system on its subjects (Hamrin, 1987, p. 288). It is significant, however, that the word for 'humanism' used in these debates, *rendaozhuyi*, is not the word (*renwen*) used by the National Essence school, nor BOBICO. The debates of 1979 and the 1980s traced ideological fissures that still fragment the Chinese political landscape, and are probably too sensitive to be incorporated into an experience that is supposed to unify, not divide. In sum, the concept of humanism has a significant history in China giving it different meanings from those assigned to it elsewhere.

In our conversation, Mr He acknowledged that communicating the notion of a humanistic Olympics would not be easy. It is not even easy to translate it into English. I also fear that this concept will be very difficult to communicate to the media, the general audience and even the IOC, though I support this effort. One problem is that it goes against the West's negative stereotype of China: the notion of 'humanism' evokes 'human rights', the main source of Western opposition to China's hosting of the Olympics. People who do not think China values human rights will not be receptive to the notion that China has an ancient and unique kind of humanism to contribute to Olympism. In November 2002, I discussed this further with Ren Hai, the director of the Olympic Studies Centre of the Chinese State Sports Administration, when we were both in Lausanne as members of the Research Council of the Olympic Studies Centre. As I am a native English speaker, he asked about possible English translations of '*renwen* Olympics': 'people's Olympics', 'cultured Olympics', 'humanistic Olympics'. I suggested 'human Olympics', but it became clear that this was not easily comprehended by non-native English speakers, and also (according to fellow member, Lamartina Dacosta) did not work in French or Spanish. I finally suggested a 'cross-cultural' or 'multicultural Olympics', which loses the flavour of the original, but keeps its intention. It remains to be seen how this concept can be communicated and marketed to a general audience.

But perhaps the bigger obstacle is that only a few obscure academics and Chinese bid committee members even think about the question: will China change Olympism? For the rest of the world, caught up in the modernist Olympic paradigm, it is not even a question. For them, because modernization is a one-way street, the only valid question is: will Olympism change China? In discussing the Beijing Olympics, Western observers so readily express a desire to change China. Why are we so concerned about changing China, and not concerned about China's changing us? My goal in this chapter has been, in the spirit of post-Olympism, to try to force Westerners to turn around and head backwards down the modernist one-way street.

4

The Global, the Popular and the Inter-Popular: Olympic Sport between Market, State and Civil Society

Henning Eichberg

The Boomerang

When the Olympics were arranged in Sydney 2000, the organizers placed a boomerang in the centre of the Games' logo. This pre-colonial throwing instrument was presented as symbolizing the idea of a 'multicultural games' and 'cultural diversity in an harmonious society, which is nevertheless united in its patriotism': Aboriginal culture should enter 'the image and the identity' of the games. For this purpose, a National Indigenous Advisory Committee was established, including representatives of the Aborigines and the Torres Strait Islanders. Besides the logo, the native Australians should also play a role in the Olympic festival of arts, in the protocol of the Olympic ceremonies, in the torch relay and in the design of Olympic medals. Additionally, an especially sponsored training camp for native athletes should be set up.

If one turns from the level of symbolic representation to concrete bodily activity, however, one does not find any boomerang throwing in the Olympic sports programme. Olympic sport is not only an arena of symbolic action, but also 'real' sport and in this field of activity, the Aboriginal contribution is missing. Olympic sport is Western sport. The absence of 'the others' not only is a question of the instrument (boomerang) and the related concrete activity, but also has its roots in the deeper patterns of sportive movement. Boomerang throwing, as well as Aboriginal games and dances in general, do not fit the basic achievement pattern of sport. That is why Aborigines may enter into the Anglo-Western sport of Australia, but their own movement culture has no relevance for Olympic-type sport. Even an engaged antiracist history of Aboriginal sport will tell us about colonization and sportization, about suppression and emancipation, but nothing about the boomerang (Tatz, 1995). From the sportive perspective, the Aboriginal tradition is non-sport.

This inequality raises questions about the relations between ideology, organization and social-bodily practice in sport and movement culture, about the contradictions of the Olympic model of sports, and about the historical connection between colonization and globalization. Together, the case calls for methodological reflections: how may a complex body cultural phenomenon like Olympic sport be analysed?

Contradictions of Movement: The Case of Jumping

Social phenomena like Olympic sport are not only entities that can be thought as a system, but also fields of contradiction. Difference and conflict may appear as unique sources of knowledge. This can be observed on the very 'elementary' level of bodily movement.

At the end of the nineteenth century, a Danish gymnastics teacher described a jumping competition between English and Finnish teams as follows:

> The English had only one thing in mind: to get over the rope, no matter how. They did nothing to conceal the exertion caused by their efforts to perform the jump and they gave the spectators the impression that the clearance of greater heights depended on certain tricks. They placed themselves at angular positions to the rope and landed on all fours. The Finns, in contrast, ran frontally to the rope, straightened their bodies as soon as they had cleared it, came down with knees slightly bent, and immediately went into an upright position as if it had been no effort at all. (Knudsen, 1895, p. 46; see also Bale, 2002, p. 180)

In this competition, as well as in its description, two models of movement confronted each other. The English sport model emphasized effectiveness in the production of a result, which is measured and quantified. The Nordic gymnastic model stressed the aesthetic of symmetrical bodily posture and of movement flow in its totality. The sportized jump is part of a system organized around the competitive production of records, objectified in a hierarchical order – citius, altius, fortius. The gymnastic jump is part of a system of pedagogical rules stressing harmony and personal fitness, correctness and the equality of all participants on as high a level as possible. In other words, one can jump either as a productive activity – producing results – or as a reproductive exercise, reinforcing health, fitness and social integration.

There also exists, however, forms of jumping that do not fit into the dual pattern of sport versus gymnastics because they neither display the raising of achievement, nor the fulfilment of the rule of posture. On the Melanesian isle of Pentecost in Vanuatu, men traditionally jump from a high tower down to the earth, on the occasion of ritual festivities, tied by lianas or vines, and accompanied by the chanting, stamping and dancing of the villagers. This Pacific 'land diving' has, in the 1970s and 1980s, inspired bungee jumping (Muller, 1970). In some villages in the island of Nias, in Indonesia, one finds large stone structures that were once used for ritual jumping. In Rwanda, certain young men had the tradition of jumping over a high installation in the context of aristocratic court ceremonies (Bale, 2002). And still today, Mexican Indians are fascinated by the game of *El voladores* where men 'fly' around a high pole (Bertels, 1993). These and similar events were, or are, related to ritual folk festivities. European folk culture knows the artistic jump as well as the comical jump of the circus clown. And children jump over each other's backs for fun. In recent decades, bungee jumping has spread as an international risk sport, as a means of psychological self-testing and border experience. Hip-hop dancers are jumping in their own way. Human beings want to fly. This is not only a dream, but also a practice – a rich world of practices, among others jumping (Behringer and Ott-Koptschalijiski, 1991; Trangbæk, 1991).

Beyond the dualism of achievement and fitness models one therefore finds models of festivity and body experience – movement as dialogical practice. By play and game, the human being does not only produce 'it' (the result), nor does it only act as subjective 'I', but it also communicates in relation to the others, it meets 'you' (Eichberg, 2002). In bodily-dialogical encounter and communicative interactions between human beings; identity is produced as 'we'.

Contradictions of Identity: Saying 'We' in Sports

Correspondingly, contradictions of movement culture can also be observed on the level of identity building. When people are playing the game, they form social patterns expressing who 'we' are. Identity develops by nostrification: 'This is us'. Identity in sports is not only harmless but also a root of soccer hooliganism and violence. In the Balkans during the 1990s, sports fan clubs have even been transformed into units of slaughter in the genocide. Playing the game is not innocent.

This requires an examination of more careful differentiations. Sport and self-identification can be linked in very different ways. This can be illustrated by three situations of saying 'we' in Danish sports. The first situation was described by a 12-year-old Dane after the European soccer championship in 1992, in which Denmark triumphed over Germany.

We travelled to Copenhagen some hours before the match should start, so we got some good places in front of the large screen, which was erected next to the city hall. At first we sat down on the asphalt and witnessed the singing roligans [fans], but later on we had to rise because more and more people arrived . . . After 19 minutes, the first goal was scored. The mood rose extremely high, and the jubilation became wilder and wilder. When halftime came, the atmosphere had calmed down a little, but there was all the time a mood of festivity and enthusiasm. After 31 minutes of the second half the second goal was shown on the screen and the mood was really boiling. Total chaos seemed to break out, and in the midst of the crowd one really had to take care in order not to fall and to be kicked down. Only with great difficulty could I keep myself upright. But even if it became dangerous at last, this was one of the greatest experiences I have had in my life. (Malte Eichberg in a school composition, 1994)

The soccer victory, and especially the fact that the final match was won against Germany, became a national event in Denmark. When the victorious soccer team was welcomed by thousands of supporters in Copenhagen, they shouted from the balcony of the town hall: '*Deutschland, Deutschland alles ist vorbei, alles ist vorbei, alles ist vorbei . . .*' (Germany, Germany, everything is over . . .). The significance of the event transgressed by far the limits of sport, and some observers related this triumph in sports to the referendum the same year, when the majority of Danes voted 'No' to the Maastricht treaty of the European Union.

The second story is about a quite different type of movement, Danish gymnastics. In 1931, the Danish gymnastic leader Niels Bukh organized a world tour with his gymnastic team. Here is what he experienced in Korea which, at the time, was under Japanese military rule:

Our good reminiscences from China and Korea are related to crowds of people and Danish flags at the reception at Mukden and Seoul railway stations and to children' s choirs singing Danish songs there. When we demonstrated our gymnastics in the Seoul stadium and let our flag down in front of 35,000 amazed people who were cheering for Denmark, and when the large students' choir was singing 'King Christian' (the Danish national anthem), we all felt stronger than ever before. How wonderful it was to be Danish and to serve Denmark. (Krogshede, 1980, p. 210)

Niels Bukh's gymnastics had its roots in the democratic farmers' *folkelig* gymnastics, but in its new form received an especially warm welcome in Japan, fascist Italy and Nazi Germany. Niels Bukh was himself impressed by the Germany of 1933, which he, though not exactly a National Socialist himself, regarded as a model for Denmark.

The third story differs fundamentally both from the sportive and the gymnastic pattern. It is about a tug-of-war contest, which was the highlight of *Fagenes Fest*, the workers' 'festival of professions' in Copenhagen 1938. The Danish daily '*Social Demokraten*' described it thus:

There was a gigantic performance. The blacksmiths quickly defeated the bakers, and the tailors could not stand for a long time against the coalmen who weighed at least twice as much. But there arose a gigantic competition between the dairy workers and the brewery men – and much to the distress of the agitators for abstinence, the beer won. The final was between the brewers and the coalmen, and here the brewery workers had 'to bite the dust'. 'This is not at all surprising', said the captain of the coal-carriers. 'You only carry the beer, but it is us who drink it'. (quoted in Hansen, 1991, p. 115)

The 'Festival of the Professions' started in 1938 as an annual sports festival of the Danish workers' movement, stimulated by similar arrangements in France and Germany. It combined sports events with more carnival-like competitions like running-matches of domestic servants with buckets and scrubbers, going-matches of pottery workers with piles of plates on their heads, hammer throw of blacksmiths and obstacle races of socialist scouts eating cream puffs on their way. Not only did the games have a joking character, as the story tells, but also during the Second World War when Nazi Germany held Denmark occupied, *Fagenes Fest* developed towards a demonstration of national togetherness. As this, the festival attracted the largest spectatorship in its history.

Production, Integration and Encounter by Movement

In the three cases of 'sport' described earlier, there are very different patterns of identification, different ways of 'we'-building and belonging. These are related to different patterns of bodily display that may remind us of the previously described trialectic of jumping.

The first pattern is characterized by *competition and result*. What emerges from it is an *identity of production*. Achievement sport produces 'goods' in centimetres, grams, seconds, points, goals, medal tables or victorious names, which are taken as indicators for 'who we are'. By linking identification to these results, the competitive encounter in sports stirs up feelings of connection and togetherness. Outcomes and records of sport are regarded as representative, as collective results: 'Two-zero for us'. The result can release strong emotions: 'We have won' – or 'We were defeated'. This model is hegemonic in most of modern sport, especially in Olympic sport and consequently in the media reception of sports.

The second pattern stresses *discipline and fitness* for the purpose of an *identity of integration*. Gymnastics contrasts to sport by being independent of the measurement of results. Competition is not needed here either, and it can be one single team alone, which arouses the impression of collective identity and the feeling of community. In this case the presentation and production of 'we'-feeling is effected by discipline and a collective demonstration of fitness. A team of dynamic young people moves in rank and file, with flag and hymn, radiating by its joint force and precision 'who we are'.

The third pattern centres around *festivity and play*, leading to some form of *popular identity*. In popular festivity, dance, play and games, all people can participate, old and young, male and female, people from different ethnic origins and different languages, top athletes as well as handicapped persons. The feeling of 'we' is produced by the encounter, the meeting in a temporary community of participation. In this situation, tradition mixes with surprise, competition and laughter, drunkenness and role-playing. Local associations may function as elements of continuity for popular sport, but the festive *encounter* is the important event – a moment of discontinuity, surprise and becoming 'high' in the here-and-now. The differences inside the group are not treated by streamlining or uniforming them, but by displaying or even over-stressing them, often in grotesque and carnival-like forms. The eccentricity of popular culture follows the logics of *mutual communication*: the truth is neither here, nor there; it is in-between.

National Identity is not One

The different types of sports can express very different types of political identities, as expressed by explicit identification. A first model is the *nationalism of production*, following the *logic of the market*. The model of competitive sport has correlations with a type of nationalism that is oriented towards achievement and production, growth and expansion. The nation is understood as an economic unit, competing with other nations in the market and developing in an historical evolution from the local to the global level. This nationalism and the corresponding sport appears as 'un-ideological', needing no explicit nationalist theory. Historically, this model has especially been developed by the Anglophone nations and sport cultures.

The second model is the *nationalism of integration*, following the *logic of the state*. The patriotic gymnastics looks much more 'ideological' than sport. It corresponds to a nationalism of integration, stressing the national-pedagogical unity of all citizens. In this type of nation building, sport may serve as a means of national representation and outward demonstration on one hand and/or as an instrument of national education and inward directed discipline on the other.

Niels Bukh's gymnastics, fascinating both Japanese militarism and German Nazism, showed some possible authoritarian and corporatist developments. However, the nationalism of integration has a much wider significance, following the logic of the territorial nation-state and its rationality of public order. As such, the disciplinary type of national identification and integrative movement culture became also visible in Jacobin France and in the Soviet Spartakiads.

The tension between state and market is often regarded as the only, or main, axis of (post)modern society. However, popular culture, as in the case of *Fagenes Fest*, shows an important underground dimension of identity building. Its social psychological dynamics are often overlooked. The third model is *popular identity* or *civic nationalism*, following the *logic of civil society*. Democracy and nation building is an action of civil society, of the people from below, or what in Danish is called *folk*. Revolution, association and togetherness in practical action have built modern political identity by saying: 'We are the people'. In the Third World, anti-colonial uprisings have had similar effects.

In Europe, the people of democracy rose for the first time, dramatically between 1789 and 1848 – the first phase of revolutionary democracy. It was no accident that this period also witnessed the genesis of modern gymnastics and sport. A new wave happened in the phase of revolutionary activity around 1900–20 – and synchronically again, sport had its breakthrough as a mass activity and became an element of personal life of the young generation. A further push occurred with the revolutions of folk identity in Eastern Europe and Central Asia around 1989–91. Festivities of sport and culture marked the change of political identity as in the revival of national springtime festivities in Tatarstan, in the wrestling festivals of Mongolia and the 'singing revolution' in the Baltic States.

In Denmark, the culture of associations and festivities of sports goes back to the *folkelig* movements of the early nineteenth century, to religious revivals and democratic self-organization around the revolution of 1848. These movements shaped the atmosphere and paved the way towards cooperative production, *folkelig* gymnastics in free associations and the alternative pedagogy of *folkehøjskoler*, the people's free academies. The modern nation was built from below.

The different models of sport – as well as those of identification and nation building – thus point in very different directions. Sport is not only one. There are alternatives in sport. There are fundamental psychological differences in identity building. Nor is there only one form of nation building. The different models are, however, also connected. Their configuration can be compared to the triad of freedom, equality and brotherhood, which once characterized the revolutionary dream of the modern democracy in 1789. The *freedom* of competition and record production corresponds to the logic of the market – survival of the fittest, the right to exaggerate (including doping), 'it is the achievement that matters'. The *equality* of discipline and integration is reminiscent of the rationality of the state and of public order – 'we are all united', standing in rank and file, in togetherness and under the same rule, responsible for our common matter, *res publica*. And the sisterhood or brotherhood of festivity and association is the base of civil society – meeting in popular self-organization and voluntary action, meeting otherness in dialogue.

The slogan of freedom, equality, brotherhood does therefore not only tell us about the harmony of democracy. It also describes a trialectical contradiction, which may lead to extremely different models of modernity.

How to Analyse Olympism?

By paying attention to contradictions of identity, Olympism can be analysed critically. Something like this was attempted in the early 1980s by confronting the mainstream Olympic model with some alternatives (Eichberg, 1984). Nowadays, enriched by recent historical evidence and with the trialectical contradictions in mind, we can ask in a self-critical way what the actual tendencies look like. Let us remember that the process of analysis went step by step from the superstructures of ideas, institutions and economic organization to the base of body cultural practice. On one hand, the Olympic model exhibited crisis. On the institutional level, the mainstream model of Olympic sport was represented by an oligarchic, self-co-opting, monopolistic organization, dominated by Western functionaries. Economic interests connected this organization with commercial corporations in the sports goods industry and the media. The practical programme of the Games was dominated by Western sports. They represented behavioural patterns and social configurations that were specific to Western industrial achievement orientation. The excesses of top sport, like chemical manipulation, misuse of children by professional training, and what sociologists have called the totalization of sports, were not at all accidental, but logical consequences of this productivism.

On the other hand, when looking for alternatives, some expectations were, at that time, tied to the awakening nations of the postcolonial 1970s. Following 'the spirit of Bandung' from 1955, radical politics in the Third World and in UNESCO were placing decolonization and the right of identity on the agenda. A New International Order – in sports as elsewhere – seemed realistic, shaping a new balance between the regions of the world (see also Galtung, 1982). In this context, the indigenous folk games attracted fresh attention and developed new national, regional and worldwide dynamics, including Europe. Opposition to the Olympic model of competition arose in the name of nature, too, and outdoor life and 'green sports' developed ecological qualities. Expressive activities like dance and modern gymnastics sprang up under the influence of Western avant garde drama and entered into dialogue with music cultures from Africa, Asia and Latin America. Meditative exercises like yoga, t'ai chi chuan and shaman practices spread in different milieux of the Western world. Whether combined with spiritual elements or not, they questioned the typical Western and Olympic separation of body and soul.

From the crisis of, and alternatives to, Olympic sport one could be tempted to predict the 'decline and ultimate fall' of this model (as did Galtung, 1982, p. 143). If not going that far, one could expect change. While remnants of Olympic sport would have future chances in the circus of showbiz and media entertainment, the democracy of body culture would produce pluralism, variety and recognition.

During the following decades many tendencies have indeed affirmed the scenario of the 1980s. Under the Samaranch presidency, the corruption of the Olympic organization has become an open secret – from the falsification of sport results to the Olympic connection with organized crime (Jennings and Simson 1992; Jennings, 1996a, 1996b; Jennings and Sambrook, 2000; Kister and Weinreich, 2000; Werge, 2000). At the same time, the economic profit of this corporation has exploded. From the rich world of non-Western sports, only tae kwon-do found recognition in the programme of the Sydney Games, but its world federation was revealed as a gang of Korean secret service agents, functionaries of dictatorship and Mafiosi, intimately cooperating with the Samaranch lodge (Jennings, 1996a, chs 9–10). The Olympic misuse of young girls has been documented in detail (Ryan, 1995). The scientific armament of achievement sport has raised doping to new intensity, though the race between East and West has become obsolete after the fall of the Wall in 1989 (Hoberman, 1992). And as Lenskyj documents in Chapter 8, anti-Olympic movements have arisen as part of anti-globalization movements, both worldwide and locally (see also Lenskyj, 2000).

However, the dualistic perspective on mainstream versus alternatives is revealed as too limited. The incipient tension between IOC and UNESCO never led to a worldwide confrontation between Olympic sports and cultural alternatives. The manifest conflict disappeared simultaneously with the weakening of the anti-colonial forces in the Third World. The well-balanced New International Order is today nothing but a memory from the past and, instead, the New World Order of one central power promises war against the disobedient rest of the world (Galtung, 2002). In sports, the Olympic model seems, likewise, to stand firm. Indeed, practices of movement culture outside Olympic achievement sport have spread widely, but as alternatives they cannot, like in 1984, be described in a dual pattern – either/or. We face a greater multiplicity.

The shortcomings of dualism do not only concern critical research. The more affirmative view, talking about a global mainstream sport on one hand and some pockets of 'resistance' on the other, must also be revised (Guttmann, 1994). Otherwise, one ends with the paradox of 'the sport' winning totally on one hand and disappearing on the other (Maguire, 1999; Nielsen, 2002). Furthermore, we have to take seriously how the mainstream prognosis from

1989 could arise: that the fall of the Wall and the end of block politics in sports would end the doping race, and that free individuals in future would compete after their own premises – and how this thesis failed. It showed an ideological construction as wrong as the prophecy of 'the end of history' (Fukuyama, 1992). 'The individual' is a non-serious and non-sociological construction, despite the intellectual attempts of Ulrich Beck and Anthony Giddens. Instead, we have to be aware of the historical shifts of societal relations and contradictions.

Historical Shifts between Civic, Public and Commercial Logics

Olympic sport has gone through different historical stages (Hoberman, 1995). These stages can be related to the (im-)balance of power between the three logics of the market, the state and the civil society. The IOC, started at the time of Pierre de Coubertin, was a lodge of aristocrats driven by idealistic pedagogical ideas, i.e. as form of a civil self-organization (Alkemeyer, 1996). Its idealistic internationalism can be compared to other civic movements like the Red Cross, the Scouting and the Esperanto movement (each of which, however, also had racialist undertones in common; see Hoberman, 1991). The national political intentions of the founders of Olympism, as well as its colonial context, paved the way, however, for the Games as a public event. In this second phase and under the impact of state rationality, the Olympics became a half-fascist festival. In Berlin 1936, the Nazi government used the Olympic Games as a means of political representation (see Arnd Krüger's Chapter 2). The public, state-political impact did not finish with the end of the Second World War but continued in the era of bloc politics. The Games entered the split between anti-communist and neo-colonial strategies; on the one hand contra 'socialist' and on the other anti-colonial strategies. Public logic drove the technological and scientific 'totalization' of elite sport (Heinilä, 1982) as well as the systematic use of doping and the political strategies of boycot. From below, anti-colonial movements in the Third World, as well as alternative body cultural practices, threatened the position of the Olympic sport since the 1960s. The Olympic model was hegemonic, but not ubiquitous. Civil society was a joker, also in movement culture.

Under this pressure, Olympism entered an alliance with the market system. A new phase of Olympism became visible during the 1980s and especially after the fall of the Wall. Under the leadership of Antonio Samaranch, the Olympic movement became a powerful machine canalizing public money into private pockets – into multinational enterprises, media corporations and mafiosi. Olympism became a sort of inverse Robin Hood: taking money from the poor – via media licences and public support – and giving it to the rich. Olympic sport functioned as an enterprise of globalization, following commercial rationality.

This history, if read as a story of change, can warn us, in a simple way, to identify the neo-colonialism of Olympic sport and with the actual globalization (Heinemann and Schubert, 2001, p. 12). The different horizons of historical time have to be taken seriously, the patterns having changed from state imperialism to market logics.

Scenarios of Olympism . . .

What is the new panorama of Olympic sports, now at the age of globalization? What we actually meet is a variety of scenarios, some more hypothetical, others more concrete.

Individual Competition

The hypothesis of individualization is based on the assumption of the lonely athlete. The Olympic sport develops – and constructs – 'the individual human being' irrespective of his or her cultural connection. You are the smith of your own luck – this corresponds to the logic of neo-liberalism and the market.

The globalized sport tries to solve the (post)colonial question by among others 'putting Negroes on skis'. In the 1990s, two Kenyan runners were brought to Finland in order to turn them into skiers. Indeed, one of them gained Olympic experience in 1998 but as soon as the media had satisfied their curiosity, the sponsor scrapped the project (Vettenniemi, 2002; more generally see Bale and Maguire, 1994). The individual athlete, free from cultural connection, is reminiscent of the description that Frantz Fanon (1961, p. 167) once gave about the 'psycho-affective mutilations' of colonial power: 'Human beings without horizon, without borders, without colour, no home, no roots, angels'. This characterized the connection between individualization and alienation.

Empirically, the hypothesis of the lonely and self-installed athlete contains an abstraction, contrasting with the collective expressions of sports by national anthems, national flags and accompanying ethno-pop, which are still customary or even expanding. It is only recently that the victory lap, the run of the winner with the national flag around the stadium, has become a general ritual. But also the teams of powerful economic corporations – for instance in the Tour de France – reveal the hypothesis of individualization as ideology: the athlete is not alone in the world. But with whom is she or he together? One answer is: the 'race'.

The Competition of 'Races'

The strong presence of African and African American athletes in certain running competitions has given rise to a new debate about 'black' and 'white' in sports, especially in the US (Hoberman, 1997; Entine, 2000). In China, experts work on medal strategies to avoid ineffective investment into disciplines like basketball, boxing and sprint, where black athletes dominate. With scientific assumptions about blood groups and similar biological factors, sport is classified by 'racial types'. Modernity has dreamt for centuries of a sport without colours. This is challenged now: is the colourless sport an illusion?

In any case, the actual 'globalization of racial folklore' (Hoberman, 1997, pp. 137–9), with its dichotomization of 'black and white', falls back before the 'tribal' differentiations, which classical colonialism had elaborated (Bale, 2002). Indeed, closer examination of the case of the Kenyan runners' successes shows that relevant ethnic differentiations exist inside the Kenyan society (Bale and Sang, 1996). Does this mean that we have to think a new ethnic tribalization?

Tribal Competitions

In 1989, the revolutionary move of 'We are the people!' spread in Eastern Europe, in Central Asia and the Balkans. Larger state-political units dissolved with the breakdown of the Soviet Union and minor national units emerged, also in sports. Not only did we witness the birth of Slovenian and Macedonian, Belorussian and Estonian Olympic committees, of teams from Uzbekistan, Latvia and Turkmenistan etc., but also there was uprising in the West. The Olympic Games in Barcelona 1992 led to Catalan 'tribal' politics of identity (Hargreaves, 2000). Scotland and other Celtic countries are developing their own sports identity (Jarvie, 1999). Will we soon meet teams and Olympic committees from East Timor and Kosovo, and then from Tibet, Pays Basque, Kurdistan, Quebec, Chechnya, Corsica, Brittany etc.? Maybe the nations of the future are barely known to us at the present time.

The new tribalizations have often undertones of cultural multiplicity and richness, of autonomy and liberation (Maffesoli, 1996; Blecking, 2001). But tribal war is another possibility. The massacres between Hutu and Tutsi in Rwanda are not located in a past time, closed and finished (Bale, 2002).

The classical national state as well as its ideological correlate, the 'individual' citizen, is thus challenged not only by the market (the transnational corporation team), but also – and in accordance with its own public logic – by tendencies towards larger units, the 'race', and towards minor units, the 'tribal' neo-nation. Meanwhile, other practices develop outside the logic of Olympic sport and public strategies try to emerge, in the directions of welfare and integration.

. . . and Post-Olympism

Welfare Sport

An increasing part of body culture is organized around health and social integration. In prolongation of the classical model of gymnastics, new practices appeal to the individual desire for fitness on one hand and to the state-political interest in public health on the other. The public is furthermore interested in social integration of 'marginal groups', as in the Australian programme of a 'harmonious society, united in its patriotism'. The Sydney case shows how welfare sport is embraced by Olympism, but the Olympic model of hierarchical achievement and the welfare model of equality remain nevertheless in tension.

Anti-sport

Quite outside the Olympic system, some tendencies of militant anti-sportive politics of the body have arisen. While earlier forms of Islam like the Egypt Muslim Brotherhood once had tried to copy – and thereby to counter – British colonial sport and American YMCA (Young Men's Christian Association) sport, some wings of the most recent Muslim fundamentalism tend to reject sport as such. Traditions of Wahabism as a special type of Puritanism gain ground. The Afghan Taliban combined the anti-sport line with a violent policy of prohibition against music and dance as well as against the popular New Year festivity *Nawroz* (Rashid, 2000).

A global strategy of prohibition is, thus, directed against both Olympic sport and its popular alternatives. This tendency arises from civil society but is striving towards a public policy of repression, with a strong male gender bias. New, surprising identities are thus growing from civil society, which appear to be far from harmless.

Popular Festivity and Non-sports

On the other side of the spectrum of civil society, 'non-sports' as they were observed already in 1984, are expanding. Popular festivities, play and games are developing and forming new organizational frameworks. Some old games have become 'new games' and found attention in the Third World (Larsen and Gormsen, 1984; Fatès, 1994). In Western countries they have given birth to a new festival culture across the borders (Barreau and Jaouen, 1998, 2001). Consequently, research has developed a new focus on play and games in civil society (Pfister et al., 1996; Pfister 1997). And inside the metropoles of immigration, the indigenous festivities and games are regarded as a way to meet the psychological and cultural problems of alienation (Emmendörfer-Brössler, 1999, 2000).

Outdoor activities have developed, too. They use nature in different ways, from high-tech risk sport to soft activities 'without leaving traces'. The Scandinavian tradition of *natur-* and *friluftsliv* is one element in this spectrum (Pedersen, 1999).

Expressive activities develop currently, among others out of indigenous dance culture and martial arts and their combination. Indonesian *pencak silat* held its first international tournament in Vienna in 1986 (Cordes 1992; Pätzold,

2000). Brazilian *capoeira* has a place on *folkehøjskoler* in the Danish countryside (Borghäll, 1997). Gymnastics as popular festivity attract large participation and spectatorship, with Zulu warrior dance from South Africa included.

While expressive activities represent an outward turn of popular movement, other activities turn inward, to the human psyche. This inward turn of body culture shows a broad spectrum, with risk sport side by side with meditative deepening, with therapeutic concentration and the ecstatic sound of drums. Bungee jumping is one example. From its starting point as a popular festivity, the Melanesian 'land diving' of Vanuatu, it was transferred to an outdoor practice in New Zealand, placed into a neo-colonial and commercial framework, and expanded further to the worldwide bungee jumping as adventure sport and risk test. By this cultural 'translation', the bungee jump is a case of what can be called the 'decentring of the West' (Maguire, 1999, p. 216).

Is there any overall pattern in these changes, or do we find just a chaotic panorama? New methodological questions are arising. When analysing globalization from below, from the body – when analysing movement in connection with identity – when analysing body culture under the aspect of contradictions – the way opens towards finding patterns in the multitude of varieties. The (im-)balance of power between market (and individual competition), state (and welfare sport) and civil society (and popular festivity) is one promising approach.

Identity on the Agenda

When asking for the social background of post-Olympic changes, we cannot overlook the 'invasion' of elderly people into sports, which has happened during the latest decades. The increase of elderly participation in sports changes the patterns of practice, so that the competitive sport of young people – faster, higher, stronger – to a lesser and lesser degree represents the general picture of people's sport. At the same time, as statistical data from Denmark since the late 1980s reveal, the spectatorship of TV sport seems to decrease. The active participation tends to surpass the mediated sport consumption quantitatively (Larsen, 2002, 2003). This is a new situation in history. As TV sport is continuing the Olympic patterns, it mirrors (in Denmark, at least) less and less the extent of popular sporting practice (Eichberg, 2000; Schultz Jørgensen, 2002). The sports and tourism markets had already begun to react to the new 'non-sportive sports' (Dietrich and Heinemann, 1989). People's new needs promise commercial profit, but their market is expanding mostly outside the world of Olympic competition. Anyway, the critical analysis of the actual scenarios around Olympic sport, of its contradictions inside and outward, leads to neither only one single mainstream – the continued expansion of Olympic productivism – nor to one single dominating dualism. Expressed in the language of fractal geometry (Mandelbrot, 1982), we meet not only a 'smooth' order in sports – either/or – but also a world of fractal contradictions. These fractal qualities in sports are coming primarily from civil society, the life-world of folk. They question the hegemonic pattern or what might be called the monotheism of productivity, which is ritually represented by the Olympic sport of result production.

We can express these contradictions and their historical change in the terms of jumping: modernity has in its very beginning brought the expansion of the gymnastic jump. But already in the nineteenth century, the sportive jump of achievement began to develop as a hegemonic configuration. This did not, however, represent the end of history. But with the appearance of bungee jumping from the depth of Melanesian folk culture, a new model has arisen. The connection of risk, self-test and psycho-experience ranges outside the classical modern achievement pattern.

However different the directions may be, in which the new contradictions as well as the scenarios are pointing, each jump and each of the post-Olympic scenarios means that social identities are newly constructed, and this in different ways. To take the example of the jump: people once jumped the equality of the nation (by gymnastics); they have jumped the record to gain a position in the hierarchy of producers (by sport); they have jumped the belonging of the village (Melanesian land diving) and they jump the self-test of risk (bungee). People are jumping different types of identities – and the Olympic jump is just one of them.

This can be related to the scenarios, as described earlier: 'the individual' understood as the individual producer of his or her own result, supplemented by the individual consumer on the global market, is only one of these identities, and its inner unequivocal consistency – me the producer (of myself) – is even falling from each other. Alternative vehicles of identification are the 'race' and the 'tribe', challenging the traditional national identity, as it is fixed in the state-issued 'identification card'. The neo-Puritan construction of the 'believer' versus the 'infidel' gains in dynamism and is, perhaps, not limited to the world of Islamic fundamentalism (Galtung, 2002). Furthermore, we are a 'target group' of welfare society. And we are the people of the popular folk culture, whether 'traditional' or 'global neo-tribes'. In other words, we experience a clash of identities, both worldwide and inside ourselves. And none of these identities is only ideological. Each identity develops in connection with social bodily practice, with movement culture.

Furthermore, none of these identities can be understood in isolation. Identity is relational – just like the body is fundamentally related to movement practice in encounter, as inter-body (Eichberg, 2002). People's identity cannot be thought without the relation to other identities. We have to think the 'between'. And this 'between' is neither restricted to the international in the sense of inter-state relation, nor to the global transfer of services and goods between different market sectors, but it has also a dimension of civil society. The inbetween of popular sport and culture is encounter from-folk-to-folk – or what in Danish is called *mellemfolkelig*, the inter-popular.

Anyway, the sociological question about post-Olympism leads to fundamental questions of identity: who are the people of sports, and who will be the people of democracy under the premises of globalization? And it leads to fundamental questions about the 'material base' of social practice. Evidently, it is easier to put a boomerang into a logo, to set multicultural ceremonies on stage and to make promising words about ethnic recognition, than to change the real practice in sports.

Whose Cathy – and which People?

In the Sydney Games 2000, the Aboriginal athlete Cathy Freeman lit the Olympic cauldron and won gold in the women's 400 metres. Giving face to the 'other' side of Australia, Cathy Freeman became the Australian celebrity of the games.

Cathy Freeman did not only lend her charming and smiling image to Olympic sport. But, being the first Aborigine to win an individual Olympic event, she also used the situation to call to public attention the fate of her 386,000 mostly impoverished fellow people. Already, at the moment of her first famous success in 1994, Freeman had run her victory lap with the red, yellow and black Aboriginal flag, which, at the time was still controversial. A special case for Freeman were those 100,000 native children, which the Australian government had taken by force from their families during the 1930s and the 1960s, who were never allowed to return to their homes. Freeman's grandmother had been a member of this 'stolen generation'. When the Australian government refused to formally apologize, Freeman openly accused the authorities. In the Sydney Olympics, Cathy Freeman's sportive achievement gave occasion to the Australian shouts of enthusiasm: 'Aussie! Aussie! Oi! Oi! Oi!' After her 400 metres victory, the runner waved both the Australian and the Aboriginal flags. This looked like an expression of Olympic multiculturalism in real life.

But it can also be seen as a form of 'reconciliation, as conceived by a Down Under version of a Hollywood production . . . As if we had erected one more glittering casino on another Native American reservation and called the slate even' (Blinebury 2000). This is how an Australian observer has commented on the Olympic finale: '*Our Cathy!*' – exclaimed the headlines of the Australian media. Whose Cathy did they talk about? And who was this 'we'?

Who are 'we'?

Cosmopolitan Olympism, Humanism and the Spectacle of 'Race'

Ben Carrington

It is the rule now that no one can take part in the Olympic Games other than as a representative of his own country. This is a first step, for previously the nationality of competitors had not always been taken into account, but merely their technical qualities. A fundamental article of the general regulations drawn up in 1894 reserves the right of the organising committees to reject any candidate whose character or previous record of conduct might reflect injuriously upon the dignity of the institution. We must establish the tradition that each competitor shall in his bearing and conduct as a man of honour and a gentleman endeavour to prove in what respect he holds the Games and what an honour he feels to participate in them . . . Such is my view of the development which ought to take place in the institution of the modern Olympic Games . . . The work must be lasting, to exercise over the sports of the future that necessary and beneficent influence for which I look – an influence which shall make them the means of bringing to perfection *the strong and hopeful youth of our white race*, thus again helping towards the perfection of all human society.

Pierre de Coubertin, 'Why I Revived the Olympic Games', 1908 (emphasis added)

Introduction

This chapter addresses a number of issues relating to the ideological content of Olympism and the extent to which it can usefully function as a progressive set of ideals and practices in our current climate of late capitalist, postcolonial modernity. I am interested in the interrelationship and articulation between 'humanism', 'Olympism' and 'cosmopolitanism' as discourses, ideologies and political projects. I want to explore the extent to which sport, and in particular the Olympics, makes possible moments when we are able to transcend our seemingly natural identity skins of racial ascription and national belonging. I am also interested in mapping how sport continues to shape and frame our understandings of ourselves as embodied social agents and the *potentially* progressive moves that sport can offer in beginning to disrupt our acceptance of racial classifications.

If John Hoberman (1997, p. xxiii) is right in his observation that sport is an image factory that intensifies our racial preoccupations then those of us committed to forms of post-racial sociality need to examine in particular those 'image factories' which operate not just regionally or nationally, but increasingly globally too. Given that ideologies are never fixed, stable entities, that they can at times be subverted, overturned and challenged, I want to add a questioning rejoinder to Hoberman's observation: that is, do we have to accept that sport *can only* reinforce our racial preoccupations? What agency is left in spectacles like the Olympics to shift, disrupt and even dismantle the dubious scaffolding that ideologies of 'race' and nationalism have erected around our self-identities? And how might a black swimmer from Equatorial Guinea and a white sprinter from Greece show us both the promise and failure of the Olympics to make real a sense of our shared cosmopolitan humanism?

Humanism and the Spectacle of 'Race'

It is clear that there are strong links between the ideologies of Olympism and humanism. Pierre de Coubertin's vision of Olympism derived from a mixture of the 'renaissance', 'romantic' and 'Enlightenment' traditions of French humanism found in the various works of Montaigne, Rousseau and Constant in particular (see Todorov, 2002) and a version of muscular Christianity that dominated the nineteenth-century British public school system.[1] Coubertin's conception of Olympic humanism was one that claimed roots stretching back to Antiquity, linking body, mind and spirit in the quest for moral uplift, social betterment and international peace. As Alan Tomlinson (1984, p. 85) notes, the revival of the modern Olympics should be understood 'as the project of an increasingly displaced or dislocated aristocrat who looked towards both the model of athleticism pioneered by the contemporary British upper classes and a world of mind-body harmony in ancient Greece, in order to breed a new generation of men to rule the modern world'.[2] The universalism of Olympism is grounded through its carefully constructed ritualistic displays of ceremony which invokes an almost sacred embrace of humanity, the human body and human creativity. Thus as John MacAloon (1984, p. 251) noted the 'transcendental ground' of Olympic rituals is the idea of an almost religious sense of human-ness itself. MacAloon continues that within such rituals, 'the symbols of generic individual and national identities are assembled and arrayed in such a way as to model, or to attempt to model, the shared humanity that is both the ground of the structural divisions the symbols condense and portray as well as the ultimate goal of Olympic ideology and practice' (ibid.).

Like Olympism, and often for very similar reasons, humanism itself has been dismissed, as Tony Davies (1997, p. 5) points out in his critical survey of the concept, 'as an ideological smokescreen for the oppressive mystifications of modern society and culture' as well as causing 'the marginalisation and oppression of the multitudes of human beings in whose name it pretends to speak' (see also Soper 1986).[3] Conversely it has been heralded as a 'philosophical champion of human freedom and dignity, standing alone and often outnumbered against the battalions of ignorance, tyranny and superstition' (Davies, 1997, p. 5). For those such as Matthew Arnold, humanism was synonymous with cultural development, where culture is read as an expression of (European) civilization, thus to be 'cultured' meant a certain 'cultivation of the mind' (Eagleton, 2000).

As it developed during the Enlightenment, humanism gave birth to modern Man. This universalist discourse was central to the development of Republicanism both in France and in the US. It is found in for example Thomas Paine's (1792) *The Rights of Man*, in Rousseau's (1762) *The Social Contract* and of course in Thomas Jefferson's (1776) Declaration of Independence. It is from this moment in the eighteenth century that 'a full-blown essentialised notion of humanity' is constructed (Davies, 1997, p. 26). Of course this construction of humankind was narrow and partial. That slave-owning could continue in the US, that the *Rights of Man* was actually about the rights of property-owning *men*, that France and other European imperial powers could see no contradiction between the doctrine of Universal Rights and the denial of these to colonial subjects, demonstrated the deeply racialized and gendered nature of humanism. Thus as Davies notes, drawing on the observations of Marx, the 'rhetoric of "Universal Man" that accompanied the revolutions of the eighteenth and nineteenth centuries tended to give way, once its ideological work was done' (1997, p. 26) allowing the promotion of narrower class interests to re-emerge. Humanism, far from challenging European imperialistic expansion and colonial control, actually provided one of the main philosophical justifications for racial terror and exploitation.

The social structures of imperialism and the popular and scientific representations that structured colonial relationships produced powerful constructions of black people as sub-human. Thus the Enlightenment project was simply thought to not apply to the 'savage' blacks who, as thinkers as diverse as Kant and Hume argued, were deemed incapable of attaining European standards of moral and intellectual development.[4] As Emmanuel Eze notes, it was Enlightenment philosophy which was 'instrumental in codifying and institutionalizing both the scientific and popular European perceptions of the human race. The numerous writings on race by Hume, Kant, and Hegel played a strong role in articulating Europe's sense not only of its cultural but also *racial* superiority' (Eze, 1997, p. 5; see also Eze, 2001). Such views are most clearly expressed in Hegel's *Lectures on the Philosophy of World History* (1975 [1830], p.128) where he asserts:

> man as we find him in Africa has not progressed beyond his immediate existence. As soon as man emerges as a human being, he stands in opposition to nature, and it is this alone which makes him a human being. But if he has merely made a distinction between himself and nature, he is still at the first stage of his development: he is dominated by passion, and is nothing more than a savage. All our observations of African man show him as living in a state of savagery and barbarism, and he remains in this state to the present day. The negro is an example of animal man in all his savagery and lawlessness, and if we wish to understand him at all, we must put aside all our European attitudes . . . nothing consonant with humanity is to be found in his character.[5]

Western anthropologists sought to prove that blacks, in their biological make-up, were closer to animals than fellow white Europeans through craniological comparisons with various primates, which was then used to explain the supposed uneven distribution in intelligence among particular 'races'. Georges Cuvier – who according to Stephen Jay Gould (1997, p. 66) was considered in nineteenth-century France as 'the Aristotle of his age', as well as 'a founder of geology, palae-ontology, and modern comparative anatomy' – argued that Africans were 'the most degraded of human races, whose form approaches that of the beast and whose intelligence is nowhere great enough to arrive at regular government' (Cuvier, 1812, cited in Gould, 1997, p. 69). Thus the disciplinary power of Western science was central in producing alterity and in constructing 'the black body' as a legitimate area for study upon which its normalizing gaze could be inscribed – measuring, photographing and categorizing, in minute detail, the various components of the black body.[6] This legitimized further racialized inquiry, which would later, during the Eugenics movement in the early part of the twentieth century, include the desperate search for the supposed innate capacitates for sporting prowess, as modern science tried to uncover the secret truth(s) encased within the black skin of African bodies.[7]

The attempt to essentialize and place that Other in a binary opposition grew from a standpoint that also allowed the idea of Europe itself to emerge. Ideologies of 'race' and white supremacy were not then minor appendages or epiphenomenal exceptions to the emergence of Enlightenment thought and European humanism, but were *from their inception* pivotal and internal to the project of modernity. It is impossible to talk about the modern construction of the subject and the 'civilizing process' of the nation-state without an account of how European racism saturated these discourses. As Sartre acknowledged, 'there is nothing more consistent than a racist humanism since the European has only been able to become a man through creating slaves and monsters' (1967 [1961], p. 22; see also Sartre, 2001).[8]

The 'dehumanization' of blacks, however, was a contradictory process. For as blacks were vilified for their supposed sub-human impulses they also, simultaneously, became the subject of a romanticized Occidental idealism, being seen as reflecting a pure state of abandonment, against the unnatural technocratic developments of a newly emerging industrial modernity. Africans became idealized/eroticized *and* despised/condemned at the same time. The colonial construction of the abject black body was ambivalent from the start, allowing constructions of the Other to remain both 'fixed' and to adapt (and sometimes to even reverse its connotations) in different historical contexts in order for it to make sense to its particular location and to 'work'.[9]

The patent gap between the rhetoric of humanism and the acts carried out under its name was critically analysed by anti-colonial writers such as Frantz Fanon and Aimé Césaire. As Césaire (2000[1955], p. 37) states in his powerful essay 'Discourse on Colonialism': 'that is the great thing I hold against pseudo-humanism: that for too long it has diminished the rights of man, that its concept of those rights has been – and still is – narrow and fragmentary, incomplete and biased and, all things considered, sordidly racist'. What is significant here, and point of departure for our discussion in rethinking humanism, was that despite the disreputable narrative of European history, black and Third Worldist intellectuals did not dismiss humanism per se. Rather the anti-colonial struggles based themselves upon 'universalist' principles of self-determination, freedom and emancipation that attempted to make real the claims made under the rubric of humanism. Their project was to expose the ethnocentric version of humanism that European thinkers had produced as a way to construct *new* bases for a universalist project of a post-racial, cosmopolitan humanism.

Cosmopolitanism and Planetary Humanism

These debates over the particular versus the universal have re-emerged in recent times in discussions concerning the possibilities to develop new universalistic political imaginaries and subject positions that can embrace the cultural hybridty and political pluralism that globalization has produced (A. Anderson, 1998; Butler et al., 2000; Balibar, 2002). If 'postmodernism' was the key buzzword of the 1980s, just as 'globalization' was for much of the 1990s, then 'cosmopolitanism' might well come to be one of the central conceptual debates for the first decade of the twenty-first century. This should not be dismissed as an intellectual fad but taken seriously as the current conditions of a postcolonial disorganized world order throw into sharp relief critical questions about belonging, civil society, identity and citizenship that cosmopolitanism seeks to address. This is a wide-ranging debate but briefly we can see that whereas internationalism sees itself as a doctrine committed to international harmony and cooperation, but still within the logic of nation-state affiliation, cosmopolitanism in its neo-Kantian form makes claims for a global civil society within which individuals see themselves as *world* citizens united, at some level, by a common sense of species connection.[10] Nation-states and national identity therefore have a much more ambivalent role to play within cosmopolitan accounts in as much as the nation as a unit is seen either as a temporary formation in light of a global public sphere or as an enabler for people, communities and organizations to develop transnational global institutions.[11] Cosmopolitanism also raises fundamental ethical questions and has been used as a way to rethink and dissolve the absolute binaries of self/other, friend/stranger, insider/outsider that have underpinned contemporary political debates, particularly within Europe, concerning migration, refugees and asylum seekers (for example see Derrida, 2001). Cosmopolitanism contributes therefore to new ways of thinking and feeling. As Ulrich Beck (2002, p. 18) argues the 'national perspective is a monologic imagination which excludes the otherness of the other. The cosmopolitan perspective is an alternative imagination, an imagination of alternative ways of life and rationalities, which include the otherness of the other'.

These discussions concerning, for example, the increased diversity of communities due to migration, the globalization and interdependence of social relations due to technological and economic developments, and the inter-cultural flows within everyday life associated with globalizing media and travel which has led to a certain cultural fragmentation (Chaney, 2002), all of which pose a challenge to nation-state hegemony, have been taken up in a variety of contexts and across academic disciplines. Within political theory discussions have centred on the rights to recognition of minority groups and the extent to which citizenship itself, for so long a central condition of nation-state identification, needs to be rethought and expanded. This has led to arguments for the enlargement of the public sphere to take account of the plurality of subject positions, calls for the United Nations' charter to be remodelled, and perhaps superseded by a 'Second Assembly' of democratic nations, to enhance the cosmopolitan basis of the international polity (Archibugi and Held, 1995; Held, 1995) and renewed engagements with developing notions of a *global* deliberative democracy in the context of multicultural societies (see Joppke and Lukes, 1999; Dower, 2000; Mouffe, 2000; Parekh, 2000; Young, 2000; Kymlicka, 2001; Balibar, 2002; Benhabib, 2002).

Within legal theory debates have focused on the legal limits and political legitimacy of the nation-state's power over its citizens against wider, more fundamental notions of *human rights*. As with the debates within political theory, this is also, in part, a *philosophical* discussion concerning the extent to which such rights can resolve particularistic claims to cultural identity and religious belief in opposition to universal responsibilities to society and the ethical duties of self/Other relationships (see Caney and Jones, 2001; Derrida, 2001; Ignatieff, 2001; De Greiff and Cronin, 2002).

Sociologists too have been concerned to trace the *social* implications and impacts of cosmopolitanism on aspects of our cultural identities – both in terms of the new risks (ecological, financial, epidemiological) these changes bring and also in terms of an increased awareness and openness to other cultural forms and aesthetics. It is argued that the erosion and destabilization of traditional markers of social identity, linked to bounded notions of localised place set within nation-state frameworks, has given way to more complex and fluid identities within which travel, the media, telecommunications and supranational identifications become more central to lived experiences of many (see Featherstone, 1995; Featherstone et al., 2002; Urry, 2003).

Within post/colonial theory these general discussions on cosmopolitanism have been developed through an examination of the continuance of ethnic absolutist politics in the context of new postcolonial subjectivities that have challenged and transrupted the logic and efficacy of dominant, monocultural nationalisms that for so long violently suppressed cultural difference (see Hesse, 2000). Paul Gilroy (2000), in his important work *Between Camps*, has argued for a rethinking of debates over cosmopolitanism and humanism and proposes what he variously calls a 'planetary humanism' (p. 17) and a 'postracial humanism' (p. 37). Gilroy's work is in many ways an attempt to map out the 'new humanism' that is prefigured in the work of earlier black anti-colonial intellectuals such as Césaire and particularly Fanon (Berasconi, 1996). Gilroy's complex argument is a self-confessed utopian position, based on the belief that raciological thinking continues to reinscribe racial difference as the central ontological point through which subjectivities are formed. Thus by failing to transcend the forms of identity formation that racial ideology produces we remained trapped within those racially overdetermined discourses which have brought such devastating effects. Gilroy's humanism, then, is an attempt to move on from the anthropological humanisms that were so marked by the discourse of racial difference. This results not in a negation of the phenomenological experiences of particularity but in recognizing that, for example, even those groups whose histories are marked by forms of oppression and denial have a duty to situate such episodes as emblematic of a wider common human history. Speaking in the context of fascism and other similar forms of unanimist political doctrines that use the modality of 'race' as forms of govermentality, Gilroy (2000) argues:

> Those of us tied by affinity as well as kinship to histories of suffering and victimage have an additional responsibility not to betray our capacity to imagine democracy and justice in indivisible, nonsectarian forms . . . diverse stories of suffering can be recognized as belonging to anyone who dares to possess them and in good faith employ them as interpretative devices through which we may clarify the limits of our selves, the basis of our solidarities, and perhaps pronounce upon the value of our values. (Gilroy, 2000, p. 230)

Following Gilroy (2000, p. 96), I want to suggest then that this re-working of humanism might be described as a *strategic universalism*. This is a deliberately political move – with echoes of both Spivak's notion of the necessity for forms of strategic essentialism and the position that it is possible to be theoretically 'antihumanist' while practising humanism – that seeks to hold on to the idea of a common, universal moral world among humans, even if one is sceptical of the absolute philosophical truth of such a claim. As Sartre (1973, pp. 45– 6) acknowledged, 'although it is impossible to find in each and every man [sic] a universal essence that can be called human nature, there is nevertheless a human universality of *condition*'.

Few of the accounts on cosmopolitanism have analysed vernacular cultures in much detail and even fewer have taken sport seriously as an object of study.[12] I want now to briefly locate sport within the general debates over cosmopolitan humanism. I want to address these discussions in terms of a general question, namely, can the Olympics be constructed as a space within which nationalism is downplayed and not reinforced and where the achievements (or indeed failures) of athletes are read as examples of achieved humanity rather than as confirmations of racialized exceptionalism?

Re-imagining the Race: Eric the Eel and the Non-white White Athlete

Two 'moments' from the 2000 Sydney Summer Olympics illustrate the contradictory nature of the Olympics in both embedding universalistic discourses whilst reframing these moments back within predictable forms of knowing. The Olympics is constructed as a space beyond the real world concerns of political antagonism, national chauvinism and racial contestation. Indeed the Olympics has often been credited as a space that can actually counter the profane world of politics. Yet as MacAloon noted, 'the Olympic Games create a sort of hyper-structure in which categories and stereotypes are condensed, exaggerated, and dramatized, rescued from the "taken for granted" and made the objects of explicit and lively awareness for a brief period every four years' (1984, p. 275).

On day four of the 2000 Games in the Sydney Aquatic Centre a moment of 'true Olympism' was made. Eric Moussambani of Equatorial Guinea turned his 100 metre freestyle race into his fifteen minutes of allotted Olympic fame.[13] With both of his competitors disqualified for false starts Moussambani, or 'Eric', as the media decided to call him, swam a determined first leg but then struggled as he came back for the final 50 metres. The *Daily Telegraph* reported that after a 'brave attempt at a tumble turn he started to struggle and poolside observers looked on anxiously as he struck for home. Officials even considered the possibility of having to rescue him as he appeared to sink beneath the water 10 metres from home before one final effort saw him finish' (Foster, 2000, p. 3). Moussambani, described in *The Times* as 'more of an energetic drowner' (Truss, 2000, p. 10) than a swimmer, was deemed to have embodied the true Olympic spirit. *The Times* reported on its front page:

Moussambani, 22, caused a sensation at the Sydney Games when he was persuaded by his coach to compete in a heat for the men's 100-metre freestyle. He learnt to swim only nine months ago in crocodile-infested rivers and assumed he had no chance . . . His family were unable to see his feat on the screen. Like most people in their remote corner of West Africa, they do not own a television. Indeed until last night, his mother was not even sure why he had gone to Sydney. She thought that his favourite sport was basketball. Other relatives and friends in the capital, Malabo, were astonished to learn that he was competing over 100 metres as he had never swum that far before without stopping to take a breath. When he practised in the sea he took a friend to watch out for sharks . . . Moussambani's proudest moment before yesterday was carrying the West African country's flag at the opening ceremony. He confessed: 'I didn't want to swim the 100 metres but my coach told me that I should do it anyway. I thought it was too much'. Until he stood at the start of yesterday's heat, Eric had never seen a 50–metre Olympic size pool . . . In a Games too often clouded by controversy over drugs and money, the African with the beaming smile had recaptured the essential Olympic spirit. (Lord and Watts, 2000, p. 1)

Moussambani's achievement was deemed of such significance that it even earned him a leader comment in *The Times*. Under the banner 'TRUE AMATEURS: Losers who climb the pinnacles of Olympic fame', Moussambani was praised for his heroic failing and for joining 'a select band of Olympians whose performances stand out for the majesty of their failure'. Thus rather than the 'superhuman', muscled torsos of the world's athletic elite, it was the human failings of the unspectacular that allowed 'us', the viewing public, to identify across nation, 'race' and geography with those 'true amateurs'. The *Times'* leader concluded, 'The further great athletes soar beyond the reach of ordinary mortals, the more reassuring are the plucky antics of the loser. For he could, spectator, be you'.

As with *The Times'* coverage, the *Daily Telegraph* also recounted anthropological stories of the Equatorial Guinea swimming team training in the 'crocodile and shark infested waters around the west African coast' (Foster, 2000, p. 3). The story was run under the title banner 'Olympian from the Equator wins at a crawl: An African who only started swimming this year helps to maintain the amateur tradition of Eddie the Eagle' (ibid.). Much was also made in the print media of Moussambani's swimwear. The *Telegraph* noted: 'In contrast to the futuristic outfits of most of the competitors, Moussambani stood at the start in traditional swimming trunks with the drawstring clearly showing' (ibid.).

While Moussambani's moment was generally read as the revival of the Olympic amateur spirit amidst the over-commercialized, drug-infested and profession- alized spectacle of modern day sports, another subtext was at work. The sight of a near-drowning black African, with string casually hanging from his Speedo swimming trunks, was greeted by the world's media with the kind of patronizing acclaim that was historically reserved for Indian footballers without boots or bare-footed East African runners. The *subtext* to the coverage was not so much about Eric Moussambani, a likeable, but largely minor figure within that summer's Olympics, but about a (re)framing of the West's knowledge of the African Other. In addition to the amusing culture clash of the modern West against traditional Africa, and the accounts of untamed wildlife roaming the waters of West Africa, Moussambani, as a signifier, shifted from and between the position of amateur Olympian to archetypal black African. Thus much of the coverage framed him not simply as an individual, or even as an individual from Equatorial Guinea, but as representative, in some fundamental way for *Africa* itself and black people in general. Even given the escapades of the British ski jumper Eddie 'the Eagle' Edwards who was sometimes read as embodying a form of English male pathos, he was never referred to as 'the European ski- jumper'. It was however the grinning African, freed from swimming away from crocodiles, who had allowed 'us', in the overdeveloped West, to once again find the pure, untarnished spirit of Olympism – supposedly putting us back in touch with Coubertin's dream.[14]

A week after Moussambani had dragged himself from the Sydney pool, across town in the Olympic Stadium, Konstantinos Kenteris left his starting blocks. A little over twenty seconds later he had crossed the finishing line, winning the men's 200 metres final. In so doing he became the first white male athlete to win an Olympic sprinting gold since Alan Wells won the men's 100 metres and Pietro Mennea won the 200 metres nearly two decades earlier and only the second Greek Olympic runner since Spiridon Louis's gold in the 1896 marathon (Guttmann, 2002, p. 192).[15] In a post-racial world in which human sporting endeavour was merely an index of human potential and creativity such a feat would have lacked any racial significance. But this was the Olympics, and a sprint final at that, a space so over-determined by racial signification that the mere presence of a 'non-black' athlete in such a setting was deemed as incongruous as a black swimming champion. As Kenteris strode away from the rest of the (black) field and crossed the finishing line with a wide smile and even wider outstretched arms, one of the key shibboleths of racialogical thinking – namely that white men can't sprint – was shattered. Here was glorious, hyper-mediated and public evidence that 'race' as biological destiny was a spurious, redundant fallacy. If the Olympics frames our perceptions of racial difference through sporting performance then the trail of languishing black athletes showed that 'race' simply did not matter beyond the human achievement of this Olympic moment. Yet even this unequivocal moment showed that the racialization of sporting feats cannot be so easily usurped. A number of narratives quickly emerged to try to 'make sense' of this threat to the racial sporting order. Commentators talked of their 'surprise' at Kenteris's 'sudden' progress. Some in the media hinted that it was not a *real* victory as Michael Johnson, for so long dominant in men's sprinting, had not competed due to his injury during the US trials earlier in the year.[16] Moreover some intimated that the world could not really be sure Kenteris was champion until the results of the drugs tests were published. As Richard Williams writing in the *Guardian* noted:

> Kenteris was asked how it felt to be the first white man to win the 200m since Pietro Mennea in 1980, but wisely chose to misunderstand the question. 'Mennea was a great athlete', he replied, through an interpreter. 'But I have my own personality' . . . Given the climate surrounding these games, such an unexpected result naturally invites scepticism . . . all Greece will be hoping that, when the results of the doping tests come in on Sunday afternoon, this does not prove to have been the Olympic 200m final that lasted three days and 20.09 sec. (Williams, 2000, p. 2)

The implicit assumption behind such commentary was that the only rational explanation for why a white athlete seemed to have so comprehensively beaten seven black guys was that the white athlete *must* have been on drugs. Once it was shown that Kenteris had not taken any run-fast supplements (or at least no more than any other top-level sprinter) a deep and fundamental problem was posed for those believers in the race-sports performance myth. Whereas the achievement of Wells and Mennea two decades earlier is seen by some not to have offered 'real' proof against racial deterministic thinking because of the American (read African American) boycott, this argument could not be employed at Sydney. True, Michael Johnson did not compete but the rest of the field were of a dark enough hue to be classified as 'black' by even the most determinist of racial fanatics. However, there was another explanation that might just restore the racial order. In a little reported but significant statement Britain's Darren Campbell, who had finished behind Kenteris, suggested that the facts might not have been as obvious as the world assumed. Des Kelly writing in the *Mirror* reported: 'SILVER medallist Darren Campbell was asked whether the victory of Konstantinos Kenteris was a turning point in the recent domination of sprint events by black athletes. Campbell replied: "He's not white, he's Greek"' (Kelly, 2000, p. 57). Unfortunately the journalists present did not press Campbell on his views. There are, at least, two ways to read Campbell's comments. The first, perhaps optimistic, reading is that Campbell was articulating something close to what a cosmopolitan Olympism position might be. In other words Campbell was challenging the premise of the question, namely that athletes should at all be read as prototypical exemplars of their 'race'. Campbell thus negates the questioner's fixation with racial difference by simply asserting that Kenteris is a runner, an athlete, who happens to be Greek – his socially constructed racial grouping having no bearing upon either his abilities or the significance of his victory: 'he's not white, he's Greek'.

The other, and perhaps more likely, reading is that to accept that Kenteris was white, that he had won (this at least could not be denied), and that in a 'fair sprint' he had beaten, with ease, seven world class black athletes, would be to accept that the whole logic of racial difference was meaningless. The self-identifications with notions of sporting superiority among black athletes are no doubt as strong as the self-*disbelief* of many white athletes. In a climate where, outside of the entertainment industries, blackness still carries strong negative connotations and where black men still face symbolic and real violence, personal discrimination and social persecution (Marriott, 2000), the embrace of sporting stereotypes within societies that offer status premiums for those who have tough, athletic and powerful bodies is not surprising. Thus Campbell simply could not accept the fact that he crossed the line *behind* a white male athlete. Given that it could not be argued that Kenteris had not won, the only other option is to resignify Kenteris, *to make Kenteris non-white*, if not quite black. The logic of the argument presumably being that those Greeks are a bit swarthy aren't they? That 'we' (middle and Northern Europeans) always had doubts about those in the South – that didn't the Moors spent a bit *too long* in Spain and Southern Italy and isn't Greece virtually a part of North Africa anyway?

What both of these seemingly innocuous episodes point to is the way in which the Olympics does throw up moments of sporting transcendence that seem to offer ways out of the binary modes of viewing ourselves that the prism of 'race' imposes. Yet, at the very same time, such sites are often over-determined by forms of racialized representations that manage to secure the meanings of these counter-hegemonic moments for dominant ends. Thus the courageous and uplifting strokes of Moussambani become re-coded as the comical actions of an infantilized *African* renamed via animalistic simile as Eric the Eel. The historic gold medal for a dedicated athlete from Greece exposes the racial signification of sport but is then reframed as an exceptional aberration or an event that simply did not take place at all.

The Politics of Cosmopolitan Olympism

As noted earlier in the chapter, Coubertin's internationalism was never cosmopolitan (Guttmann, 2002, p. 2; see also Hoberman, 1995). This contradiction at the heart of Olympism, an ideal that posits the universal bonds between humans through the pursuit of individual greatness, but also an ideal that defers to the supposed natural bonds of national allegiance, has never truly been resolved. Guttmann is right in this context to remind us that although the Olympic Charter:

> proclaims that the games are contests between individuals, not between nations, the IOC created an institutional structure based on national representation: no athlete can compete as an individual; every athlete must be selected by his or her country's national Olympic committee; every athlete . . . must wear a national uniform; when a victor is honored, a national flag is raised and a national anthem is played. (Guttmann, 2002, p. 2)

In contrast, cosmopolitan Olympism challenges the saliency of national teams, emblems and allegiances. It decentres nationalism and nation-state symbolism and promotes the sense of human achievement; it avoids a spurious amoral universalism and embraces a contested and explicitly political sporting democracy; it engages and extend sport's human rights discourse and the basis upon which those rights are formed thus politicizing the IOC's own statements; it questions the focus on the elite and the body beautiful at the expense of the participatory while centring the importance of the para-Olympics. As the Olympics is awarded to *cities* a radical opportunity is opened up to constitute the ethical position of hospitality to the stranger which is behind Derrida's arguments for 'cities of refuge' within which the open city, rather than the closed nation-state, redefines its borders as porous and would 'welcome and protect those innocents who sought refuge' (2001, p. 17). It would be interesting to see how eager national governments were to 'host' the games if the condition of such a privilege was predicated on the hosting city being redesignated open to all who seek sanctuary.

A key question then is the extent to which such a cosmopolitanism is feasible, given the current climate of resurgent ethno-nationalisms and the assumed naturalness of nation-state identification? Yet this is to concede too easily to the supposed necessity of the nation as a unit of political mobilization and the impossibility of imagining different forms of belonging. The question of nationalism clearly presents a problem for (leftist) critiques that, while sceptical of the liberal and conservative accounts of nationalism that dominate much of the literature in the field, nevertheless still defer, in the last instance, to the nation as a key agent of social change. Yet our current post-anti-colonial situation shows how effective authoritarian and xenophobic mobilizations of nationalism have been in contrast to any putative socialist alternatives. As Clifford observes, the 'hope that "popular" nationalisms will ultimately be different from other nationalisms is surely utopian' (1998, p. 364).

Despite the claims of those who wish to downplay the significant transformations to nation-state hegemony, it remains the case that nation-states are increasingly decentred in a context where there are pluralized, diasporic cultural identities, multiple legal and judicial frameworks, increased forms of devolved power to regions and cities, and a weakening of the ties between territorial residency and civic responsibility, driven, in part by a new global stage of the world economy (Benhabib 2002, pp. 180–1). Moreover it is within the realm of culture and the everyday that forms of *banal cosmopolitanism* have developed through the normative embrace and consumption of music, youth cultures, television, Internet, sport and food. The proxy contestation as the Roast Beef Dinner battles it out with Chicken Tikka Masala for 'The Nation's Favourite Food' serves only to highlight how such food styles are *already* adaptations, re-formed and displaced combinations of culinary habits that are unthinkable outside of the processes of imperial globalization and banal cosmopolitanism. As Beck (2002, p. 28) argues it is this 'banal cosmopolitan culinary eclecticism', found on supermarket shelves everywhere, that is now promoted and celebrated on TV cookery programmes and in ever popular cook books as 'the new normality'. Beck concludes: 'So world society has taken possession of our kitchens and is boiling and sizzling in our pans. Anyone who still wants to raise the national flag, when it comes to food, founders on the ever more hollow myths of national dishes, which at best are no more than islands in the broad stream of the dominant and by now banal culinary cosmopolitanism' (Beck, 2002, p. 28).

It is not so much that we need to create a cosmopolitan humanism that is removed from our present location. The notion that societies change from one social formation to another as an epochal shift is mistaken. Historical rupture and cultural change is always 'a jagged process' (Buck-Morss, 2002, p. 2). As Pollock et al. (2002, p. 12) note, 'we already are and have been cosmopolitan, though we may not always have known it. Cosmopolitanism is not just – or perhaps not at all – an idea. Cosmopolitanism is infinite ways of being'. The question then is whether we are able to recognize, in these times of absolutist nationalist and racial politics, that the multiple forms of attachment between peoples that will/may provide the basis for cosmopolitan solidarities already exist. That is although the formal institutions of global democracy, a clearly delineated global civil society and a functioning global public sphere remain in nascent forms, the wider sense of world connectedness and interdependence has been realized since the birth of the world's modernities. Yet it is this very *inter*connectedness, this very cosmopolitan humanism that also makes possible, and in some ways creates the conditions from which, forms of ethno-nationalism, racism and ethnic chauvinism have been able to emerge. Thus as Balibar notes:

> real universality is a stage where, for the first time, 'humankind' as a single web of inter-relationships is no longer an ideal or utopian notion but an actual condition for every individual; nevertheless, far from representing a situation of mutual recognition, it actually coincides with a generalized pattern of conflicts, hierarchies and exclusions. It is not even a situation in which individuals communicate at least virtually with each other, but much more one where global communication networks provide every individual with a distorted image or a stereotype of all others, either as 'kin' or as 'aliens', thus raising gigantic obstacles to any dialogue. 'Identities' are less isolated *and* more incompatible, less univocal *and* more antagonistic. (Balibar, 2002, pp. 154–5)

It may be that we should think of cosmopolitanism as an ethical disposition rather than a political organization (Benhabib, 2002, p. 183), though that does not reduce its political significance or rule out the necessity for political experimentation of cosmopolitan parties (Beck, 2002, p. 42). Cosmopolitanism is itself directed towards both the nature of the world or universe (*cosmos*) *and* the political ordering of human society (*polis*). However, one of the problems for the political position of cosmopolitanism is that it does not offer any pre-set political programmes. As James Clifford has observed:

> Discrepant cosmopolitanisms guarantee nothing politically. They offer no release from mixed feelings, from utopic/dystopic tensions. They do, however, name and make more visible a complex range of intercultural experiences, sites of appropriation and exchange. These cosmopolitical contact zones are traversed by new social movements and global corporations, tribal activists and cultural tourists, migrant worker remittances and e-mail. Nothing is guaranteed, except contamination, messy politics and more translation. (Clifford, 1998, p. 369)

One of the questions that remains is can the modern Olympics be transformed if it is so tied to those very same origins of racially exclusive European humanism? Allen Guttmann has argued that for the Olympics to survive it needs to decentre itself from those Eurocentric doctrines which privilege 'the West' over 'the Rest' and that gave modern sport its identity. Thus 'the root difficulty is that modern sports, like the universalistic political ideals institutionalized in the Olympic Games, are themselves a product of Western civilization. Paradoxically, the success

of the baron's dream is one of the things that prevents the dream's full and complete realization' (Guttmann, 2002, p. 194).

The Olympics as presently organized is now so closely connected to and implicated with forms of corporate capital that the space for effective critique of those very same structures has been radically reduced. As Tomlinson correctly observes, 'the Olympics has endorsed a global consumer culture quite as much as any noble historical ideal of international cooperation and universal peace' (Tomlinson, Chapter 9 in this volume). Yet this undeniable complicitness may also be a way in which the human rights discourse can be used to highlight forms of global economic inequality as the travelling road show of the Olympics dramatically connects those forms of economic commodity production to their consumption in the overdeveloped West – a connection many transnational companies go to great lengths to hide. Despite the fact that, and even because, Olympism was born of the same singular universalizing and imperialist logic of European modernity that came from its parents of philosophical humanism and the polity of nationalism, it may prove to be a site that can be reworked to transrupt its Eurocentric impulse.

Conclusion

In this chapter I have raised a few questions concerning the legacy of Olympism as an ideology and its links to European humanism. I have suggested that recent discussions on cosmopolitanism may offer analytical insight into the continued fascination with and contestation over the modern Olympic Games. The (admittedly critically agnostic) analysis has attempted a political reading of what might be a *post-Olympism*, that is an Olympics shorn of its dependency on nationalism and that allows us to move beyond our continued resort to forms of raciological thinking and seeing. If this is to be realized we perhaps need to work towards a deeper *theorization* of cosmopolitanism than the suggestive historical-descriptive account that I have offered here. Whether the term is merely a normative disposition or has real analytical purchase (it could indeed be both) and the extent to which it provides an ethical basis upon which tangible political projects can be built or is itself a retreat from materialism into the world of metaphysics, are serious and urgent questions. We need to establish how vernacular cosmopolitanisms feature as aspects of everyday life in affecting peoples' sense of identity and lived experiences as against the condition being the preserve of cosmopolitan (intellectual) elites. In other words a cosmopolitan reflexivity is needed that sees the universal as a political horizon rather than the basis from which politics starts and that embraces diversity even whilst it critiques the limits of insular and fixed identitarian politics. In this regard Beck (2002) is right to warn against a naive belief in the teleological march towards the Cosmopolitan Subject. The undeniable development of new forms of cultural attachment, the reconfiguring of national space and the opening up to *processes* of cosmopolitanization 'should not deceive anyone into believing that we are all going to become cosmopolitans. Even the most positive development imaginable, an opening of cultural horizons and a growing sensitivity to other unfamiliar, legitimate geographies of living and coexistence, need not necessarily stimulate a feeling of cosmopolitan responsibility' (Beck, 2002, p. 29).

Out of these philosophical, cultural and historical inquires we may begin to develop a credible ethical-political understanding of what I have termed in this chapter a *cosmopolitan Olympism*. Recent discussions linking Olympism and sport to the wider human rights discourse is one example of this.[17] Such work holds out the promise of linking the philosophical debates over (post)-humanism with the practical issues over representation, citizenship and rights, within the messy terrain of real world politics.

Olympism is not just an abstract ideal. Embodied in the actual Olympics (whether the Winter or Summer Games) the opportunities to realize a sense of global, post-national belonging that is grounded in the politics of the local, the city, the regional is opened up every few years. It allows, however temporarily, for wider solidarities to be produced and new senses of self to be formed. The fact that such a politics remains indeterminate is all the more reason to see Olympism as a possible site for progressive forms of intervention. If it is true that the only thing wrong with Olympism is the Olympics itself then we might require greater intellectual and political commitment into reshaping its current complicit form. The question remains however: is the Olympics itself still worth fighting for?

6

Post-Olympism: Olympic Legacies, Sport Spaces and the Practices of Everyday Life

Douglas Brown

today we have a surfeit of knowledge and methods as far as structures are concerned, and we are impoverished as soon as we have to study operations, transformations, in short, movement.

Michel de Certeau, *Culture in the Plural*, 1974, p. 145

This chapter is impressionistic and collage-like. It is an effort to study the culture of an Olympic legacy, an Olympic sport and a community of people. It represents a sporting space and sporting lives. With the collage-like presentation, I am attempting to expose and analyse the richness of cultural life in a highly defined (some might say rarified) sporting space. It is a synthesis of images, memories, emotions, characters and theoretical considerations that have converged and diverged over a period of two years at a post Olympic Games speed skating facility. During this two-year period, the pattern of my everyday life intersected with the everyday lives of speed skaters at Calgary's Olympic Oval on the campus of the University of Calgary. My experiences and the production of this text is a response to the ideas of Michel de Certeau and other critical thinkers for whom the patterns of everyday life are a source of knowledge about human agency and social and cultural institutions. This text integrates facts, inventories and definitions with theoretical propositions and anecdotes. It attempts to illustrate the ways Olympic Games, Olympism and Olympic legacies can impact the daily lives of human beings. I have organized these impressions and reflections into four sections: the space, the sport, the skaters and the 'Olympians amongst us'.

The prefix 'post' evokes sentiments that range from optimism to pessimism, playfulness to anxiety. It implies a paradigmatic shift away from the clear and singular rationalism of modernist discourses; it evokes a pluralistic and murky irrationalism associated with postmodernist discourses. With this chapter, I have opted for the playful, rather than the pessimistic. I want to play-around with the literal, figurative and poetic possibilities of exploring a humanistic legacy within the material remains of an Olympic Winter Games. At the most literal level, this chapter examines a post-Olympic Games facility. However, I am concerned with the lives that bring historical, social and cultural meaning into the materiality of this Olympic legacy. On a more abstract level, this investigation also extends from my own postmodern identity/sensibility. The theme of post-Olympism is evident in the pluralism of my observations and reflections. I am not turning my back on my reality where practice straddles ideology; the present straddles the past, representation straddles presentation and disinterested scholarship straddles personal growth and passion. In other words, my disposition towards reflection, investigation and writing is an openly murky convergence of my own identity as athlete/skater straddling academic historian. Somewhere in between these binary concepts I hope to discover something of the *life histories* that *flesh-out* the institutional and ideological history of the Olympic Games.[1] Theoretical, methodological and analytical choices help emphasize the intervals within the binary concepts that tend to shape our understanding of the Olympic Games.[2] These intervals are recognized literally and figuratively. They exist in the architecture of Calgary's Oval, the history of Calgary's Olympic Games, the community that uses this space and the programs that have been developed at the Oval following 1988. I hope that the tactics I employ will decentre conventional discourses that exceptionalize events and experiences associated with the Olympic Games, the Olympic movement and Olympic legacies. This text explores an Olympic legacies by focusing on the mundane, banal and 'everyday'. I will try to demonstrate that the way this Olympic legacy is consumed ought to encourage us to recontextualize relationships between the Olympic Games, themselves and the cultivation of sporting communities and athletic/sporting identity.

No single theory of space, cultural practice, and especially physical culture, seems to satisfy my curiosity about how human beings find meaning in this post Olympic Games space. Understanding lived experiences in a milieu where the Olympic Games, sport history and postmodern society loom large seems destined to be an ongoing struggle where identity is negotiated polemically between practice and imagination. Cultural theorist Victor Burgin (1996, p. 27) suggests that Henri Lefebvre's discourse of human space and everyday life provides a problematic of space theory that is, at least, adequate as a point of departure for the analysis of identity, humanness and representation. For the purposes of exploring everyday life at Calgary's Olympic Oval, I agree that

Lefebvre's ideas provide interesting and provocative triggers. In particular, his three analytical focuses (space, spatial practice and representations of space) provided a structure for organizing ethnographic and autoethnographic observations. By blending both types of observations, I am hoping to expose the precariousness (and absurdity) of forcing a disinterested perspective in humanistic research (Sparkes, 2002).

Since the early 1990s, I have become increasingly aware of the fact that most of my colleagues and I expend great amounts of energy finding ways to study sport that negates our own passion for this type of cultural pursuit. We have subjugated (or denied) our personal (and most likely deep) knowledge of sport culture in an effort to advance a more legitimate image of critical sport studies to the larger academic community. As a consequence, we have produced rather shallow and predicable socio-cultural critiques of sport that tell us very little about human beings who find meaning from participation in sport and physical culture. In a sense, this chapter is a coming out for me. I am attempting to come clean about my own intimate and passionate relationship with the subject that led me to an academic career in the first place. Although I accept many of the strongest negative social critiques of sport, I remain an insider whose personal life is shaped and directed by my own participation in competitive, organized modern sport.

In Lefebve's theory, ethnographic and autoethnographic observations are the loci of cultural meanings and identities that converge (temporally and spatially) in the realm of the physical and psychological (Burgin, 1996, p. 28). Burgin argues that identity can only be understood as a complete convergence of the physical and psychological. In other words, and like many other theorists of culture practice, Burgin emphasizes inbetween*ness*, point of divergence or interval as a possible focus for understanding the production of cultural meaning.

The Space

[Space] is first of all my body, and then it is my body counterpart or "other," its mirror-image or shadow: it is the shifting intersection between that which touches, penetrates, threatens or benefits my body on the one hand, and all other bodies on the other. (Lefebrve, quoted in Burgin, 1996, p. 30)

The Olympic Oval is concrete, aluminum, steel, ice and space that is consumed by skaters, runners, jumpers, cyclists and observers.

26,000 square metres
200 metres by 90 metres
21,000 cubic metres of concrete
180 kilometres of piping

2000 permanent spectator seats
2000 temporary spectator seats
400 metre oval ice track
25 metres, inner track curve radius
29 metres, outer track curve radius
4 metres, inner track width
5 metres, outer track width
113.57 metres, hub distance
2 Olympic-size ice rinks
1, 2 lane 450 metre running track
8, 100 metre sprinting lanes
1 pole vaulting pit
1 long jumping pit
25 stationary bicycles
60 square metres of stretching mats. (*Official Report*, 1988, pp. 145–51)

Since the late 1950s, Calgarians have conceived of and represented their Olympic speed skating oval in many different forms. Like many grand projects, the Olympic Oval has a considerable pre-history that began in 1959 when the Calgary Olympic Development Corporation first bid for the right to host the 1964 Olympic Winter Games (King, 1991). Through the 1950s, 1960s and 1970s, Calgary's bid committee only imagined that some space would be allocated to the sport of speed skating in the event that the bid was successful. However, the Oval's pre-history and history converged in 1981 after the city won the competition to host the 1988 Olympic Winter Games. For a number of years after the successful bid, the space of the Oval was imagined, conceived and at times represented, but not present. Different sites and architectural concepts came and went. As the 1980s progressed, Calgary's role as host of the Olympic Winter Games became entwined with federal and provincial discourses on sport progress in Canada. These discourses reflected a modernist project for sport where centralized high performance sport infrastructures were promoted as the rational first step in moving Canada's sportspeople higher in the rankings of international sport (Macintosh and Whitson, 1990). Consequently, a sophisticated, permanent, indoor and state-of-the-art facility was conceived. The cost of the Oval was CDN$40 million. This particular expense was paid for by the Canadian government as one of three major capital investments expected to improve Canada's international sporting reputation (*Official Report*, 1988, p. 145). The Oval was no longer simply thought of as a place to accommodate the speed skating competitions in 1988; it was conceived as a space where the sport of speed skating in Canada could be nurtured and cultivated for future generations. Finally, in November 1984 construction began on the

Olympic Oval which began to amass a spatial history (a presence) that included geographical, architectural and human materiality (*Official Report*, 1988, p. 147). The Oval opened for competition in 1987. Its conceived space was now consumable space. Since 1988, the Oval has been recognized as one of the most effective Olympic legacies of the Games. Its three official stake holders are Canadian speed skaters, the University of Calgary students and staff and the local Calgary community. In 2000, the Olympic Oval's *Annual Report* estimated that the facility experienced one million people visiting during the year.

Michel de Certeau suggested that negotiating everyday life is a process of strategic or tactical manoeuvres. He described strategic operations as instrumental uses of a culture practice. It reflects a sanctioned and expected way of consuming culture. Access to strategic ways of operating is a factor of social power or the will to power. When people's lives intersect with the Oval and its programmes, they discover a rather limited number of strategies. Officially, these strategies help provide succinct answers to questions concerned with who, what, where, when, how and for the most why people should use this facility. First and foremost, strategies for operating in this space are granted to those who come to the Oval to be physically active. Once you are down at the level of the sport surfaces, spectators can barely be accommodated. Passers-by are physically displaced by the active bodies that surround them. Out of necessity, observers migrate towards the periphery of the different sporting surfaces. Staking out a space to watch is nearly impossible. Even on the periphery, static bodies tend to get in the way. The space designed for spectators is regularly reconfigured by bounding, hopping, lunging, side-stepping and running athletes. The tiered spectator seating provides the added resistance of gravity to indoor training programmes. Sometimes this space is also reconfigured by sleeping, courting, visiting and even studying students. Movers (and some sitters) have tactically created more ways of operating in this space. Unlike the Olympic Games, themselves, Calgary's Olympic Oval does not promote the bicameral spectacle of modernity. In fact, the spectator is more or less always out of place in this space. More than anything, this is a rational and functional space for high performance training. The ice surfaces and supplemental services are maintained for athletes whose goals are logical and linear.

He could be a character concocted by the writers of a classic American sitcom like *Friends* or *Seinfeld*. I'll refer to him as Crazy Mr. Skating Backwards Man which is actually an abbreviation for Crazy Mr. Always Skating Backwards Man (Four Cuts Left and Four Cuts Right, Four Cuts Left, Four Cuts Right, Wearing Hockey Gloves, Powder Blue Sweat Suit, and Discman). During public skating, noon and night, Crazy Mr. Skating Backwards Man moves freely to a decidedly non-modernist beat. In a community facility that is known for producing Olympic and world champions, Crazy Mr. Skating Backwards Man is more recognizable, and possibility more discussed within the general community, than two time Olympic gold medalist, Catronia Lemay Doan. He asserts an individualism that defies this apparently rigid and rationalized functional space. There is one other amazing thing about Crazy Mr. Skating Backwards Man . . . I don't think he is really that crazy.

Calgary's Olympic speed skating facility is responsible for some of the sport's more recent modernist refinements. By moving the sport indoors, elements of nature, like wind, humidity and even seasons, have been eliminated.[3] The ability to produce 'fast ice' on demand is one of the Oval's unique and utterly distinctive contributions to modern winter sport history. The expertise of Calgary's ice makers is now sought out by other indoor speed skating facilities. For example, Mark Messer was seconded from Calgary's Oval by the Organizing Committee of the 2002 Salt Lake City Olympic Winter Games. Ice making, as refined by the technicians at Calgary's Oval, intersects logically with the ideological motto of the Olympic Games: Citius, Altius, Fortius. At the Oval, ice making is characterized as a discourse that transcends science and art. Among the elite skaters who make the Oval their training centre, the technicians who maintain the ice seem to be respected in much the same way as coaches are respected. Since 1988, the careers of the ice technicians at Calgary's Oval have become entwined with the temporal patterns of the Olympic Games quadrennial cycle. As the sport festival moves from new location to new location, Olympic Games hosts and International Skating Union administrators are challenged continually to build new facilities that incorporate the latest science of ice making. This ensures that Olympic speed skating competitions are record breaking events. While the Games may never come back to Calgary, the Oval's contribution to the technology and teleology of *ice making for record breaking* will likely be a legacy to the sport of speed skating for many years to come. Although Calgary's Oval can no longer claim the majority of world speed records, its place in the history of record breaking will remain intact.[4] As conceived, presented, represented and consumed space, the Oval will always be part of a modernist discourse of sport where progress and record breaking are central organizing concepts.

The Sport

I began speed skating in 1997 when I arrived in Calgary with a freshly minted PhD and ambitions of becoming a faculty member. As a sessional instructor, I felt displaced and conspicuous in the area designated for faculty offices. I thought I would find anonymity and relaxation down the hall at the Olympic Oval. Like many other people within whom I have spoken, I was attracted (and perhaps betrayed) by the visual impact of the sport of speed skating; the fluidity, rhythm and grace of the movement magnified the power and athleticism of the athletes. Immediately, I began picturing myself on the ice, moving in unison with the other skaters as they trained together lap after lap. Within a week or two, I had decided to join the Calgary Speed Skating Club. The coaching programme for adults began a week after classes started. I was a complete novice with shaky ankles, rented skates, running tights and a baggy turtleneck sweater. I was also shy and self-conscious. The visual pleasure and thrill of watching elite speed skaters turned to devastation and embarrassment when I realized that I had no intuitive skill for this particular activity. In fact, the perfect glass-like ice conditions of this indoor facility magnified the deficiencies of my own body and athleticism. My self-consciousness and insecurity was only heightened when I discovered that the coach for my 'Never skated before group' was a 2nd year Kinesiology student. Thank goodness, I did not realize that two of the young women in this 'Never skated before group' were part of the faceless mass of 200 students in my history of sport class. If they had not chosen seats in the back of the auditorium during the first week, they mostly likely had done so by the end of the second week. I only discovered their identities as 'my students' a month or so later after I had entertained them with a number of spectacular crashes.

The Oval is a paragon of sporting excellence. The architectural structure fulfils the Oval's singular function with distinction. It is represented in local, national and international media as a place where world records in long track speed skating are made. For modernists, the achievement of world records is an expression of human progress in its most definitive form. The idea of endless human progress is only enhanced when recognizing the activity that this space was designed to accommodate. Long track speed skating is a sport that exemplifies high modernist ideals:

- precision
- efficiency
- linearity
- unidirectionality
- minimalistic
- sterilized
- individualistic
- technological
- form following function
- standardization.

Few physical activities restrict the freedom of human movement like Olympic-style speed skating.[5] The combination of perfectly manufactured ice, the shape of the blade and the structure of the human skeleton converge and prescribe a very limited range of possibilities for generating forward propulsion. The best skaters are able to contort their bodies over and around a 16–18 inch blade that pivots longitudinally at the ball of the foot. The blade is flat filed (unlike a hockey or figure skating blade that is ground into a concave surface). As speeds increase, skaters' bodies must submit further to the laws of physics. This is especially true in the corners. To suggest that skaters negotiate corners is misleading. At speeds that range from 40–60 kilometres an hour, very few options exist for entering, passing through and exiting a 100 metre long arc with a 25 (to 29) metre radius.[6] Hips must be inside the arch of propulsion produced by the feet; the skater's centre of gravity and the pivot where the blade is fixed to the boot must align; shoulders must be parallel to the ice surface and pointing in the same direction as the hips and feet; feet must push perpendicular to the circumference of the corner. When the body transgresses these prescriptions non-skating results: crashes, bail-outs or shut downs.

The Skaters

Prior to 1981, when Calgary won the right to host the Games in 1988, its speed skating community was typical by North American standards. The sport was established but was hardly prominent in the community's sporting consciousness. When the facility was inaugurated with a compulsory Olympic Preview World Cup Race in December 1987, state holders like the University of Calgary, the Organizing Committee of the Olympic Games, Speed Skating Canada and especially the community in Calgary could only imagine the culture that might emerge after the Olympic Games had come and gone. Even the Oval's mission statement, although decisive in its wording can only represent an imagined community and culture.

Our Mission

To operate a world class speed skating and ice sports facility and to provide program opportunities which promote excellence, health, wellness and quality lifestyle to all users, through high performance, sport and human resource development, competition, education, research, and recreation.[7]

Certainly, mission statements and programmes of operation provide structures that help guide the development of communities in most cultural institutions. Dance historian Susan Leigh Foster (1996) draws on the work of Michel de Certeau to advance a cultural understanding of lives that pass through the institution of dance. According to Foster, the value of de Certeau's ethno-sociological studies is partially found in his data collections methods: 'tracking of the meandering and errant traces left behind by ordinary persons moving through their day' (Foster, 1996, pp. 5–6). According to Foster, de Certeau argues:

that many of these traces, rather than conform to dominant social specifications of behaviour, document the thought-filled gestures of those who, having assessed and rejected the normative, simply move in a different way. Erratic, impervious to statistical investigations, these gestures constitute a vital reservoir of resistance to the overwhelming force exerted by dominant orderings of the social. (Foster, 1996, pp. 5–6)

The Oval definitely promotes a dominant ordering of the social. Although the Oval's current mission statement seems to promote a wide range of programmes as well as a culturally diverse population of users, programmes that have emerged in spite of this mission establish a framework in which 'us' and 'other' is clearly evident in practice. Ultimately, the system that categorizes the Oval's consumers outlines social specifications of behaviour that are extensions of the rules and objectives of Olympic-style speed skating. The 'us' is then equivalent to 'athlete-speed skaters' and 'other' is for everyone else, speed skater, recreational skater, runner, jogger, walker, etc.

Among the different user groups that the Oval supports, speed skaters have a strategic advantage at this Olympic legacy facility. The Oval provides a multitude of ways to be a speed skater, but not all speed skaters can use the facility strategically. The production of social identity and athletic identity among the participants is bound to a strict definition of who speed skates, where they speed skate, when they speed skate, how they speed skate and especially why they speed skate. This prescription results in a system of sub-categories of consumers, **A**, **B**, **C** and **P** skaters. **A** signifies National Team and National Development Team, **B** stands for athletes who have met specific time standards and hope to challenge for a position among the **A**s. For the most part, **B**s must be registered in the coaching programmes run by the Oval. **C** stands for club skater which includes children, teens and adults. **P** stands for public skaters who wear speed skates during public/open skating times but do not skate in an organized programme.[8] When foreign skaters come to train at the Oval, they are generally accommodated within this system of categories.

B skaters serve a vital function in the operating strategies of the Oval. **B**s constitute a time and space division between serious speed skaters and other speed skaters. This time and space division is an important factor in determining the culture and community in which skaters identify. This system is the basis for the institutionalized strategies that define the errant traces of skaters' daily lives as they move through the Oval on a yearly basis. **C**s are separated categorically, physically and temporally from the **A**s by the **B**s. They are separated by time and space. **A**s have access to the ice during mid-morning and mid-afternoon. **B**s have access to the ice in the early morning and later part of the afternoon. **C**s have access to the ice in the evenings after the **B**s have skated. Officially, the ability to move around within this time and space structure is a factor of athletic merit. For **A**s, an unwritten code exists that allows them to go onto the **B** ice or **C** ice if they so desire. For **B**s, an unwritten code exists that allows them to go onto the **C** ice if they so desire. **B** skaters with promise may be invited onto the **A** ice. No code, whether written or unwritten, gives **C**s the opportunity to encroach on the **A**s' or **B**s' ice. In addition to the **A**s, **B**s and **C**s, there are also the **P**s, or general public, who can skate on the speed skating surface with whatever type of skate they own or choose to rent. For the most part, **P**s access the ice only after the **A**s, **B**s and **C**s are finished for the day.

> From 1997 to 2002 my cultural currency changed at the Oval. My skill level has improved dramatically and my confidence has been boosted as well. In other words, I sense that my skill has improved to such an extent that I no longer make my students feel uncomfortable when they realize we inhabit the same space. In fact, a former student even offered to lend me her skin suit to wear in my first big race. Skill and fitness has enhanced the legitimacy of my skating in this space. It legitimizes my self-identification as a speed skater. I suspect that it has also enhanced the ability of my students to identify their professor as a speed skater. Am I a speed skater? My ability to go 30.4 seconds in a flying 400 and hold 33 second laps for a 1500 has opened up an entirely different way of operating in this space, the same space that I entered so tentatively several years earlier. Some obvious strategies are available to me and my peers for simple reasons of safety. My speed and proficiency permits me to hold my line through a corner while lesser skaters are responsible for peeling outward toward the periphery. When I train with my peers, we fill the C ice. Our program sets the pace for the others. Our movement, power and speed displaces the slower C skaters, literally. For 'us', the 'others' are left up to their own devices to 'make-what-they-can' of the space that is available to them. They must be creative, even tactical, to ensure their own safety and presence on this ice. The merit of my ability to go 30.4 in a flying 400 and hold 33 second laps for a 1500 ranks me near the bottom of the Bs. Still, as a 41 year old professor, I will never be invited onto the B ice. While I may be able to self-identify as a speed skater, I am less certain of my identity as an athlete-speed skater.

Beyond explaining how people operate strategically within cultural systems, de Certeau suggests that people also operate tactically. Strategies are an instrumental use of culture that confirms social identity. When an individual misuses or usurps a cultural activity, de Certeau describes this as a tactical or fragmentary use of culture. If strategic uses of culture are associated with social power and the will to power, then tactical uses of culture are primarily the domain of the weak, the disenfranchised or the 'other'. Tactical uses of culture are equated with 'making do', exploiting or reconfiguring the relationship between practice and meaning. The value of this theory of cultural use, especially in terms of the practices of everyday life, is provocative because de Certeau forces us to consider the way cultural practices and their presumed meaning or significance is susceptible to alternative uses.

The **A**, **B**, **C** and **P** organization of skaters at the Oval reflects the social instrumentality of sport at the Oval, in Calgary, in Canada and in the eyes of the International Olympic Committee and International Skating Union. But this organization of skaters it is not impenetrable. While it is effective at defining generic types that certainly constitute the greater lived culture at the Oval, it cannot fully accommodate all of the creative uses that individuals might find within these categories. In other words, categorization of skaters into **A**, **B**, **C** and **P** groups answer questions related to who, when, where and how, but it cannot always answer the question why. This system does not fully restrain human beings from making-do, exploiting and reconfiguring their relationship between speed skating, this speed skating space and the personal identities they derive from their participation. Two years of observation revealed that the use of tactics is, at least, somewhat apparent among the **B** skaters, but most obvious in the ranks of the **C** skaters. Self-identification as *speed skater or other* and *athlete or other* is a dynamic application of tactics by some members of the **C** group. In this group of skaters, a great variety of social identities converge in shared time and space. For many **C** skaters at the Oval, including myself back in 1997, the use of tactics began at registration. The Calgary Speed Skating Club is a family-based association where parents fill the board of directors to ensure that their children have a positive experience in the sport. In spite of their best intentions, adults without children who are registered in the club are sub-categorized as others. While there is some evidence of change in the marginalization of adult skaters, their coaching, competition and even social needs are clearly secondary to those of the children members of the club.

Initially, everyone uses tactics when they attach speed skates to their feet and step on the ice. From then on, gaining proficiency and attaining speed is a constant application of strategies and tactics. The extent to which strategic ways of operating prevail over tactical ways of operating in this physical activity is very much an extension of the everyday bodies that come to the Oval. To be blunt, some bodies work better than others. Some conform to the equipment, ice and movement quite naturally, others do not. Like all sports, physical ability is equivalent to cultural capital. Skaters with less of this type of cultural capital must make tactical decisions about how to use this activity as a means of forming their identities. Besides physical capital, other aspects of **C** skaters' everyday lives determine the cultural capital and subsequently the strategies or tactics that they employ to operate in this field of cultural production (Bourdieu, 1993). For example, Dutch or Norwegian ethnic identity certainly carries some weight. In the theory of Pierre Bourdieu, this is regarded as symbolic capital rather than cultural capital. Also, a family's history in the sport is an another example of symbolic capital that is especially valuable to skaters in the **C** group. Inevitably, martial status, age, gender and sexuality constitute particularly interesting variables that contribute to one's symbolic capital in this sporting community.

> Arnie Schotlz (an alias) holds a world record in speed skating. He began his speed skating career in Calgary and is living proof that hosting Olympic Games can have a significant impact on the development of new sporting communities. Were it not for the Oval, Arnie probably would have never taken up the sport. At competitions, most people know of Arnie's world records and show their appreciation for his talent when he races. In spite of his success, he remains down-to-earth and approachable and shows a genuine interest in other skaters' accomplishments. At a recent competition in Calgary (CANAM 2002), Arnie's races set the tone for the rest of the competitors. In his mid-70s, his times are usually the second slowest regardless of the distance. His principal age-group rival does not quite have the raw power that Arnie possesses. The slowness of his speed skating, especially at longer distances, alters the typical progression of a competition. For example, most adult male skaters at the recent CANAM competition finished the 5000 metre race with times between 7 and 8 minutes. Arnie's race took 14 minutes. Because Olympic-style speed skating is basically a race against the clock, athletes race in pairs. When one pair is finished racing, the next pair begins. All of us who were competing in the CANAMs knew that Arnie's race would be approximately 15 minutes and gauged our own warm-up and race preparation with this in mind.

From a technical perspective, Arnie's body defies the modernism of this sport. Although very fit and healthy, his 70-year-old skeleton and muscles do not allow him to conform to the blades and the ice. Furthermore, these limitations effectively keep Arnie moving at approximately half the speed of average adult male skaters. According to numerous principles of technique and technology, Arnie does not speed skate. And yet, Arnie is a speed skater with clap skates and a skin suit, world age-group records and respect from his peers and surrounding community. He has created his identity as a speed skater tactically. At Calgary's Olympic Oval, Arnie Scholtz seems to be the embodiment of postmodernism. He seems to have rejected many of the modernist ideological tenets that define how this ultra serious sporting space is used and consumed. While this may be an extreme example, it encourages us to reflect on all of the other lives that also defy the linearity, rationality and homogeneity of this paragon of sporting modernism.

Within the C category the question of athletic identity is quite problematic. Ironically, becoming fast among the Cs can also produce a sense of otherness. If you skate fast – if you speed skate – and you are under 20 years of age and want to skate faster, institutionalized strategies at the Oval enabled you to operate legitimately in this space. In other words, the question 'why speed skate?' is presumed. The system of athletic meritocracy answers the question and defines the utterly predictable and logical routes that are opened up in front of you.

B ice becomes your field of cultural production. It provides you with a logical foundation to construct an athletic and social identity. However, if you are over 20 years of age, skate fast and want to skater faster, the strategies at the Oval begin to fail you. Among the adult **C** skaters with no children in the club, the opportunity to self-identify as a speed skater-athlete becomes increasingly tactical the faster you get. In other words, the question '*why speed skate?*' cannot be answered so conveniently. The system of athletic meritocracy that provides the pattern of operation for the Oval's **A, B, C** and **P** categories cannot accommodate the notion that alternative meanings/values/motivations may be derived from the will to accelerate one's body though this space and in this culture. And yet, the Oval is becoming a space where athletic and social identities are challenged aggressively, disassembled or perhaps just lost in the intervals between social, cultural, historical and even Olympic discourses that order normative ways of operating.

The organization of space, time and programmes at the Oval might easily be described as an overwhelming force of the dominant orderings of society. But, is this organization also susceptible to the thought-filled gestures of those who have assessed and rejected the normative? At the ground level of the Oval, official delineations of normative behaviour and normative identities are made vulnerable by the real movers and shakers of this community. At ground level, designated training areas, surfaces and equipment are exposed to the meandering paths, firm trajectories, resounding voices and arrant gazes of socially pre-identified consumers sharing a space and time. While the consumers of this space may allow their physical movement to be guided and confined by these specialized areas, their social identities carry far more transcendent power than these boundaries. For the most part, the athletic identities of the consumers are determined by their chosen physical activity. But these identities are also bound to lived experiences that consumers bring to the Oval. These include social identities like man, woman, boy, girl, father, mother, lawyer, engineer, roofer, grocer, professional athlete, stay-at-home dad, student and professor.

At certain times in the yearly pattern of life in the Oval, convergences of social identity and athletic identities are intense, even extraordinary. Saturday morning time-trials provide an interesting and complex example. Beginning in late October, speed skaters begin testing themselves on Saturday mornings. These time-trials are open to anyone. Although skaters are seeded according to ability, it is common to find Olympic champions and world class skaters from all of the leading skating nations racing and warming-up among novice and master skaters. During the first few weekends of time-trialing, boundaries based on athletic identity appear to be quite insignificant. Easy and comfortable exchanges can occur between all levels of skaters and their respective friends, families and coaches as well as members of the general public who are training for other sports at the Oval. This rather utopian environment is not permanent. Once the World Cup season begins, ways of operating at these Saturday morning time-trials change. The elite skaters begin traveling internationally and are rarely present on Saturday mornings. When they are back training at the Oval between championships, they tend not to participate in these informal time-trials. The elite athletes who have not been named to an international team begin to narrow their focus and increase the intensity of their participation in these practices races. The easy exchanges and signs of shared community identities between elite and club athletes are rare. Initially, one might argue that the first few weeks of Saturday morning time-trials are evidence that moments of liminality do, indeed, occur at the Oval. Certainly this argument requires that any liminal moments are products of both temporal and spatial convergence. During a few weeks in late October and early November, the Oval appears to offer a temporary separation or suspension of athletic and social identities. Although I do not discount this theory of cultural space, my observations suggest that sharing this space does not always lead to a common or shared identity among the different participants. The convergence of people with different social identities, especially sporting identities bound to a common space, sport and pastime does not necessary produce new freedoms to reconfigure one's athletic identity. Although the 'never skated before group' may tighten their skates while sitting on the same bench as an Olympic champion who is removing their skates, differences and otherness are preserved and roles are confirmed by a multitude of strategies and tactics. Age remains the most distinctive social identity that cannot be transcended by this shared space or by the shared activity.

'Olympians Amongst Us'

Last night following my ice session, I was stretching on the carpeted area at the periphery of the Oval's interior space. The University of Calgary's varsity cross-country running team was stretching on the carpet beside me. As I eaves-dropped on their conversation, I realized they were discussing the famous Canadian speed skaters with whom they share the facility. In essence, they were discussing the idea of sharing space as opposed to the experience of sharing space. I realized this as the three young men tried to agree on a composite picture of what Jeremy Wotherspoon looks like. 'How tall is he? Does he have sort of spikey hair? Ya, I know who he is'. Not surprisingly, it was clear from their comments that they knew exactly when their paths had crossed with that of Catriona (Le May Doan). Le May Doan is probably the most widely recognizable Canadian female athlete since the late 1990s. Her two Olympic gold medals and distinctive good looks have made her a true celebrity in Canadian society. For most non-speed skating athletes who train at the Oval, the presence of Canada's most notable speed skaters is experienced as an idea that is cultivated in the local media and in personal discussions among peers. In this sense, the Oval's community with 'Olympian's Amongst Us' is part of a much broader interpretation/representation of the Oval and the way people operate in its space.

On the surface, the Oval seems to reflect a harmonious blend of the everyday and the extraordinary. A slogan that Oval and University of Calgary promotional departments use from time to time is 'Olympians Amongst Us'. In the months leading up to the most recent Olympic Winter Games, a glassed-in showcase at the entrance of the Oval promoted the theme, 'Olympians Amongst Us'. The display encouraged Oval users and university students to consider the 'Olympians Amongst Us'. This slogan asked everyday skater-athletes to contemplate the juxtaposition of their banality with the extraordinariness of some of the Oval's athletes. There is an interrogative quality in the slogan 'Olympians Amongst Us'. We begin to ask ourselves, where are these out-of-the-ordinary individuals among us? In the context of the showcase, observers are left to contemplate when and where their own errant meandering paths through the Oval have crossed those of Olympians.

The slogan 'Olympians Amongst Us' proposes a strange and artificial concept that is entrenched in the history of sport culture and the Oval's imagined sense of community.[9] The slogan sustains the notion that being named to an Olympic team constitutes a type of social transformation that is linked to athletic identity. It promotes the myth that athletic achievement ought to be recognized as an enduring social attribute. Once an Olympian, always an Olympian! In practice, the transformation of identity that the slogan promotes is far more fluid and considerably less awe-inspiring. In the year-in-year-out life at the Oval, the reality of 'Olympians (living) Amongst Us' is expected and inevitable. This is only intensified by the history of the space, itself, and the fact that it is one of only two premier training sites for Canadian speed skaters. The other major training centre of speed skating in Canada is located on the outskirts of Quebec City. As successive generations of children begin speed skating at the Calgary Oval, the emergence of some 'Olympians Amongst Us' is almost guaranteed.

In early January 2002, Canada's best speed skaters congregated at Calgary's Oval for the Olympic Team Trials. As a speed skater and researcher, I went to the Oval expecting something really special and out of the ordinary. Instead, what I experienced was one of the strangest and most anti-climatic competitions I had ever witnessed in any sport. First, only a handful of athletes had met the international standards to compete in the trials. For the most part, they were all already members of Canada's National Team. They all looked the same in their bright yellow suits that paid homage to their principal sponsor, Cheerios. As the races were contested, it became apparent that more than the outcome of the day's races determined the organization and selection of the team that would compete in Salt Lake City. Some complex series of standards had to be achieved over a specified number of events and within a certain period of time. Only a small number of athletes who competed in the trials actually qualified for the Olympic Games as a result of these races. The greatest revelation I had during the competition was the utter banality of becoming an Olympian, at least a Canadian speed skating Olympian.

Additionally, from the standpoint of athletic excellence, I realized just how narrow the margin is that distinguishes an Olympian from a non-Olympian. For the incredible athletes who competed at these Olympic team trials, the idea of the 'Olympians Amongst Us' must have carried a somewhat ominous tone. As the performance standards were achieved (or not) by tenths and hundredths of seconds, the community that appeared to be homogeneous in athletic excellence and Cheerios yellow suits, was fracturing into a community of 'Almost Olympians' and 'Olympians Amongst Us'.

As a type of metanarrative, 'Olympians Amongst Us' can also be explored with a different, and possibly less pessimistic, focus. Over the span of an Olympiade, the lives of hundreds of international athletes become entwined with the lives of club and elite skaters for whom the Olympic Oval is truly regarded as an extension of their backyard. The yearly comings and goings of these international athletes factor significantly into the economic viability of the Oval. International skaters paid a considerable sum of money to train at the Oval. Canadian athletes paid a small fraction of this sum. Beyond the economic benefit of hosting national teams from all of the leading speed skating nations, one might presume that their presence also enriches the cultural practices and construction of identities and sense of community among the wide range of Oval consumers. While their bodies literally fill (consume) the space alongside Canadian Olympians and the general skating population, these foreign 'Olympians Amongst Us' exist largely in a figurative context. In the day-to-day, week-to-week (and sometimes month-to-month) patterns of life at the Oval, the foreign Olympians preserved their outsider status. For the average speed skater, and certainly for the general public, most Olympians are anonymous individuals who have participated at remote and unpalpable sporting events. For foreign Olympians, even Olympic gold medalists and world record holders, training at the Calgary Oval is also a mundane, day-to-day, year-to-year experience. It is what they have to do to stay competitive in this sport. Within this space, their identity as Olympians has far less to do with their bodies and their skating, than is does with their team uniforms and distinct coaching groups. Although Gerard Van Velde, Adne Sondral and Annie Friesinger may be skating around the 400 metre ice surface, their Olympian status is far more imagined than it is experienced. For all but a very few of the serious local speed skaters at the Oval, the identities of foreign Olympians are only evident in the abstract, a fast skater with a non-Canadian national team racing suits. In this sense, they are imagined Olympians. But this status of imagined Olympian is not restricted to foreign skaters at the Oval.

Last year I skated with the Calgary Speed Skating Club on Tuesday and Thursday evenings. As the 2002 Olympic Winter Games in Salt Lake City approached, our way of operating in the Oval space changed. New ice schedules were introduced to accommodate an increased volume of foreign athletes who chose Calgary's Oval as a training facility before they headed down to Salt Lake City. The large number of visiting athletes seemed to have an impact on the way Canadian Olympians operated in this space. As the urgency to fine-tune skates and bodies increased, we club skaters occasionally discovered a Canadian national team athlete skating among us during our evening C ice time. While duly impressed, most of us had no clue of the athletes' names or accomplishments. More than the athletes' exquisite skill and easy speed, it was the national team suit that made the impact. I can remember a number of discussions in which my peers and I attempted to narrow down the identity of the 'Olympian Amongst Us'.

Regardless of our success at putting a name to the body, the experience of sharing the ice with an Olympian was a curious combination of knowledge and experiences. The athlete's differences were constituted visually, physically and intellectually. As days, months and years pass at this athletic facility, micro-communities emerge. At the Oval, these micro-communities reflect skating ability, age, employment status, commitment to the sport, and a host of other variables. The effect is that everyday use of the space and the activity is patterned by more or less familiar people. As the 2002 Olympic Games approached, micro-communities, like my Tuesday and Thursday club skating group, experienced ruptures in this pattern. The presence of the odd Olympian skating during club ice time provided unusual opportunities to reflect on identity and sense of community in this sporting space. The problem is discovering what meaning emerged from these ruptures. When the national team athlete skated during our club time, his difference was visually and intellectually evident. But this was very superficial. This difference was signified as a generic-type, a national team athlete and a possible Olympian. Not all national team athletes were successful at establishing a position on the Olympic team. Based on this visual distinction of their bodies and their skating ability, most of us could still not attribute a name to the body. When these athletes glided past us with power, grace, ease and spectacular bodies, their physical presence could be experienced in the purposeful rush of wind as we moved momentarily, clumsily and precariously alongside of them. Although the sensation was exhilarating, the athlete's identity as an Olympian and his impact on our sense of community remained generic. Any one of a thousand powerful speed skaters could have evoked a similar rush. Only our imaginations played an important role in the way we made sense of this experience.

Conclusion

Because this chapter was presented as a series of impressions of an ongoing ethno-graphic process, conclusions as such are inappropriate. In place of a conclusion, two postscripts illustrate a central concern that has provided much of the inertia for this study. Both of these postscripts illustrate the important relationship between time, cultural space and construction of identity and community.

Postscript One

In a presentation of this chapter in Aarhus, Denmark on 11 September 2002 I suggested that some of the administrative structures at the Oval would never fully legitimize mature adults who wished to pursue high performance skating. I argued that mature skaters (like myself) wishing to skate faster would need to continue pursuing their sport tactically and creatively (rather than strategically or with institutional legitimization). Furthermore, I suggested that opportunities to self-identify as a speed skater-athlete are limited by barriers that have been constructed from an elaborate and unchallenged system where traditional modern notions of athletic identity are contingent on the teleological logic that sustains the modern Olympic Games. Upon my return from Aarhus, I was surprised to discover that a new programme had been created during my brief absence. The programme is call 'Link' and is designed for skaters who have followed unorthodox routes into the realm of serious (or high performance) speed skating. In other words, 'Link' provides serious coaching and **B** ice time for skaters who are too fast for **C** ice, but not necessarily pursuing an athletic identity or life course that will lead to the Olympic Games. The Oval's Director of Coaching encouraged me to join this programme. Certainly, there are reasons to be sceptical of the programme and the motives of the Oval administration. Are we simply a new source of revenue that supports the true elite programmes? Is this a public relations gesture to convince the larger community that the Oval supports a diverse range of interests and abilities? In the three months since its institution (and my own participation in the programme), 'Link' has provided former odd-balls ('others') with what appears to be a strategic way of operating in this high performance space. Furthermore, it appears to have legitimized our identities as speed skater-athletes. With a simple administrative gesture, the need to operate tactically and creatively in this space has been reduced.

Postscript Two

In the presentation of this chapter in September 2002 I suggested that the physical layout of the Oval, and the management of the facility, provided some interesting opportunities for diverse populations to share a common sporting space. I tried to demonstrate how the everyday lives of very different people could potentially cross and intersect in this massive interior space. Furthermore, I argued that the space, itself, was managed in such a way that very fluid and spontaneous human interaction could occur in spite of apparent physical, social and athletic barriers.

I attempted to convey optimistic impressions of a cultural space where the potential to develop new and unique athletic identities was enhanced by the fact that many different lives converged in shared time and space. Upon my return from Aarhus, I was discouraged to discover that a new system for controlling access to the Oval had been instituted. Access to the observation deck is now completely restricted. This has effectively curtailed the opportunity for students and staff at the university to use spectator seating as a casual hangout between classes or during lunch breaks. Access to the ground level (ice surface, running track, stationary bikes, stretching mats, etc.) is now monitored by paid staff. A system of plasticized membership cards was implemented to ensure that only paying members of the Oval use the space during specific times. This intervention has effectively restricted drop-in use of the Oval, especially for the running track and stretching mats. Granted, some of the chaos experienced during peak hours has been eliminated and potential legal liability of the Oval has been reduced. At the same time, however, some of the most poignant juxtapositions of athleticism and physical culture have been eliminated. The opportunity for Calgary's senior citizens to use the running track while Olympians glide past them on the ice is a thing of the past. The opportunity for groups of school children to hang over the bumpers and encourage hi-fives from members of Canada's national speed skating team is remote. With a simple administrative gesture, the opportunity to tactically and creatively operate in this space has been reduced.

'An identity implies not only a location but a duration, a history. A lost identity is not only lost in space, but in time. We might better say, in "space-time"' (Burgin, 1996, p. 36).

7

The Future of a Multi-Sport Mega-Event: Is there a Place for the Olympic Games in a 'Post-Olympic' World?

Richard Cashman

This chapter reflects on the future viability of a multi-sport event such as the Olympic Games, identifying potential threats to their exalted status at the pinnacle of world sport. Since any threat also represents an opportunity, the chapter also considers the capacity of Olympic organizers to respond to such challenges. The future of multi-sport mega-events is explored in the context of Asia for a number of reasons. Asia is one of the dynamic frontiers of world sport and will play an important role in the future global sports system because the countries of East Asia – China, Japan and South Korea – are becoming increasingly important in global economic and political terms. Asia is one area of the world where the Olympic movement is holding its own with its chief rival, the football World Cup. In many other continents – such as Africa and South America – devotion to the World Cup is much greater than the Olympic Games. The capacity of the Olympic movement to maintain its position in Asia will be critical to its future.

This chapter will revisit the Allen Guttmann thesis, elaborated in his *Games and Empires*, that the Olympic Games have long been deeply Eurocentric. Guttmann in this seminal work has stated that

the modern Olympic Games began as a European phenomenon and it has always been necessary for non-Western peoples to participate in the games on Western terms . . .

The most important consequence of European and American control of the Olympic movement has been that all the sports included in the Olympic programme have their origins in the West or are represented in the distinctly modern forms developed as part of Western culture. (Guttmann, 1994, pp. 120, 137)

Guttmann does not directly address the issue as to whether the Eurocentric bias of the Olympic Games represents an impediment to greater Asian involvement since he is wary of defining cultural imperialism as the dominant strand of ludic diffusion. Cultural imperialism is a factor but not necessarily the factor behind this process. In his conclusions Guttmann cites many examples of cultural appropriation and even resistance by colonized peoples so that an imperial games ethic, so far as it existed, was often undermined and even subverted.

So the question remains as to whether the Olympic Games may be lumbered by its past in any future shift in the balance of world sporting power. Or, does it really matter to many South-East and East Asians that badminton, table tennis and volleyball for instance – sports in which many Asian countries now excel – began as European and North American sports? Is it a concern to Indians that cricket began as an English sport because, to the people of that country, the game looks decidedly Indian? Is it necessary for the future viability of the Olympic Games that there be a greater representation of Asian sports on the programme such as the martial arts of karate and wushu and maybe even the South-East Asian sport of sepak takraw and South Asian sport of kabaddi? Have the Olympic Games become sufficiently multicultural since 1964, with the staging of the Summer Olympics at Tokyo, and the introduction of sports of Asian origin (such as judo) and other sports that are popular in Asia (such as volleyball)?

The Contemporary Global Sports System

Before contemplating the future, it is necessary to begin with an overview of the evolution and operation of the contemporary global sports system. Maarten van Bottenburg (2001), in *Global Games*, suggests a number of general features. First, the global sports system is undergoing rapid change:

> The global sporting system is marked by internal differentiation and is subject to constant change. One sport exercises far more appeal than another. Some grow in popularity, while others lose ground. New sports are constantly being created, as the model of established sport is applied to old and new activities alike. (Van Bottenburg, 2001, p. 9)

Van Bottenburg notes, second, that while a transnational culture of sport has emerged, a uniform culture of sport is far from being complete, nor is a mono-cultural system of global sport likely to occur in the future. The sports practised by most people in the world, he adds, have been diffused from four main countries: Britain, Germany, the US and Japan. Before the Second World War the global sporting system was dominated by Britain and Germany. Guttmann would probably add France to this list because of the country's contribution of cycling in particular (Guttmann, 1994, p. 2). Since 1945, the US and Japan have become more influential in a world sporting culture and Guttmann contends that Americans finally supplanted Britain as 'the primary agents in the diffusion of modern sports' (Guttmann, 1994, p. 2). The reason why these four powers play a dominant role in the global sporting culture is because they have 'occupied positions of international power' from the mid-nineteenth century onwards (Van Bottenburg, 2001, p. 197).

Third, differentiation in world sport continues to occur because countries appropriate the global sports system in a variety of ways. So while soccer is by far the most popular sport in Europe, Africa and Latin America, other sports are more prominent in North America, parts of Asia and some of the countries of Oceania. Van Bottenburg contends that this diversity of global sport is likely to continue in the future.

Fourth, television and other forms of media, including the Internet, have given birth to what Joseph Maguire referred to as the 'global media-sport complex' (Maguire, 1999, pp. 144–75). While 'Anglo-Saxon elements predominate, other cultural traditions are increasingly mingling with them', suggests van Bottenburg. This has occurred in part

> because the media are less exclusively bound to superpowers, and because their reporters and cameramen are standing by in almost every part of the world. And partly it is attributable to increased 'bottom-up' influence: large-scale migration from poor to richer regions means that people in prosperous countries are increasingly encountering new cultural phenomena, from areas about which they were previously quite ignorant. (Van Bottenburg, 2001, p. 206)

There is then the implied possibility, fifth, that the world sporting culture may be more multicultural and less Anglo-Saxon in the future. There has already been a transition in the twentieth century that the global sporting system that is European to one that includes North American and Japanese components. So there is the possibility a future world sports system may be more multicultural. Globalization does not necessarily mean greater homogeneity of world sport.

Guttmann warns that there are limits to the potential diversity of the contemporary global sports system. With the 'standardized universality' of modern sports there has been a 'loss of diversity when contrasted with the bewildering variety of traditional sports'. Modern sports he suggests (quoting Ommo Grupe) are inherently cosmopolitan in that 'their language, symbols, and rules . . . are universally understood' (Guttmann, 1994, p. 188).

Van Bottenburg provides evidence of an increasing diversity of global sport. The Japanese martial arts of judo and karate have become popular in many European countries – and judo has been part of the Olympic programme since

1964 – even if judo has been transformed in the process so that, as Gutmmann noted, Olympic judo 'is shorn of almost all traces of its Japanese origins' (Guttmann, 1994, p. 138). The Korean martial art of taekwondo has increased its global spread in recent decades, becoming an Olympic sport in 2000. While politics was obviously a factor in the selection of taekwondo as an Olympic demonstration sport in 1988 and an Olympic sport in 2000, taekwondo could not have achieved this status without some degree of global spread.

Van Bottenburg (2001, pp. 207–14) includes some interesting figures on the participation rates of some sports of Asian origin in a number of European and Middle Eastern countries demonstrating how these sports have penetrated the European market. Judo ranks as a significant participant sport in thirteen of the twenty-four countries selected and is now the tenth most popular global sport. Judo ranks third after soccer and tennis in France. Karate is represented in six countries. Although taekwondo has been globally prominent for a shorter period than judo and karate, it ranks in the top fifteen in three European and Middle Eastern countries (see Table 7.1).

A sixth feature of the global sports system is that because of the extended reach of global media, there has increased competition between mega-sporting events. Since the 1970s, there has been a proliferation of world cups and world championships in individual sports. There has also been a greater variety of Games, mega-sporting and cultural events, each of which is keen to carve out a global market. Van Bottenburg states that 'the dissemination of standardized sports is approaching its absolute geographical limit'. I take this to mean that world markets are becoming saturated with competing global sports and sporting events so that there are relatively few new markets and frontiers. The successful promotion of a new sport or global sporting event can only take place at the expense of some existing sport or event.

This chapter identifies five threats to the continuing status of the Olympic Games. It will attempt to weigh the significance of each threat and the capacity of Olympic organizers to respond to each challenge.

Increased Competition

The first threat is the increased competition due to the proliferation of global games and mega-events in recent decades. On the website of the Amateur Athletic Foundation of Los Angeles (AAFLA) in his 'International Games Resources' Daniel Bell has identified many types of games, the majority of which date from the post Second World War period. Bell notes that there 'are currently over 200 kinds of international multisport competitions held every four years':

Table 7.1 *The Ranking of Asian Sports in Twenty-four European and Middle Eastern countries (based on participation rates)*

	Judo	Karate	Taekwondo
Austria (15)	–	–	–
Belgium (15)	5	15	–
Bulgaria (15)	–	–	–
Cyprus (10)	9	6	7
Czechoslovakia (former) (14)	11	11	–
Denmark (15)	–	–	–
Finland (15)	14	–	–
France (15)	3	12	–
Germany (15)	15	–	–
Great Britain (8)	–	–	–
Hungary (10)	10	–	–
Iceland (15)	14	–	–
Ireland (13)	–	–	–
Italy (15)	8	–	–
Luxembourg (9)	–	–	–
Netherlands (15)	–	–	–
Norway (15)	–	–	–
Poland (14)	–	–	–
Portugal (10)	6	–	–
Spain (15)	4	5	13
Sweden (10)	–	–	–
Switzerland (15)	–	–	–
Turkey (15)	9	11	10
Yugoslavia (former) (15)	10	–	–

Note: This table has been extrapolated from van Bottenburg (2001) which lists the fifteen most popular sports in these countries. However, in some countries fewer sports were listed. The figures in parentheses indicate the number of sports listed.

Ranking: 1 = most popular participant sport; 15 = fifteenth most popular participant sport.

Games are organized for certain regions such as the African Games, Asian Games, or Central American Games. Certain occupations have organized competitions; for instance the World Medical Games, or World Police and Fire Games. Many games are also available for certain age groups such as the World Youth Games, World University Games and World Masters Games. (Bell, 2000)

The Games can be divided into four broad categories: global games such as the Olympic Games; regional and inter-regional games such as the Asian Games and the Commonwealth Games; religious, ethnic and cultural games, such as the Arab Games and the Maccabean Games; and special category games such as the World Medical Games or the World University Games. However, there has also been a significant increase in many other global sporting festivals. Although the first world cup (soccer) was played in Uruguay in 1930, it was not until the 1970s that there was a proliferation of world cups in other sports such as cricket (1975) and rugby (1987). World cups for men have been replicated with women's world cups in cricket, soccer and rugby for instance. Every sport now has either a world cup or a world championship. The first swimming world championship was in 1973 and the first track and field competition was in 1983. World championships in swimming and track and field were originally held once every four years but now operate on a two-year rotation basis.

The increase in the quantity of global sport has led to increased competition between cities to gain the right to host a mega-event; between sports to gain access to a premier global sporting event such as the Olympic Games; and between one sporting festival and another to secure public interest, media and sponsorship support. Because there is already significant literature on place competition between cities to host major sporting and cultural festivals I will focus on the latter two forms of competition.

No fewer than fourteen sports applied for admission to the Athens 2004 Olympic Games. The sport of water skiing was the only one that met all the requirements of the Greek organizers; however, the International Olympic Committee decided to add no new sports to the Athens programme. The campaign by the International Water Ski Federation for inclusion in the Olympic Games had begun in 1991 and was led by the Colombian, Andrés Botero Phillipsbourne. He expressed his disappointment with the result and the process:

I'm very disappointed . . . it has cost us almost three million dollars and taken me to a lot of strange places in the world . . . If they would only let us know what they want. There are no clear rules on how a sport gets included in the Games — or gets kicked out . . . Non-Olympic sports like us have not got much money, and I think it's becoming almost impossible to ever join the programme. (Vestergård, 2003)

The Olympic Games, it seems, have reached saturation point. Dr Jacques Rogge, president of the IOC, has decided that the programme of the Olympic Games has reached its maximum size and for the time being, the number of sports, events as well as competing athletes, has been capped. Under this system, new sports can be added in the future only if some existing sports and events are deleted.

There is another form of competition that have been less noticed in sports literature, such as competition between mega-events staged in one country. This became evident at the time of the 2002 World Cup finals. South Korea is a relatively small power in East Asia that, as Kang Shin-pyo noted, has invested heavily in mega-sporting events. He stated that the 1988 Seoul Olympic Games involved 'total social and cultural mobilization' (Kang et al., 1987, p. 85).

South Korea had been successful not only in winning the bid to co-host the Football World Cup in June 2002 but was also selected to stage the Asian Games at Busan, from 29 September to 16 October 2002. It was reported at a seminar held at Inje University in July 2002 that the Asian Games were struggling to secure sufficient sponsors because they had invested heavily in the World Cup. While some 160 sponsors had signed up for the World Cup the Asian Games had trouble finding a mere 16 by late July (Eighth de Coubertin Youth Conference, Inje University, 2002).

Australia, like South Korea, is another small country that invests in what John Hoberman has referred to as 'sportive nationalism' (Hoberman, 1993, pp. 15–36; Cashman, 2002, pp. 233–8). The hosting of events by various Australian cities from 2000 to 2006 demonstrates both the competition within one country to stage mega-events and the mixed responses to six major sporting festivals that have been or will be held in this period. After the 2000 Olympic and Paralympic Games in Sydney, Brisbane staged the Goodwill Games in 2001 and Sydney the Gay Games in 2002. Sydney staged the Rugby World Cup in 2003 and Melbourne will host the Commonwealth Games in 2006.

No fewer than five Australian cities (Adelaide, Brisbane, Darwin, Melbourne and Perth) expressed some interest in bidding for the 2006 Commonwealth Games, which were awarded to Melbourne. Despite a great Australian enthusiasm for these Games, there were some who wondered about the future viability of these Games and others questioned whether the Games were a 'colonial relic' and an 'imperial anachronism' (Smith, 2002).

The Games, when they were first held in Canada in 1930, were a celebration of the 'white empire' that gained dominion status in 1931. They have been held only twice outside the 'white'-dominated countries, once in the West Indies (Jamaica in 1966), once in Asia (Kuala Lumpur, in 1998). The Commonwealth Games have never been held in Africa or in South Asia though New Delhi has been awarded the 2010 Commonwealth Games. The countries that sustain the

Commonwealth Games are largely Australia, Canada and New Zealand (in 2006 the Games will have been held in Australia for the fourth time), and Canada and New Zealand have each staged the Games three times.

The threats as a result of increased competition can be summarized under two headings. Because there is an increasingly crowded calendar of global sporting events, there are some sporting festivals, such as the Goodwill Games, that have folded. There are others, such as the Commonwealth Games, that have dwindled in significance, losing some of their original purpose because the British Empire and then Commonwealth had declined as a significant inter-government agency since 1930. The Commonwealth Games will probably survive propped up by voluntary support rather than a high profile commercially driven mega-sporting event.

The second challenge for the organizers of a multi-sport event, such as the Olympic Games, is to incorporate new sports which as van Bottenburg noted 'are constantly being created' when the Olympic programme is already crowded to capacity. There is a need to work out the appropriate balance with the established sports and the new sports on the Olympic programme. This can be achieved only through selective pruning of some less popular sports.

Alternative Visions of Sport

The organizers of a multi-sport festival face the continuing challenge of a proliferation of new sports that stretch the boundaries of what constitutes sport and incorporate alternative visions of sport. There are, first of all, the sports of youth. Triathlon developed a tough and youthful image, after its invention in the US in the 1970s and enjoyed a rapid rise in popularity particularly in Australia and other Pacific countries. It was incorporated into the Summer Olympics programme in 2000. Extreme sports, which are also popular with youth, have also enjoyed a rapid increase in popularity. They are not easy to incorporate in an Olympic programme because of the time involved in events, such as ultra-marathons, and in some instances the level of violence that is part of some sports such as extreme fighting. There are a whole new range of sports that are linked to technological innovation, such as water skiing. Then there are regional sports such as Asian martial arts and kick-boxing.

The Asian Games have become an important site for new sports. The Asian Games, like the African and other regional Games, were encouraged by the IOC as second tier Games and they continue to be organized by the Olympic Council of Asia. The Asian Games were first held in New Delhi in 1951, when there were only eleven countries involved in six sports. The Busan Games involved forty-three countries – from East, West, South and South East Asia – and featured thirty-eight sports.

The Asian Games had their roots in the Far East Championships, primarily through competition between China, Japan and the Philippines between 1913 and 1934. East Asian countries have dominated the Games. When the Games were held in Beijing in 1990 China won 60 per cent of the gold medals. The Asian Games have been used as a stepping stone for Asian countries that want to stage am Olympic Games. Because of their smaller size the Asian Games have been able to incorporate many new sports into the programme. In the four Games from 1986 to 1998 sixteen new sports were added to the programme:

- 1986 bowling, fencing, judo and taekwondo
- 1990 canoing, kabaddi, sepak takraw and wushu
- 1994 baseball, karetedo, modern pentathlon and soft tennis
- 1998 rugby, billiards, snooker and squash.

The Asian Games have become more diversified than the Olympic Games. While the 2000 Olympic programme included 28 separate sports and some 301 events, the programme for the 2002 Games at Busan, Korea, consisted of 38 sports and 420 events. In addition to a full range of Olympic sports, the Asian Games included the most prominent martial arts of the region – karatedo, judo, taekwondo and wushu – the martial arts practised in Japan, Korea and China. The Games also include sports that are popular in particular regions of Asia, such as kadabbi and sepak takraw. There are other sports that are popular in Asia such as bodybuilding, bowling and squash and yet other sports, such as billiards, golf and rugby, that are not part of the current Olympic programme.

It is interesting to note that although there was an unprecedented expansion of the Olympic programme during the Samaranch years (1980–2001), the increase in the number of sports and events – seven and eighty respectively – was far more modest than the Asian Games in the equivalent period. The new sports on the Olympic programme, from 1988 to 2000, were:

- 1988 tennis, table tennis
- 1992 badminton, baseball
- 1996 softball;
- 2000 taekwondo, triathlon.

The competition between the four martial arts to gain access to the Olympic programme demonstrates the dilemma of those who construct the Olympic programme. Judo was admitted in 1964 and taekwondo in 2000. Karate has long been waiting in the wings and the push by China to include wushu in the 2008 Beijing Olympic Games has so far been unsuccessful.

Karate has, long since, fulfilled the IOC requirements for an Olympic sport. It is the 'tenth biggest sport in the world, with approximately 50 million practitioners'. Despite its Asian origins, Europeans now dominate the sport. The problem for karate is that in the mind of the IOC the sport is too similar to taekwondo and 'there cannot be too many martial arts' on the Olympic programme (Vestergård, 2003). Taekwondo gained Olympic recognition despite 'a shorter history and a smaller international spread'. Taekwondo had the benefit of the advocacy of IOC vice-president Un Yong Kim, who also led the World Taekwondo Federation (Vestergard, 2003).

The IOC has long had a de facto policy to include some regional sports in the official or unofficial programme (as a demonstration sport) and often one or more sports that are popular in the host country have been added. Judo and volleyball were added to the programme when Japan hosted the Olympic Games in 1964; taekwondo became a demonstration sport at Seoul in 1988 and an Olympic sport in 2000; softball became an Olympic sport at Atlanta in 1996 and triathlon at Sydney in 2000.

Given the stance of the current IOC president on the size of the programme, the IOC has very little room to move on the issue of adding regional sports. The Olympic Programme Commission acknowledged this problem in its August 2002 report:

Regional sports

The possibility of including 'regional sports' within the future Olympic Programme was reviewed. The Commission felt that this would cause similar challenges to those acknowledged with the demonstration sports in previous Games, and would reduce the continuity which was a key success factor of the Programme. The Commission concluded that the regional popularity of a sport should be a factor in considering any requested changes; however, regional popularity should not be a sole factor permitting the admission of a sport to the Olympic Programme. (Olympic Programme Commission, 2002, p. 6)

It is likely to become more, rather than less, difficult to maintain the balance between old and new sports in a far more pluralistic sporting world. Given the past practice of the IOC, to include a sport popular in this host country, China might well feel aggrieved if the campaign to include wushu in the Beijing 2008 Olympic Games is not successful.

The Pragmatic and Loose Definition of the Olympic Programme

A third source of weakness, but also a possible strength, is the pragmatic and loose definition of the Olympic programme. The Olympic Games carries baggage from its nineteenth- and early-twentieth-century origins. It was a product of a European-led 'idealistic internationalism' that included an 'artistic cosmopolitanism', as John Hoberman (1995, pp. 1–37) has noted, though the Cultural Olympiad struggles to gain any real notice and exists on the margins of the Games. The Olympic Games are sports festivals that still bear the marks of the world fair Games, a loosely integrated smorgasbord of events, of which it was part in 1900 and 1904.

The Olympic Games draws on an older concept of sport: the programme consists of a loosely related amalgam of sports. Some of the events of the early Games, such as the tug of war and the obstacle race in swimming, reflected this context. Tug of war was omitted from the Olympic programme after 1920 not because it didn't fit the definition of an Olympic sport – because there was no precise one – but because it lacked an international federation to defend its interests.

There remains only a very general definition of an Olympic sport and what constitutes the Olympic programme. The official criteria, repeated in the 2002 *Review of the Olympic Programme*, are suitably broad and flexible. Some of the principles include the following:

- . . . changes in the structure of the Olympic Programme must result in a benefit for the Olympic Movement and an increased value and appeal of the Olympic Games
- Some flexibility should be inherent in the future Olympic Programme
- The Olympic Programme must contain a mixture of types of sports (team and individual, indoor and outdoor, sports of a different nature)
- The traditions of the modern Olympic Games should be retained and reflected in the future Olympic Programme
- The inclusion of sports within the Olympic Programme should be supported through analysis of each sport against identified criteria. (Olympic Programme Commission, 2002, p. 4)

The global spread of a sport – it should have a significant presence in seventy-five countries for men and fifty-five for women – and the issue of a sport being accessible to both men and women are the two most important 'identified criteria'. However, Anders Vestergård has identified other unofficial requirements – money, politics and television interests – that affect the shape of the programme (Vestergard, 2003).

This loose and pragmatic character of the Olympic programme may enable the Olympic movement to adapt in the future to changing global sporting priorities. Whether the IOC has the capacity and the political will to do so is another question because of vested interests, tradition and politics. The proposed deletion of three sports for the Beijing 2008 Olympic Games – baseball, modern pentathlon and softball – represents a big challenge for the Rogge leadership. In the past it has been far easier to add rather than subtract sports.

The Changing Geography of World Sport

It is interesting to compare the global spread of the Olympic Games with the World Cup of soccer since both these mega-events were Eurocentric in their initial decades. Soccer was first organized and codified in England in 1863 and the world governing body for the sport, FIFA (Fédération internationale de football association), was set up in France in 1904. During the 1920s football provided a convergence of interest for the two mega-events. Uruguay became a powerhouse of world soccer in the 1920s, winning the football competition at the Olympic Games in 1924 and 1928. Its Olympic success provided a platform for its successful staging of the first World Cup in Uruguay, that the host nation won.

Since that time, World Cup football has captured the imagination of European, South American and African countries in particular. The World Cup has been staged in South America six times in five different countries: Uruguay, Brazil, Chile, Argentina and Mexico (twice). Brazil has won the World Cup five times, and Argentina and Uruguay each twice. The Olympic Games, by contrast, have made less progress in this continent though the Olympic Games were held at Mexico in 1968 and Buenos Aires lost by only one vote to Melbourne for the right to stage the 1956 Olympic Games. It is interesting to note that while the Football World Cup has been staged in South America six times, Buenos Aires has been one of the perennial Olympic bid losers: it failed on six occasions to win a bid to host the Olympic Games (for the Games held in1936, 1940, 1956, 1960, 1968, 2004). IOC president Rogge stated in 1999 that it was important for the Olympic Games to be staged in South America and Africa in the next two decades (Rogge, 1999) – though whether this occurs appears problematical.

Football's World Cup was not staged in the Asian region until 2002, by which time four Summer Olympic Games and two Winter Olympic Games had been held in the Asian and the Pacific regions.[1] The Asian region lags behind the powerhouses of world football, Europe and South America, in terms of success in the World Cup competition. Even Africa appears to have advanced further in international soccer than the countries of the Asia-Pacific: Cameroon was the winner of the Olympic gold medal in 2000 and Senegal (as well as South Korea) was a 2002 World Cup quarter-finalist. South Korea is the strongest football country of the region having competed in the World Cup for the sixth time in 2002, when it reached the semi-finals. However, before 1986 South

Korea played in the World Cup only once, in 1954. Japan reached the World Cup for the first time in 1998 and China in 2002. North Korea reached the quarter-final in 1966.

There is, by contrast, a longer history of nations of the Asian and the Pacific regions in the Olympic Games. This is in part because even small nations, such as Australia and South Korea, can compete successfully in a particular sport in an Olympic Games. The following list, of Olympic Games staged in the Asian and Pacific regions is an impressive one. The Olympic Games have been awarded to countries of Asia and the Pacific nine times from 1936 to 2001. Six Olympic Games had been held in these regions by 2000. The frequency of Games held in these regions has increased since 1988:

- 1940 Tokyo (Summer Games) but not held
- 1940 Sapporo (Winter Games) but not held
- 1956 Melbourne (Summer Games)
- 1964 Tokyo (Summer Games)
- 1972 Sapporo (Winter Games)
- 1988 Seoul (Summer Games)
- 1998 Nagano (Winter Games)
- 2000 Sydney (Summer Games)
- 2008 Beijing (Summer Games).

Although the World Cup of soccer started more than three decades after the modern Olympic Games, it could be argued that it has outstripped the Olympics in its global spread.

Asia represents an important testing ground for the future appeal of the Olympic Games. To sustain this advance of the Olympic Games in the Asian and Pacific regions, there is a need to be sensitive to Asian priorities, culture and sports in the way future Games are run. Since 1964, the Olympic programme has catered more for sports of Asian origin and sports in which Asians excel. After judo and volleyball were added to the programme in 1964, table tennis became an Olympic sport at Seoul in 1988 and taekwondo a demonstration sport.

Although table tennis was invented in England, it has taken deep roots in Asia, and China now dominates this sport. After China shared the four gold medals with Korea in table tennis at the 1988 Seoul Olympic Games, China has since won eleven of the twelve gold medals contested achieving a clean sweep – men's and women's singles and doubles (and mixed doubles in 2000) – at the 1996 and 2000 Olympic Games. Badminton, also invented in England, has a similar history to table tennis. Asian countries have dominated badminton since it was introduced to the Olympic programme in 1992: the thirteen gold medals have been shared by China (five), Indonesia (four), Korea (three) and Denmark (one). This sport is particularly important for Indonesia, because the country's success in any event in the Olympic Games has been rare. Indonesia won the men's and women's singles in 1992, and the men's doubles in 1996 and 2000.

South Korea not surprisingly dominated taekwondo – which is a Korean martial art – when it was introduced at the Sydney 2000 Olympic Games. South Korea was allowed to compete in only four of the eight events – as were all other countries except the host nation – and won three gold and one silver medals.

The Olympic movement has advanced its prospects in Asia with the staging of the Olympic Games in Japan, South Korea and China and with the introduction of sports that are of Asian origin or are prominent in Asia. The staging of the Olympic Games in Beijing in 2008 is propitious because China is likely to play an increasing role in global sport of the future. The advance of the Olympic movement in Asia has yet to be replicated in other non-Western countries, notably Africa, South America and the Middle East, where the Olympic movement lags behind the football World Cup.

Copying Olympic Ceremonies

Anthropologist John MacAloon has analysed the significance and power of Olympic ceremonies that brand the Olympic Games as a special ritual event. He has observed that the opening ceremony of an Olympic Games is the most expensive and sought-after event, even though it includes no sport, because it is the greatest display of 'globally powerful and evocative' ceremonies (MacAloon, 1996, pp. 29–43). Ceremonies in a sense brand the Olympics as a special event. The power of such ceremonies are enhanced by their quasi-religious character. Bill Baker has noted that de Coubertin consciously borrowed from Catholic ritual to invest Olympic ceremonies with a religious quality (Baker, 2000).

However, can Olympic branding and quasi-religious ceremonies sustain the Olympic Games in the future? Can Olympic ceremonies be copied by other sporting festivals? Will the increasing number of mega-sports festivals reduce them to the mundane? With the application of soap opera techniques to television broadcasting as Joan Chandler (1991) has noted, the high mass of Olympic ceremonies may descend to kitsch.

There was something memorable in the unprecedented achievement when Mark Spitz won seven gold medals at the 1972 Munich Olympic Games. However, swimmers today have a myriad of opportunities for multi-medal hauls. After Ian Thorpe won three gold medals at Sydney 2000 Olympic Games, he gained six gold medals at the 2001 world championships in Japan. He almost went one better at the 2002 Commonwealth Games when he secured six gold and one silver medals. Winning a swag of medals and breaking his own world records has almost become routine for Ian Thorpe.

There is a danger that the increasing amount and variety of world sport that the Olympic Games will become just another sports spectacular in a crowded sports programme. However, the ceremonies, the traditions and branding provide the Olympic movement with a unique advantage over any rival sporting festivals. The torch relay, which begins at the site of the ancient Games at Olympia, and the lighting of the cauldron at the opening ceremony invest the Olympic Games with great symbolic capital.

Review of the Olympic Programme, August 2002

The August 2002 *Review of the Olympic Programme* endorsed the view that the Olympic programme had reached its optimum size so that any expansion in 2008 could take place only at the expense of some existing sports. The commission recommended the deletion of three sports: baseball, modern pentathlon and softball. The review identified a number of reasons why baseball and softball should be deleted: their restricted global spread, the cost of constructing appropriate stadia and because Olympic baseball does not attract the best athletes in the sport (Olympic Programme Commission, 2002). It has also recommended the deletion of some events within a particular sport such as race-walking in track and field, the synchronized swimming team event, the mixed doubles in badminton and a number of other events.

Golf and rugby sevens were two sports recommended for admission to the 2008 programme though there was no reasons for the inclusion of these particular sports. Karate was listed as a sport for possible review. If it is considered, its status will be reviewed in comparison with judo and taekwondo. Wushu was not recommended for inclusion.

The commission was complacent about the current mix of the programme. It concluded 'that the current structure was very successful, and therefore an argument could not be made for changing it'. However, at the same time 'it was agreed that there may be opportunities to add value through change, and to allow access to the Olympic Games for different athletes and sports' (p. 6).

Conclusion

This chapter has focused on threats (and challenges) to the future of the Olympic Games mainly in regard to Asia and ability of the Olympic movement to adapt to a changing global sports system. The chapter has concentrated mainly on issues relating to the Olympic programme and whether it may be sufficiently flexible and sensitive to changing priorities in the future. Threats to the future viability of the Olympic Games may come from other sources which are less easy to evaluate such as the increased appeal of alternative sporting festivals and problems within the movement such as excessive commercialism, drugs and even security and insurance costs. The ability of the Olympic movement to reform itself after the scandals of 1998 and 1999 is obviously another factor.

What does the past history of the Games tell us about the capacity of the organizers of the Olympic Games to deal constructively with these threats considered in this chapter? Can the Olympic Games be reinvented to take account of a rapidly changing global sports system?

The Olympic Games have been reinvented many times to adapt to a changing global sports system and it would be foolish to underestimate the capacity of the Olympic movement to operate even in a 'post-Olympic' world. The award of the Games to Tokyo for instance opened new possibilities for global expansion particularly in Asia. The open acceptance of commercialism and professionalism after 1980 transformed the character of the Olympic Games.

The Olympic Games remain a Western-dominated movement, both in terms of political power and the origin of sports on the programme as Guttmann (1994) has suggested. It does not seem that this Eurocentric bias represents a handicap to the global spread of the Olympic Games since many of the sports on the programme have become cosmopolitan sports, understood by sports communities globally. Thus many European countries are strong in Asian-origin sports, such as judo, while Asian countries now dominate in sports of European-origin such as archery, badminton and table tennis.

The crowded calendar of world sport and the increasing competition between sporting festivals is likely to affect more second tier global sporting festivals – such as the Asian, Commonwealth and Goodwill Games – than the Olympic Games. However, the Olympic Games are vulnerable in terms of their balance and size. If it is conceded that the Olympic Games have reached their optimum size, it is a matter of great sensitivity to get the balance right between new and old sports, the sports of youth and the traditional sports of the Olympics as well as 'regional' sports. This is not an easy task and one that requires great inter-cultural sensitivity. It is not something that should be dictated by the interests of television companies or the sponsors.

It might be prudent for the Olympic authorities to include wushu rather than golf or rugby sevens in the programme of the 2008 Beijing Olympic Games. It would demonstrate that the IOC recognizes the importance of China as perhaps the last great frontier of world sport. It would indicate inter-cultural sensitivity and a recognition of alternative visions of global sport. It would demonstrate that it is possible for the programme of the Olympic Games to evolve to take into consideration the changing global sports system.

8

Making the World Safe for Global Capital

The Sydney 2000 Olympics and Beyond

Helen Jefferson Lenskyj

DANGER! You have just been handed an illegal leaflet containing unAustralian sentiments, from an Olympics criminal . . . The Olympics – keeping Sydney safe for global capital.

On 17 September 2000, members of the Sydney-based Anti-Olympic Alliance challenged Olympic legislation by handing out *illegal* materials to visitors at a downtown plaza that had been designated an Olympic 'live site' and, hence, one of the many areas of the city subject to the full force of new laws controlling public behaviour. The protesters' message was clear: the Olympic Games serve the interests of global capital first and foremost.

This was not, of course, the first time that anti-Olympic activists had made the important connection between the Olympic industry and global capitalism, or had challenged Olympic sponsors for their complicity in environmental destruction, human rights abuses, and the widening gap between rich and poor countries, and between rich and poor within a country. In the words of one Salt Lake City protester, the central problem with the Olympics is 'the role that transnational corporations are playing in bankrolling, selling, and exploiting the athletic competition'. The best tactic, in this critic's view, is 'to directly, continually, and unabashedly screw with the advertising and marketing attempts of Olympic corporate sponsors' (Nutrition, 2001).

Just as anti-globalization protesters condemned the virtually unfettered power of transnational corporations, many of which boasted greater assets than those of small nation-states participating in Olympic sporting competition, anti-Olympic critics argued that the IOC itself shared some of the most repressive features of these global giants. For example, as an autonomous, unelected body, the IOC has the power, through Rule 61 of the Olympic Charter, to shape domestic policy, at least in the short term, by requiring host cities (and by extension, host nation-states) to guarantee that there will be no political protests in or near Olympic venues. As history has shown, such guarantees can only be made through enacting legislation that suspends the basic right to freedom of speech and freedom of public assembly cherished by most democratic societies (Lenskyj, 2000).

Indeed, the climate for political protest – whether anti-globalization or anti-Olympic – has become significantly more repressive since mass protests against the World Trade Organization meeting in Seattle in 1999. Moreover, many international anti-terrorist initiatives that were put in place after the 11 September 2001 attacks on New York and Washington provide a convenient rationale for police crackdowns on peaceful protests and public assemblies, as events in subsequent G8 summits, most notably Genoa and Quebec City, demonstrated. Even before September 2001, legislation in many US and Canadian cities criminalized nonviolent protest activities such as marching without a permit, hanging banners, blocking traffic, altering billboards, and wearing satirical masks or balaclavas (Mackinnon, 2000). Since that date, free speech has been repeatedly threatened by draconian laws in the guise of anti-terrorism measures.

Mainstream media coverage of these protests typically – and erroneously – depicts all participants as young, masked anarchists hurling missiles at police. While there is a broad social and political spectrum of anti-globalization protesters, including progressive academics and other public intellectuals, radical Olympic critics are more difficult to find in the academy. One popular liberal perspective holds that there are progressive men and women, including academics, who share the concerns of the more radical critics, and are working within the system to try to bring about change. In my own experience, it has been suggested that I should be collaborating with these colleagues, rather than aligning myself with grassroots activists who dare to criticize these learned Olympic scholars. It is true, of course, that many well-intentioned and left-leaning people, including academics, join Olympic bid and organizing committees in the hope that their presence will influence the agenda (and I have met with some of them to discuss these issues off the record), but there is little evidence of their success in this venture, and ample evidence of silencing, co-option and disenchantment (see, for example, Lenskyj, 2002, ch. 6).

Olympic Resistance, Past and Present

Urban anthropologist Charles Rutheiser (1996) coined the term *imagineering* to describe the process by which Olympic organizers, business people and politicians collaborated to engineer a new image of Atlanta as a 'world class' city, an international tourist destination, and a site for corporate investment, in the lead-up to the 1996 Summer Olympics. Olympic bid and host cities have been relying on these costly imagineering campaigns since the 1970s or earlier, while, for their part, Olympic critics have been trying to put the real questions of Olympics costs and benefits on the public agenda, with varying degrees of success.

Among the most pressing concerns raised by anti-Olympic activists is the practice of transferring scarce public money from affordable housing or other social service programmes into urban window-dressing projects designed solely to impress Olympic visitors. Promises of affordable housing have been a constant feature of recent Olympic bids, but have failed to materialize in most post-Games cities. In the same vein, undemocratic decision-making on Olympic budget issues has often resulted in taxpayers' shouldering a huge Olympic debt for years after the Games are over. Specific examples of these trends include the following:

Mexico City, Mexico

In October, 1968, before the Olympics began, thousands of Mexican students protested the huge amount of government money that had been redirected to Olympic-related projects, most notably US$200 million transferred from social services budgets to urban re-imaging campaigns. Like earlier popular uprisings, the student protests were violently suppressed by the Mexican military and paramilitary forces, with hundreds massacred, and thousands arrested and beaten (Paz, 1972).

Montreal, Quebec

The 1976 Olympic Games are infamous for the CDN$1 billion debt that Montreal taxpayers continued to pay off throughout the 1990s. Many critics (e.g. Auf der Maur, 1976; Ludwig, 1976; Wright, 1978) blamed undemocratic local government, under the leadership of Jean Drapeau, a mayor who had the dubious distinction of having boasted that the Olympics could no more have a debt than a man could have a baby.

Denver, Colorado

The IOC awarded the 1976 Winter Olympics to Denver in 1970, but, following residents' concerns over the potential tax burden, negative environmental impacts, and uncontrolled urban and regional growth, the issue was put to state and city referenda in November 1972. The outcome was a negative vote and Denver took the unprecedented step of rejecting the IOC's offer to host the Games (Katz, 1974).

Seoul, Korea

This city's preparations for the 1988 Olympics prompted major urban redevelopment, and there were documented reports of forced evictions of over

1 million people. Residents in some neighbourhoods organized resistance to Olympic construction, but their protests were violently suppressed by riot police and private security personnel. So-called Olympic beautification programmes included government-ordered demolition of 'slum' housing visible from main roads, hotels, Olympic venues and torch relay routes. Sex tourism was a feature of the government's marketing of Korea to the rest of the world (Asian Coalition for Housing Rights, 1989; Mulling, 1990).

Barcelona, Spain

Before and during the 1992 Summer Olympics, there were police crackdowns on petty crime, street sweeps of homeless people and sex trade workers, and arrests of dissidents (Cox et al., 1994). A group called NOOOOO a la Barcelona Olimpica challenged the city's costly bid by forming a coalition of over twenty tenants' rights, environmental and other social justice groups. Concerns included undemocratic decision-making, threats to the environment, and public money redirected into Olympic construction and urban image-making campaigns instead of housing and recreational facilities for working-class communities. Although the city had promised subsidized housing in the post-Games Olympic village, by 1992 most of the 6,000 units had been sold at market value (Montalban, 1992). As Olympic construction took priority over subsidized housing, there was an increase of over 50 per cent increase in the number of residents leaving the city in 1992, when compared to outmigration figures for 1986 (Cox et al., 1994, pp. 37–9).

Amsterdam, Netherlands

A coalition of groups called No Olympics Amsterdam opposed that city's (unsuccessful) bid for the 1992 Olympics. Their *People's Bidbook* documented numerous environmental, financial and social concerns, as well as the usual problem of insufficient public consultation. The coalition demanded that politicians give priority to urgent social problems, particularly housing shortages and lack of funding for local recreational programmes and facilities. On a global front, protesters pointed out that the Netherlands' business links with South Africa could prompt boycotts, with obvious implications for budget projections and possible debt to be borne by local governments, and hence, by taxpayers.

Calgary, Canada

Federal, provincial and local governments directed about CDN$461 million towards the construction of Calgary's Olympic village and other facilities in preparation for the 1988 Winter Olympics (Walkom, 1999). Problems experienced by Calgary's low-income tenants, including displacement and forced evictions, have been well documented (Olds, 1998). Over 2,000 people were temporarily or permanently evicted to provide accommodation for Olympic visitors, while houses in low-income neighbourhoods near the Olympic stadium were given a 'facelift' to enhance the city's tourist image. Like Olympic construction in other host cities, approval for the Olympic stadium development, to be built in a low-income inner-city neighbourhood, was fast-tracked by a provincial government order-in-council with minimal community consultation (Macintosh and Whitson, 1992; Olds, 1998). In other protests, First Nations people and their allies targeted Petro Canada, a crown corporation that had been implicated in the exploitation of Native lands and resources, and was also an Olympic torch relay sponsor.

Melbourne, Australia

During the 1989–90 bid process for the 1996 Olympics, Toronto's anti-Olympic Bread Not Circuses (BNC) Coalition worked with a Melbourne group of the same name, and both groups subsequently produced alternative bid books that documented the real costs to the taxpayer. Not coincidentally, both Toronto's and Melbourne's Olympic bids were unsuccessful.

Melbourne BNC demanded that the government give priority to urgent social problems related to employment, environment, health, housing, public transport and social services. The group pointed out that close to half of the Melbourne bid committee were corporate representatives, eleven corporate donors or representatives had financial dealings with South Africa, and twenty companies had poor environmental records.

Nagano, Japan

In the late 1980s, a Japanese group, the Anti-Olympic People's Network, organized to oppose Nagano's bid for the 1998 Winter Games. A 1999 letter to Juan Antonio Samaranch, then president of the IOC, identified these concerns:

- environmental destruction
- huge and expensive facilities financed with taxpayers' money but not serving the needs of local communities
- restrictions on citizens' freedom of movement and civil liberties during Olympics
- Olympic venues and infrastructure given priority over more important public services
- distortions in local economy and hindrance to sustainable economic development
- commercialism of athletes, sport and sport venues, resulting in damage to individuals and the environment. (Anti-Olympic People's Network, 1999)

In 1990, the Nagano group was one of several that participated in an anti-Olympic rally in Tokyo, in solidarity with the Toronto Bread Not Circuses Coalition. On the occasion of the IOC meeting to select the 1996 Olympic host city, two BNC representatives flew to Tokyo (with airline tickets donated by a Toronto businessman) to convey the message that there was extensive community opposition to Toronto's bid (see Lenskyj, 2000, ch. 4).

Berlin, Germany

The Berlin NOlympic group, organized in 1993, opposed Berlin's (unsuccessful) bid for the 2000 Olympics. Like their counterparts in other bid cities, they identified the environmental threats and the negative social impacts resulting from public money being diverted from housing and social services to Olympic projects. The Greens, a political party active in Europe, Australia and elsewhere, participated in Berlin's anti-Olympic efforts. In Rome, too, Green Party members in 1997 joined an alliance that opposed that city's bid for 2004.

The International Network Against Olympic Games

In 1998, four European groups organized the International Network Against Olympic Games and Commercial Sports to oppose their city's bids for the 2006 Winter Games and to draw attention to the environmental threat posed by hosting the Olympics. The larger aim of this network was to address problems caused by Olympics and all commercial sports, and to bring about an end to the Olympics as presently constituted. Since 1999, twelve new anti-Olympic groups have been established in Europe (Anti-Olympics Committee in Turin, 2002).

This brief review of international Olympic opposition demonstrates how coalitions of existing community groups worked together, often in the face of formidable Olympic industry opposition in the form of generously funded public relations campaigns, to raise citizens' awareness of the problems that have plagued Summer and Winter Olympics for decades: the exacerbation of existing housing and homelessness crises, environmental damage, and the diversion of scarce public funds from much-needed social services and infrastructure to the Olympic juggernaut. While individual member-groups often focused on single issues, the experience of working in anti-Olympic coalitions broadened participants' understanding of the connectedness between social, political, economic and environmental issues.

Sydney 2000 Protests

Legislation passed in 1997 and 1998 in New South Wales significantly strengthened state power over public behaviour and peaceful assembly, and even small anti-corporate protests were forcibly closed down by police (Lenskyj, 2002). By 2000, the stage was set for state intervention in any anti-globalization or anti-Olympic protest, despite police assurances that 'law-abiding' demonstrations would not be impeded. With extensive Olympic-related legislation in place, however, it was virtually impossible to mount a 'law-abiding' protest in Sydney's downtown and harbour-front areas, or in any of the suburbs hosting Olympic events.

The World Economic Forum (WEF) held its Asia-Pacific Economic Summit in Melbourne in September 2000, just before the start of the Sydney Olympics. A number of WEF's corporate members were Olympic sponsors – Nike and Coca-Cola, for example – and had been implicated in environmental destruction, human rights infringements and/or poor labour practices.

The Melbourne-based S11 Alliance, a coalition concerned about corporate power and globalization, organized a blockade, daily protest rallies and a programme of forums and workshops to strengthen the international anti-globalization movement. Their goal was to take a stand 'against the right of global capital to rule the world' (Earthworker, 2000). Many of the S11 groups, which ranged from the Green Party to Greenpeace, also participated in the anti-Olympic protests in Sydney.

The Sydney-based Olympic Impact Coalition, formed in February 2000 and later renamed the Anti-Olympic Alliance, represented a broad spectrum of community and social service organizations, ranging from the Salvation Army and Red Cross, at the conservative end, to radical groups such as Reclaim the Streets and Critical Mass at the other. The more political groups made the links between local and global issues in a variety of ways, including protest marches, street theatre, direct actions, and independent media websites. For example, one member-group, the Campaign Against Corporate Tyranny with Unity and Solidarity (CACTUS) held protests against Shell Oil, Nike, McDonald's and Westpac Bank – all Olympic sponsors – as well as against the Sydney Organizing Committee and the WEF. As its literature explained, CACTUS sought 'to support a cross-section of people, unions and issues in combating the common foe of corporate power.' Sessions on the WEF and the Olympics, globalization and women, and racism and imperialism were held as part of a CACTUS-sponsored teach-in during June, 2000.

In other street actions, Nikewatch, an international watchdog organization associated with Oxfam, held an alternative Olympic opening ceremony in Victoria Park, Sydney, and a Socialist youth group, Resistance, organized a protest against the Olympics and its corporate sponsors, including Nike and McDonald's. And about a thousand cyclists joined Critical Mass, an international group that organizes a global celebration of non-motorized transport on the last Friday of every month in over a hundred cities, in a peaceful demonstration on Sydney Harbour Bridge.

More Resistance: Vancouver and Whistler

In 2001, Vancouver and Whistler, in British Columbia (BC), Canada, announced their joint candidacy for the 2010 Winter Olympics. Two Olympic watchdog groups, the Impact of the Olympics on Community Coalition (IOCC) in Vancouver and the Association of Whistler Area Residents for the Environment (AWARE), quickly organized to raise critical questions about financial, environmental and social impacts, and to challenge the secrecy that has become standard for Olympic bid committees. The IOCC's member groups included longstanding environmental organizations such as the Society Promoting Environmental Conservation (SPEC), housing advocates and community groups working with low-income, elderly and/or homeless populations.

Early in 2002, two Whistler residents, Van Powel and Troy Assaly, set up a website that offered critiques of the Olympic industry and the Vancouver/Whistler bid, and invited questions and comments from the community. Both groups organized regular public meetings and invited speakers with experience in Olympic resistance, including Glen Bailey from Salt Lake City, and Michael Shapcott and me, representing the Toronto-based Bread Not Circuses Coalition that had opposed that city's bids for the 1996 and 2008 Olympics.

In March 2002, on another global front, residents discovered that Whistler Council had been secretly negotiating with the World Economic Forum to host its 2004 meeting. Another interactive website, www.whistlerinfo.net, set up by Powel and Assaly, gave the full details behind the WEF plans and identified the serious problems of undemocratic decision-making. A petition opposing the deal, with over 1,300 signatures, was presented to Whistler Council, which subsequently passed a set of stringent conditions to be met before approval was given, thereby virtually ensuring that the WEF would not find Whistler an appropriate meeting site.

Later in 2002, it came to light that the province's public automobile insurance company, the Insurance Corporation of British Columbia (ICBC), had given nearly CDN$1.8 million to the Vancouver-Whistler Olympic bid early in 2001, around the same time that it increased auto insurance premiums. Furthermore, this was only one of several crown corporations that had made cash or value-in-kind (personnel/office space/marketing) donations to the bid. The province's Lottery Corporation and BC Hydro, for example, each contributed over CDN$1 million. Activists from the No Games 2010 Coalition launched a class action lawsuit against the bid corporation and ICBC in December, claiming that the ICBC payment was outside the powers granted to it by the Insurance Corporation Act, and thus an illegal transaction, and that the bid committee directors ought to have known that this was the case. The plaintiffs demanded that the money, plus interest, be recovered on behalf of ICBC rate-payers/ shareholders – BC citizens – and that the bid committee repay the sum immediately (Class Action Lawsuit, 2002).

Resistance in Salt Lake City

Several years before the IOC bribery scandal, Utahns for Responsible Public Spending, an Olympic watchdog group, had tried to get a question on the state ballot ensuring that Utah taxpayers would not have to cover debts incurred by the Olympic Games. In 1995, a coalition of minority, anti-poverty, women's and disability rights groups, called Salt Lake Impact 2002 and Beyond, began to address issues such as post-Games affordable housing and protection of the civil liberties of homeless people during the Games. The group also demanded a more open and public process with relation to Salt Lake Olympic Committee documents and board meetings, but with limited success. As another Salt Lake anti-Olympic group, the Citizen Activist Network, pointed out, rather than accepting the rhetoric that the Games were an 'investment in Utah's economic future', social justice activists 'would prefer to see similar excitement about investing in education, affordable health care and housing, environmental clean-up, and other community needs' (Citizen Activist Network, 2002).

The February 2002 report card issued by Impact 2002 gave the organizing committee low grades in most of these areas. Evictions of low-income tenants were an ongoing concern, and the 1996 promise of affordable housing as an Olympic legacy that would benefit the entire community largely failed to materialize. By 2002, the number of affordable units had dropped from 360 to 156, and relocatable units dropped from 470 to 42 (Salt Lake Impact, 2002).

In two of the most illuminating examples of Salt Lake City landlords' Olympic greed, an *Observer* (UK) journalist described the appalling treatment of permanent residents in 'budget' accommodations. In the first example, hostel residents who used to pay US$110 per week for substandard rooms were given three 'choices': pay US$2,800 per week during the Olympics, renovate 'the derelict attic' and live there for the duration, or move out. In the second case, motel residents could either pay a threefold rent increase or leave. In the immortal words of this motel owner, 'I don't run a charity, and every other hotel in the city is doing the same . . . I don't feel guilty about taking advantage. *This is what capitalism in America is all about*' (Donegan, 2002, emphasis added). These were precisely the kinds of abuses that Olympic watchdog organizations had been trying to prevent for many years, while, on a bigger scale, anti-globalization protesters had been addressing the abuses of global capitalism.

Threats to the civil liberties of homeless people and of groups planning Olympic protests were key concerns for community groups, including Impact

2002, the American Civil Liberties Union (ACLU) of Utah, the Citizen Activist Network and the Utah Animal Rights Coalition (protesting the inclusion of rodeos in the Games' cultural programme). Taking the position that Salt Lake City's public streets and sidewalks constituted 'traditional public forums' where First Amendment Rights to free speech were protected, the ACLU of Utah began lobbying the organizing committee and the city council in 1998. By February 2001, with no official disclosure of the locations of and rules governing free speech (protest) zones, the ACLU of Utah filed a lawsuit against the Utah Olympic Public Safety Command (UOPSC), a public agency comprising approximately twenty law enforcement services. The ACLU expressed disappointment that it had to resort to the courts to gain access to public documents on proposed police treatment of peaceful protesters, despite several years of meetings with UOPSC (ACLU, 2001). For their part, American law enforcement agencies had been concentrating more on surveillance and infiltration operations targeting anti-Olympic protest groups in Salt Lake City and elsewhere than on open communication with civil liberties and community groups.

Officials eventually developed plans for a few free-speech zones accommodating small numbers of protesters, and established a system of permits to be allocated to approved groups for limited periods. Not surprisingly, civil liberties advocates strenuously objected to what they saw as First Amendment tokenism, and eventually the plans allowed greater numbers of protesters in free speech zones and unlimited numbers in parades within a given timeframe. Ironically, the mayor of Salt Lake City, Ross Anderson, was a former ACLU attorney.

The Poor People's Economic Human Rights Campaign, a Philadelphia-based group led by poor and homeless people to raise the issue of poverty as an economic human rights violation, organized a non-violent March for Our Lives in Salt Lake City to coincide with the Olympic opening ceremony. As their informational materials pointed out, while 'the United States welcomes the Olympics, it has abandoned the poor people of this nation'. The government's expenditure on the Olympics was close to double that of the 1996 Summer Games, with US$230 million in state and local funds, as well as an additional US$1.1 billion of accelerated federal spending directed towards Utah highways and other infrastructure that Olympic organizers and Utah politicians demanded (Bennett, 2002). About four hundred protesters joined the March for Our Lives, and police arrested five of the leaders – all women, including one nun – when the marchers approached the Olympic Stadium. In other actions against state repression, activists marched through downtown streets protesting unprecedented levels of surveillance and security spending. Ironically, while these peaceful protesters were the focus of considerable police and security force attention, as well as disapproving media coverage, the so-called 'beer riot' – the fighting and vandalism that resulted when groups of young, white people had been turned away from a Salt Lake City bar – was played down in the local and national mainstream media (Wise, 2002). Meanwhile, on another continent, Sweatshop Watch groups in Amsterdam held an alternative opening ceremony to protest the purchase of Burmese sportswear for Olympic torchbearers, and to urge the IOC to boycott all such products because of the brutal military regime and questionable labour standards in Burma.

Conclusion

This review of Olympic resistance since 1968, and the detailed examination of protests organized in Australia before and during the Sydney 2000 Summer Olympics, reveal unequivocal solidarity between anti-Olympic and anti-globalization critics. Furthermore, events in Salt Lake City before and during the 2002 Winter Olympics, and in Vancouver and Whistler during the bid process for the 2010 Winter Olympics, provide further evidence of the strength of these alliances, and reflect activists' critiques of the Olympic industry's role in global capitalism and its exploitation of people and environments.

9

The Disneyfication of the Olympics?
Theme Parks and Freak-Shows of the Body

Alan Tomlinson

Introduction: Survival and Transformation

The Olympic Games sells itself as the most prominent recurrent global event in the contemporary world. Combining a focus on elite performance and athletic excellence with a principle of universal participation, it claims to represent peaks of human endeavour while fostering international friendship, peace and harmony, and to cultivate new generations of internationally tolerant young people. It is in the context of such a set of values that, in this chapter, I want to explore more sceptically the nature of the event itself, focusing upon the Sydney Summer Olympic Games, and my experience of those Games in Sydney itself – as flâneur, fan, investigative researcher, media observer and critical social scientist. In doing so I will consider the parallel experiences of the leisure consumer in contemporary consumer culture, and assess the extent to which it makes sense to talk of the Disneyfication of the Olympic Games.

In the late 1970s, nobody wanted the Olympic Games. Massacres of militants in Mexico City (1968), terrorism on television in Munich (1972), boycotts and near bankruptcy in Montreal (1976) and the prospect of a communist extra-vaganza in Moscow (1980) meant that, as a troubled International Olympic Committee coped with this multiple-M factor, few cities and national Olympic committees were lining up with offers to host the 1984 Summer Olympics. Tehran, Iran, was an unconvincing looking runner but when it withdrew its candidature, only Los Angeles was left. The Los Angeles (LA) bidding team could write its own terms, and as some commentators (see Tomlinson and Whannel, 1984) were quick to observe, recast the Olympic mould on the basis of sponsorship deals, marketing, mobilization of volunteers, and limited formal political responsibility for the successful staging of the event. The LA 1984 Olympics was a symbolic moment in the history of the modern Olympic Games, embodying its transformation in terms of media profile, marketing opportunity and potential source of profit and personal aggrandizement for those purporting to live by the ideals of the Olympic movement. They were also the first Summer Games at which Lord Killanin's successor as president of the IOC, Juan Antonio Samaranch, presided. His career as one of Franco's political appointees in fascist Spain (Simson and Jennings, 1992) was to stand him in good stead. His capacity to strike exclusive deals with major multinationals and television companies was to reward him well in his regal lifestyle in Lausanne, on the banks of Lake Geneva. The LA Olympics not only symbolized the survival of a shaky antiquated-sounding ideal, but also shook and stirred that ideal into a new shape, and international sporting events of this profile were never to be quite the same again. It could be seen as the pivotal moment when the Olympics were steered down a path towards their Disneyfication, and the extent to which this can be claimed is the theme of this chapter. Before outlining the parameters of Disneyfication, as a process and a noun, it is useful to remind ourselves of some of the continuities in rhetoric and practice of those professing the Olympic ideals, representatives of what is often labelled (particularly by those representatives themselves) the Olympic movement or the Olympic family. It is useful because if the Olympics can be said to have been Disneyfied, then this is a process that is identified in counterpoint to the values and claims of these sorts of movement or family apologists.

Baron Pierre de Coubertin was no slouch when it came to self-promotion. Hobnobbing with the political and business elite was his forte, a natural vocation for a suave young aristocrat raised in the sporting and social culture of the leisure classes in the last quarter of nineteenth-century France (MacAloon, 1981; Tomlinson, 1984). De Coubertin excelled at hyperbole, hailing his 1894 Congress in Paris as the moment when a 2,000-year-old idea was restirred in 'men's hearts today as in days past, an idea that satisfies one of the most vital instincts and . . . one of the most noble' (de Coubertin, 2000, p. 531). The idea was the restoration of a notion of physical exercise rooted in de Coubertin's reading of Greek Olympism: 'Character is not formed by the mind, it is formed above all by the body. This is what the ancients knew, and that is what we are relearning, painfully' (2000, p. 532). Later in the same year, speaking to a literary society in Athens, de Coubertin recalled his delegates listening to choirs singing the hymn to Apollo, unearthed at Delhi:

> In one of those mysterious glimpses that music sometimes gives us of lost worlds, for a few seconds those gathered at Paris perceived Greek antiquity in all its splendour.
>
> From that moment on, Gentlemen, the Greek genius was among us, transforming a modest congress on athletic sports into a quest for moral betterment and social peace. My goal had been achieved. (Coubertin, 2000, p. 533)

For de Coubertin, the Olympic project had philosophical, historical and educational dimensions and goals: 'everything in the restored and modernized Olympism', he wrote in 1931, 'focuses on the ideas of mandatory continuity, interdependence, and solidarity' (2000, p. 603). De Coubertin puffed up his conception of Olympism consistently for more than forty years, inscribing it in the expanding rituals and protocols of the Olympic event, and claiming a remarkable continuity and expansion of impact and importance of the Olympic movement and family. It was a heady mix of lofty ideals and grandiose ambition, and that the notion is still engaging the attention of so many in the contemporary world testifies to the power of the idea. John MacAloon speaks of what he considers to be the real heart of the Olympic phenomenon, the volunteers, in terms that bear comparison with de Coubertin's articulation of core Olympic ideals. MacAloon has subjected numerous Olympic flame or torch relays to anthropological scrutiny and cultural analysis, and sees in the commitment of the thousands of individuals evidence of 'dramatic and transformative' dimensions. Of the volunteers committed to the 1996 Olympic flame relay for the Atlanta Games he writes:

> No one had to tell these volunteers that Olympism is or should still be a social movement, a human movement for peace and intercultural encounter, a ritual encounter with human diversity and common humanity. Indeed, I believe these volunteers and others like them around the world could tell Olympic leaders a thing or two about the Olympic Movement . . .
>
> Volunteers are people seeking to be and being touched by the Olympic Movement . . . the *real* Olympic Movement. (MacAloon, 2000, p. 25)

So for MacAloon, it is the volunteers who 'hold a key to the future of Olympism as a bona fide social movement' (ibid.). MacAloon is rightly critical of Olympic leaders for whom the Games are no more than 'just another branch of the sports industry', and locates the more idealized possibilities of Olympism in the everyday culture of people drawn into their volunteering roles.

De Coubertin was never at a loss for ways of talking up his project and dream, writing after the 1908 London Games of the 'quite apparent . . . colossalism' of the event (2000, p. 416), despite the peripheral status of the event as a whole in relation to the international Franco-British expedition (Roche, 2000, p. 90). With 90,000 people turning out for the final event, the Marathon, it is true that the 1908 Games can be claimed as some sort of turning point (Wallechinsky, 2000, p. xxi). But regardless of the material circumstances of their staging, pitched from the start as a phenomenon of modern, worldwide significance, framed within a set of historically specific classicist ideals, the Olympics has generated an aura of seriousness and vastness of scale. Talk of Olympic family values and the Olympic movement perpetuates this, and runs the risk of underestimating some more mundane aspects of the Games as a social phenomenon and cultural reality. Evaluations of Games are often characterized by the very discourse that such evaluations ought to critique. For instance, an interesting contribution to the study of the changes in Barcelona's urban environment brought about by the Barcelona Games is marred in its conclusion by an effusive enthusiasm: 'the city has become more welcoming, friendlier, cleaner, more athletic, more pleasant, more cultivated, more urban, more Olympic and all of this is a consequence of having organized the Games of the City' (Millet, 1995, p. 202). What would be lost here if the word 'Olympic' was omitted from the sentence? What might be gained, in terms of cultural analysis, if the word 'Disneyesque' took its place?

Disneyfication: Process and Outcome

To talk of Disneyfication is to refer to the process whereby the Walt Disney business empire emerged from its Hollywood base to dominate particular forms of popular cultural production and associated consumer markets, across a range of cultural forms from animation to feature films and theme parks. Wasko (2001, pp. 177–8) notes that the term has been applied to cultural texts and literary works, as well as in analyses of urban planning. There have been numerous studies of the making of a particular cultural product, such as the 1940 film *Fantasia* (Culhane, 1983), on a descriptive level (though there are interesting issues of interpretation contained in such works, as when Culhane observes that on its re-release in 1969, the film could now be seen as 'a psychedelic experience'). One of the earliest deconstructionist approaches to the Disney question argued that the manufacture of fantasy characters constituted a threat, representing 'the manner in which the US dreams and redeems itself, and then imposes that dream upon others for its own salvation' (Dorfman and Mattelart, 1975, p. 95). These authors were pioneering for their reading (first published in 1971, in Chile) of the apparently innocent world of the Disney imagination, identifying deeply entrenched ideologies in the narratives and values of Disney productions. This has been a strong recurrent emphasis in critical work on Disney, and Giroux, looking at the consumption of Disney products by children in the US and beyond, has claimed that beneath 'Disney's self-proclaimed role as an icon of American culture lies a powerful educational apparatus that provides ideologically loaded fantasies . . . Fantasy is a marketing device. A form of hype rooted in the logic of self-interest and consumption' (Giroux, 1999, p. 158). The strand in work on Disney relating to the urban environment is eloquently represented by Zukin, who notes that the multimedia precedents for Disney World's imaginary landscape were the World's Columbian Exposition in Chicago in

1893, and New York's 1939 World's Fair in Flushing Meadow: 'Both world's fairs featured the four kinds of attraction that Disney World would later integrate to perfection: amusement parks and rides, stage-set representations of vernacular architecture, state-of-the-art technology, and a special construction of an ideal urban community' (Zukin, 1991, p. 225). In the construction of the Olympic stadium, the production of ceremonial shows, design of the Olympic Village, modern Olympic host cities may well be seen to have committed themselves to cultural projects comparable to those of the world fairs and Disney World itself.

Bryman (1995) has discussed how the Disney theme parks exhibit characteristics akin to processes of McDonaldization (Ritzer, 2000), in which control, predictability and efficiency are at the heart of the consumption process and experience. Ritzer's fourth dimension, calculability, is seen as less relevant to the Disney sites and products. Wasko also reports Bryman's identification of four elements of 'Disneyization' – 'theming, dedifferentiation of consumption, merchandising, and emotional labour' (Wasko, 2001, p. 178) – and makes no attempt to dispute that the trend towards this process has been increasing. Bryman's (1999) analysis is indeed convincing, linking the understanding of Disney with broader analyses of cultural productions and consumption, such as theme parks and shopping malls more generally. It is my intent in this chapter to attempt if not a complete rethink of the Olympics, then at least a rethinking of its place in consumer culture, in the light of some of these wider themes established in critical cultural analysis of contemporary cultural productions and associated forms of consumption.

Wasko, and the many Disney analysts whom she cites, have shown how the stories and characters in Disney narratives 'typically go through a process of Disneyfication, which involves sanitization and Americanization' (Wasko, 2001, p. 113). The dominant themes and values of what she calls 'Classic Disney' are individualism and optimism; escape, fantasy, magic and imagination; innocence; romance and happiness; and good's triumph over evil (Wasko, 2001, pp. 117–19). Wasko also draws upon Bryman's analysis of the Disney theme parks, and discusses seven economic and ideological themes identified by analysts of the parks. There are synergy, across a range of cultural products; commodification and consumption, interweaved with entertainment; commercialization and corporatism, generating sponsorship as a form of legitimation of capitalism; huge levels of tourist visits; state-of-the-art technologies underpinning forms of 'backstage magic'; forms of organization based upon predictability and consumer expectations; and 'control, control, control' (Wasko, 2001, pp. 157–70).

The outcome of the process of Disneyfication is a set of characteristics, or features, of the Disneyfied phenomenon. The epitome of such a phenomenon is undoubtedly the theme park, and, culled from Philips (1999) as well as the sources on Disney discussed above, the theme park can be seen to be characterized by the following ten features:

- It is beyond the city but with ease of access
- It is a reclaimed site, a converted space
- It is strongly sited, but with no reference to local culture
- It is, in Philips' (1999) words, 'insulated from the outside world'
- It is a source of fantasies, dreams and passions
- It is dedicated to hedonism or pleasure
- It represents a breach with traditional time
- It provides spaces that are themed as stories
- It fosters a carnivalesque of the body
- It is a celebration of modernity, commerce, trade and consumerism.

The following observations on the Summer Games in Sydney 2000 are offered in the interpretive light of these features of the theme park/Disneyfication phenomenon.

Scenes from Sydney

Scene 1 – Ceremony and the Spectacular: Fairy Tales do Come True for Hero Girls, from Kylie to Cathy[1]

All Olympic open and closing ceremonies try to balance regional (city), national and global interests. Sydney had a go at this with its unsuccessful mascots. Syd the platypus was the city's. Millie the echidna spoke for the millennium. Olly the kookaburra was named after the event itself. They were so unsuccessful though that they were left offstage as the ceremonies played out the modern Olympic narratives of national rebirth and international and global cooperation, and Olivia Newton-John and Australian former Essex-man John Farnham sang songs of welcome to the world.

Birch's opening ceremony was widely hailed in Australia as a masterpiece of showbiz presentation, an uninhibitedly ambitious show of national and historical pride and cosmopolitan sincerity. What follows is a reminder of the primary themes and narrative, blended with my commentary, from close to ringside.

Sydney's Welcome to the global audience in the world's most watched television event was like an advertisement for your local riding school. Or outdoor overcoat supplier. One hundred and twenty riders draped in dry-as-bone Ozzie bush-coats romanticized the taming of the Australian outback. Riders aged 15 to 77 astride their Australian stockhorses kept their cool in front of the 111,000 in the Olympic Stadium. The horse master didn't mince words: 'We're breaking world records with this event and its scale will blow the world away'. And sitting fifteen rows back, the emissions from the panting horses' nostrils wafting into the faces of the A$1,400 onlookers, it was certainly stirring, as the riders also sang the Australian national anthem. There weren't many more live animals to come after that – a couple of stray dogs or dingoes. But there were lots of imagined ones – imagined in a little girl's dream, and realized like a playschool orgy of the fantastic.

Olympic ceremonies share the same preoccupations. The host nation wants to show that it can put on a global show, but must also feature a quota of Olympic-style spirit – youth, universalism, peace and the like. Such a recipe can draw and hold the audience, for we all become gleeful spectators again, watching vastly sophisticated technologies reduce complex histories to showbiz formulae. For Sydney 2000 the Sydney Symphony Orchestra worked overtime backing a line-up of Australian popular singers, as well as haunting soloists and choirs, in pop classic and middle-of-the-road numbers stressing dreams, heroism and the power of the symbol of the flame. And political messages get slotted in there too. The Governor General of Australia, representative of the United Kingdom of Great Britain and Northern Ireland's Queen, told the world that the Olympics was 'a powerful tool for reconciliation'. But it's the cultural spectacle that grabs you the most, that takes you back to the front row of the stalls or the big-top.

The beginning of Sydney's cultural spectacle, after its welcome to the world, echoed the four-year long Olympic arts festival, which had opened with the theme of Aboriginal dreaming, the life-force and spiritual basis of the longest-surviving of human civilizations. Deep Sea Dreaming placed centre-stage the Hero Girl, an innocent Shirley Temple look-alike, or a refugee from the cast of Peter Pan, who descended into the depths of a pool of fish, and so began a bizarre dream-sequence journey guided by the great tribal dancer Djakapurra, the Songman. Hero Girl, suspended at great height, performed somersaults in the sky, chased by several glowing yellow creatures; they turned out to be young swimmers training, bellowed on by legendary Australian swimming coach Laurie Lawrence in video close-up. She can't keep up, and the giant figure of the Songman waits to save her and guide her safely to salvation. Then followed Awakening, revolving around the uniting of diverse Aboriginal nations, and the appearance of Wandjina, the creation spirit, arching the stadium like a sunrise, and igniting bushfires that prefaced the third theme, Fire, as a creative not a destructive force. Circus-time this, with an array of fire-eaters. This elemental emphasis persisted in the theme of Nature, the Australian landscape and its plants and animals emerging out of the chaos of fire, with just the one swift guest appearance from a kangaroo, then sidelined by the organizers as an undesirable national symbol, after the scathing response to the bicycling kangaroos that had represented Australia in the handover phase of the closing ceremony of the previous Summer Olympics at Atlanta. The threat of a dark force of modern culture was then represented in a Tin Symphony, which included Ned Kelly types in iron masks (several performing flying feats), dancing cog wheels, and then merry fiddling music ushering in cheerful jigs. At the end of this segment, Hero Girl looked like she was about to be gobbled up by a mechanical dragon – or was it a horse? She survived, though, and after a few British sailors arrived on a contraption resembling a penny-farthing bicycle, and the penal colony roots of Western settlement were conveniently overlooked, the dream could continue.

Arrivals, the sixth theme, depicted the arrival (all fit and dancing) of groups of immigrants from all over the world, hailing the New Australia of multi-culturalism, celebrated ultimately (an Australian in-joke, I knew instantly from my time promenading the suburban streets of New South Wales) in a move from shanty-town to suburbia, represented in the opening up of gyrating packing-boxes, transformed into jovial domestic gardeners, the lawn-mower their dancing partners. The last segmental theme, thankfully, didn't live up to its name. In Eternity, the blue-collar egalitarianism of Australia was celebrated, workers building an enormous bridge on which a thousand tap dancers beat out an anthem of celebration, Songman and Hero Girl reconciling in the centre of things.

Some experienced Australian commentators were nervous at the world's reaction. Would this be too Australian, too parochial? A concentration on the Aboriginal roots of the country, an encomium to the Australian countryside (the bush) and the making of the industrial culture, dominated. Multiculturalism, ethnicity and reconciliation were central to the display, hailing the cultural diversity and cosmopolitanism of the New Australia. Artistic director and producer David Atkins states that the Sydney ceremony is important because it is about Australians themselves, and no other culture could have attempted what they did: 'They couldn't have matched our mixture of youth, naiveté and larrikinism'. Larrikinism is the term in Australia for that streetwise, even 'connish', wit and cunning that helps you get on in life. It's an illuminating claim, showing how strong that 'see what we can do' spirit is in an Australian consciousness still afflicted by a deep-rooted sense of inferiority, and undoubtedly fuelled by the continent's geographical marginality.

After the host city/nation's narrative, like a magician's trick, fire and water were reconciled in the official ritual of the lighting of the Olympic flame. The last lap of the torch relay was inside a fountain. Far from extinguishing it, this streamlined the flame, a still more dramatic effect when the cauldron burst into flames. It was runner and soon-to-be gold medalist Cathy Freeman who emerged to light the flame, rounding off the ceremony's depiction of the history of Australia as an Aboriginal metanarrative.

This was the new Australia, reworking its history and its tensions, offering a vision in which Wendy learns to fly and all, however different, live happily ever after. Fairy tales do come true after all. Birch stated confidently that the Sydney spectacle would be 'the greatest ever' opening ceremony. That is until next time, when the likes of Birch and his team, or some rival outfit, will be there in Athens, telling the same story anew and making us all instant classicists and historians.

Scene 2 – Centre and Periphery: the Little Olympics and the Everyday Audience, from Bondi Beach to Rooty Hill [2]

Sydney 2000 was the Bumper Summer Olympics. It welcomed more than 11,000 athletes, several thousand officials and coaches, and as the sixteen days whizzed by estimates of the number of mediafolk in town reached 21,000, although official estimates had been initially put at around 15,000. Athens 2004 plans to cater for 18,000 media. The Main Press Centre at the Olympic Park was vast, and the International Broadcast Centre was dominated by US broadcaster NBC, who had paid 705 million US$ for the rights, and mobilized a workforce of more than 2,000. More athletes, more sports, more professionals. Bigger, bigger, bigger.

The International Olympic Committee claims that the vast majority of the world's population able to access a television will have watched the action, the opening ceremony pulling in several billion – though such claims are beyond corroboration, and more reputable estimates by independent researchers have put the figure at rather less than half the one trumpeted by the IOC. But it is beyond dispute that the Summer Olympics claims one of the biggest television audiences of all time. Australians, and Sydneysiders especially, responded to the Games with passion and a determination to shout and support their own competing hopefuls, and then in the 24 hour pubs of Pyrmont and the like to party through till dawn. Gold was won by the scantily clad blonde women beach volleyballers at Bondi Beach, by the muscular concrete-pillar necked water polo girls in the Aquatic Centre, as well as by the beach bums of the swimming squads and the fated and feted bridge to Aboriginal/Australian reconciliation, Cathy Freeman.

When the big hopes were competing, the venues were a sell-out and the great live sites of Sydney – Circular Quay, Martin Place in the Central Business District, Tumbalong Park at Darling Harbour, Pyrmont Park, The Domain atop the Royal Botanical Gardens, Belmore Park at Central Station – were throbbing with nationalist enthusiasm. The home crowds were raucously supportive of their Australian hopes, and always ready with a jeer and a boo for the athletes from the UK and the US. If there was no serious Australian competitor in an event, the crowd cheered any compatriot it could locate. At the boxing, this gave a moment of celebrity to a number of Australian referees.

It was nevertheless enthralling seeing a nation of 20 million people chasing the US and China in the medal table, and celebrating this by waving or being draped in a national flag dominated by the flag of the United Kingdom of Great Britain and Northern Ireland. The victorious side of the Olympics for the host nation quickly became a metaphor for both the reconciliation embodied in the dignified presence of Cathy Freeman, and the success of the new Australia of multicultural mix (Wensing and Bruce, 2003). The silver medal in the first-ever Olympic women's pole vault was won by a blonde beauty from Adelaide, with the most New Australian of names, Tatiana Grigorieva – complete too with a recent nose job by the look of it, maybe since she relocated herself from Russia in 1996. So many of the Australian women were blonde, leggy and en route to if not already packaged up in modelling contracts. Tatania had already got the glam shots of her, in far less than her pole-vaulting outfit, ready for the world press.

The organizers of the Games, the much-maligned SOCOG (Sydney Organizing Committee for the Olympic Games) could claim an Olympic record in ticket sales, 80 odd per cent and above the sales figures for Atlanta 1996. But there weren't many sell outs for the women's soccer semis, or the softball preliminaries, or the Graeco-Roman wrestling, or the handball. I'd decided to take a look at some of the less glitzy sports, across Olympic Park, city centre venues and the western suburbs. Ones too that normal people like most of my taxi drivers might be able to afford – not the 455 dollars a go for the Aquatic Centre and a partial view only of the pool; or the 1,400 dollars for the opening ceremony. Or even the 105 dollars for the later rounds of the beach beauties over at Bondi. I thought I'd go where on a professorial salary I might have been able to afford to take my family when they were younger, had some interest in sports, and might have enthused if the Olympics Games were in town.

Western suburbs was a bit of a misnomer. Getting to Olympic softball was deserving of a special Olympic award. It was based in the Olympic Softball Centre at Blacktown. Well, that's what the programme said, but it wasn't really in Blacktown at all. There, a good ride out of town, it already felt like we were half-way to the Blue Mountains. Another train took the increasingly blue-collar crowd to Doonside, where fleets of buses carted us in to Rooty Hill.

Rooty Hill was flat, making the south-east of England look mountainous. This seemed another Australian trait. Back in Newcastle, New South Wales, I'd visited a house in Cooper's Hill, on the flattest bit of central Newcastle. So I was ready enough for this – the Olympic Softball Centre was on a flat dustbowl called Rooty Hill. From Central Sydney this had all taken close to two hours.

The compensation was that I'd been able to feel nostalgic for the Blue Mountains, I'd mingled with some of the local population rather than the worldwide media, and I was now able to watch what was billed as some of the world's top women athletes in one of the newest sports on the Olympic agenda.

Softball is essentially a copy of baseball. The women dress pretty much the same as men in baseball. They use a stick that looks pretty much like a baseball bat, though it's thinner. And the critical player in the squads is without question The Pitcher (some squads have loads of these). The basic principle of the game is that The Pitcher throws the ball underarm (men in baseball pitch overarm) very hard – high or low, it varies – in a fashion designed to prevent The Batter from hitting it at all. This means that The Batter can't then score a run by hitting the ball – white, and bigger than a baseball, but not at all soft-looking to me – high and beyond the perimeter of the stadium, and running around all the four bases. If you hit it high but not far enough you get caught. Nobody drops a catch in softball, as the players have on one hand a giant mitt, that looks like the kind of soft toy Australian gold medallists had become fond of cuddling on the medal rostrum. If you don't hit the ball or if you hit it just a short distance then you can run like mad to one of the four bases. For ages in this game, if the teams are evenly matched, there's no score. Then The Pitcher might get tired or The Batter might get lucky, and the softball is hit longer and harder and some runs might be scored. You also get a run if you can get around all those four bases while someone else is having a go with the bat. Some teams play cunningly, getting different players on the bases, knowing that it's unlikely that many players will hit the ball out of the playing area. The Canadian team did this very cleverly against Japan. Trailing 3–0 to some impressive Japanese swinging and thwacking, they had got a couple of players on the bases, and a mighty swing from Wood connected and thrashed the ball into the crowd. All three players then trotted around the four bases and suddenly the match was all-square, or tied-up, as the commentators liked to say. At first, looking at the woman who crouches behind The Batter to catch the ball that nobody's likely to hit, who's adorned in a suit of armour and mask that would delight the local S-M community, I'd thought that tied-up was a sub-text for more exciting Games. But it turned out to mean level, and the Japanese brought on The Really Big Pitcher. This was a rather older-looking woman, of more than ample proportions, who had something special in her wrist action. She went on to mesmerize the Canadian players and eventually, in complex tie-break rules, the Japanese got home 4–3.

There are interesting moments of tension in softball. Like when the ball's mishit and seems to be coming at your head in your spectator seat, at a million miles an hour. Then it hits the safety net. And The Batters swing the stick with serious menace, and you think that they can't go on missing it for so much of the time. But when there's a bit of a mismatch it can look embarrassing. That's true in any competitive sport. But how can you have this in team sports at the Olympics? The Cuban women lost 7–0 and began to look as if they feared the wrath of Castro long before the end of their encounter with the lean and wiry looking Chinese. The Cubans looked like they'd been left out of the track and field squads throughout their lives, maybe not quite got the mobility skills for volleyball, but in line with Cuba's philosophy of sport for all – 'massivity', they've often translated it in Cuba (Sugden et al., 1990) – they had to come to the Olympics and do something. Not to beat about the bush, the Cuban team was a bunch of fatties. Softball might have looked the soft option for some of these, but as China accelerated its desperate bid to host the 2008 Olympics, nothing was going to halt the momentum of its attack on the medal table.

The Olympics is a bloated beast, but one grain of optimism, as some of us try to salvage some positive values from the debacle of consumer excess, organizational scandal and jingoistic nationalism, is that the proportion of women competing at the Games has risen dramatically. The old Soviet Union and other East European states always knew how to win lots of medals. Pick obscure sports, people with some physical aptitude, train up on drugs and dedicate lots of resources to esoteric activities. Do this with your women athletes too and most of the West's hopeful beauties won't stand a chance. China's followed the formula well. So has Australia, where it was clear that the general profile of women's sports, and the country's position in the medal table, would rise if more women's sports got on the programme. So the Australian Olympic Committee supported, prepared and sent loads of impressively athletic and fearsomely competitive women to the Games. And it makes an interesting counterpoint in Australia to the nation's top four team sports – rugby union, rugby league, cricket and Australian rules football. All male and not on the Olympic programme. Not to mention the major Australian sport for women and girls, netball.

But there were not very many people at Rooty Hill rooting for the teams of China, Cuba, Japan and Canada. Some of those teams always have hired support, colourfully attired and led by choirmasters in neat rows of officially sponsored supporters, often in front row seats. But most of the parts of the crowd voluble at all at Rooty Hill were high-voiced pubescent and early-adolescent Australian kids. Go Cuba Go, squeaked a few dozen of these. Behind the big moments of the Olympics, those with the 112,000 crowds, there's the Little Olympics. Modest crowds, esoteric sports, ambitious administrators – the Argentine boss of the International Softball Federation now has millions of dollars of revenue from the IOC as well as gongs and awards and all the trappings that come with the ceremonial culture of world sport. No wonder he looked plump, contented and happy as he received one of these before the China–Cuba game.

Softball had its debut at Atlanta, when the US beat China 3–1 to get gold. These countries are big markets for the men behind the scenes of the expansion of women's sports. But if you go to some of these Little Games, and don't hide in the suites of Sydney's top hotels, or get tempted to the delights of the Blue Mountains, you'll see what really goes on.

Before the Games started, I'd joined a group of media people on a tour of the Olympic Park, at Homebush Bay, out in the western suburbs 19 kilometres from central Sydney. Here, for an expectant world media, SOCOG and its partner, the state government's Olympic Coordinating Authority (OCA), puffed up their accomplishments. Things hadn't gone too well that morning. The new Olympic Park train wasn't running that day, and some camera crews were late. Sydney knew what the press corps did to Atlanta when there were delays and transport problems. You don't get long in a seventeen-day event to overturn initial media impressions that, within hours, become worldwide opinion. So the organizers were nervous at the start of the tour. But it didn't put them off their stats. This will be the biggest sports event ever, with thirty-four sports and disciplines and an Olympic village catering 'for the first time in Olympic history' for all athletes, and housing a total of 15,300 athletes and team officials. The Olympic Park is 160 hectares in size – 'the largest land regeneration project in Australia', surrounded by the 440 hectare Millennium Parklands. Australia has made a A$3.3 billion commitment (two-thirds from state taxpayers in New South Wales). More than 50,000 a day were anticipated coming in to the park by train and bus, 100,000 flocking around Darling Harbour in central Sydney. The new station cost A$95 million; 5,500 will use the main press centre as their working base. The International Broadcast Centre, on the edge of Olympic Park, covered more than 70,000 square metres of facilities, including one monitoring studio housing 402 screens, servicing more than 180 broadcast organizations and 12,000 or so accredited Rights Holding Broadcasters. Some 47,000 volunteers were trained to ensure that the event went smoothly. This was the language of the Las Vegas taxi-driver, drilling into your consciousness with his statistics on electricity and water usage in the themed hotels of the Nirvana of gambling.

Homebush Bay was essentially a toxic dumping-ground for the Sydney area, and it took A$137 million to clean up the site to make this 'Disneyworld of sport', as SOCOG's Steve Cooke put it, for athletes and participants from all levels from the Olympic elite to community teams and family groups – and as the Games got under way, it was still not clean throughout. The official

Olympic telephone wait-in-line voiceover had said that 'this will be the biggest event ever held in Australia'. The stakes were raised on the trip around the park. Albeit a little sheepishly, our hosts announced that 'this will be the biggest peacetime event in the world'. The crowds at Sydney's Olympic Disneyworld were like any holiday crowd at a day out at the local theme park – as long as they could afford the admission to something, they'd have the day out for ever. At Rooty Hill it was in a sense the same, but also very different. It was an eight-hour round trip that reminded me of nothing if not the dutiful attendance at the school fete.

A Disneylimpics? Challenging Stale Olympic Ideals

The modern Olympic Games is without doubt characterized by features that one can call Disneyesque, and manifests many of the characteristics discussed in the second section of this chapter as typical of the Disneyesque phenomenon or the theme park. The Sydney Summer Games certainly sanitized history, in its evocation of an Australian multiculturalism that smoothed over the injustices and inequities of historically entrenched forms of Australian racism. The Olympics is Americanized in forms of both its essential economic infrastructure and its primary forms of representation, as can be seen respectively in the line-up of US-based multinationals on show in the privileged sponsorship spaces at the event and in its broadcast coverage, and in the showbiz LA-84 model of self-representation that flavoured the opening and closing ceremonies (Tomlinson, 2004c). The Olympic Programme sponsorship scheme entered what the IOC calls its fifth generation in 2001, and the line-up of these ten super-sponsors, accounting for 16 per cent of reported IOC revenue, was predominantly US-based: Coca-Cola, John Hancock, Kodak, McDonald's, Panasonic, Samsung, Sema, *Sports Illustrated*, Visa, Xerox. Local sponsorship contributed as much again (18 per cent of overall revenue), and the 50 per cent of total IOC revenue from broadcaster fees has come in large part from North American broadcasters.

Olympic Parks are essentially theme parks, speaking not just for the history of a sport event but for the reclamation of blighted spaces and landscapes. The Olympic Park in Sydney's Homebush Bay was precisely this, a futuristic converted space beyond the city, but easily accessible by the specially extended urban transport system. During the course of the event itself, it was in a very real way cut off and insulated from the external world, helped by the IOC propaganda on the healing powers of an Olympic movement consistently committed to the ancient Olympic ideal of an Olympic truce. The Games certainly fuel forms of fantasy, dreams and passions in the identification of the fans with performance and victory. These are widely nationalist in nature, though not exclusively so.

Identification with a particular sport performer or celebrity can certainly transcend the national. Such forms of identification are enmeshed in schedules and narratives exclusive to the Games, providing a world of its own – self-contained sites for pleasurable sights. The Olympics allows the presentation of physical specimens of all kinds – the powerful and swift in the sprint classic, the grotesquely focused in the weightlifting, the self-sacrificially slight in the Marathon, the eroticized woman in the regulation scrap of clothing in the beach volleyball, the sublimely heroic in the endurance event. There is no equivalent event in history to have legitimized such a range of examples of the carnivalesque of the body, on public display. And since 1984, and the end of the Cold War in particular across the late 1980s and the early 1990s, the Olympics has endorsed a global consumer culture quite as much as any noble historical ideal of international cooperation and universal peace. When musing on the nature of the Olympics during the months preceding the 2000 Sydney Olympics, by consulting the IOC website, it was not easy to escape the marketing speak and the warnings about copyright and the statements of the sponsors' interests. Much, if not all, of the self-promotion of the IOC and of the Games' organizers was cast in an aggressive tone of product exclusivity and market protectionism.

For some, this has become too much, and the whole Olympic phenomenon is beyond repair or redemption. Investigative reporter Andrew Jennings (Jennings and Sambrook, 2000) is unambivalent on this. Lincoln Allison (2000) has also argued that the Olympics is hardly worth persevering with, at least in its current form, proposing that it should, if it is to persist at all, recapture its amateurist ideals and reconstitute itself genuinely around youth and participation. Football fanatic Tim Parks, chronicling the fortunes of his local top-level but humble football side Verona, expressed his anger at the delay of the start of the football season. The Italian League Serie A put the start of the season back a month, 'so as not to clash with the Olympic Games, that intolerable mix of noble sentiment and growth hormones' (Parks, 2003, p. 4). For Parks, nothing could compare with what is at stake when his beloved lowly Verona takes on the might of Milan giants Inter, certainly not 'the prurient pantomime of synchronised swimming' or 'any of that grim athleticism and loathsome armchair nationalism' (Parks, 2003, p. 4). Parks captures the absurdity of the Games, though misses the drama of the contest that no packaging of the event could ever undermine, as well as the fun of simply being there. But to recognize a Disneyesqe element to the Games is not to consign it to the past. Whatever the dubious and at times corrupt premise of the organization's survival and prosperity in the post-Samaranch era, an organization that can sign up every nation in the world for a regular sport competition should not be dismissed out of hand. Three points bear consideration here. First, the Olympic Games must be recognized as a remarkably resilient historically rooted international phenomenon, an internationalist initiative whose appeal, however hyperbolic, has been wide enough to captivate expanding and enormous publics, appealing in adaptable but recurrently para-religious fashion to its successive audiences (Tomlinson, 2004a). Second, the Games – in more ways than can single-sport based mega-events – embody intriguing and memorable forms of heroic human endeavour, feats of the body, agonistic narratives of the most compelling kind – of triers, and losers, as well as of supreme and sublimely accomplished champions. Eddie the Eagle, trundling down the ski-slopes and scavenging in the dustbins of Calgary in 1988, Eric the Eel thrashing through the waters of Sydney in 2000, as well as Cathy Freeman running for the history of her people in September 2000, or Steve Redgrave rowing to historic five-Olympiad glory at the same Games. Third, it is inherently interesting, historically and social scientifically, that the Games are the foremost example of regional cultural productions to which cities and governments subscribe, whatever the vague retrospective analyses of the benefits of the event. That in Sydney, every blue and yellow-outfitted volunteer in beige outback hat and badly cut trousers who smiled at you seemed to mean it, was remarkable: a 'G'day' meant with a smile was an innocent form of cosmopolitanism that is markedly preferable, in terms of any internationalist aspirations, to excesses of national pride and aggressive jingoism.

Conclusion

This is not to say that a Disneyfied Olympics does not need internal reform. I conclude with a five-point agenda of Olympic challenges. First, the IOC would do well to look closely at the elements that actually sustained it in its arrogated forms throughout its three-century spanning history. The so-called family and movement should revisit its history, downgrading the claims made for its significance in the cultural, social and political history of its time. Whatever de Coubertin was, he was not a sociologist or a rigorous social historian, and his enthusiastic interpretations of the impact of early Olympics should be subjected to adequate neutral, systematic scholarly scrutiny. Second, it should learn its audience. It flatters its audience, and itself, with the help of uncorroborated statistics on the global audience and the events' impacts. But we need to know more about this audience, about the mundanities of its receptivity, the routineness and transience of its commitment. The hyperbole of the apologists of Olympism should be tempered in the light of a better and more informed understanding of the nature of the audience. Third, it should trim the programme, excluding prima donnas and Dream Teams (the US basketball players, for instance), freak shows of the body and esoteric physical practices, and include only truly international sports. Fourth, it should review the place and profile of the Olympic partners, the sponsors, in the staging of the Games. The New South Wales police and sometimes the IOC-hired heavyweights denying access to the hotel bars and lobbies of central Sydney in September 2000 are protecting crass privilege, and denying basic human rights, an abuse of market consumer rights underpinned by public expenditure. Finally, if the IOC and its partners came clean in public, they should revise their rhetoric and recognize more openly the fantasy and the fun that fuel the contemporary Disneyfied Games. It would make them sound less pious, and far more credible. Some of us might not like it. But the youthful global consumers on whom the future of the Olympics will depend – fully Disneyfied or otherwise – will recognize the party for what it is, and keep coming. And without them, and the family outings to the Olympic theme site that fill with life the soulless modern quasi-boulevards of Olympic Parks, the Olympics is nothing.

Essences of Post-Olympism:
A Prolegomena of Study

Synthia Sydnor

Proem

Pierre de Coubertin wrote of the Olympic Games of 1896:

> It is . . . difficult to know why and how an idea is born – emerges from the tide of other ideas which await realization, takes on substance and becomes fact. This however is not the case regarding the Olympic Games. (Coubertin, 1966 [1896], p. 108)

He goes on to explain that the idea of the Olympic Games revival was not a 'passing fancy' but the logical culmination of a great movement (Coubertin, 1966 [1896], p. 108). In this third millennium, I think that we can agree that whatever its faults and complexities, the Olympic Games have been a great movement. However, I want to begin my chapter by disagreeing with Coubertin's idea that the Games are not a passing fancy. I want to claim that perhaps we should consider the Olympics in our post-age to be a kind of once-every-four-years (in tribute to the ancient Greeks) passing fancy, one in which people, athletes, spectators, collectors – 'players all' as Bob Rinehart (1998) refers to them – get to create, invent traditions and remake the Olympic Games. Some involved in the post-Olympic Games will be athletes – the best in this world; others will be watchers or shoppers, some will compose rules of contests while they watch the games, others might design computer/virtual games at special game design chambers. In this chapter, I identify what I call 'essences' of which such post-Olympism and Olympic Games are composed. The essences I discuss within include performativity, aesthetics, transcendence and acceleration. My writings about these essences are preliminary, a prolegomena for the study of post-Olympism.

Imagine then, a post-Olympism that connotes nothing of nationalism, which celebrates essences of sport such as competition, beauty, sacrifice, awe, extreme performance, coming community, fantasy. What would such Olympic games be like?

Although I want to forward ruminations on what such Olympic Games and philosophies of Olympism may encompass and look like, I am not sure that this is an attainable post-Olympism, so I suppose one can call my chapter a thought exercise. I am not a futurologist, nor am I an expert in new-age technologies. Although there are, of course, urgent problems related to technological advances upon Olympism and Olympic Games, what I concentrate upon here is a framework for celebrating these 'advances' and later, further ideas about acceleration that allow us to envision the Olympic Games and post-Olympism in ways to coincide with new times. This said, I critique myself a little at the start, relying upon Robert Nirre's 'The Genealogy of Dead Space'. Nirre writes of the myth of cyberspace, which this and more I quite celebrate in my chapter:

> What is this, exactly? Clearly it isn't amenable to our . . . understanding. There is neither a physical nor even a conceptual space. There are places but nothing between them, no interspatiality; one navigates a sprawling agglomeration of webbed-together billboards, of insides without exteriors, of islands of hyperdense information adrift on etherealized seas. (Nirre, 2001, p. 3)

I realize that virtual/cyber Olympism and its potentials for idealizing and reconstituting communities, bodies and landscapes can be romanticized with 'fantastic powers'. Many have pointed out the nostalgia that people like me have for 'dream landscapes', cautioning that these involve a 'myth revealed for what it is: a poignant imaginative lunge that illuminates exactly what will be denied us. A nostalgia for a world that will never come to be' (Nirre, 2001, p. 9). I also understand that there is only a small portion of the world's population that has access to this fantastical world, yet I still want to engage in this exercise.

My rationale is that I am a doctor of philosophy whose calling is to create knowledge and converse about the human condition. From the tenets of the humanities, we write and talk with the hope of contributing a small bit of love, peace, justice, beauty and community (whatever these are, and these are the things we debate in the humanities) to the local spaces that we inhabit; we provide research, writing and academic doings that significantly make us messengers (e.g. Ward, 2000, p. 15) of possibilities. That is, an historian, I am concerned not solely with 'the past', but also with understanding and troubling the ongoing documentation, preservation and interpretation of 'present-day' history (e.g. White, 1978; Culler, 1988). We can historicize what is 'to be' in the history of health, fitness and physical activity, and in this case, post-Olympism.

Cultural Adaptation

We know the 1990s' proliferation of the World Wide Web, video, computer, online, virtual, simulation, fantasy and cyber games-sports-play as a unique moment in the history of the world. Exercise sites, network and multi-player gaming, online sport gambling, fantasy-team competitions, virtual participation in real sport events, exercise chat groups, celebrity-athlete 'stalker' sites, the latest scores, recruiting, sport news and statistics, and sales of online athletic clothing, souvenirs and equipment spawn millions of daily Internet hits. There are enhanced technologies in photography, super-slow motion film and holography. Humans of the developed world are obliged to understand reality as experienced not only directly, but also through immersion in filtered, enhanced, distorted mediation of the Internet, television, film, editors, creators and artists. Sports competitions of all sorts are the object of a spectrum of lens, i.e. from youth games in the US where the spectator stands are filled with parents adjoined to video cameras, to computer game contests and role-playing in which players view spaces through data streams. Video artists create fragmented, blurred, gorgeously coloured and musically choreographed rushes of sport scenes for advertisements that provide opportunities for aesthetic experiences for viewers and players. For example, Nike had a commercial that shows various kinds of athletes in the seconds before the start of their competitions. It is a beautiful piece that seems to evoke universal singularity. Photography, videography, literature, cinematography (in journalism, television, film, personal computing, music videos, and advertising) are as much sites of 'Olympism' today as are traditional sport sites and cultural spaces, such as the biomechanics lab or the football field.

Although such modes of sport represent an enormous historic and cultural change in the way millions of people play and contest, they have not been interpreted very deeply except to criticize these complex narratives such as through studying themes of violence, sexism, racism, alienation and consumerism that are illuminated in them and from which humans are supposed to be safeguarded. Yes, cyberspace/video games are often violent, bloody, gory. They too are often sexist, sometimes close to what I, as a mother, would call pornographic. Later in this chapter, I'll try to use the philosopher Giorgio Agamben (1994, p. 50) to say that we have to 'wrest a good from commodities in decline'. Critics also point out how tragic, that in these technological, televisual times, we are a world of sickly watchers and voyeurs instead of healthy doers; others seek to raise awareness about 'issues related to the way in which technology is becoming increasingly overwhelming within sports' (http://www.dmu.ac.uk/In/fast).[1] And all of these same critiques are applied to Olympic sport; the current state of games and Olympism are forwarded as if they are negative.

Yet, such virtual and simulated contest, sport, play and 'physicality' are perhaps not bad or overwhelming, but a cultural adaptation to the world that we have created and live in, a world that Lévi-Strauss called a 'hot society' (1966, p. 233; see also Slowikowski Sydnor, 1993, p. 1) committed to ever-moving change. That humans are especially and extremely involved and fascinated in such simulation and virtual reality is a kind of cultural response to the world we face – the world as sophisticated video game, speeding through an agglomeration of images, interspatiality, screens and keyboards. Roberts et al. (1959) in their classic 'Games in Culture' article, argued this point half a century ago: things that occur in a regular, universal fashion are enculturating or selectively useful for human survival – to individual and cultural well-being. More recently, Mark Pesce (2001) claims that because of the new technologies and the Internet, humans play in entirely new ways, ways that would not have been conceived of just a few generations ago, ways that would have once been considered magical. Pesce (2001) says of the Web:

> Never in the course of human history has any innovation taken hold so rapidly or so completely ... it draws millions of us in, day after day, offering an endless exploration of the catalogue of humanity, all its stories and wishes and horrors and facts. Every day it becomes more indispensable, more unforgettable, more important. (Pesce, 2001, p. 170)

The Web, argues Pesce, 'will create new forms of culture and require us to learn a new language; our own languages can't quite cope with the confusion of tongues, mixed meanings, and ambiguities.' A present-day example is 'the incredible power of the PlayStation 2 [which] opens the door to entirely new types of computer simulations, works of art, education and forms of play that we've only just begun to imagine' (Pesce, 2001, p. 213).

Classic Olympism

To attempt to apply some of these like ideas to the study of post-Olympism, to theorize and categorize the elements and formations, the issues and themes of future Olympic Games festivals is a huge, almost infinite task. I wonder if we should not begin this task by returning to re-reading the idealist aims of Olympism as the foundation upon which post-Olympism can be constructed. Written in an old notebook from the early 1980s are my notes from an Olympic Games class taught by Professor John Lucas at the Pennsylvania State University. They read:

> Olympism: The pursuit of physical and moral excellence, international cooperation, and goodwill, a link between sport and aesthetics. Olympic programs: literature, cultural museums, fashion shows, film festivals, music, arts. Olympism uniquely proclaims the integral

participation of sport in the organic whole of human life. It is devoted to educational achievement, to devout and exuberant sense of religious piety, to the noblest and most judicious expression of humility and integrity and to the most sublime and creative sense of beauty and peace.

Transcendence

I take this classical Olympism, at which I once scoffed, and place it now in the third millennium. One concept embedded in classical Olympism that stands out is 'religious piety'. Can religious piety be linked to Olympism today? I have been studying the thought of an academic movement called radical orthodoxy which, using medieval thought and post-structuralism, has as its core the idea that a theological sensibility and a sense of the sacred lies at the root of all knowledge and performance work, and that the task of understanding and revitalizing a theological sensibility and sense of the sacred is part of postmodernism's project, a hope that has yet to be fulfilled (for example, Certeau, 1971; Milbank, 1993; Ward, 1997b; Pickstock, 1998; Wyschogrod, 1998; Milbank *et al.*, 1999; Ward, 2000; Milbank and Pickstock, 2001; Ward, 2001). That is, in radical orthodoxy, all of philosophy, every discipline and more, is theological. Radical orthodoxy claims that for all humans, to live in the world is sacramental/liturgical and that postmodernism offers a language to recover for our time the world before and beyond the secular (Ward, 1997a, p. xxxix).

In this so-called post-secular age, our process of showcasing sport and contest at the Olympic Games could be enriched by illuminating the ideas of the sacred/mysterious/invisible not only having to do with new sport forms, but also in previous understandings of older forms (e.g. Huizinga, 1955; Novak, 1976; Pieper, 1998 [1952]), practices and representations of sport, competition and play. For instance, in David Sansone's (1988) definition of sport as 'the ritual sacrifice of human physical energy', the athlete is both sacrificer and sacrificial victim. Such a definition helps us to understand what may be a universal essence of sport as it manifests itself today in versions extreme and as it did in much earlier times – but is little mentioned today – in mystic ways that connect the athlete and audience with ineffable meanings of life and universe. The ongoing elaboration of, and emphasis by ticket-buyers and media of, the Olympic Games' opening and closing ceremonies since 1984 speaks to this point: our desire to engage with a sense of transcendence, sacramentality.

Aesthetics

As I have argued in other work, to study sport, we have to utterly loosen our definitions of sport and of the essences of sport. The birth and proliferation of x/extreme sports have aided us in making fluid the definition of sport from a grassroots level. Extreme sports have called our attention again to this need of sport to remind us of such things as that sport is art; that such art perhaps touches the transcendence and sacramentalism discussed above. For example sky surfers speak of themselves as not competitors, but artists; one surfer states 'Contrary to popular belief, we're not hard-core thrill seekers. We're pioneering a new form of art' (Anon, 2002d). Motifs associated with these x-sports are ubiquitous in everyday life – they decorate our back yards, streetwear, language, lunch boxes, the World Wide Web, MTV, ESPN and advertising of every sort. The fashion magazine *Vogue* asks 'What's cooler than snowboarding?' and answers 'Snowboarding clothes' (Chen, 1998). Perhaps Olympism can unabashedly celebrate our desire for such desire.

Skyjumping from a plane while riding a water heater, wagon, golf cart or automobile through the air at 150 mph (AXN, 1998), lawn-mower racing, toe skiing, waterfall skiing or low altitude parachuting. Participation ranges from the casual to the obsessed, from leisure/recreational enthusiasts to hard-core professionals, and from samplers to experts. One begins to realize that some of these athletes are simultaneously engaging in serious sport and making fun of the paradoxes and canons of sport from this alternative sport vantage point. Can post-Olympism incorporate such a terrain, sometimes paradoxical and satirical (e.g. McGrath, 2002) into its agenda?

Performativity

As in the examples given, sports are performative, but must they be competitive? Sports as somehow 'beautiful' as dance; creations that blend artistic and musical compositions with virtual reality and computer/graphic design (e.g. Bertine, 2002) and beyond: sports whose genres/materials/essences we cannot now imagine. For instance, are Olympic Games for humans? People themselves are robotic/cyborg and we see the utmost enjoyment all over the world with which they are engaged with virtual and computer-generated sport. If competition must be a criterion of sport, imagine: an Olympic festival revolutionized to consist of multidimensional imaging, of people on-site and continents away designing contests: the designing of the sport contest is itself an Olympic event; imagine Olympic robot and drone wars. I noticed a sign posted in a gaming area in Seattle, 'STOP PLAYING COMPUTER GAMES, ENTER THEM'. The University of Illinois at Urbana-Champaign's National Center for Super-computing Applications, along with the university's Department of Kinesiology and several others, are constructing the world's largest six-sided virtual reality chamber (Integrated Systems Laboratory).[2] Perhaps this 'cube' will be one of the origins of huge chambers that could be situated at a permanent Olympic Games space (perhaps in northern Greece?) that would enable humans to play with, to be fascinated with, the possibilities of faster-higher-stronger in their greatest festival, the Olympic Games.

Acceleration

How else might I contemplate post-Olympism? Most significantly, as I allude to in the Proem, 'acceleration'. Humans celebrate acceleration in travel, communication, perception, performance, sight, imagination and the organization of space because such speed prolongs and enriches life, and, as the philosopher Paul Virilio (1997, p. 12) notes, it enables us 'to conceive the world more intensely'. Accelerated technology enables us to see things in extremely slow motion. Conversely, the notion of acceleration is also envisioned by many as an instrument of social, geological and biological destruction (as in the acceleration of modern technological surveillance, pollution, lack of affordable housing, weather catastrophes and body ageing). Institutionalized and governing bodies and practices survey and predict such acceleration. And, when Olympic organizing bodies and institutions strive for 'green' Olympics or to provide permanent housing for the homeless who are deposed from Olympic Games areas in the months before the Games, it is acceleration that is at the core of what is being confronted. As James Gleick (2000) notices, acceleration is a state of simultaneous freedom and imprisonment. An exploration of the concept of acceleration should be undertaken by sport scholars whose initiatives could further understanding and create sophisticated knowledge concerning acceleration across a spectrum of epistemological and theoretical possibilities. Related to post-Olympism and the Olympic Games, such possibilities could investigate the following themes with regard to acceleration.

Urbanization and Movement Vectors/Architecture

By this phrase I mean increased 'megalopolitan hyperconcentration' (Virilio, 1997, p. 12) (for example, rapidly expanding cityscapes as venues themselves for post-Olympic events such as skateboarding or BASE (building, antennae, span, earth) jumping) and its synthesis with sport (again, loosely defined). Iain Borden (2001) pioneers such study. But there is more: inspired by the transformation of our world since the early 1990s, artists and athletes are mastering techniques and environments to express sport, move, play and contest in novel ways and venues. Some brief current-day examples include robots that play underwater hockey with humans. At an art museum in New York City, free-form ping-pong in which the table has four sides, all rounded, with a lily pond in the middle. Visitors to the art museum are encouraged to play this sport, in which the shape of the playing field encourages invention of rules and simultaneous violation of them. Or, choreographers and sportspersons have created spaces on cliff sides at American national parks upon which dancers use the apparatus and skills of rock climbers to perform for audiences composed of park goers. Or, SlamBall, a 'human video game action played on a revolutionary trampoline and spring-loaded surface' (Robbins, 2002). SlamBall is described by a player as follows:

> Take the flying freedom of a trampoline, the fantasy of stepping into a video game and add the fear of an extreme sport. 'It's just like I dreamed about in street ball, that I could do a certain dunk in midair and the man I just dunked on was Michael Jordan, The dream came true in SlamBall'. (Robbins, 2002)

The creator of SlamBall was inspired by the idea of

> an extended highlight clip, designed for the attention-deficit generation . . . the sports landscape, and I thought about the phenomenon of the X Games and the whole video-game culture and how that all runs on excitement, it runs on nonstop action and it runs on level of fantasy fulfillment. (Robbins, 2002)

Remember the classical Olympism from my old class notes? That Olympism highlighted fashion shows, film festivals, music, arts, religious piety, sublime and creative sense of beauty. Humans approach these things when they dream, fantasize, dance on cliffs – why not these essences showcased in post-Olympism?

Accelerated Education

I wonder: at this moment in time, in terms of cultural adaptation, is expertise in virtual and simulated reality more important than is fitness, sport, physical education and elite athleticism as we traditionally compete in, teach, measure and envision them? In terms of virtual alternative sport and the cyberworlds of youth sport: are its representations, discourse and therapy for related injuries to be made into policy and possessed by health professionals, coaches, trainers and physical educators? For example, video game technologies bring forth hand injuries such as repetitive stress syndrome, carpal-tunnel syndrome, 'nintenditous'. Could physical education classes and Olympic formation programmes work on making hands stronger and more adaptable to screen play? Are projects like these legitimate endeavours for Olympic committees and formation programmes? The debate of such questions and issues involve post-historians like us.

Technology Utilization; Acceleration and Dynamics in Sensor Dynamics

Just as running shoes revolutionized track and cross-country, kayaks constructed of the new material hypalon (Anon., 1997, p. 80; see also Wagstaff, 1998) and snowboard cores made of piezoelectronics that sense a body's balance and direction, are the 'stuff' of our times. Take also the Gravity Boarding Company's Hyper-Carve – a skateboard with a digital readout on the nose that indicates the current and maximum speed (Parks, 1998) – these present-day technologies serve as an exemplars for theorizing new sports via 'speed' and the equipment of post-sport.

Time Studies of Sport Acceleration as Art; Virtual Velocity; Holographic Art; Stop-motion Photography

Sport has always contained genuine artistic elements, but as C. L. R. James, *Beyond a Boundary*, pointed out in the early 1960s:

> our enjoyment of it can never be quite artistic: we are prevented from completely realizing it not only by our dramatic interest in the game, but also . . . by the succession of movements being too rapid for us to realize each completely, and too fatiguing, even if realizable. (James, 1963, p. 197)

Now, our amazing technologies (and perhaps the nutrition and energy of new times) enable us to bypass James's obstacles ('too fast', 'too fatiguing') to more completely realize and recognize sport as form, as art. In light of these developments in time studies, I believe that post-historians should revisit in their studies the aestheticization of sport.[3] Because we now see sport (and also other things such as colour, sound and human bodies) in different ways than in the 1950s, this changes how we compete in, spectate, view and judge sport. I turn your attention again to skysurfing, where the camera flyer is integral to the sport, as elite an athlete as the skysurfer being filmed. When the skysurfing is competitive, the video that the camera flyer creates, composes and turns over to judges upon landing is how the sport is judged. Photographic and video composition is the essence of this sport. Susanna Howe (1998) reiterates this difference in snowboarding: without stop action photography, videographers and photographers themselves, the sport of snowboarding would not exist for most of us.

Miniaturization/'Nano' Studies; Acceleration of Performance Enhancing Drug Use and Development

Nanotechnology is the name Eric Drexler at MIT gave to imagined molecular or even atom size devices, such as a whole computer the size of a grain of sand, (Pesce, 2000) that would surely change the face of the earth (not to mention our concept of Olympism). The closest things we have to nanotechnology today are the surgical cameras that can be swallowed and the attempts by researchers to create artificial blood. Drexler and others envision a time when nanorobotic scanners are injected into bodies to diagnose and heal them, and when what he calls repirocytes – nano-scale diamond spheres holding highly compressed oxygen (atom scale machinery) – dispense oxygen on an as-needed basis (Pesce, 2000). Gordon Moore's Law, that semiconductors (transistors and integrated circuits) improve at a fixed rate (every eighteen months they decrease in size by a factor of two and increase in speed by a factor of two), has proved true. In the year 2000, semiconductors were approximately 10 million times smaller and 10 million times faster then they were in 1964 (as explained by Pesce, 2000). How will such miniaturization transform post-Olympism and our philosophy of such?

Mind/Soul Acceleration into 'Higher' Knowledge and Consciousness

A century ago, philosopher Henri Bergson scrutinized terrain in terms of bodily spaces that gave what he called 'ballast and poise' to the mind. In his work, *Matter and Memory* (1991 [1896], p. 173; see also Benjamin, 1969a [1936], p. 180), Bergson argued that 'space, by definition, is outside us, yet the separation between a thing and its environment cannot be absolutely definite and clear-cut; there is a passage by insensible gradations from the one to the other' (Bergson, 1991 [1896], pp. 202, 209). This abstraction of insensible gradations from bodily spaces to environmental ones was consequential for later thinkers, and, I argue, too, for the ways in which we can read post-sports such as skysurfing which may someday encompass the canon of Olympic sport. Another example: Gilles Deleuze's introduction to 'Mediators' considers the categorical spaces of sport, forwarding a unique touchstone for not only the biomechanical analysis of sport, but also the culture and aesthetics of sport and post-olympism:

> Many of the new sports—surfing, windsurfing, hang-gliding—take the form of entry into an existing wave. There's no longer an origin as starting point, but a sort of putting-into-orbit. The basic thing is how to get taken up in the movement of a big wave, a column of rising air, to "come between" rather than to be the origin of an effort. (Deleuze, 1992, p. 281)

Coming Community/*Whatever*

This kind of space is also a metaphor for the space of the times in which we live: we are working on transforming our sense of what it means to live, to be, in other times and different spaces, both human and historical (Bhabha, 1994, pp. 245, 256). Giorgio Agamben (1994, 2.1, pp. 106.5–107.5) uses the word *whatever* to describe the possibility of new spaces in the world for what he calls a 'coming community'.[4] Agamben says that in the coming community 'there is a good that humanity must learn to wrest from commodities in their decline'.

This good involves linking 'together image and body in a space where they can no longer be separated, [thus forging] the *whatever* body' (Agamben, 1994, p. 50). The coming community of these whatever bodies is made up of liminal passages, inside/outside spaces such as might not only be in sport contests of the Olympic Games, but in the crowds hanging out at Olympic Games festivals, and in things such as architecture, colours and music surrounding the Olympic Games (as we predominantly saw beginning with the 1984 Los Angeles Games). How many times have you heard from people and friends who upon their return from an Olympic Games pilgrimage said something such as this: 'I simply enjoyed being there, in the crowds, experiencing huge throngs and the entertainment. Going to the sporting events wasn't necessary . . . I'll go to the next Olympics and just hang out; it was fun shopping for Olympic souvenirs and trading pins.' 'Hanging out in the crowds.' Of course the reason that these Olympic Games' pilgrims had fun was perhaps because they had the economic power to afford such a trip; the negative back regions (homelessness, pollution, citizenry's lack of political freedom) are 'hidden' from such travellers. (My chapter can be criticized for taking no notice of such problems; assuaging them in order to celebrate post-Olympism; I hope to contemplate the problematics of post-olympism in forthcoming work). This said, one of the objectives of this chapter has been to urge scholars to once again admit that Olympism *does* highlight world brotherhood, community, beauty, whether we critics want to admit it or not. Olympism is also comprised of liminality, thresholds – thresholds moments are liquid, indefinable, and themselves and memories of them are exciting, dangerous, wondrous (e.g. Turkle, 1995; McCorduck, 1996). Thresholds are magnified in virtual and computer sport, cyberworlds of sport, new spaces of sport. There are already countless video and arcade games/experiences in which the participant's body is interfaced (through keyboard, cathode screen, dataglove or datasuit) to a sport contest or performance. In this way, Virilio calls the body the last urban frontier: 'Having been first *mobile*, then *motorized*, man will thus become *motile*, deliberately limiting his body's area of influence to a few gestures, a few impulses, like channel-surfing' (Virilio, 1997, p. 17).

This urban frontier may be celebrated in post-olympism: the ultimate motile body – motionless, yet also virtually, dramatically, somehow beautifully representing faster, higher, stronger. Real space *is* giving way to virtual space. How will the glory of the physicality of sport be perfected in such space as Olympic festivals? Again, in *Beyond a Boundary*, James (1963) anticipates this question. He writes: 'I believe that the examination of the stroke, the brilliant piece of fielding, will take us through mysticism to far more fundamental considerations than mere life-enhancing. We respond to physical action or vivid representation of it, dead or alive, because we are made that way' (James, 1963, p. 203).[5]

Speed, time, space and acceleration are central issues in the ontology of post-sport and festivals. Recall again classic Olympism: physical and moral excellence, link between sport and aesthetics, cultural museums, fashion shows, film festivals, music, arts, devout and exuberant sense of religious piety. An initiative to study Olympic Games and post-Olympism in relation to some of the essences of performativity, aesthetics, transcendence and acceleration could spur glorious collaborations/coming communities drenched with sacramentalism, athletes, scholars, street people, filmmakers, advertisers, virtual/fantasy players – post-Olympians all. In this prolegomena I suggest rudimentary frameworks for pondering and dialoguing about specific essences of sport that imprint Olympic-related ideals, practices and representations into the emerging post-world.

Sportive Nationalism and Globalization

John Hoberman

Early Globalization and Olympic Sport

On 25 November 1892, at a meeting of the Union des Sports Athlétiques in Paris, Pierre de Coubertin, founder of the modern Olympic movement, declared: 'Let us export our oarsmen, our runners, our fencers into other lands. That is the true Free Trade of the future, and the day it is introduced into Europe the cause of Peace will have received a new and strong ally' (Anon., 1992, p. 198). This proposal to invent and implement a symbolic version of free trade on behalf of international relations reminds us that Coubertin's Olympic project remains among the most durable monuments of the early phase of what we may call modern globalization (Hoberman, 1995). The Olympic movement originated, in fact, in a *fin-de-siècle* world that anticipated our own age of globalization in important ways.

'Perhaps the greatest myth about globalization', Nicholas D. Kristof (1999) notes, 'is that it is new' (see also Stille, 2001). By the end of the nineteenth century, as Harold James points out, 'the world was highly integrated economically, through mobility of capital, information, goods and people. Capital moved freely between states and continents. The movement of capital would not have been possible without improved mechanisms for spreading news and ideas' (James, 2001, p. 10). The first era of globalization was made possible by steamship lines, free trade, foreign investment, low trade barriers and mass migration of labour at a time when passports were not required for international travel. Like the second era of globalization of the last decades of the twentieth century, this early version of globalization was made possible by technological breakthroughs such as telegraphic communication, which functioned as the Internet of its era. This was the global civilization that offered the Olympic movement the political and economic circumstances in which it could fulfill its unique international mission.

The last decades of the nineteenth century also saw a remarkable proliferation of transnational movements and organizations that were meant to serve both practical and idealistic purposes. An example of the first type was the General Postal Union, founded in 1874 by representatives of twenty-two countries. The better known 'idealistic' internationalisms of this period include the International Committee of the Red Cross (1863), the Esperanto movement (1887), the Olympic movement (1894) and the Scouting movement (1907). Because the idealistic international movements of this period represented novel strategies for dealing with anxieties about war and peace, it is not surprising that all of them incorporated evangelistic promises of redemption from the international tensions of this period. Every idealistic internationalism of this period offered its own path to the fellowship of reconciliation.

This evangelistic impulse often stimulated a confidence in future developments that in retrospect looks positively utopian. 'The optimism of the age', James notes, 'can be used as a testimony to its internationalism or cosmopolitanism. Some analysts believed that the dynamic of integration was so great that it could not be halted by anything – indeed, that it made war between highly developed industrial states impossible.' The classic formulation of this optimistic doctrine, Norman Angell's best-selling book *The Great Illusion*, was published in 1910.

> International finance has become so interdependent and so interwoven with trade and industry that . . . political and military power can in reality do nothing. [Angell wrote] These little recognized facts, mainly the outcome of purely modern conditions (rapidity of communication creating a greater complexity and delicacy of the credit system), have rendered the problems of modern international politics profoundly and essentially different from the ancient. (Beinart, 1997, p. 20)

According to this theory of international relations, the complexity of modern commerce and the interdependencies it created made war unthinkable. Angell was knighted and won the Nobel Peace Prize. Four years after *The Great Illusion* was published, the First World War demolished the first era of globalization and the optimism that had sustained it. The enduring appeal of the Olympic movement is evident in the fact that it, along with some other prominent transnational organizations, managed to survive the abrupt collapse of internationalism in August 1914.

The 'rapidity of communication' celebrated by Angell was best exemplified by the telegraphic technology that evolved over the second half of the nineteenth century. But the significance of telegraphic communication to the early phase of globalization transcended the practical advantages of a technology that was revolutionizing the commercial activity of this era. In addition to economic ambition, the telegraph inspired a euphoric sense that the end of international conflict was in sight. 'Optimism about the peacemaking potential of the telegraph was still widespread at the close of the century,' Tom Standage (1999, p. 161) writes, 'even though there was no evidence that it had made any real difference one way or the other.' Preachers evoked biblical passages that suggested global telegraphy was nothing less than a fulfilment of ancient prophecy: 'Their line is gone out through all the earth, and their words to the end of the world' (Psalms 19). The authors of *The Story of the Telegraph* (Briggs and Maverick, 1858) predicted that 'the whole earth will be belted with electric current, palpitating with human thoughts and emotions. It shows that nothing is impossible to man.' At a banquet held in 1868 in honour of the inventor of the telegraph, Samuel Morse, the British ambassador to the United States toasted 'the telegraph wire, the nerve of international life, transmitting knowledge of events, removing causes of misunderstanding, and promoting peace and harmony throughout the world' (Standage, 1999, pp. 82, 91).

Coubertin participated in this wave of optimism without succumbing to the giddy euphoria that is so evident in some of the other pronouncements of this period. 'His notion of international harmony', John MacAloon (1981, p. 262) points out, 'was fundamentally rationalistic; war and peace were matters of knowledge and ignorance.' 'To attain this end,' Coubertin wrote, 'what better means than to bring the youth of all countries periodically together for amicable trials of muscular strength and agility?' What he called 'true internationalism' accepted national differences in a way that a less discriminating 'cosmopolitan' *bonhomie* did not (MacAloon, 1981, p. 189). More credulous global evangelists of this period were inspired, as we have seen, by the seemingly miraculous effects of telegraphy. 'What can be more likely to effect [peace] than a constant and complete intercourse between all nations and all individuals in the world?' the British ambassador had declared in 1868 (Standage, 1999, p. 90). Sportive internationalism could not offer such an innovative and dramatic version of human fellowship; for the political effects of Olympic Games were based, not on instantaneous contacts through wires, but on the slower work of building personal relationships over time and distance.

The euphoric vision of globalization's harmonious effects has been encouraged during the second era of globalization by another communications revolution. Peter Beinart has pointed out that 'in today's America, as in Norman Angell's Britain, there is a strong intuitive sense that globalization is connected to wondrous new developments in communications technology: satellites, faxes, the Internet' (Beinart, 1997, p. 22). It is also clear that the Olympic movement has benefited mightily from the optimistic dogma that inheres in this 'intuitive sense' that contact between different groups of people promotes peace in the world. In this context the satellite television systems that broadcast the Games around the world are the new telegraphy of instantaneous human relations.

In both eras of globalization, optimistic and even magical thinking about human reconciliation has been challenged by contrary interpretations that find a different kind of potential in human nature. A particularly sceptical visitor to the 1896 Athens Olympic Games was Coubertin's countryman, the reactionary nationalist Charles Maurras. Disquieted by the implications of this new type of international festival, Maurras wondered 'what would be the meaning of an Olympiad open to the entire world? Finally, this *mélange* of races threatened to result, not in an intelligent and reasonable federation of modern peoples, but in the vague disorders of cosmopolitanism' (Maurras, 1929, pp. 56–7). Maurras was greatly relieved when he realized later in life that 'in our age, when several distinct races are put together and constrained to mingle, they are repelled from each other and distance themselves at the very moment they think they are mixing' (Maurras, 1929, p. 59). As a nationalist and a racist, he welcomed what he mistakenly saw as the failure of an internationalist initiative whose success would inevitably promote a pan-racial globalism.

Disillusion with the results of what the British ambassador called in 1868 'a constant and complete intercourse between all nations and individuals in the world' is an important development of our own era of globalization. 'My main concern', Ted Turner once said, 'is to be a benefit to the world, to build up a global communications system that helps humanity come together.' The man who originated the first global news network (CNN) during the late twentieth century shared the optimism of his predecessors a century earlier. 'But this technological togetherness', George Packer argues, 'has not created the human bonds that were promised. In some ways, global satellite TV and Internet access have actually made the world a less understanding, less tolerant place.' The 'constant and complete intercourse' made possible by satellite communications and the Web produce 'superficial familiarity – images without context, indignation without remedy', leaving our media-saturated globe 'a parochial place of manifold suspicions, rumors, resentments and half-truths.' In the context of this analysis I would suggest that the Olympic Games too offer the ideal, but not the reality, of genuine reconciliation, and that they have always occupied what Packer calls the 'halfway point between mutual ignorance and true understanding' (Packer, 2002).

The Olympic doctrine formulated by Coubertin can thus be understood as an original contribution to the early doctrine of globalization that emphasized transnational ties and exchanges of people and products as instruments of international conflict management. He also intuited the iconic status of sheer dynamism and the homogenizing logic that would become standard features of the globalization model a century later. 'The tendency today', he wrote in 1901, 'is toward a total culture. It is not just democracy that is pushing in this direction, but especially the transformation of labour, the industrial character of the epoch, the almighty goddess Activity who already reigns uncontested' (Coubertin, 1901, p. 199). Sport is needed to counteract what he calls the 'intensive character' of a 'pulsating and complicated' civilization (Coubertin, 1913, p. 27). At the same time, it appears that Coubertin did not foresee that global sport would eventually become a powerful symbol of the competitive ethos that constitutes the driving ideology of economic globalization.

Globalization as International Competition

Globalization is frequently depicted as a fateful competition among corporations or nations or regions of the world. Whether one supports or opposes the globalization process that takes the form of multinational corporate expansion will have much to do with how one assesses the advantages and disadvantages of making competition the animating principle of international and commercial relations. An unfettered 'Darwinian' competition may have consequences for the economic or cultural ecology of the world that competing nations might want to avoid. For example, US trade negotiators who insist that subsidies for national film industries create 'unfair' international competition do so despite the fact that 'the free movement of American movies in the world spells the death knell of national cinemas elsewhere, perhaps of all other national cinemas as distinct species' (Jameson, 1998, p. 61). Addressing the consequences of what he calls 'intensifying world market competition,' Giovanni Arrighi points to the wretched fates of societies that are regarded by the rest of the world as the losers of this global competition: 'Entire communities, countries, even continents, as in the case of sub-Saharan Africa, have been declared "redundant," superfluous to the changing economy of capitalist accumulation on a world scale' (quoted in Jameson, 1998, p. 65). Small wonder that prominent sub-Saharan African voices have protested against the tyranny of Darwinian competition between the nations. 'It has been said', Kofi Annan remarked on 5 June 2000, 'that arguing against globalization is like arguing against the laws of gravity. But that does not mean we should accept a law that allows only heavyweights to survive (United Nations, 2000). 'We do not accept', Thabo Mbeki declared in 2002, 'that human society should be constructed on the basis of the savage principle of the survival of the fittest' (Anon., 2002a).

Commentaries on global competition are suffused with sportive imagery because elite sport models both the sheer intensity and the civilizing potential of competition. The charisma of athletic competition consists in the fact that it features dramatic conflicts that are held in check by rules and regulations.

The utopia of regulated competition is the universe of 'fair play' that is possible in sport and virtually nowhere else. For the ideologues of competition, the sports world thus offers a profoundly deceptive, and therefore politically useful, idealization of 'fair' competition that sporting events have made known throughout the world. Many people will automatically equate fairness in sport and commerce because both are forms of competition: 'fair' sport makes it possible to imagine the 'fair' commerce that is supposed to be the principle of free-market globalization.

The problem is that the ideal of fair play disregards important inequalities among the competitors, such as political power and technological development, in order to focus exclusively on 'the rules of the game.' Suffice it to say that this procedure affects human welfare far less when it is enforced on the playing field than it does when it is applied to commerce or politics. The US trade officials who insist on 'fair play' while disregarding the profound asymmetry of power that characterizes the relationship between the American and foreign film industries are exploiting a charismatic ideal of fairness that belongs exclusively to the world of sport. Fairness in international trade is a more complex ideal that can be ignored by powerful interests if they succeed in substituting the 'fair play' of sport for the fairness criteria that are more relevant to the world of politics and business.

Sport and the larger world of economic and cultural globalization are in constant thematic intercourse with each other. Just as a sportive concept like fair play can be imported into the world of international business, so can the larger world of globalization extend its norms and practices into the world of sport. This process was described with much enthusiasm in an editorial that appeared in the *International Herald Tribune* during the World Cup of soccer in June 2002. 'Globalization, a word heard so often in other contexts,' we are told, 'has effectively leveled the playing field' in world soccer. 'International soccer's aristocratic pecking order has proved no match for the opening of national borders, which in turn has increased the flow of talent among nations and allowed players from soccer's developing countries to refine their skills in countries with richer traditions and historically high standards of play' (Anon., 2002b).

This text belongs to a special genre of sports commentary that takes pleasure in moving back and forth between the sports world and the larger world for the purpose of promoting the encouraging idea that a nation's success in sport can compensate for the inequalities and injustices of history. Such portraits of the sports world dare their readers to dissent from the general proposition that globalization creates equality; the technique here is to offer a series of gratifying incongruities that evoke an alternative political universe in which the weak are strong and the strong are weak. In the 'aristocratic pecking order' of this political universe, a country like Brazil is at the top, while the superpower to the north ranks as a 'second-tier country'. In a similar vein, Senegalese players who have played professionally in France can now give a (soccer) lesson to 'their nation's colonial parent'. Like Indian computer programmers who study in the US, 'when these players fly home to wear their national colors, their countries benefit.' Soccer becomes a microcosm of globalization, since 'there is now one global market place for soccer talent.' Globalization creates another kind of unity by 'forging a convergence in playing styles, in much the same way that it has homogenized popular culture' (Anon., 2002b). Once again, economic globalization and sportive globalization merge into a single realm where the 'level playing field' prevails.

The fact that a nation's sportive stature often does not correspond to its political stature creates a fantasy space in which competition can produce apparent 'miracles' on the 'level' field of play. The victories of small countries over large ones can evoke the utopian possibilities that always attend the dramatic emergence of a new order of things. 'Sport at this level', a British journalist wrote during the 2002 World Cup, 'carries significance beyond its purpose, and in this year of national presidential elections, the euphoria is inseparable from politics' (Hughes, 2002). 'As the [South Korean] national team kept winning,' an American reporter wrote, 'the country became united and self-confident in ways that people could not have imagined'. A political science professor in Seoul saw an opportunity for Korea to leave its 'historical inferiority complex' behind (Longman, 2002).

Sports imagery can also express national feelings about the threats posed by unregulated competition. Boxing metaphors can convey the apprehensions of globalization's losers (Kofi Annan's indignant reference to bullying 'heavyweights') or the feisty ambition of a small country like Norway that is determined to 'punch above its weight' in the international arena (Anon., 2003a, p. 12). 'We are in a worldwide competition,' says a French high-tech executive. 'If we lose one point of productivity, we lose orders. If we're obliged to go to [a work-week of] 35 hours it would be like requiring French athletes to run the 100 meters wearing flippers. They wouldn't have much of a chance winning a medal' (Friedman, 2000, p. 12).

The irony is that the spectacle of national competition does not reflect economic reality in an age of globalization. 'The obsession with nations in competition', William Greider (1998) points out, 'misses the point of what is happening: The global economy divides every society into new camps of conflicting economic interests. It undermines every nation's ability to maintain social cohesion. It mocks the assumption of shared political values that supposedly unite people in the nation-state.' This is, of course, a counter-intuitive model for people whose image of the state and its roles has been shaped by two centuries of nationalism. 'The truth of our age', President Bill Clinton declared in 1993, 'is this and must be this: open and competitive commerce will enrich us as a nation. It spurs us to innovate . . . And so I say to you in the face of all the pressures to do the reverse, we must compete, not retreat' (Greider, 1998, pp. 18–25). It is the emphasis on competition between nations that prompts Greider to consign the speaker to 'the old order' that antedated the age of multinational products that 'originate' simultaneously in a number of national economies. His point is that globalization does not unify national workforces like teams; on the contrary, it is the national sports team that creates by analogy the illusion of a national workforce that is in reality less unified than it appears to be. While national workforces appear to compete as 'teams' in the complex 'game' of globalization, teams of athletes representing nations enact the international sports competitions that can be mistaken for models of economic globalization. Because the Olympic movement is an international arrangement that exists to promote these competitions between nations, it has faithfully preserved the old model of national economic competition into the age of globalization.

The transient and illusory political achievement of an Olympiad – the reconciliation of the nations – is based on presenting international competitions within the idealized context of the human family. The territory we are exploring here is what Liisa Malkki (1994) calls 'the processes and practices that allow the contemporary system of nation-states to be imagined as an international community, a "family of nations".' The family celebrations of this global community take the form of what she calls 'ritualized evocations of a common humanity that occur precisely through the construction and celebration of an egalitarian diversity among peoples or nations' – in other words, ceremonial occasions such as the Olympic Games and international beauty pageants such as 'Miss Universe' or 'Miss World.' 'The expectation encoded in the imagined community of nations,' she writes, 'that we are all "International Friends," and that anyone can put on a national costume that would accurately represent their kind, is a cruel and magical fiction' (Malkki, 1994, pp. 41, 52, 25).

Sportive Nationalism and International Competition

The political reality that lurks behind this 'magical fiction' is the nationalist feelings that persist within the internationalist arrangements that are constructed to regulate them. Coubertin's Olympic doctrine was realistic enough to acknowledge the dynamic tensions that tied sportive nationalism and internationalist idealism to each other. He understood that internationalism existed in a dynamic tension with sportive nationalism, the doctrine that promotes sportive success in international competitions as an instrument of national self-assertion. The explicit content of this doctrine is the claim that triumphant athletes promote national prestige. Implicit in sportive nationalism is also the more urgent idea that victorious athletes are indispensable symbols of national vitality who contribute to the survival of the nation through role-modelling effects. In this sense athletes can function as symbols of national willpower and strength.

The ubiquity and tenacity of sportive nationalism indicate that, on an unconscious level, elite athletic performances can signify nothing less than national survival for large numbers of people in many different societies (Hoberman, 1993, pp. 18–24).[1] Fantasies of national grandeur, xenophobia and triumphalist celebrations that appear to be cathartic releases of popular emotion are among the familiar characteristics of sportive nationalism. Governments allocate national resources to the production of Olympic medals on the grounds that this benefits both the morale of the nation and its general standing in the world (Hoberman, 1993, pp. 261–2).[2] Sportive nationalism can also be promulgated on more pragmatic grounds. During the 2002 Soccer World Cup competition, for example, the president of the German Association of Employers stated that: 'Sports victories create a better mood which leads to an increase in consumption that is good for business' (Anon., 2002f). Between 1992 and 1994 the Norwegian Prime Minister Gro Harlem Brundtland waged a brilliant (if ultimately unsuccessful) campaign to persuade her country that the Olympic medals won by Norwegian athletes, and the hugely successful 1994 Winter Olympic Games in Lillehammer, demonstrated the nation's fitness to compete in international markets in general and the European Union market in particular. Indeed, it is tempting to establish a special category for small-country sportive nationalism that 'plays a "normal" [as opposed to a pathologically xenophobic] symbolic role for smaller nations that have few opportunities to assert themselves against much larger states. If this is the case, then the more civilised forms of sportive nationalism may have to be recognised as an inherent right of the "minor" nations that participate in international sport' (Hoberman, 1993, p. 21).

Sportive nationalism can also take the form of a kind of masochistic self-reproach that blames the nation for its inability to meet global standards of excellence. Thus, a Nigerian magazine editor bemoans the fact that 'the nation has been lucky to record some successes in the field of soccer, especially at the junior level before the players were injected with the national virus of inefficiency' (Omotunde, 1994, p. 6). The Nigerian dictator, General Sani Abacha, declared in his 1994 budget speech that 'government can no longer watch with indifference when those charged with the heavy sports administration in the country dissipate so much energy in endless bickerings, thereby making us a laughingstock in the international community' (Augustus-Ndu, 1994, p. 30).

We should recognize that the nationalist self-consciousness of this unscrupulous autocrat does not really differ from that of some other politicians in democratic societies. The important difference between autocratic and democratic politicians in this respect is that the ambitions of the former can often be translated directly into policy. Generally speaking, however, sportive nationalism can be used by politicians in a variety of political systems to dramatize national resolve for their own purposes.

Sportive nationalism appears to be entirely compatible with the globalization process if we define the latter as a gigantic competitive arrangement that rewards sheer performance and efficient technique. This unofficial global competition is made up of various kinds of national performances that can even include assessments of the competitive fitness index of the nation itself. For example, in 2001 Finland occupied the top ranking conferred by the World Competitiveness Report (Anon., 2001c). Humanitarianism, too, can become a competitive event, as when the United Nations declared the same year that Norwegian society did more to promote human development than any other society in the world. These are competitions small countries can win; at the same time, these mini-states must also compete in more difficult and fateful contests that directly affect the national security. The director of the Norwegian Research Council thus invokes a sportive motif to emphasize the competitive dimension of science and technology: 'Research is not a local championship, but rather a high-level international competition in which other countries invest more intensively than we do' (Hambro, 2000). Even Japan, the world's second-largest economy, has adopted the same competitive approach to research. In 2001 a national commission created to inject new energy into Japanese science set about to devise a strategy that would enable Japan to win thirty more Nobel Prizes in the sciences in the course of the next fifty years. 'What we need to create', said one Japanese scientist, 'is job insecurity rather than security to make people compete more.' An administrator at Japan's ministry of education, culture, sports, science and technology says: 'We've been trying to increase competitiveness and career mobility in science because we recognize this as one of the most important problems we have to tackle' (Anon., 2001a). Given that job insecurity defines the existence of any elite athlete, this approach to extracting the maximum performance from employees may be termed the athleticizing of labour for the purpose of ensuring global competitiveness.

The relationship between sportive nationalism and national survival in a global economy belongs to a much larger repertory of relationships between various national performances and fantasies of national vulnerability and the symbolic performances that are supposed to boost the morale of the nation. For example, the collapse of Swissair in 2002 serves as an excellent paradigm of a failed national performance that acquired profound symbolic importance for a small nation. The Swiss psychoanalyst Sonja Wuhrmann (2002) has pointed out that this event was not simply 'an economic disaster'; on the contrary, 'a traditional national institution' had literally ceased to exist, leaving in its wake a traumatized national identity. This enterprise had relied on the stature of two kinds of male performers – the men in the executive suites and the men in the cockpits of the planes. Like the trainer of a national soccer team, the director of Swissair had, 'in the eyes of the people, the task of positioning Swissair as an independent, successful and significant airline in the world.' This chief executive was nothing less than a father figure, an *Übervater* endowed with 'almost magical abilities'. The charismatic figure of the pilot also promoted deep feelings of dependency on the part of ordinary citizens. 'Flying,' Wuhrmann (2002) notes, 'unlike any other form of transportation, 'demands a blind faith in the abilities of the pilots'. The markedly 'irrational' dimension of sportive nationalist passion suggests that many people feel an analogous faith in the abilities of athletes.

Denationalizing Global Competition

A year after the Swissair implosion the chairman of the now renamed airline ('Swiss') declared that the very concept of a national airline was becoming outdated. 'The nationality of an airline will not carry much weight in the future,' he said (Anon., 2003b). In a similar vein, the denationalization of global sport has been underway for decades as the performance principle has displaced nationalist sentiments. Multinational professional soccer teams coexist with national teams that are frequently managed by foreign coaches whose skills are considered superior to those of native candidates. The global labour market for athletic talent confers a kind of dual citizenship on elite athletes that frequently devalues service to the nation in favor of service to their professional clubs. The same labour market subverts the racial concept of nationality by integrating 'racial aliens' of African origin into European national teams (Gerald Asamoah in Germany, Emmanuel Olisadebe in Poland). Training methods and management principles of foreign origin can challenge and undermine national values and traditions.[3] Sportive nationalism can thus end up promoting political ideas, such as individualism, that are customarily regarded as consequences of a globalization process that favours denationalization rather than nationalist self-assertion.

At the truly denationalized end of the spectrum, the globalization of sport creates venues for the display of technological achievements and the mastery of these new technologies that require the best equipment and the best expertise money can buy. It should come as no surprise that the participants in these contests show little regard for the nationalities of those who make success possible. This development eventually culminated in the vaguely absurd spectacle of three billionaires, two American and one Swiss, scouring the planet for the sailing talent that might win the 2002 America's Cup. It was only fitting that this spectacle was won by the team assembled by Ernesto Bertarelli, the Swiss heir to a pharmaceutical fortune, who hails from a country that is hundreds of miles from the nearest salt water.

The cosmopolitan potential of such spectacles was best exemplified by the Seattle telecommunications entrepreneur Craig McCaw, who stated that his objective had always been to create 'a global gathering of talented people with a conscience' who would prevent the America's Cup from 'degenerat[ing] into an entrepreneur's ego contest with the biggest war chest determining victory.' His America's Cup effort was dedicated, he said, to raising the visibility of the One World Environmental Foundation (Anon., 2001d). The director of the foundation said that McCaw had even investigated the possibility of sailing under the flag of the United Nations. But this most cosmopolitan solution would have violated the rules of the competition. The United Nations cannot afford a yacht club (Anon., 2002c).

12

The Vulnerability Thesis and its Consequences: A Critique of Specialization in Olympic Sport

Introduction

According to official Olympic ideology, the Olympic Games are festivals for the celebration of a series of values and ideals as expressed in the official ideology of Olympism. As it is stated in principle number 2 of the Olympic Charter:

> Olympism is a philosophy of life, exalting and combining in a balanced whole the qualities of body, will and mind. Blending sport with culture and education, Olympism seeks to create a way of life based on the joy found in effort, the educational value of good example and respect for universal fundamental ethical principles.[1]

However, based on the development of the Games in the twentieth century, the idea of high performance sport as a sphere for culture and education has been seriously challenged. Olympic sport is among the most popular products on the international entertainment market. The Sydney 2000 Olympic Games were watched by 3.7 billion people in 220 countries and territories, making the Games the most televised in Olympic history, and the most watched sporting event in the world.[2] Critics argue that values and ideals of Olympism serve as a false ideology that covers rather harsh Olympic realities. The driving forces of the development are based on a cynical wrapping up of extraordinary athletic performances as commercial entertainment to reach external pay-offs in terms of profit and prestige, as exemplified in several chapters in this book.

In this chapter, I shall take a closer look at one particular value tension between the Olympic ideal of sport as 'combining in a balanced whole the qualities of body, will and mind', and the high degree of specialization we find in a series of sports. The reason for my focus is that I believe that highly specialized demands on performance constitute one of the primary causes of the most serious moral problems facing high performance sport today; those linked to the development of new and radical performance-enhancing means such as doping and genetic technologies.

First, I shall sketch out the basic elements of an athletic performance and define more specifically what I mean by 'specialization'. Second, and on this basis, I will formulate what I shall call the vulnerability thesis that states that the higher degree of specialization in an athletic performance, the more vulnerable this performance becomes to morally problematic manipulation. Third, I will discuss the premises for the vulnerability thesis and some of its implications in terms of sport policies. In a final section, I will comment upon possible objections to my argument.

Before proceeding, I should add that my discussion is not limited to Olympic sport but should be relevant to high performance sport in general. However, Olympic sport serves as a good case for demonstrating the vulnerability thesis for two reasons. First, we deal here with sport at its highest level of performance that can be said to be at the forefront of innovative manipulation of performance. Second, and different from other sport events, Olympic sport can be critically evaluated on the background of clearly articulated value claims as found in the Olympic Charter. Among them is the view of sport as serving the overall, harmonic development of athletes. Here, then, the critique of specialization becomes particularly relevant.

Athletic Performance

A clarification of the meaning of specialized performances must build on a more general idea of what an athletic performance is all about. On what factors are athletic performances built? Advanced human performances are paradigms of human functioning at its most complex. According to Dreyfus and Dreyfus (1986, p. 30), performing at the expert level is best understood in non-analytic, creative and intuitive terms. It seems impossible to capture fully their holistic character. For a discussion of the development of such performances, however, some analytic distinctions can be drawn.

An athletic performance is the result of a high number of genetic and non-genetic influences (Bouchard et al., 1997, pp. 3ff., 384; Schmidt, 1991, pp. 127ff.; Martin, 1991, pp. 24ff.). In this context, I will distinguish between genetically programmed basic abilities and learned skills.

Basic abilities can be grouped in bio-motor and mental abilities (Bompa, 1994, pp. 259ff.). Bio-motor abilities include strength, endurance, flexibility, speed and coordination.[3] Mental abilities include sensation, motivation, emotion, cognition, and personality characteristics.[4] A gradual development of genetically programmed bio-motor and mental abilities is necessary for what we hold to be normal human functioning.

Such a development is a complex process (Bouchard et al., 1997, p. 384). An individual's genetic make-up is the random product of what is often referred to as 'the natural lottery'. Each outcome represents one among hundreds of millions of unions of sex cells, and one particular arrangement among perhaps as many as a hundred thousand genes encoded by 3 million chemical pairs of DNA. In what follows, the genetically defined predispositions to develop relevant bio-motor and mental abilities to succeed in a sport, will be called 'talent' for that particular sport.

'Talent' in the sense used here exists in its pure form only at the moment of conception. As all human phenotypes, an athletic performance is the product of genetic predispositions and environmental influence combined. Differentiation and specialization of cells are the results of an infinite number of interactions between genes, and between genes and the environment. Environmental influences on performance include everything from the very first nurture and psychological and social stimuli via influences from the general physical and socio-cultural environment, to sport-specific influences from training, access to facilities, equipment, coaching, and other kinds of expertise.

Different from abilities, skills are not directly genetically programmed and must be learned in interaction with the environment.[5] Skills can be of general and specific kinds. For instance, general motor skills include walking and running, and human beings are probably genetically predisposed to develop them. Specific skills are related to particular practices such as sport, where they are given a framework, and often a certain description, in the rules. In sport, it is common to distinguish between technical (motor) and tactical (cognitive) skills. A rule for technical skill in tennis might be 'look at the ball when you hit!' A rule for tactical skills in soccer might be 'when the opposing team is superior, play defensively and concentrate on break downs and quick turnovers!'

To sum up so far, we can say that an athletic performance is a product of talent, or genetic predispositions to develop the relevant abilities for a sport, and of environmental influences in the development of abilities, and in the learning of general and sport-specific skills. Given this background, I will take a closer look at the idea of specialization.

Specialization

In a sense, all athletic performances are specialized performances. The sprinter specializes in running the 100-metre as fast as possible, the soccer player specializes in playing soccer, or perhaps in certain roles on a soccer team, the decathlon participant specializes in the ten events that make up the decathlon. However, my use of the word here will be different. On the basis of what has been said above, it is possible to be somewhat more precise. Although all athletic performances are the products of an infinite number of genetic and non-genetic factors, the significance of various abilities and skills varies greatly between sports. Without a well-adapted nervous system and a high percentage of fast twitch muscle fibres, a track and field sprinter will have problems succeeding at a top level. As Sir Roger Bannister (1997) says, 'the faculty of speed is inborn'. Performance in sports with more complex technical and tactical requirements depends to a lesser degree on one-sided advantageous predispositions for development of abilities. For instance, one soccer player might be a little slow whereas another has great speed. Both players can become top performers. The slower player might have excellent working capacity and tactical skills, the faster player might compensate for a certain lack of working capacity with speed and strong technical skills.

In other words, we can say that in some sports, such as the running events in track and field, tend to narrow what is measured as a relevant performance in a particularly radical way. Whereas playing soccer, or competing in the decathlon, is based primarily on learned skills, the successful Olympic 100-metre performance depends upon a fortunate genetic predisposition for, and a systematic and extensive development of, the bio-motor ability of speed. Here, then, specialized performances mean *performances that are based primarily on one or a few bio-motor abilities.*

The Vulnerability Thesis

There is nothing wrong with specialization per se. Highly specialized sports are often sports of great beauty. Many of them, such as track and field, represent variations over basic movement patterns – the run, the jump and the throw – in elegant ways, and performances take place within a fair and just framework. Athletes perform on their own and separated in time and/or space, there is little interaction in performance and hence few possibilities for cheating, aggression and violence.

Moreover, in a culture predominated by a strong belief in (quantifiable) progress, highly specialized performances take on strong symbolic meanings. To a larger extent than in team sports in which performances are relative to an opposition, specialized performances can be measured in exact mathematical-physical entities within strictly standardized frameworks which again provide a basis for objective comparisons of improvements and the setting of records. For instance, in the current home pages of the IOC, athletics – the paradigmatic example of a record sport – is viewed as the very embodiment of the Olympic motto citius, altius, fortius (see http://www.olympic.org/uk/organisation/index_uk.asp).

Nevertheless, as noted in my introduction, I believe that it is within sports with high degrees of specialization we find the most dramatic ethical challenges. Highly specialized performances build on the development of one or a few genetically programmed bio-motor abilities. Such programming can be mapped in the genome; the total set of genes in the nucleus of a cell. Moreover, genes are codes for the production of various enzymes (catalysts of biochemical processes) and structural proteins, which are the building blocks of cells and tissues. Hence, bio-motor abilities can be manipulated by bio-chemical substances and more or less advanced medical technology.

In modern Olympic sport, this possibility causes problems. The increased social, political and economic significance of athletic success has lead to an increased flow of knowledge and resources into sport. Research on performance-enhancing means and methods has reached rather advanced levels. The use of performance-enhancing drugs is the standard example (Hoberman, 1992). Possible use of a rapidly developing genetic technology represents future possibilities (Munthe, 2000). What is at stake here is not just internal moral codes of sport itself such as fair play and sportspersonship, but what a sport performance, a human performance, and, more generally, what a human being, is all about.

Now it is possible to formulate what I will call the vulnerability thesis.

For any athletic performance goes that the stronger degree of specialization (the higher significance of basic bio-motor qualities and the lesser significance of technical and tactical skills in performance), the more vulnerable a performance becomes to bio-medical and bio-technological manipulation.

Let me comment on Table 12.1 in which I have sketched some examples of how sport performances can be mapped according to their vulnerability. A good performance relies heavily on the ability for developing speed. Speed is based on reaction time, explosive strength and an efficient running technique. This integrated capacity for speed is to a large extent based on a genetic predisposition that can be manipulated in various ways. It suffices to point at the efficiency of anabolic steroids to improve explosive strength. Therefore, sprint running is a vulnerable sport.

The sprinters' only tactical rule is simple: full speed from start to finish! Other running events in track and field, such as the 10,000 metre, include a tactical element as well. Since this is a relatively long race, athletes have to dispose their energy optimally during the race. Depending upon whether it is a record attempt and race against time, or a championship in which the main goal is to cross the finishing line first, tactics play a slightly different role. In all races, however,

Table 12.1 *Sport Performances and the Vulnerability Thesis*

	One/a few-round bio-motor abilities	All-round bio-motor abilities	Technical skills	Tactical skills
Sprint – track and field	X			
10,000 metres – track and field	X			(X)
American football – defender/running back	X		(X)	(X)
American football – quarterback		X	X	X
European football, tennis		X	X	X

endurance is a critical quality, and endurance can be efficiently enhanced with, for instance, EPO (erythropoietin) that stimulates the production of red blood cells and enhances the capacity for oxygen transport.

The vulnerability thesis does not primarily distinguish between sport events but between various forms of sport performances. Although not an Olympic sport (yet), American football can serve an example of a sport that includes both vulnerable and less vulnerable performances. This is a complex sport but with specialized role requirements. A defender has to be strong in mass velocity, which again is based primarily the bio-motor abilities of speed and strength. A running back depends upon speed although the ability to tactical runs and catching the ball are important. Both the defender and the running back can improve significantly with the use of, for example, anabolic steroids. A quarterback needs good technique, good tactical understanding of the game and good all round bio-motor skills. The use of steroids will be of less significance. This is the position that requires the most complex skills and that has the lowest degree of vulnerability.

European football and tennis are built on less specialized performances and are therefore less vulnerable. These sports require primarily complex technical and tactical skills. There are no pills or injections that can enhance significantly technical and tactical skills. Of course, favourable genetic predispositions for the development of various abilities are important, but good players need an all-round profile in order to learn. And skills are learned through extensive practice, primarily in social interactions. In both sports we find elite players with a diversity of talent, abilities and skills.

I have formulated the vulnerability thesis and sketched with a few examples how various performances have various degrees of vulnerability to bio-medical and bio-technological manipulation of performance. However, the argument should not be taken on face value. In order to reflect critically upon whether it is reasonable or not, there is need to clarify its basic premises.

The Underlying Premise: Sport as Moral Practice

The very premise for the vulnerability thesis is that certain kinds of bio-medical and bio-technological performance-enhancements are morally problematic. The justification is to be found in the view that as a human practice, sport should link up with morally valuable ideas of human development. This is a key thought in Western justifications of sport and has roots in the British amateur ideology, in Olympic ideology, and, more systematically developed, in works in sport ethics such as in my own interpretation of fair play (Loland, 2002). In sport, individuals and teams should stand forward with responsibility for their own performances that are cultivated primarily through their own efforts. Inequalities with systematic and significant influence on performance upon which individuals have little control and influence, and for which they therefore cannot be claimed responsible, should be eliminated or compensated for.

These norms are reflected in the way sport competitions are structured and organized. Ideally, we eliminate or at least compensate for inequalities in external conditions, in technology or sport equipment, and for inequalities in weight, height, gender and age in performances where such inequalities have significant and systematic influence. Of course, part of the justification of these regulations is the quest for even competitions with uncertainty of outcome. However, I still think the deeper, regulative idea is one of fairness. Sport should measure and compare individuals based on inequalities that they can influence and in part control, and for which they can take responsibility. In this way, sport can become an arena for human development and growth. Philosophically speaking, sport can become an arena for the realization of what Rawls (1971, p. 426) calls the Aristotelian principle, which is considered a key characteristic of human flourishing:

Other things equal, human beings enjoy the exercise of their realized capacities (their innate or trained abilities), and this enjoyment increases the more the capacity is realized, or the greater its complexity.

The Aristotelian principle represents a valuing of, and respect for, individual differences. To be of moral value, then, sport has to offer possibilities for an all-round development of individual talent based on own efforts. In this understanding, specialized performances are problematic for two reasons. First, specialization encourages the development of only one or a few narrow human abilities and leads to monolithic sport cultures in which human diversity and complexity are undermined. Second, specialized performances are based on bio-motor abilities that can be manipulated by external bio-medical and bio-technological expert systems. Hence, athletes easily lose insight in and control over their performances. The responsibility for performance is moved gradually from the individual to the supporting system. This makes the individual vulnerable to exploitation and to treatment as mere means in the quest for external rewards. Such a development somehow drains sport of moral value.

Policy Implications

If the vulnerability thesis is accepted, several critical questions arise. How can Olympic sport in particular and high performance sport in general deal with this? What are the policy implications? I will sketch out and comment upon two possible reactions, the one of status quo, and the one of modifying the logic of specialization in vulnerable sports.

The status quo policy, I assume, is the standard position of established sport systems today. It is politically difficult and very unlikely for the IOC to acknow-ledge that some of the classic sports such as running in athletics are vulnerable to moral problems and ought to be modified or changed. In official Olympic ideology, sport itself is the carrier of moral values. The view is that excessive use of morally problematic ways of performance-enhancement is an expression of individual moral weakness or degenerate subcultures and does not indicate a problem with the logic of performance in sport. The challenge is not at the systemic level but practical-political in kind: to implement tough anti-doping strategies with rules, tests, and sanctions that make bio-medical and bio-technological manipulation of performance impossible or at least very difficult.

Indeed, there are many good reasons to support anti-doping work from a moral point of view. However, there are good reasons for certain scepticism towards the success of such work as well. If the vulnerability thesis is correct, the potential pay off of doping use is high in specialized performances and there will always be individuals and groups that will use this possibility to reach their aims. On this background, anti-doping work seems as a reactive strategy, more designed to repair the damages that to deal with the core of the problem.

A somewhat different approach would be to see the logic of specialization as a degenerative logic and call for change or modification on the systemic level.

The vulnerability thesis should encourage alternative, proactive thinking about how to make sports less vulnerable. Elsewhere I have concentrated on a critique of the record idea and explored alternative competitive principles in more detail (Loland, 2001). I have argued that the continuous quest for new records in specialized performances can be understood as a small-scale version of the eco-logical crisis, and that alternative schemes of development can be inspired by the ecological ideal of a sustainable development. Key ideals, valid for both ecological and cultural systems, are diversity and complexity. These ideals, I believe, have interesting implications for sport.

A diverse sport culture includes a variety of performance ideals and has the potential for the flourishing of a large number of different talents. In a complex sport culture, individuals have a high number of potential ways of realizing their innate or trained abilities. Complexity is the very antidote to specialization. For instance, for a performance to be complex, it has to be based on many and varied elements that combine bio-motor abilities and technical and tactical skills. In my suggested reconstruction of record sports (Loland, 2001), I have shown how the ideal of complexity can be implemented in a vulnerable sport such as running. In sports with high degrees of specialization in certain roles, such as American football, other measures have to be taken. However, there is no space here to go into detailed discussions on these measures. My aim has been to formulate and justify what I consider to be a significant problem on the systemic level in Olympic sport. I will conclude by commenting upon some possible objections to the argument.

Conclusion

One obvious objection concerns its very premise – that there exist dilemmas linked to specialization in high performance sport at all. I have described how the vulnerability thesis builds on particular premises, or a particular sport view. Alternative sport views would lead to other conclusions.

One alternative view could be to reject the whole idea of performance-enhancing means outside of competitions as particularly problematic and endorse a new sport paradigm. High performance sport is about transcending human limits – technological, biological, and moral. Ideas of vulnerable sports do not just make sense. Moral ideals internal to competitions such as fair play and sports-personship are accepted. However, whatever athletes do outside of competitions are up to them and their supporting systems. The history of sport is full of more or less successful attempts to restrict the quest for improved performance. Time has come to abandon these restrictions and to liberate sports from its repressive forces. In Olympic high performance sport, the new human being will appear, freed of its biological chains and of moral restrictions and with performances created in his or her own image (Tamburrini, 2000).

Another possible objection builds on another view. The argument could be that my critique is not going far enough. Specialization is only a symptom of a more serious problem. High performance sport in general is a degenerate social system based on unhealthy competition, self-interest, and a blind belief in unlimited growth (Rosenberg, 2002). High external pay-off in terms of prestige and profit of Olympic success encourages those who are willing to do whatever is necessary to win. A new kind of sport, and a new world order, has to build on other values – cooperation, solidarity and moderation – in which there is no room for Olympic sport as it is practised today.

Although pointing to different solutions, both the above objections have in common that they concern the basic premises of my argument. More specifically, both of them are based on different sport views than the one I have presented here. In a more extensive discourse, critical and systematic comparison of alternative sport views is both necessary and interesting. In this more limited argument, there is no place for this. I present the premise for, and the substance of, an argument about specialized performances as particularly vulnerable to problematic performance-enhancement. If the premise is rejected, there is no reason to discuss the further argument. If the premise is accepted, we can turn to a critical review of the ideas of specialization and vulnerabilities. I will look at two possible lines of critique here.

If the vulnerability thesis holds water, it should be possible to confirm it empirically. Is it the case, then, that what I portray as the most vulnerable sports are the sports in which we find the most use of bio-medical and bio-technological performance-enhancement? Here, objections come easily to mind. For instance, whereas professional cycling has had great problems with doping, a sport such as marathon running seems to have had fewer cases. According to my scheme, both sports require highly specialized endurance performances and should be equally exposed.

My response would be that the vulnerability thesis should not be understood as an empirical thesis without qualification. The thesis deals with the social logic of high performance sport and their various requirements on performance. The fact that some performances that end up in the vulnerability category have differing doping histories can be explained by the social and cultural contexts in which they have developed. Professional cycling has a long tradition for bio-medical experimentation on performance (Waddington, 2000). Marathon running is part of a relatively strict track and field tradition in which doping is more frequently controlled for and sanctioned. However, there is reason to believe that as high performance sport develops, sport-specific histories and traditions are replaced by a harsh ethos of efficiency. The question is not whether a particular kind of performance-enhancement is acceptable, but whether it works. In such a situation, the vulnerability thesis can predict which sports will face the most troubling consequences, and which sports that are less exposed.

The final critique concerns the possibilities for modification and change in Olympic high performance sports. Are not the forces in the direction of specialization too strong to be challenged by alternative kinds of performance logic? Is not what I have presented an ideal argument far removed from the real world of Olympic sports?

By no means do I expect that a set of academically developed principles such as mine will cause any revolutionary changes in Olympic sport. My ambition is simply to point out that Olympic sport has problems on the systemic level, and in order to solve them, there is a need for changes at that level. However, independent of my argument, the development within high performance sport might go in other directions than established sport organisations are prepared for. Specialized, vulnerable sports built on the ideals of *citius, altius, fortius* might lose their fascination among the future generation and can become spheres for those who are especially interested. Technical and tactical complexity belongs to the world of sporting games, such as soccer, basketball and volleyball, that actually are the most popular sports in terms of public attention. Moreover, new sports with new ideas of progress and growth are appearing on the scene. The so-called board sports such as surfing, skateboarding, snowboarding, wake boarding and kite boarding, are good examples. With their relatively non-precise measurements of technically (and tactically) complex performances, and with their lack of standardization, they represent an openness and complexity that might constitute a less vulnerable sport performance paradigm in times to come.

13

Doping and the Olympic Games from an Aesthetic Perspective

Verner Møller

There is no doubt that the modern Olympic Games have been an enormous success if the sole criterion is growth: increases in the number of participants, intensified media awareness, boosted economies, improved levels of achievement, and so on. Over the years the modern Olympic Games have, as John MacAloon has stated, 'grown from a *fin de siècle* curiosity into an international culture performance of global proportions' (MacAloon, 1988, p. 279). There is, however, good reason to wonder at this growth, not least in the light of the parallel growth of destructive forces that have caused considerable erosion of Olympic ideals.

In 1936 the Olympic Games were harnessed to the Nazi propaganda machine. In 1968 they staged a setting for the 'Black Power' protest. In 1972 they were the scene of the greatest tragedy in the history of the Olympic Games, when eleven Israelis lost their lives as a result of a Palestinian terror action. The games again became the scene of international political conflict in 1980 when the Americans boycotted the Moscow Games and in 1984 when the Soviet Union boycotted the Los Angeles Games (see Hoberman 1986; Hulme 1990).

In addition to political abuse, the Olympic Games were also exploited by commercial interests with the result that the original amateur ideal was completely eradicated. During the 1960s, Avery Brundage still attempted to maintain amateurism as the foundation of the Olympic movement but he was up against too strong economic interests. After the Olympic Winter Games in Grenoble, Brundage circulated an indignant letter in which he complained about a number of rule infringements. He was outraged when he saw that special Olympic butter, Olympic sugar and Olympic petrol were being sold, and that not only had an enormous mercenary mentality infiltrated the games, but also the participating associations were blatantly flouting the rules. Allen Guttmann (1992), in his book *The Olympics*, vividly describes the massive problems faced by Brundage.

> The Fédération Internationale de Ski, for instance, had violated its pledge to remove advertisements from ski equipment. Athletes had been tempted for decades to accept small

sums of money for advertisements painted or sewn on their equipment or clothing, but the opportunity to reach a global television audience made advertisers frantic. Athletes were corrupted, rules and regulations were mocked, money flowed, and hypocrisy flourished. The French National Olympic Committee was said to have paid 300,000 francs to an Italian ski manufacturer so that [Jean Claude] Killy could be released from his contract and freed to endorse a rival French brand. When Killy was told by Olympic officials not to brandish his trademark skis in front of the television cameras, he submitted to an extravagant congratulatory hug from a friend who held *his* trademark gloves in front of the cameras.

Worst of all, many athletes boasted openly of their enormous under-the-table incomes and, in effect, dared the IOC to take punitive action against them. (Guttmann, 1992, p. 128)

When the Olympic Games – assisted by effective electronic media coverage – had become a global success, the obvious commercial possibilities became a greater temptation than amateur ideals could resist in the long run. It is hardly an exaggeration to say that the popularity of the Olympic Games stimulated greed, and prepared the ground for a number of corruption scandals (see, for example, Jennings and Simson, 1992).

The merging of political and commercial interests in sport created good growth conditions for another element, which came to be perceived as subversive – the use of doping. When we are talking about doping we refer to a problem fundamentally different from corruption. Nevertheless, doping as well as corruption is considered to be a direct consequence of political and rampant economic interests. The typical example of politically determined doping misuse is the systematic doping of ignorant athletes in the former East Germany. The typical example of the correlation of commercial interests and doping problems is the temptingly large sums that companies are willing to pay for contracts to successful athletes. The best athletes can live a glamorous life whereas the less successful ones – if they are professionals at all – are constantly threatened in their livelihood, and therefore will be tempted to make use of performance-boosting measures (see, for example, Hoberman, 1992).

There is no doubt that political and economic factors contribute to intensification of doping problems. But I consider that this is only valid as part of the problem. The advantage of claiming these factors as a complete explanation is that it affords a possibility of regarding athletes as victims, and of exonerating sport as such. If we can pretend that it is political and commercial forces that are the cause of the whole mess, then we can justifiably begin to combat them for the salvation of sport. If, however, we realize that sport itself contains the seeds of doping use, and that commercial and political interests are only growth-boosting factors, then this results in a far more awkward consequence, namely that doping can be eradicated only if we implement an efficient battle against sport, which must be regarded as the root of the evil.

My perception, that I will attempt to make plausible in the rest of this chapter, is that the impact and continued success of sport is intelligible only if we regard it as belonging to the field of aesthetics. This is not to say that sport is art. It shares certain features with art, but it differs from art in one decisive point. In contrast to art it is not created for the purpose of conveying a message. As the Danish professor of philosophy David Favrholdt (2000) has pointed out, art is created by artists in order to convey an inexpressible message. Sculpture, paintings, poetry etc. are chosen as a mode of expression, in order to present a sentiment or experience, which is impossible to be expressed in everyday language. Sport is not performed with that aim in mind.

Sport as an aesthetic phenomenon is more closely related to wine. Wine and sport are in themselves devoid of meaning, but can certainly be attributed meaning. Sport, just as wine, can be of excellent or of inferior quality. It may lead to joy or despair. We may prefer one type rather than another. But fundamentally what attracts us are first and foremost aesthetic qualities. If we regard sport as an ethical matter, we convert it into something other than it is, just as when religious wine is called the blood of Christ. When we now speak of the crisis of the Olympic Idea, and even of sport itself, this is not least because of Pierre de Coubertin's attempt to convert sport into a religion and ascribe ethical meaning to it.

In London in 1908, Coubertin made his famous speech, 'The Trustees of the Olympic Idea', in which he spoke of the threats to the Olympic ideal of fair play that he suspected. Accordingly he cited Bishop Ethelbert Talbot's dictum that, 'The important thing is not winning, but taking part' and extended it by saying, 'The important thing in life is not victory, but the struggle; the essential is not to conquer but to fight well' (Coubertin, 2000, p. 587). By this Coubertin emphasized the pedagogical aims of the Olympic games. However, that Coubertin's and the bishop's pedagogical ideals were not in complete agreement with the attitudes of the athletes, and the fundamental character of Olympic sport, was amply illustrated during the same games. The marathon race thus had a dramatic conclusion. The leading runner, Dorando Pietri, collapsed just before the finishing line, and had to be carried over the line by officials who took pity on the totally exhausted athlete. During the race he had, like many competitors, taken some form of strychnine as a stimulant, and in his eagerness to win he had almost run himself to death (see Rodda, 1979, p. 59). This episode was almost a repetition of the drama at St Louis four years earlier where the winner of the marathon, Thomas Hicks, had also used strychnine to improve his performance. He managed to finish the race without further assistance, but collapsed afterwards and had to be resuscitated (see, for example, Voy, 1991).

Thus, long before the games were involved as the scene of international political conflict, and before commercialization had made winning a particularly lucrative business, the pedagogical ideal that it was not about winning at any price was contradicted by the practice of sport. Right from the beginning, modern Olympic Games have apparently fostered ambition, to such an extent, that the ideal of winning was not the most important has never been acclaimed, except in speeches and tributes to sport as an educational project. The curious figures of 'Eddie the Eagle' at Calgary 1988 and 'Eric the Eel' at Sydney 2000 in no way contradict this viewpoint; quite the contrary. They precisely draw attention, as bizarre contrasts, to the typical Olympic athletes who have competed uncompromisingly since the beginning of the Olympic Games. Coubertin liked to view sport as a means of developing the character of youth, and wanted the Olympic games to assist in the moral upbringing of athletes. This is illustrated in the ceremony of the games, and not least in the Olympic oath, which was sworn for the first time at Antwerp in 1920. The long and even more spectacular opening ceremonies usually contain a moral message to the world, about peace, equality, harmony, and room for all in the universal Olympic spirit. One of the most moving demonstrations of this was Muhammad Ali's conduct when he lit the Olympic torch at the opening ceremony in Atlanta 1996. In his essay, 'Carrying the Torch for Whom? Symbolic Power and Olympic Ceremony', Alan Tomlinson (2000b) argues convincingly that Ali's faltering performance was an abuse of a living legend in the Olympic Games commercial circus that it *also* is. In a certain respect, the staging of the Olympic Games has become more and more of an invocation and its moral appeals more and more hypocritical.

It was probably not with this in mind that a popular Danish football commentator, Carsten Werge, summed up the opening ceremony of the World Football Championship in the US 1994 with the words, 'In my opinion a beautiful opening. Moving atmosphere. Good music. Colourful. And also praiseworthy that it was limited to approximately half an hour. Not so much in football but, in the Olympic games, there has been a tendency to draw out the opening ceremony. It will now be nice to get started with the genuine article'.

In his decidedly non-highbrow report of the opening ceremony, Werge makes an important point, namely, that there is a staging divorced from sport, which reflects an external will, an ideological message, and there is the genuine article, which is not necessarily in agreement with the ideological superstructure.

As previously mentioned the modern Olympic Games have from the beginning been marketed as a pedagogical project, with emphasis on the aspect of character formation and raising moral standards. But the Games do not remain true to the ideals by which they are marketed. Nevertheless the Olympic Games is such a strong brand name that companies in thousands are willing to pay large sums of money for the right to exploit it. This is remarkable evidence that it is necessary to differentiate between the genuine article – sport itself – and its ideological ornamentation. It is a fallacy to believe that scandals in sport are expressions of a fundamental alteration of the driving forces of sport. It is rather an expression that the values, which have been attributed to sport for ideological purposes, are false.

In order to avoid the confusion that often arises when sport is referred to without differentiating, for example, between exercise sport and elite sport it would be useful to define what I mean when I use the word sport, which is characterized by the following:

1. The activity takes place in a competition, which is taken seriously, even though the competition does not serve any external purpose and, in a certain sense, could be regarded as inconsequential.
2. The activity is organized and functions within an institutionalised framework, within which results are noted and are assigned signification.
3. The activity is controlled by a set of written rules, which is administered ideally by an impartial referee.
4. The purpose is to win and to better one's position within the hierarchic structure of the activity.

These criteria include, without exception, all the sports on the Olympic programme but are sufficiently narrow to exclude a number of cases, which would prevent a consistent analysis if they were to be included under the heading sport. A fun run or a cycle tour – even on a racing bike at good speed – with friends or alone, would fall outside the category sport. The same would also apply to unorganized badminton and squash matches at a fitness centre, a wrestling match on the lawn, or a race where who comes first to the garden gate. These activities can also be designated competitive games, but they are not sports in accordance with the definition given here.

When sport has been praised as being healthy and character forming, sport has been ascribed a value for which there is no basis. It is, in fact, a misleading trade description. And Olympic scandals constantly remind us of it. It is also worth noting that when Ben Johnson's positive doping test is referred to as a scandal, and not simply as breach of regulations; it is a demonstration that the illusion of sport as a good and moral matter still applies.

Even when boxers knock each other out in Olympic boxing matches, no one refers to it as a scandal, even though it would not be too implausible, from a humanitarian viewpoint, to regard it as scandalous that two human beings compete as to whom is the best at punching each other. When it concerns boxing and other martial arts, the ordinary sports-interested person is in no doubt whatsoever that these sports are not about health or spiritual and moral improvement. Many people are keen on boxing in spite of the health risks connected with this branch of sport, and hardly because they let themselves be duped by the apologists of boxing, who have no compunction about speaking of the pedagogical value of this sport (see, for example, Oates, 1987).

When it is a question of doping, attitudes are much more uncompromising and, in the wake of a positive doping test, the word scandal is on everyone's lips. Even though it is reasonable to point out the simple difference, that doping is cheating, and therefore a violation of the ideal of sporting fair play, whereas the knock-out in boxing is not, it is not a sufficient explanation of the difference because there is so much cheating in sport that is not condemned to the same degree. For example it was clear to everyone who saw the slow motion television replays of Maradona's first goal against England, in the World Cup in Mexico 1986, that he had cheated by scoring the goal with his hand. However, he was acclaimed as the world champion when, as the captain of the Argentine team, he lifted the cup on high at the close of the world championships. Furthermore, if the scruples were due to a refusal to accept cheating as a possibility in sport, it could be possible to simply choose to legalize medical treatment as a part of the preparations for competitions in the same manner as training, sport psychology, physiotherapy, and other methods that elite athletes make use of. But this proposal is regarded not only as being cynical but also downright heretical, because it strikes right at the heart of *the image* of sport.

The German sociologist Eugen König (1996), has made the point that the problem of doping is not a problem for sport, but a problem for the technical discourse concerning sport. He points out that normal, morally based criticism regards doping as an attack against sport itself. This criticism represents doping as a threat to the concept of sport, its ideals, values, spirit, purity, origins, humanity and authenticity – the whole meaning of sport. It is possible to continue along this course, and regard doping as betrayal, an abuse and destruction of pure sport and, in this way, establish a degeneration perspective of sport. But, as König points out, this mental image is founded on a number of suppositions that are not self-evident. For example, it is not so simple to explain the true meaning of sport and, if we set ourselves the ambitious goal of deducing the true meaning of sport based on its practice, idealism immediately flies out of the window. In the practice of sport, it is difficult to find convincing support for the moralist's idealistic perceptions, which is why König, with justification, can assert: 'The hopelessness of doping criticism is an expression of the impotence of the moral- pedagogical-minded ideal of sport, as opposed to the actual nihilism of sport, the "*morality*" of which has always served only as an ideological lubricant for technological processing of the body' (König, 1996, p. 224).

Nevertheless the ideological standpoint is defended with tooth and nail. Every time an athlete is exposed for doping, it is represented as an isolated occurrence; an unsporting degenerate who has tried to gain an unfair advantage and has thus acted contrary to the true spirit of sport. Consequently when the athlete in question was punished, order was restored and noble and equal competition could continue in a true sporting manner. It was for this reason that the great doping scandal during the Tour de France in 1998 was such a fierce threat to the image of sport. With one terrible blow it was now made impossible to explain away doping abuse as isolated occurrences. It revealed that the image of sport was false. It was therefore interesting to observe reactions of the sporting world to this exposure.

Cycle sport was quickly segregated. It became a new isolated occurrence. It was not a real sport. It was in reality a commercial circus. Suddenly it was remembered that this particular sport had never really, at any time, been true to the ideals of amateurism either. Cycle sport became a sort of pariah. And when this view was established, it was again possible to carry on treating instances of doping, in other branches of sport, as isolated occurrences – for example when subsequent reports of doping instances in football began to appear. Prominent names, such as the Dutch players Edgar Davids (Juventus), Frank de Boer (Barcelona) and Jaap Stam (Lazio) were all tested positive within the year 2001. Nevertheless they were all treated as isolated occurrences. The same happened to the Spanish cross-country skier Johann Muehlegg who fell into the trap during the 2002 Winter Olympic Games.

One of the most important anxieties connected with doping problems in sport is that the financial wells could dry up. The sports associations' striking rejection of doping sinners could indicate that they regard doping as a threat to the business. It is a fear of the destructive consequences it would have for the image of sport, if it were not possible to retain the conviction that doping was an example of an individual athlete's morally degenerate lack of sportsmanship, but, on the contrary, doping was an irresistible temptation provoked by sport itself.

It has been interesting to follow developments since 1998. The main sponsor of the Tour, the newspaper *l'Equipe* did reconsider its sponsorship but retained. Coca-Cola used the incident to reduce its sponsorship from £2.95 million per year to under £590,000 but is still a highly visible sponsor of Tour de France. In Denmark where a professional cycle team was first established in the wake of the success in 1996 of the Danish Tour de France winner Bjarne Riis, doping scandals did cause some concern and anxiety. When the Belgian Mark Streel, one of the most prominent riders in the biggest Danish team Home/Jack and Jones, was tested with too high a haematocrit value, this caused the estate-agent company 'Home' to withdraw its sponsorship of cycle sport. This retreat by

'Home', that was ethically motivated, was immediately seen as a confirmation that sport could not survive, in the long term, as a business, if the use of doping was not eradicated. However, today we can establish that the former Home/Jack and Jones team (now CSC) has a much larger budget than previously. New sponsors have willingly kicked in, and the success of the team has grown steadily. With the American Tyler Hamilton the team came second in the Giro d'Italia. With the Frenchman Laurent Jalabert the team won the polka-dot mountain jersey in the 2001 and 2002 Tour de France and with the Dane Jacob Piil the team has won the Tour of Denmark. The business performs faultlessly, and so do the riders, and in 2002 a record number of spectators followed the Tour of Denmark race from the roadside. Cycle sport, just as other sports, is still going strong, in spite of all doping exposures.

All in all it would seem that interest in sport is not reduced when sport does not live up to the ideals of fair play and sportsmanship or to Bishop Talbot's assurance that the important thing was not winning, but taking part. When sport, in spite of all scandals, still appeals to a huge audience, it must be that its primary quality – the aesthetic – is in no way compromised. And by changing the focus from the ethic to the aesthetic, it is now possible to avoid the unsatisfactory explanation of doping abuse as an expression of an individual athlete's unsporting and immoral behaviour. On the contrary, it is now possible to regard doping as amoral and, to a high degree, sporting behaviour. Athletes use doping for the same purpose as artists use stimulants. They do it to achieve the optimum: to reach their highest level – to transcend themselves. In other words there is a kinship between the phenomenon Orlan, who makes art by transforming herself through plastic surgery, the orchestra musicians who take beta-blockers, mentioned by John Hoberman (1992) in *Mortal Engines*, and the athletes who make use of testosterone, EPO etc.

In his book *The Body Language*, Andrew Blake (1996) argues that sport lacks an aesthetic theory. This absence is due, he maintains, to the fact that: 'both aesthetics and those who discuss aesthetic theories are elitist and that sports, especially as the elite see them, are popular. This elitism prevents people on both sides of the high/mass culture divide from seeing that sports belong in the same domain as theatre, ballet, opera and dance' (Blake, 1996, p. 194). However, as far as sport is a game we can establish that the culture historian Johan Huizinga already in 1938 argued that sport belongs in the realm of aesthetics. In his classical work *Homo Ludens*, he writes:

> Play lies outside the antithesis of wisdom and folly, and equally outside those of truth and falsehood, good and evil. Although it is a non-material activity it has no moral function. The valuations of vice and virtue do not apply here.

If therefore, play cannot be directly referred to the categories of truth or goodness, can it be included perhaps in the realm of the aesthetic? Here our judgement wavers. For although the attribute of beauty does not attach to play as such, play nevertheless tends to assume marked elements of beauty. Mirth and grace adhere at the outset to the more primitive forms of play. In play the beauty of the human body in motion reaches its zenith. In its more developed forms it is saturated with rhythm and harmony, the noblest gifts of aesthetic perception known to man. Many and close are the links that connect play with beauty. (Huizinga, 1955, p. 6)

Sport is exactly an advanced form of play that gives the spectators an experience of rhythm and harmony. And to this must be added the drama that is enacted in sport and induces mythological acclaim. Roland Barthes (1957) called atttention to the mythological signification of the Tour de France in his book *Mythologies* and, in keeping with this, the German professor of philosophy, and former Olympic rowing champion, Hans Lenk emphasizes the positive role of modern Olympic games as secular mythology. 'The sporting myth', he says, 'appears in a sporting competition as a symbolic drama' (Lenk, 1996, p. 105). And he claims that it is quite simply this drama that fascinates both athletes and spectators alike.

Lenk has a clear eye for the fascination aspect of sport. It is sport as drama and mythological narrative that casts a spell over the mass of spectators. Lenk appears to have understood the reason why sponsors and television networks are willing to spend millions of dollars on such ventures. As a former Olympic champion, however, Lenk tends to give sport too much credit. Lenk seems to insist on describing Olympic sport as being positive in a broader context. He is not content that sport is fascinating simply because of its aesthetic qualities. He also wants sport to be expedient in a broader context. For this reason, he mentions the pedagogical images of sport, as being important for the attraction of sport. But as König (1996) has demonstrated, this is a romantic representation without foundation.

The continuous popularity of sport despite the evident erosion of the sporting ideals seem to suggest that sport does not need any ideological superstructure for it to thrive. It does not need to be harnessed to a pedagogical wagon in order to be financed. As an aesthetic phenomenon it will continue to be attractive so long as its dramatic qualities remain intact. We can, of course, personally dissociate ourselves from doping sport, but it would appear to be impossible to argue the viewpoint that the use of doping makes sport generally less attractive. I will therefore draw on König's analysis and suggest that the impression of a crisis of the Olympic Games is first and foremost a crisis of Coubertin's original Olympic ideals. Olympism as a concept has become an empty shell containing a number of sporting events, which fascinate by virtue of otherwise imperfect qualities.

In other words, the age of Olympic ideals is over. But the enterprise will undoubtedly remain intact at least into the foreseeable future. For when the ball rolls and the show has begun no one worries about the sportsman's future suffering. Here the sportsman shares the fate of the artist. As long as the music, the poetry, the ballet or sportsman fascinate and elevate, the audience will not care much about the anguish, the deprivation that lie behind it all. When there is sometimes a case where activities in the aesthetic sphere may end fatally for the performers, their tragic fate becomes part of the mythology. Tragedies within sport are taken as proof of the seriousness that the performer has put into the activity, but they are not in a wider sense taken seriously by the spectators – the foundation of the enterprise – as a societal or ethical problem. Therefore the death of the doped Danish rider Knud Enemark Jensen at the Olympic games in Rome 1960 or the early death of the fastest woman ever, Florence Griffith Joyner, does not seriously harm the Olympics. In fact it may well be that they contribute to enhance the attraction of Olympic sports.

14

Post-Olympism and the
Aestheticization of Sport

Søren Damkjær

The question of post-Olympism is an interesting one. The prefix 'post' refers to a number of contemporary discussions of postmodernism, deconstruction, high modernity and similar approaches to society in general and social institutions in particular. These discussions, having taken place during the 1980s and 1990s, are now, with a characteristic delay, affecting sport – including Olympism and the Olympic Games. This raises the question of the essence of sport as a social institution and the character of individual sporting activities. The question of the aesthetics of sport is related to questions of modern and postmodern sport. The modern legitimization of sport has relied upon a number of moral and functional premises. The Olympic movement and Olympic sport have, since Coubertin, referred to moral and universal forms of legitimization. On the other hand, the actual practice of the Olympic organization has continually involved political compromises, bureaucratic misuse and, recently, fundamental questions of its ideological foundation and practice. Critiques of sport, as will be explained later, have had, as their privileged object, the Olympic movement, the IOC and the Olympic Games. For better or worse, Olympism epitomizes the essence of modern sport in a way that no other sports or sports organizations do.

If the traditional and modern legitimization of Olympism is no longer valid, indeed, if one has to talk of a situation or even an era when the concept of post-Olympism is more appropriate, a number of questions arise. This is where the theme of the aesthetization of sport, and particularly Olympic sport, comes to the fore. Can the aesthetization of Olympic sport save the future of the Olympics? If the moral and functional legitimizations are invalid, can the aesthetics of the particular events, and of the Games, provide a new legitimization?

The above question introduces the idea that something is fundamentally wrong with Olympism. The question presupposes a number of critiques – that modern sports are in such a state that their philosophy and practice must be reconsidered. So, the implications of post-Olympism can be stated in two related types of reflection. One is that Olympism in its modern sense has changed to such an extent that we have to deal with a radically different object. The other is that the form of analysis has to change, implying the application of postmodern analysis and deconstruction.

The phenomena that point to a change in Olympic sports are often stated in a number of critiques. These phenomena can be divided into several levels. There is the level of the individual athlete and the body; for example, body-modification by means of drugs, excessive training, immoral and aggressive behaviour on the field of 'play' and immoral behaviour outside sporting venues. This could be called the denaturalization and moral degradation of the body. Furthermore, there are the problems at the level of the sports event. These include transgressions of rules and fair play, rigging of events and results and the exclusive focus on winning and the winner. This could be called the demoralization of the ideals of modern sport. Similarly there are criticisms concerning inequalities in the preconditions for entering sports events at the individual or national level; that is, inequalities between individuals, genders and nations in terms of financial and training conditions. These inequalities divide nations into a hierarchy with the majority of nations having practically no chance of Olympic success. The question of gender inequality is raised, partly at least, because the number of events for females is fewer than that for males. To this are added all other questions of gender inequalities in elite sport in general and specifically in Olympic sports. These could be called the inherent and growing inequalities.

Other forms of criticism point to the preponderance of the contextual, that is the pageants of openings, rituals, ceremonies or the massive media influence on the staging and performance of the Olympic Games. In short, this critique points to the Disneyfication of elite sport, leaving the actual events as a mere pretext for a spectacle involving all contextual and media devices that make the Games attractive to sponsors and the media business. This could be called the hegemony of the context.

To all these forms of criticism could be added the malpractices on the level of the organizational structure: game fixing, corruption and the extravagant life of top-level Olympic officials. Related to this, the commercialization of the games and events are also critiqued. Finally, the sportsperson is seen as a mere puppet in a media show involving scientific manipulation of the body solely for the sake of performance. These phenomena are seen as connected and somehow involved in a spiralling process, presumably without end – a megalomanic performance, losing the connection to the spirit of modern sport. All this points to a change, the magnitude of which indicates a change of Olympic events from a modern to postmodern perspective.

What is Olympism?

Before one can answer the question of post-Olympism, an analysis of Olympism is necessary, involving a historical, a sociological, and more contemporary perspective. Olympism is the ideology, practice and organizational apparatus associated with a specific phenomenon in early modern and modern sport, the so-called Olympic movement and the Olympic Games that comprises the ideology of the promulgation of sport in the modern world, eventually the mission of modern sport as an institution with a variety of functions. The ideology comprises a reference to a foundational myth, the body culture of ancient Greece, and the idea of its revival in modernity, and the mission of sport in promoting health, character and peace. The ideology bears the imprint of its founding father, Pierre de Coubertin, and the birthmarks of the cultural climate at the time of its birth. This birthmark was undoubtedly modern, though modernity was and is never a clear-cut ideology. Olympism emerged as a mixture of aristocratic, modern, cosmopolitan and nationalistic ideas. But its origins also included a number of limitations in terms of democratic ideals, particularly regarding gender equality. The basis was originally also based on the cultural superiority of the European and American forms of body culture. During the twentieth century certain elements have been retained, others have been modified, some have disappeared and some have been realized. The whole ideological concept is couched in a quasi-religious language, equal to other modern secular ideologies.

The Olympic movement is supposed to transmit and promote these values to humankind, globally. The IOC was established to implement these ideals. It is a transnational organization, based on cooption of its members. It is neither democratic, nor responsible to others but itself as sole arbiter of the ideology of Olympic sports practice. The main, but not only, activity of this organization lies in organizing the quadrennial Olympic Games. The IOC has the *de facto* monopoly of these events, staging them and deriving whatever profit, leaving the actual staging to cities according to procedures of application and delegation. These events have shown a remarkable ability to survive and even flourish in recent decades as a profitable business. This makes the Olympics different from mono-disciplinary events like World Cups or multi-sport events on a continental basis. They are also different from commercially arranged single sports events like tennis or cycling (e.g. Tour de France). Other sports disciplines also lack the explicit missionary ideology, the idea of a movement and, indeed, a mission.

The Meaning of Sport

Play, games and sports are sensuous forms, combining body, movement, time and space in a particular form. The particular form of the game is then placed in a context and an organization and eventually related to other cultural and political forms. On a more philosophical level, the meaning of sport consists of the correspondence between a number of levels of meaning, that is the structure of the singular game and the code of the activity, i.e. winning or losing. Furthermore the result of a singular event enters into a series of other events, that is, a tournament where winners meet winners. The supercode of modern sports consists in the accumulation of results. Sport is in that sense a social institution, producing institutional facts like any other social institution. The institution of sport assumes a cultural and political significance depending on a historical and cultural situation. This 'construction' also includes the intentions and attitudes of individual sportpersons and their bodily dispositions. Modern sport is a modern institution that is founded on a correspondence between all these levels of meaning. What makes modern sport modern is exactly the characteristic traits of modernity and modern institutions. If some, or indeed all of these levels of meaning are circumvented, corrupted or brought out of alliance, the meaning of sport will change into a situation of two values, first the assumption of partial or totally new values, and second, the loss of meaning. As will be seen later, this is exactly where the postmodern critique of modern sport finds its pivot of deconctruction. The postmodern and deconstructive stance in general looks on all social forms, institutions, subjectivities and identities and meanings and tries to exhibit the dislocation between cultural meanings, institutional orders, activities and subjects. This is evident in the postmodern discussion of sex and gender, of the postmodern condition in general, of morality and of personal and social identities. In general, the postmodern critiques point to the absence of absolute referents, the existence of multiple meanings, of arbitrary or contingent meanings. This can be couched in different forms of postmodern or deconstructive terminology, depending on the particular forms of the founding fathers of the postmodern stance. The result of these forms of deconstruction is a change in perspective towards an aesthetization of the particular forms of social and cultural life. If there is no ultimate foundation, social life, including sport, is disseminated into local and particular aesthetic and individual forms.

This is where the discussion of post-Olympism comes in. In a sense, the postmodern critique is far more radical than other forms of critique. I shall therefore divide the following into both a Kantian and a postmodern critique of sport.

Modern Critiques

The first three critiques are modern in a Kantian sense, by which I mean an investigation into the categorical preconditions of sport as a phenomenon. By this I suggest that sport can be analysed in a number of different ways. The three critiques are historico-sociological, ethical and aesthetic.

The historico-sociological critique has definite political implications. The premises of this critique are that sport is a historical form of movement culture and like all historical forms it is subject to change. This form of critique first states the difference between antique forms of body culture and Olympic sport – the premodern and the modern. There are a great number of varieties within this form of historico-sociological critique. The result of this form of critique is to relativize the claims of Olympism.

The ethical critique implies that modern sport is associated with a specific ethos. There must be ethical rules appertaining to the integrity of the body, the observance of rules of fairness, the ethos of participation, of honouring the opponent, indeed a whole array of ethical prescriptions associated with modern sport. The ethical critique in a Kantian sense has acquired a specific relevance because of the character of modern sport and the ethical questions raised by body modification, doping, cheating and the preponderance of winning at all costs. The ethical critique is, arguably, still in its infancy. The problem is the relevance of the traditional ethical distinctions and positions when one analyses sport. Is an Aristotelian or neo-Aristotelian ethical analysis of virtue relevant? Is a Kantian categorical analysis relevant? What about a material ethic looking at the intrinsic values of the game itself? The typical form of ethical critique is the confrontation of the values of sport with the actual practice of sport. In the case of Olympism this consists in the confrontation of the original values of fair play and the integrity of body, of the unmodified body and its doping and cheating.

The aesthetic critique will be analysed in depth later. It implies that the essence of sport consists in the aesthetic qualities of sport or at least that sport also has a number of aesthetic qualities that have to be taken into consideration. The typical theme is the comparison between sport and art. This critique, until recently, has been marginal to discussions on sports, one reason being the overwhelming influence of a biological and bio-functional type of analysis that persists even today. Even the historical and sociological perspectives on sport as movement forms have had problems in thematizing the field of sport studies.

Each critique, in a Kantian sense, has its proper domain of questions, and each critique is related to the other in subtle ways. My main emphasis will be on the aesthetic critique. The main points of the three critiques will now be analysed in greater depth in order to provide the background for the far more radical postmodern and deconstructive forms of analysis of modern and even postmodern sports.

The Historico-Sociological Critique

The essence of the historico-sociological critique is in a relativization of the claims of Olympic ideology and the past and present practice of the Olympic

Games. The historical relativization has been mentioned above in the brief presentation of the three forms of critique. This essence is to point to the difference between the Olympic Games of Ancient Greece and Rome, and the historical variability even in the history of modern Olympism. Ideals, practices and organizational forms have changed also in relation to the context of society and politics. In this perspective, Olympism is less the eternal guardian of sport's sacrosanct ethical values, than an organization intent on its own self-preservation and prey to global political pressures.

On the sociological level one could point to an ideal model of modern Olympism, which could be used as a standard of comparison with the actual policies and practices of Olympism. If one summarizes this ideal type of ideologies and practices, modern Olympism would comprise the following model of truly modern sport. Modern sport is characterized by its autonomy on the institutional level, meaning the independence from political pressure and the autonomous running of events, organizational apparatus and the jurisdiction over all controversies of sport within its own regime. Modern sport is further devoted to a set of essential values: fair play, equality of opportunity, magnanimity, respect for the opponent, acceptance of the outcome of the contest. Additionally, outside the arena the sportsperson is a paragon of virtue on the basis of the universal virtues of sport. This also includes a number of values concerning the body, placing restrictions on what can be done to one's own body and the body of the opponent, or put differently, a number of requirements for the body, notably that the body must be modified only by training and nutrition.

To this are added various requirements for the events that are governed by rules and regulations to ensure fair and equal competition. As the sports event where this modern definition of sport is paramount, the context is subservient to the event. The venues and arenas of sport are, so to speak, neutral and functional spaces that serve to guarantee the preconditions of the event as such. The spectators and the media are witnesses and judges of the orderly procedure of the event and not actors in their own right. On the organizational level, the sports organizations, including the IOC, are the servants of the events. The organizational structure exists to guarantee the orderly and regular sequence of events.

Although Olympic sports are organized on a national level, the values and practice of Olympism refer to the transnational and universal values of sport. This means that modern sport is modelled on the universalistic ethos of other modern institutions. These forms can be incorporated into various modern forms of statehood, democratic or totalitarian. Even if this incorporation relativizes a number of the modern and essential forms of modern sport (autonomy for example), ethics of modern sport still exemplify modern ethics: universalism, impartiality and equality of opportunity. The history of modern sport is the instantiation of these modern principles: the extension of sport to all nations, the inclusion of all types of groups, whether based on sex and gender, race and religion. This would culminate in the apogee of global modernity. In this case modern sport is a modern institution, sharing the main features with other modern institutions, though admitting certain specific features.

The aesthetics of modern sport is an aesthetic of functionality in the case of the hard types of sport and the cultivation of aesthetics standards in the types of sport where an aesthetic judgement is part of the evaluation (gymnastics, skating, ice dance, etc.). The historico-sociological critique takes this ideal type as its point of departure for a critique. Typically that takes the form of a comparison of ideal and reality.

The Forms of Critique

A form of critique in sociological analysis implies a basis of critique that is a point of reference for the critique. Then there is a form of critique on the basis of this reference. For example, a prevalent form of critique is the confrontation between the ideals of Olympism and the reality. The basis of critique consists of the ideals of Olympism.

Three types of critique of modern Olympism can be recognized. The first is very simple: there is no critique at all. This form is *apologetic*, meaning that everything is in order. The ideals of Olympism coincide with the reality of present practice. There might be minor transgressions of the Olympic ideals, but these be can easily be corrected. The apology can assume several forms. A recent form asserts that, despite scandals and criticism, the Games are still a success, meaning that the Games are a commercial success. This seems today to be the only apology and legitimization of the Games. This is a pragmatic apology. The legitimization is inherent in the success. If the critics of the malpractices were right (referring to doping, corruption, abuse of bureaucratic power), the Olympics would already be dead. Despite problems, the Olympics have survived, so this is proof of their viability. Underneath this argument is, of course, the view that Olympism's ideals are still valid, but instead of referring to the ideals, this argument refers to the success and viability of the Games. One could regard this as the pragmatic ideology of modern Olympism

The *partial* critiques are the prevalent forms of critique and focus on a number of elements within the ideology and actual practice of Olympism. This form of critique often compares ideals and reality, being based on some ideal of Olympism, often the professed ideals as expressed in the Olympic Charter or in Coubertin's philosophy. These critiques include a number of elements and the essence of the partial critiques implies that, in principle, the questionable elements can be changed or eradicated. The partial critiques concentrate on a long list of partial elements. A number of prominent typical elements include corruption on the organizational level, the extravagance of the officers of the IOC, the deals for organizing Olympic events, and the devious ways of bidding for the staging of the events in the competition of host cities. Eventually accusations of downright fraud and corruption arise. Similar forms of critique concern the commercialization of the Games, the preponderance of the commercial show, the appropriation of the Games by corporate business (e.g. Nike, Coca-Cola). Additionally, critiques are raised concerning doping and other malpractices and the negligence or downright tolerance of these deviant practices in the Olympic events.

Furthermore, there is a list of problems related to the of the context of the Olympic Games in the form of pageantry and trappings at the opening and closing ceremonies, presumably overshadowing the ideal content of the events. Often these partial critiques assume almost an accumulative weight relating the partial critiques to the *total* critiques. The total critiques, however, are not only an accumulation of partial critiques. The total critiques are more radical.

Evidently, the historical critique can be, and is, often combined with the partial critiques. The historical critique assumes that change is endemic to all elements of Olympism, the ideology, the practices, the politics, the political environment and so on. The crucial question to a historical critique is the magnitude of change in recent years. Has Olympism changed to such an extent that the modernist and partial critiques are no longer relevant? The evaluation depends to a large extent on the particular philosophy of history and the particular history of sport.

The total critiques differ from the partial critiques for a number of reasons, the main one being a shift in perspective. Whereas the partial critiques assume that the ideals of Olympism, at least in principle, can be restored, the total critiques imply a total rejection of the ideology, organisation and practices of Olympism. For a variety of reasons, the total critiques discard the practice and ideals of Olympic sports in their totality, the most obvious examples being the various marxist views from the 1960s and 1970s. Brohm (1978), for example, saw sport as part of the ideological state apparatus of capitalism. The mode of production of capitalism and the various forms of concrete societal forms provided the determination for the state apparatus and the other forms of apparatus in the superstructure. Sport belonged to the ideological instance in the superstructure. Capitalism was doomed to produce its own destruction, and so was the ideological state apparatus called sport. As the former Soviet Union, the former East Germany and China were, in fact, varieties of capitalist modes of production, their sports systems were also doomed. Brohm's Althusserian analysis promoted his Trotskyite view of sport. The total critique of capitalism included the total critique of sport. The basis of this total critique of sport is a total critique of capitalism.

Post-Olympism

The term post-Olympism is coined according to the models of postmodernism, postfeminism and postcolonialism. The prefix 'post' alludes to a situation where the elements of modernism have changed radically to create a new situation where the usual type of analysis is no longer applicable. As noted in this volume's Introduction, the prefix 'post' is ambiguous. Postmodernism can refer to a temporal sequence – something after the modern, a historical sequence of premodern, modern and postmodern. But the prefix can also refer to a radically new institutional arrangement meaning that postmodern institutions and social relations have changed into something radically different from the modern institutional order. This means that the object of a postmodern analysis, namely postmodernity, is a different sort of social order. The fixed order of modernity is supplanted by a multiplicity of floating arrangements of particular orders. The philosophy of postmodernity is the philosophy of these multiple institutional orders and fractured subjectivities. Postmodern sociology tries to emphasize the changes that have taken place, its emphasis being on the death of legitimizing referents and moral orders, the elements of social construction of social identities and the lack of essential features. This implies that all the elements of Olympism are subjected not only to the forms of modernist criticism mentioned above, but also to a more radical form of subversion. The postmodern critique is different from the three forms of critique mentioned above. The historico-sociological, the ethical and the aesthetic critiques all assume an essence of sport, a deeper or original point of reference of what sport was, is and is supposed to be. In short, the modernist analysis of sport presupposes some kind of universal reference. But postmodernist and deconstructionist strategies aim at the destruction of all kinds of universalism and absolute points of reference. If one looks at the Olympic movement and the Olympic Games a number of features easily fall prey to postmodern analysis and deconstruction. Olympism is the metanarrative of modern sport. It is even a totalizing narrative claiming in the Olympic Charter that the Olympic movement its responsibility for all sports activities universally (Anderson, 1998).

Postmodern in Olympism

As mentioned earlier, the prefix 'post' is ambiguous. It can refer to a temporal change from modern to postmodern. It can refer to a sharp distinction on the structural level between modern Olympism and post-Olympism. To imagine a stage of post-Olympism a series of steps are necessary. If we are at this stage, it is a subject for discussion. If we model the stage of post-Olympism on the model of postmodernism and postfeminism, the 'post-model' would reverse some, if not all, of the characteristics of modernism. Postmodern Olympism or post-Olympism would mean both a temporal and structural change from the ideals and practicies of modern Olympism. This would mean the erosion of original and modern values. Original values are not only corrupted and circumvented. They are not only obsolete in a historical sense. There were never any original values. Doping and other malpractices were part of modern sports from the beginning. A postmodern critique or deconstruction would accumulate all the forms of critique mentioned above, but would add a new perspective.

If the universalist norms were never operative or were circumvented and corrupted from the beginning, there were actually only particular forms of a hegemonic European body culture. The so-called European and US universal standards of sports practice are in fact, from the postmodern perspective, only a particular instance of cultural imperialism in body culture. The ideals of fair play and the restrictions on the body are only reflections of a moralist stance on the individual sportsman and sportswoman. The modern rules of the game and restrictions on body modification are arbitrary and essentially moralistic. So why not accept the changes already happening?

If some, if not all, restrictions are raised, one could accept radical changes in Olympism and the Olympic Games. If the restrictions are loosened on the rules of the game, one could imagine all kinds of games, having different standards and rules. One could imagine that the standards applying to the body (unmodified, sacrosanct) would be changed. Body modifications and enhanced performances by doping would be allowed for a number of reasons.

Whereas the context, despite the present day pageants and ceremonies, is still subservient to the Games, one could easily imagine a situation where the context of the Games assumes priority over their content. Finally, one could imagine a situation involving the total loss of sport over its own affairs. This would mean the loss of control of the individual athlete, of the organizational framework for sponsors, corporate interests and media networks. This would paradoxically probably mean the ultimate ascendance of the individual sportsperson as the media focus. To sum up, a postmodern sport reflected in post-Olympism would mean a total change in the meanings of modern sport – or maybe a total loss of meaning.

Deconstruction

Deconstruction, postmodernism and poststructuralism are often combined. Where the contours of a particular philosophy can be pinpointed by looking at the founding father, often French, they are in the Anglo-Saxon versions often combined into a mixture, drawing on various sources. So what are distinct contributions in a French intellectual climate, are often presented as an amalgam of Baudrillard, Derrida and Foucault in the Anglo-Saxon context.

Deconstruction is different from the critiques mentioned above. Critiques of sport are squarely located within the modernist paradigm. Deconstruction is different. I know of only one example of deconstruction of sport, that by Verner Møller (see chapter 13) in this volume. This form of deconstruction is known as critical cultural analysis. The deconstructive strategy consists of turning the argument upside down. The moral stance, that is the moralizing attitudes connected with the modernist critique, is abandoned. Phenomena like doping, regarded in the modernist stance as corruption or degradation, are put into a different perspective. The moral absolutism of the modern Olympic philosophy is discarded, not only because of the clash between ideals and reality, but also because of a radical change of perspective.

The phenomenon of elite sport is not seen as an ethical phenomenon and a modern social institution, but as a phenomenon of inbuilt transgression of ethical and moral barriers. The essence of sport lies in transgression, not in ethical and political moderation. This deconstruction changes the whole perspective on sport. The 'object' sport as historical and contemporary fact was never a moral affair, but actually an aesthetic practice. The modernist understanding of modern sport was wrong. The phenomenon of elite sport is not an ethical matter, but an aesthetic phenomenon. Sport is presumably not art, but akin to art.

The idea in this form of deconstruction is to change the fields of understanding and analysis from the socio-ethical field to the aesthetic field. This has a number of consequences. The most important is the right of the sportsperson to pursue his or her strategy of transgression in the pursuit of the ultimate or extreme performance in spite of arbitrary rules and regulations. Møller advocates the understanding of this transgressive urge instead of moralizing arguments.

This aestheticism of sport is an aestheticism of the transgression of the limits of both the human body and of the specific type of sport. The aesthetics lies in the transgression. This creates an analogy with art, where some artists, in pursuit of the aesthetic effect, have used performance-enhancing drugs. Artists are not subjected to the same kind of moral contempt for their use of prohibited drugs. Why then the moral approbation for elite sportspersons? In a certain sense, postmodernist critiques are not of the same type as the other critiques. All the critiques mentioned above are critiques in the name of modernity. They refer to a point of reference, typically the discrepancy between ideals and reality: No such thing for the postmodern temper. In a sense, postmodern analysis accepts all as it is, while at the same time asserting that what is at stake in elite sport is totally different from modern moralism. There is therefore no ethical judgement involved, regarding the metamorphosis of the present day Olympics. The deconstructive stance immediately raises two questions. The first regards the ethics of sport and the second the aesthetics of sport. If the legitimization of sport lies not in the ethics of sport, it must lie somewhere else, presumably in its aesthetics.

The Ethics of Sport

The ethics of modern sport are rooted in modern ideals of fairness, impartiality and the integrity of the body. This creates a universalist form of sport morality similar to other modernist forms of ethics. Now postmodern critiques of ethics and morality have questioned this universalism. It is supposed to be in fact a partial, ethnocentric, phallocentric example of white male Western hegemony. This is evident in the discussion of postmodern ethics. The whole idea of universalism is questioned and the idea of a universal foundation of ethics is questioned. This means the disappearance of foundational ethics. Instead emerges a fluid, multifaceted ethics.

Such a view has consequences for the ethics of sport because they are founded on the claims of universalism. If this claim is false, the whole idea of the ethics of sport as the foundation of sport is wrong. And if the actual practices of elite sports continually transgress the ethical standards, a strong argument can be raised against the foundationalist philosophy of elite sport and Olympism. In fact, the critique of the moral foundationalism meets the critique of immoral practices in the same form of argument. This is the essence of a postmodernist critique of sport. This is also what makes this critique different from the modernist forms of critique – and this is also Møller's argument. If the ethics of sport have no foundation then the foundation must be found in the aesthetics of sport. Sport as an institution must have some kind of meaning.

A Model of Postmodern Sport

Before undertaking an analysis of the aesthetics of sport it could be useful to project an idea of a sport without the moral restrictions, applied to modern sport and its modern ethos. A truly postmodern sport can be regarded either as a utopia or a dystopia. This would be bodily activities that have discarded all restrictions on the modification of the body and all restrictions as far as the ethics of the activity is concerned. This would be a sport, where the aesthetization of the context would be preponderant. The context would assume hegemony, reducing what is going on to a mere pretext for contextualization for all kinds of mediatized representation. This would allow all forms of organizational machinations, all kinds of scientific experiments with body, activity and equipment. This might have a certain aesthetic quality. It might involve elements of violence. It might have enormous popularity as a part of postmodern culture in general. It would relegate old-fashioned Olympism to the dump of sports history.

This kind of sport would be focused entirely on the individual event, the individual sportspersons involved, the individual context and the individual organizational structure. For philosophical reasons any comparison of events would be impossible, excluded or irrelevant. A result would be reduced the specific mode of production of the specific result. The organizational apparatus would not be judged according to modernist ideals of Olympism or historical ideas of the founding father. It would be judged only according to financial and mediatized success. The contexts – the staging, venues, architectural and media context – would assume absolute hegemony. It would be a postmodern equivalent of the circuses of Rome. Now this situation has already happened in Formula 1 and basketball since the introduction of the Dream Team. So the question of post-Olympism is highly relevant, although the types of analyses of the consequences are faulty. The fact that there are tendencies in that direction in Olympism and post-Olympism does not necessarily mean that Olympism has entered into a new stage. However, question of a post-olympic sport is a useful device for diagnosing a number of questions of Olympics sports and elite sport in general.

Sport and Art

If the modern analysis of sport is not valid, and the postmodern deconstruction is right, that is, if the morality of sport and the ethics of sport is no longer valid, there seems to be a strategy of changing the perspective. The legitimization of sport would not lie in the distinct modern and factual aspects: universality, respect for the rules of the game, respect for restrictions on the body. These are all based on a foundational ethics of sport, as mentioned earlier. The legitmization is to be found elsewhere. That is in the aesthetics. Sport is to be compared, if not to art, then to an activity akin to art. The critiques of sport, as mentioned above, are therefore misguided, appealing to an ideal of modern sport that can be restored, a foundational ethics that can be restored. This can only be a misguided and hollow appeal to morality or moralizing and even victimizing the sportsperson that transgresses the rules of a moralistic Olympic sport. This seems to be Møller's view, as presented above.

This, of course, requires an analysis of the aesthetics of sport and as a model of comparison, the aesthetics of art. If the foundational ethics of sport is gone for philosophical and practical reasons, then sport as an artistic phenomenon might provide a new foundation, if one can talk of a foundation in the postmodern and deconstructive sense at all. Art has no foundation in a philosophical sense, especially postmodern art.

On a superficial level, sport has a number of aesthetic aspects: an elegant exercise in gymnastics, an elegant kick in soccer, executed by more or less beautiful bodies. But sport also has activities that are grotesque and bodies that are ugly from most points of perspective. Race walking, an Olympic discipline, is not particularly elegant. Sumo-bodies are excessively fat. In general the aesthetics of modern sport is a functional aesthetics.

In other respects sport differs from art because of the standardization, the repetition of games and exercises according to fixed and very detailed rules and regulations. In art there are rules and models of presentation, but these rules are there, at least in modern art, to be broken, circumvented and subverted. This is evident in ballet, an art of movement that can, on a superficial level, be compared to sport and gymnastics. But dance and gymnastics are two different genres of movement, and the aesthetics are radically different.

Art

If sport was art or a form of art, the whole legitimization of sport would change. Of course, this is to venture into a comparison of sport and art. In this context art consists of forms of sensuality, that are transformed, presented and represented in such a way that the original sensuous inputs are transformed into formal categories that are the end forms of sensuous material as form. This means that the original affection is transformed into affect and perception into percept. Affect and percept are, so to speak, the crystalline form of the original affection and perception. Percepts and affects are objectified sensuous forms. They are artistic objects. What happens is that artistic forms, be they painting, dance or music, are processes of transformation, metamorphosis and retention. Furthermore, art sets its own rules. They are intrinsic to the process of creation and the presentation of the final work as on object of art. There might be more or less fixed stylistic rules and conventions, even verging on stereotyped artistic conventions in music, dance and painting. But these rules are, in modernity, always open to revision, conversion or rejection. Art forms are sensuous forms crystallized into artistic objects in the forms of affects and percepts. As objects of art they present a challenge to the perception of the object, i.e. the perceptions and gaze of the spectator (Deleuze, 1983).

The Aesthetics of Sport

But sport is not art. Art as form and sport as form are different. Sport is related to art, because sport forms are sensuous forms constructed according to rules that combine bodies, movements, time and space. But in sport the rules are fixed, whatever the activity. Even if ice dance as a form of sport resembles dancing, the rules are fixed, as the activity is subjected to the code of evaluation of the technical and so-called artistic features. Ice dance and sports dance are dance forms subjected to the rigid rules of sport and therefore different from dance as such. Art is characterized by forms of presentation and representation but is remembered in a peculiar form. Art consists of an artistic object.

Sport can be represented in art, as can everything else. But the code of sport is founded on the difference between winning and losing. And the outcome counts as a result in an institutionalized system of results. Sport is not representation, but presentation of a singular sportive event, related to a series of events. The aesthetic is derivative, that is, dependent on the character of the event and the position of the singular event in the series of events.

The aesthetics of sport lie in the form of the sportive event. This aesthetic is an aesthetic of presentation, not representation. Sport can be represented in media, literature, and in narratives in news coverage. But strictly speaking, the event is pure presentation of real bodies in real time and real space, all governed by the rules of sport. This is what makes sport into sport. It consists of rule-governed activities. This means that sport constitutes an aesthetic field of its own, different from art. The aesthetics of sport consists of the form of the sportive event. The form of sport is exactly the way roles combine bodies, movements, time and space into an event, and a series of events into the hierarchy of winners meeting winners in a tournament. The aesthetics of sport is therefore constituted by the event, that means, concretely the particular rules of the activity, (a soccer match, swimming). So sport has an overall aesthetics, being a form of play. Play is a specifically sensuous form for human activity, different from pragmatic considerations in other social institutions like work. This gives play a certain autonomous status in all cultures, but it is exactly this status that makes play and its subclass sport, able to interrelate in numerous ways with other institutions by way of analogy, homology, metaphor or blending. The aesthetics of sport is the aesthetics of the sensuous form of sport. The rules define the relationship of body, movement, time and space. This means that the essence of sport, and one has to state a form of essentialism, consists of the sportive event. This is also the point of departure for a discussion of the aesthetics of sport. The aesthetics of sports is the aesthetics of the event. And the aesthetics can never be higher than the ethics of the event. If the ethics are faulty by ways of cheating and other malpractices, the aesthetic qualities will be low.

One could take as an example the case of football. The aesthetic qualities are defined by the code of winning or loosing in the individual game. In football, additional aesthetic qualities are derived from the absolute difference between offence and defence. This makes football a good example of the structural properties that define the aesthetic qualities of a particular sport. In all team sports there is on the structural level a difference of offence and defence. Sociologically this means that all team-mates are partners, and all members of the opposing team are opponents. The aesthetic structure of the game is mimicked by the social organization of the players. The aesthetics is defined by the game as a structure of rules, bodies and the particular aesthetic qualities by the distribution of offence and defence. This gives every game or every sport activity and sport event its particular aesthetic structure. Football is, as a corollary, defined by the rigid distinctions, and by the alternation between attack and defence, plus the alternation between absolute immobility and explosion. Energy and destruction of energy of the opponent define team sports. This is an aesthetics of presence. The moments of the game and the final result are irrevocable and cannot be disputed. The aesthetic attraction lies in the finality of the result. This is different from the aesthetics of art (Gumbrect, 1998).

The aesthetics of sport are fundamentally connected with the individual event and the singularity of the individual event. The singular event is decisive. But the singular event is also placed in a series of events, that is, a tournament. And the decisiveness of the singular event depends of course on the placement in a series. The decisiveness of the first rounds in a soccer tournament is limited, whereas the finals are decisive or definite. So we have an interplay between the singular event and the series of events. The results of the singular events are accumulated into the standing of the individual or team. But the aesthetics of sport consist in the logic of the event, depending on the position of the event in a series of events.

From an aesthetic viewpoint there are four forms of sport. First, there are the direct and hard forms, the sportive event in its purist form: the 100 metres sprint, javelin and high jump. These events, typically in track and field, have a particular form. The aesthetics of these events is purely functional. That means that aesthetics is subjected to the logic of winning. One can imagine changes of distance of running to make an event more aesthetically pleasing. A 100 metres event can be extended to 120 metres to provide for a longer and presumably more elegant race. But as the aesthetic qualities are derivative and subsumed to the inherent arbitrary length of the race, this is no solution. One can only within certain limits 'improve' the aesthetic qualities. In general one would only substitute one arbitrary rule for another. Changes to please the mediatized representation are only superficial as the mediatized aesthetics is always secondary and even tertiary.

Second, there are games like soccer or hockey that do not exactly conform to this category. They represent an aesthetic of the events, but they are not clean and pure. Each game has is own aesthetic form, like the example of American

Football noted above. This form represents the particular rules and relations between the body, movement, time and space. Only within a certain level can games be 'improved' to make them more aesthetically pleasing. Of course a modification of certain rules can make a soccer match quicker, but these changes are only superficial. One can replace one form of arbitrariness with another. But the element of the arbitrary is inherent to sport.

Third, there are the types of sport where the aesthetics are part of the event, and subjected to a specific form of evaluation in conjunction with an evaluation of the technical performance: figure skating, sports gymnastics, dressage and synchronized swimming. These are also founded on the aesthetic of the event. The difference between dance as a sport and dance as a presentation of all possible kinds of meanings of movement is evident in the forms of sport where types of dancing are subjected to the codes of sport, like sports dance and ice dance. In these, dance forms are literally subjected to the code of sport and typically evaluated in accordance with the technical performance and the expressive quality. In order to conform to the standards of sport, these dance forms have to assume a stereotypic form, both as far as the body is concerned and as far as the aesthetic qualities are concerned. Body, dress and dance movements are modelled according to a stereotype of body, movement and expression.

Fourth, there are, of course, a number of gymnastic forms that are not subjected to the code of sport and cannot be subjected to the code of winning or losing. These will represent individual forms of gymnastic excellence. Essentially these forms define, each in its own way, a number of aesthetic features of the body and of the activities, often in a definitive, even stereotypical way. These gymnastic forms range from Swedish gymnastics to non-competitive aerobics. They are perhaps very similar to the choreography of dance, but they are still exercises subjected to rules and standards of correctness. What is at stake here is a self-defined standard of the exercises.

Aesthetics at the Olympic Games

The hard and direct disciplines, exemplified by track and field athletics, are still the core of the Olympic Games. Very little can be done to change their aesthetics to make them more pleasing. On the contrary, the arbitrary element and the functional aesthetics are inherent. One cannot aestheticize these forms of sport beyond the functional aesthetics already there.

Disciplines based on an evaluation of technical and aesthetic performance, both in winter and summer events, have grown in number while others are replaced according to the renewal of the events. They are there for a number of reasons. They appeal to new athletes and young audiences. The existence of the technical and artistic sports raises of number of interesting questions both in relation to the philosophy of sport in general and to Olympic and post-Olympic sports in particular. Gymnastics, even gymnastics as highly codified as Swedish Gymnastics at the beginning of the nineteenth century, were once part of the Olympic programme and competitions. But, properly speaking, this kind of gymnastics is not amenable to the codes of sport. Historically they were excluded and figured only as part of a gymnastic 'performance', and rightly so. This form of gymnastics, like a number of other gymnastic forms, cannot be sportified.

The sportified forms of technical and artistic exercises (such as synchronized swimming) have multiplied, but they do not conform to the Olympic motto, citius, altius, fortius. The Olympic motto fails to include a considerable number of growing sports on the Olympic programmes. And all the technical and aesthetic activities follow a different logic, namely a logic of evaluation.

Strictly speaking, only the 'direct and hard' sports conform to the Olympic motto – but not even these really do so. Logically these events require only the adherence to the code, winning or losing. The event is singular, as each event is singular, depending on an unlimited number of circumstances. The Olympic motto is, philosophically speaking, a misnomer. Faster, higher, stronger may conform to the striving of the individual sportsperson and to the ideology of the sports system but, interestingly enough, not to the logic of sport. The motto of citius, altius, fortius is simply wrong for logical reasons. The motto mixes different levels of analysis and is finally based on an erroneous philosophy of sport. The logic of sport is the individual event as a unique event that can, with certain qualifications, be compared to other events. The pragmatics of sport, of course, require that events be compared. But lots of events do not end up with a record. The record is meaningful only under severe restrictions. The logic of the individual event in competitive sport is winning or losing. This leads to a result. Some results, but not all, can be represented as a record. Some world records remain unchanged for years and some national records stand unchanged for decades. The record is only derivative to the individual event from at systemic point of view. Certain records can strictly speaking not be compared to earlier records, because the conditions are not comparable. So, even for the direct and hard events, the motto should be renamed 'Fast, high, strong, technically brilliant, aesthetically pleasing'.

The Philosophy of Olympism

One crucial problem of Olympism is that the philosophy is in total disorder. The actual practice is not in accordance with the foundationalist ideology. The extreme pragmatism is not in accordance with the ideology. In that sense Olympism can be compared with other modern and global institutions. In a sense all these contradictions are so pronounced that all the questions of Post-Olympism are relevant. Are the games changing their form from a moral occupation to an aesthetic show? Møller's deconstruction rightly challenges the platitudes and hypocrisies of the ethos of Olympism and top level sport. But Olympic sport is bound to be modernist and founded on an ethics of the activity and the body. The aesthetic aspects of sport can never be higher than the ethical aspects. If the results are derived from cheating and illegal modification of the body, the aesthetic aspects are low. The aesthetic aspects found in sports are founded on the ethics of the game, the event and the performance according to standards of excellence. This brings one to the crucial question: can the aestheticization of Olympic sport save Olympic sport? The answer is no. As mentioned above there are severe limits to the aestheticization of the direct and hard forms of sport, and a proliferation of the technical and aesthetic disciplines does not solve the problems. One cannot aestheticize the hard and direct forms. As mentioned above one cannot change the elements in the structure to make it aesthetically more pleasing. The element of arbitrariness is inherent.

What about the addition of the types of sport where an aesthetic element is crucial? As noted above, these sports have grown in number. But they have their own inherent problems. There are serious problems with the arbitrary judgement of referees. There is the element of alliances of referees, and the plain element of error.

Post-Olympism Reconsidered

Olympism cannot change into post-Olympism. The real problem of Olympism today is that it is in danger of becoming meaningless if it loses in foundationalist ethics. An aesthetization will not save Olympism because the aesthetics can never be higher than the ethics. The aesthetics of sport lie in the logic of the singular event and the ways events are concatenated into a series of events. The meaning in sport arises in the correspondence between the cultural significance, the institutional arrangements, the codes and rules of the sports event and the individual sportsperson's construction of meaning.

If there is a serious disjuncture between these levels of meaning, modern sport loses its meaning. It that case, the structure of modern sport deconstructs itself. Postmodern or deconstructive forms of analysis, like the form suggested by Møller, emphasizes the discrepancy between the official and moral rules of sport, and the actual practice and attitude of the individual sportsperson. But the postmodern perspective and deconstructive stance miss the point. Sport can be modern only in the sense of being founded on a number of universalist premises.

Whatever happens in other modern or postmodern institutions, sport cannot change into something postmodern. Now there is no perfect synchronization between different institutions in modern, high-modernity or postmodern society. Art as an institution can move in directions that sport cannot. Dance as a movement activity has no limitations of rules of presentation and representation, except certain rules of ethics. Movements in dance define their own rules, whereas the rules of sport are given as fixed and universal rules of execution and performance.

Postmodern activities are thinkable, if one imagines activities with codes different from the winning or losing code, with the context as preponderant, with organizational structures organized to totally different purposes than the promulgation of sport as a modern and universalist form of activity. Post-Olympism can, from that perspective, mean the following: the end of Olympism in its present form; that the content of the activities change beyond recognition; the total loss of meaning; and the acquisition of totally different meanings.

Conclusion

One can imagine all sorts of things. But Olympic sports are doomed to be modern. The postmodern perspective can highlight this situation. Aesthetization cannot save the Olympic movement or the Olympic Games. There are serious limitations to aesthetization because the aesthetics consist of the aesthetics of the event. This is simply because sport is not art. Sport can never transgress its essence. The price would be a loss of meaning. Recent examples of transgressions of the ethics of sport amply demonstrate this.

15

Laying Olympism to Rest

Kevin B. Wamsley

Introduction

In the early years of the twenty-first century, the multibillion dollar Olympic Games remain sufficiently intriguing to the sport entertainment connoisseur. In spite of, or perhaps due to, the numerous crises, real and imagined, over the past hundred or more years, the games have become entrenched in what might be referred to as the global imagination – a contrived cultural space positioned as the pinnacle of athletic competition. Further, the games have been carefully orchestrated to portray 'high' values, ethically and morally situated above such competitions as the World Cup of football and US professional sports. And, certainly, given this, and its long, firmly entrenched history of controlling and organizing international competition, the IOC will have considerable influence in the shaping of sport for the foreseeable future. *The* 'core value', *raison d'être*, the fundamental tenet historically invoked as the essence that separates the Olympics, elevates it beyond all other sport competitions, is 'Olympism'. From the writings of de Coubertin, to the Olympic *Charter*, to the popular promotional rhetoric of today, Olympism remains the marker of distinction, a deified space once shared only by the notion of amateurism. But to suggest that a common global understanding or one underlying philosophy is responsible for the popularity and resiliency of the games and, thus, the long-term sporting influence of the IOC, would be a tremendous overstatement. People are attracted to the games for a multitude of reasons well beyond the scope of any singular study. My purpose here, under the guise of post-Olympism, is to provide a social critique of the notion of Olympism and the idea of the Olympics with respect to some of the more prevalent and contentious historical and current issues, to argue that in many respects the two are incongruous and to show how, during the twentieth century, the nebulous concept of Olympism became the structural apologetic for the Olympic Games.

Officially, the IOC's *Charter* promotes the idea of 'Olympism' as the guiding philosophy of the games and the cultural infrastructure that supports them (IOC, 2003) and further a philosophy of life that promotes a balancing of body, will and mind. These Fundamental Principles listed in the *Olympic Charter* provide certain guidelines – the core of Olympic thinking; however, the inherent vacuity in this array of terms such as 'harmonious development' and 'preservation of human dignity' render them almost meaningless, or at the very least open widely to interpretation and application in a variety of contexts – in a sense, as a metaphoric empty flask to be filled by the next political, economic, educational opportunist.

Olympism is promoted at the basic level through mediated broadcasts of the Olympic Games; by the IOC through its Celebrate Humanity campaign (http://www.olympic.org/uk/passion/humanity/index_uk.asp); through 'Olympic education' in the form of Olympic academies; through its official publication *Olympic Review*; and through the various promoters of Olympic education in public elementary and secondary schools. Thousands of people who are Olympic supporters, critics, boosters and fanatics are familiar with the term. At times the mediated message can be deafening; indeed CNN International ran Celebrate Humanity advertisements thirty times per day for eight months for a total airing of 6,500 commercials focused around the Sydney Games of 2000 (IOC, 2003). The campaign was 'designed to communicate the core values of the Olympics and why the Olympic Games are special' (IOC, 2003). Its television commercials provided heart-warming stories about Olympic athletes, such as the US speed skater Dan Jansen, who had prevailed over various difficult, personal circumstances. Evidently, the campaign's producers poured over hundreds of hours of Olympic film footage to find stories 'which give the Olympic Games their true meaning' (IOC, 2003). Although the campaign targets Olympic consumers, according to the IOC, it is as much designed for commercial sponsors of the Olympics to 'provide a positive platform for the advertising sales effort' and to 'secure ownership of the Olympic broadcast in the minds of the viewing public by broadcasting the announcements on a regular basis' (IOC, 2003). Brand identification and association has been a significant IOC marketing strategy since the 1980s (Barney et al., 2002) and the 'human values' invoked through the organization of the Olympics and related programmes have been marshalled since de Coubertin's earliest musings to the present day. Arguably, it is through television broadcasting that the majority of Olympics consumers currently receive messages and meanings about the games. For many, this means at least a generation of exposure to various preconceived notions, and multiple interpretations, about the Olympics as positioned by the IOC, sports leaders, governments and by myriad broadcasters and sponsors, if not locally by coaches, teachers and parents. Consequently, millions of people who consume the games through some sort of spectatorship or interest, and most athletes, would be hard pressed to identify the particularities of meaning associated with Olympism, or at least an approved definition of this concept.[1]

As determined by IOC surveys, people identify the Olympics as something quite different from other high-profile international sport competitions (www.olympic.org). Capitalizing upon, and sustaining, this distinction of course provides the foundational impetus of the current social and economic trajectory of the games, and for both The Olympic Partners (TOP) sponsorship programme and multibillion dollar television revenues collection. The IOC has profited immensely by encouraging people to 'think Olympic' (Barney et al., 2002). At local and national levels, organizing committees of host nations also have extensive campaigns to 'educate' citizens, particularly children. The Beijing organizing committee (http://www.beijing-2008.org/eolympic/ztq/5–21/5–21.html), for example, announced that:

An extensive media and education campaign will be devoted to communicating the Olympic Ideals to the people and athletes of China, particularly through education programs on Olympism in schools, the hosting of international forums on 'the Olympic Movement and Human Civilization', and finally, the implementation of the Athletes Education Programs to encourage the athletes themselves, as national role models, to take an active interest in Olympism.

A handful of scholars promote the idea of Olympism through their work at conferences, through research and writing, in the classroom. Essentially, they suggest, the Olympic project is worthwhile, the Olympic ideal is something tangible, and there is hope that the Olympic Games can create a better world – a worthy intent no doubt. Without question, during the twentieth century, thousands of athletes, coaches, spectators, even academics have benefited directly from their experiences, travel and fame or association with the Olympic project. And the fact that nations spend millions of dollars to prepare and participate, now billions to host either Summer or Winter Games, in addition to the hours that television spectators spend watching, is reason enough to consider what place the Olympics might have in a globalizing culture. But a fundamental critical assessment of the supposed organizing principle of Olympism, by classes of intellectuals, the professoriate or otherwise, has not been forthcoming.

The immense popularity of the games aside, some critical scholars have successfully and thoroughly established that, historically, the Olympic Games are not what they are claimed to be. Some have gone as far as to argue that the Olympics have done harm to some segments of society (Brohm, 1978; Hoberman, 1992; Wamsley and Heine, 1996; Booth, 1999; Lenskyj, 2000). Yet, even with this growing body of literature and the mass exposure of extensive corruption and bribery within the IOC, bidding processes, and hosting (Booth, 1999), cities are still bidding with not inconsiderable frenzy, and the games continue to generate significant excitement for travelling sport tourists and television spectators alike. This is an important signal to those interested in the directions that sport might take in the twenty-first century.

Olympism

Obviously, the Olympic Games will not live or die by any academic evaluation of their real or imagined merits. But at least academic scholarship has been in part responsible for calling into question the issues of race, gender, and athlete health in Olympic matters. To a certain extent, it should also be credited with correcting some of the more pervasive mythologies reproduced for popular consumption in the press and for Olympic television broadcasts (Kidd, 1984; Young, 1984). Although seemingly insignificant, it is the Olympic stories, and selective histories, the nostalgic rhetoric that reaches the average citizen. But, as shown in the case of apartheid in South Africa, from time to time powerful social institutions can have an impact on broader social movements if the proper chords are struck within advocates who have vested political interests. But, generally, given the evidence of the twentieth century, it is suggested here that we cannot look to the IOC or the Olympic Games to initiate and sustain a human-centred peace movement, one of the fundamental tenets of Olympism. Indeed, the problem with Olympism *is* the Olympic Games. All things considered, the Olympic Games of the twentieth century are a paradox. The basic contradiction is that the games, in their contemporary incarnation, are the antithesis of the very Olympic ideals they ostensibly cherish. From this assertion emanate two suppositions for exploration: first, the Olympic Games do not need Olympism, they negate it, and would be much more honest, and therefore humanistic, without it. Second, that Olympism does not need the Olympic Games.

Post-Olympism

On pages 8–9 of the current print edition, the *Olympic Charter* invokes the practice of sport as a human right and one of the Fundamental Principles of the Olympic movement, but in the same section proceeds to define the limits of inclusion – and exclusion – defining who is permitted to belong, and who will be officially recognized by the IOC. This juxtaposition may appear to be too simple and too binary to be cogent – but during and since Pierre de Coubertin's time as founder of the Olympics, the IOC has gone to great lengths to position itself as the sole arbiter empowered to determine inclusion and exclusion, by attempting to ensure that other sport organizations and international bodies would be either absorbed or dismantled, positioning the IOC as, essentially, supreme lord over international sport. As early as 1930, and certainly implicitly evident long before this, de Coubertin (IOC, 1930, p. 14) in his 'Charter of Sports Reform' called for the outright 'suppression of all world-wide Games which are merely useless repetitions of the Olympic Games and which have an Ethnical, Political, or Religious character' defining the games as one of the solutions to combat what were identified as various abuses of sport. How the Olympic movement arrogated to itself the authority to distinguish between use and abuse, naturally remains un-stated. This exercise in power of course has been well documented in the literature (Espy, 1979; Guttmann, 1984; Senn, 1999) but persistently ignored by Olympic supporters. Minimally, however, at issue for advocates of the Olympics as any sort of humanistic endeavour *must* be the lineage of policy as it relates to practice.

In this respect, it is fair to conclude that Olympism, in structural terms, is an apologetic for past practice both immediate and distant. de Coubertin, himself, wrote in 1920 that 'neo-Olympism also means responding fully to the needs of the present age' (Müller, 2000, p. 477). de Coubertin's words are methodologically instructive. The promoters of amateur sport, the intellectual advocates of Olympism, were bourgeois – elites of various participating countries (Espy, 1979), without any organic connection to working-class, average people. In this sense, it follows that Olympism, indeed the Olympic Games, have always been organically disconnected from the lives of average people, excepting their immediate experiences with invocations of nationalism and national identity (Dyreson, 1998). The Olympism of de Coubertin's age brought nations together in competition, similar to the world's fairs of his era; the Olympism of his age sanctioned and reaffirmed that competitive sport was to be an enclave for the wealthy, an institution that provided a podium for the celebration of competitive, physical masculinities in contradistinction to other masculinities and to femaleness (Hargreaves, 1994; Wamsley and Schultz, 2000). Thus, the IOC's incorporation of women's athletics was a strategic response necessitated by political considerations, and not by an ethical principle employed towards the 'improvement of humankind', an ideal proposed in the *Charter*. Indeed, the outcome – that more women participated in a variety of athletic activities – was really brought about by the Cold War posturing of the Soviet Union, and by the resistance of athletic feminists to the Olympism of their era.

de Coubertin's rhetoric spoke of peace and brotherhood, no doubt an expression of his own view of humanity, but it can not be doubted either that his Olympism was loaded with negational antecedents, explicitly founded in the common desires of men of his age who were concerned about nationhood, readiness for war and cultural competitiveness. Prior to the inauguration of the modern Olympic idea, when de Coubertin spoke to the Literary Society at Athens in 1894 he said:

Of course, it is absolutely noble and beautiful to engage in manly exercises with the intention of defending one's country better and fulfilling one's duties as a citizen better. But there is another thing that is more perfectly human, if one dare speak in such terms. That is to seek in athletics a marvel[l]ous solidification of the human machine, a delicate balance of mind and body, the joy of a fresher and more intense life, the harmony of the faculties, calm and happy strength. Athletics can best serve the interests of a nation and enrich its destiny when viewed in this light. (Müller, 2000, p. 534)

In this sense, de Coubertin's vision was inherently limited by the logic of the argument it sought to express, and this became readily evident. Of course, there are numerous, often cited examples of the tensions between peace and nationalism (Matthews, 1980). Case in point, de Coubertin's organization was deeply politicized, and hence the scars that the two world wars inflicted on de Coubertin and his successors made it impossible for them to live up to the founder's lofty ideals – national political expediencies overwhelmed the ideals of international brotherhood: IOC political policies prevented the defeated nations of war from participating at the Olympics. Hitler's Olympism, perhaps, is more instructive. Hitler's vision for the future Olympics was to host them in Germany in perpetuity within the boundaries of a newly constructed Nuremberg, his planned utopian city (Mandell, 1971; Paton and Barney, 2002). His visions for humankind were those of a despot and fanatic but, arguably, his views on the essence of race were widely held, in principle, by many in Europe and North America and the Berlin Olympics became the venue to posit these social distinctions. Certainly the American experience of slavery and its treatment of Aboriginals was just as brutal; but even now, decades after the Holocaust, desegregation and anti-apartheid measures, colonized Aboriginals and many other groups around the world still remain subject to commonly held views and practices that invoke race as a social distinction, and Olympic ceremonies organizers, as recently as Sydney in 2000 and Salt Lake City in 2002, still sought to trade on these demarcations and colonial narratives (Wamsley and Heine, 1996; Forsyth, 2002; Watts, 2002). That Hitler's values could be positioned in the same cultural space as de Coubertin's is a state that Olympics supporters have yet to extricate for the idea of Olympism.

The root of many difficulties for modern sport, including the dehumanizing aspects of competition, has been the notion of progress as an ideal that may be most visibly expressed through the quantification of human performance. It has been well documented that Cold War era science wielded through the politics of competitiveness has created numerous crises for athlete health and well-being (Hoberman, 1992). The quantitative (or time-distance-weight) sports are more readily associated with the performance principles of the Olympic motto, *Citius, Altius, Fortius*. However, throughout the twentieth century, the qualitative sports federations, too, in events such as gymnastics and figure skating, have responded in kind to the lusts and lure of progress endemic in the games by increasing risk and difficulty in routines. Single somersaults have turned to doubles, then triples; routines are more complicated and dangerous. The results of this process have been horrifying (Ryan, 1995). Progressive performance standards in these sports, predicting strength to body weight ratio in association with age, have led to the emergence of the child athlete (Donnelly, 1997, 2000), one who trains several hours per day from a very young age, one who may suffer from eating disorders or crises in body concept (Ryan, 1995).

Not oblivious to the organizing principle of performance, de Coubertin himself recognized that the success of the Olympics, even the *raison d'être* of the games, was bound to the breaking of records as an index of human progress through physical improvement. de Coubertin admonished in his 'Charter of Sports Reform' that the Olympics must survive at the expense of other festivals, such as the Workers' Olympics and the Women's Olympics. This declaration, he recalled, demonstrated his 'desire to clear the ground around the Games in order to give them greater emphasis, greater prominence, and greater grandeur' (Müller, 2000, p. 749). Responding to the 'non-sportsmen' who criticized the notion of excess in competition, de Coubertin's citation of the Charter (p. 749) was as telling as it was ominous:

> For one hundred to go in for physical education, fifty have to go in for sport. For fifty to go in for sport, twenty will have to specialize. For twenty to specialize, five will have to show themselves capable of astounding 'feats'. It is impossible to get away from this basic truth. Everything is closely bound up with everything else. Thus the athletic record stands inescapably at the very summit of the sports edifice, like the 'external axiom' referred to by the French writer Taine concerning Newton's law. You cannot hope to remove it without destroying everything else. Resign yourselves, therefore, you partisans of the unrealistic Utopia of moderation – which is quite against nature – seeing us continue to put into practice the motto Father Didon used to quote his students, and which has since become that of Olympism.

Coubertin's Olympism as it developed from the 1930s onward, and after his death in 1937, was about human performance as physical performance – *Citius, Altius, Dortius* – as much as anything else. Ideas of common chivalry and decorum were supposed to gentrify this creed, of course. Indeed, the mode of organization, the forum, the display, and ultimately the medium that expressed this constellation of the ideologies of social evolutionism, embodied in a motto that made perfect sense to its period observers, has delivered the Olympic Games through the decades to its present state, even though the broader significations have changed. Consequently, Olympism became the apologetic for the short-comings of the games, the twentieth-century materialization of Didon's motto, and for the multifarious social distinctions and divisions manifested through sport, as it had been for the demarcations of social class, race and gender of the previous era. Olympism became the endemic principle by which physical, social, symbolic, cultural, economic and academic capital (Bourdieu, 1986) was traded within the field of the Olympic Games.

During the period of the 1980s, when Reaganomics and Thatcherism exacted significant changes to our societies, people spoke of the dream of wealth; economic and political policies assured the interests of elites; and capitalists were held up as successful champions. The theory was that wealth would trickle down to the lower levels of society. These shifts were evident in the Olympics, as IOC president Juan Antonio Samaranch reaffirmed. Our own sport policies suggested that if we followed this model for sport, particularly Olympic sport, then more people would participate. The Olympics of the 1980s certainly brought more people to their television sets (Barney et al., 2002) but perhaps not to the athletic fields. Now the language has shifted from trickle down economics to globalization.

The often-cited Olympic motto operates in perfect synergy with the conditions currently being established throughout the world engendering the flow of global capital. These conditions favour the wealthy and powerful nations, couched in the rhetoric of 'free markets' – the freedom to accumulate wealth and power, to mobilize and exploit labour for profit (Greider, 1998). The Olympic Games have been utilized strategically to promote such values since the waning years of the Cold War era and, obviously, the alignments struck between global corporate sponsors and the IOC (Barney et al., 2002) are manifestations of deliberate strategies to trade on such ideologies. The corporate athlete of the twenty-first century is not unlike the imperialist muscular Christian of the late nineteenth and early twentieth centuries. At the levels of nation, sports leader, individual, there was and is a tremendous impetus to be a significant part of the order of the day – some seek to organize, to control, to lead, others to participate, to win, to reap the social and economic rewards (Dyreson, 1998). The problem with Olympism is that similar to the previous era, and resembling some notions about globalization, it promises that being human is the only qualification that one needs to have in order to share in the rewards provided by the so-called Olympic movement. That implicit claim is completely fraudulent. Even de Coubertin recognized that the athletic exercises of his era would not change inequalities in social conditions. His ideas about egalitarianism through sport were primarily related to the supposed due consideration that individuals would receive on the playing field – a social levelling, but only through the context of participating in sport at any particular moment (Müller, 2000, p. 214). Given problems with race, nationalism and politics at all levels, however, indeed the evidence of the past hundred or more years, de Coubertin's assumptions hold no basis in Olympic fact.

Even with such difficulties aside, many simple but interminable problems remain for Olympism: who gets to the field in the first place? When, in the twentieth century, did competitive sport at its highest levels balance the 'whole qualities of body, will and mind' (IOC, 2003)? How, under the supreme authority of the IOC can sport be organized and managed by independent sport organizations? How can sport possibly be a human right when the bidding process alone demands a minimum of US$40 million and holding the games requires billions of dollars in infrastructure and the building of many sports facilities not even remotely accessible or relatively useful to the average citizen? Of course, these are only a handful of many basic problems with respect to claims about Olympism. A more significant issue perhaps for future research is the current place of the Olympics in the political and economic ordering of the world. It is interesting to note that corporations have long used the language of sport to canonize their competitive champions and business processes; it is perhaps just as significant that the latest crisis in the US – the long, hard, fall of major corporate executives caught cheating (Enron, for example) has not been described in Olympic or sporting terms, in what would be a rather appropriate symbolic equivalent, related to the fall of the Olympic athlete to drugs and the IOC itself to scandal (Booth, 1999).

The IOC is essentially a European-based organization, largely dependent on US capital, and at least dependent upon AustralAsian, African, and South American participation and endorsement. Frankly, George Orwell (1949) was not too far off the mark in his novel, *Nineteen Eighty-four*, not an insignificant year for the new corporate era of the Olympic Games (Barney et al., 2002). Olympism was the *doublespeak* of late-twentieth-century sport, signatory to its colonization process and the Olympic cultural boundaries thus delineated. It was more than just a guiding philosophy or set of values to direct ethical aspirations; olympism was and is used explicitly as a marketing tool, one that influences the flow of billions of dollars in capital and serves a legitimizing function for the organization of human relations through an historically specific version of worldwide competitive sport. 'Coca-colonization' is the term often invoked (Bairner, 2001) to describe processes of globalization, ones that homogenize economic relations and often create multiple dislocations between cultural traditions and modernized forms of consumption. Similar to notions about the impact of globalization, it has been argued that the Olympics are a form of global sport monoculture (Donnelly, 1996), delimiting how people come to understand sport, how they participate in it, actively rendering alternative sport forms irrelevant or even unthinkable. However, in response to claims about globalization's homogenizing economic and political forces, Bairner (2001) argues that events such as the Olympic Games can promote resilience in national identities and ethnic nationalisms, indeed resistance to broader trends in globalization. The games still pit nation versus nation. But, resiliency of distinct forms of nationalism and identity politics aside, the Olympics, the IOC more specifically, structure the boundaries of organization, participation and spectatorship. People still find ways to celebrate nationalism and local identities – to engage the games uniquely; but the Olympics remain a venue over which they have little control or creative influence.

Entangled between pillars both uncritically promotional and ostensibly educational, Olympism does not even question the *idea* of the Olympics as a point of departure. And remarkably, Pierre de Coubertin is still invoked as the spiritual leader of Olympism in a time so different and so distant. In de Coubertin's name, the Samaranch era has produced unprecedented funds for spreading the Olympic word to every corner of the world. His final act of sporting imperialism as IOC president, after successfully converting the political currency of the Cold War Olympics into the economic currency of the multibillion dollar post-1984 era of commodification, was the declaration of Beijing, capital of the world's most populous country, to host in 2008. What need now for Olympism?

Conclusion

In spite of its contradictory tendencies and its failure to achieve the goals of international peace that de Coubertin envisioned for modern sport, Olympism will not be laid to rest for the moment. There are more missionaries involved and there is more money invested in promoting Olympism, whatever that might mean, than ever before. The Olympics provide a venue to celebrate competitiveness, to place the strong on the podium as the winner of a fair contest – the obfuscatory signature of global capitalism. Of course, the physical achievements of the individual and the team are paramount and the defeat of others is a critical part of the spoils. There are tremendous symbolic, cultural and economic rewards available for a limited population that benefits directly from the games. Elite sport competition is intense, cut-throat, and sometimes comes at many costs – there is really nothing peaceful about it. But people love it, participants, coaches, parents and spectators alike, now more than ever.

There are some basic reasons why the Olympics of the twenty-first century will not achieve what twentieth-century Olympism claimed as its ends. For one, there is no responsibility attached to the process. The twentieth century has shown us that anyone can promote Olympism or determine what it is for that matter, from the good and the ethical to the Hitleresque. The kinds of ideals that Olympism lays claim to cannot be engaged at the level of spectacle, performance, ceremony – or at the level of the national, the religious, the legal. Peace, equality and human rights are far too important to be relegated to the abstract, or the institutional, and must be inherently embraced at the level of the personal. All societies are rife with issues and problems related to race, class and gender. Racism does not disappear with desegregation and gender equity programs do not work without engagement at the level of the individual. And this is to say nothing about cultural traditions that have been completely marginalized or absorbed by the Olympic process, another rather deep contradiction yet to be resolved. Standing shoulder to shoulder in a stadium is exciting, perhaps uplifting for some, but has nothing to do with addressing social issues and other people, directly and it says nothing about the problems endemic to sport itself. But rather than to consider the sportive process reflectively and proactively, the IOC has typically reacted to the visible symptoms of any crisis by responding on the basis of political expediency; and, further, it has been much more efficient to blame the participants for endemic problems such as doping. This in spite of one of the consistent, most presumptuous aspects of the Olympics – the claim to know, to represent, even to adjudicate the values and hopes of athletes. It is no oversight that the IOC refuses to contemplate publicly why elite athletes really participate in the Olympics.

Unless the *idea* of the Olympics is systematically and regularly questioned, then charters, lists of ethics and organizations like the recently established World Anti-Doping Agency (WADA) remain only significant cogs in the cultural apologetic for the games. It is important, in the long term, that critical scholars continue to unravel the social processes inherent in this vast cultural phenomenon, how people engage them, how the Olympics relate to the broader processes of globalization, how bodies are bought and sold and what that means.

At one level, at the present time, the contradictions in twentieth-century Olympism cannot be resolved. At another, the Olympic Games do not require further promotion of Olympism. We are grossly uncomfortable with the contradictions seemingly inherent in sport. We continue to apologize for sport, unable to concede that we enjoy forms of culture that are often not purely ethical or honourable, and even harmful. Spectators and fans are quite content to flock to the current product with or without WADA. Athletes pursue gold medals willingly at the expense of their own bodies. Tearing away the layers of hyperbole, the glorious rhetoric and grandiose ethical proclamations, revealing the Olympics as the sport spectacle they are just might make the games of the twenty-first century a bit more honest. Make no mistake, there is and always will be hope for peace and understanding in the world. Such things are worth striving for but not through something as abstract as the Olympic Games; indeed, if we are *really* prepared or motivated to take on these challenges and find peace, then we would best start with an honest engagement with the people around us. As long as we believe the social Darwinist notion that competition is natural or right and good, and that it brings out the best in the human spirit, then we will not have peace and equality. When people are prepared to engage one another without coveting, without trying to get ahead materially, socially, culturally, nationally, intellectually, physically, then we will have honestly addressed the idea of competition. Indeed, the best indication on the world's cultural landscape that we are prepared for peace and equality, that Olympism and these often quoted values have finally triumphed, is that the Olympic Games will be gone.

Notes

Chapter 2

1. Using the cues from this case, my next monograph dealt with continuity in the German sport system (Krüger, 1975b).
2. For the propaganda circulars see Bohrmann (1993). Most of the *Circulars* for the 1936 Games are in vol. 4; for a general view see Bernett (1985).
3. The Japanese later asked Hitler about his position towards the Japanese people and were reassured that they were not treated like Jews in Germany; see Nakamura (2003).
4. Goebbels kept himself well informed about the discussions at the AAU conference to debate US participation in the Olympic Games (Fröhlich, 1987). Brundage was later recompensed by a huge sum of money as his company received the order to build the new German Embassy in Washington, DC.
5. Baillet-Latour in a letter to Ritter von Halt (26 May 1933), *IOC Archives Lausanne*, 'Jeux Olympique de 1936 et la question juive' (quoted hereafter as *IOCA*). Germany kept that option open until the very end. However, see Krüger (1994).
6. Baillet-Latour in a letter to the German IOC member, Count von Mecklenburg (21 May 1933), *IOCA*.
7. Edström in a letter to Baillet-Latour (8 May 1933), *IOCA*.
8. There has been a long tradition of national Olympics in Germany that was particularly strong in the *Turner* movement but also nationally during the time when Germany was excluded from the Games (1920–8), see Krüger (1994).
9. There are two records from this interview, one by the interpreter (Schmidt) *Political Archives of the German Foreign Minister*, P.A. Olympiade 36, A.Z. 86–26, vol. 1 and one by Hitler's personal advisor (Meissner), *Federal Archives, Koblenz*, B.A. R. 43, II/729 (Reichskanzlei/betr. Olympiade 1936).
10. For the difficult situation of the IOC president, Count Henri de Baillet-Latour, see Lennartz (1994).
11. Hand-written letter by Sherrill to Bailley-Latour (30 August 1935), *IOCA*.
12. On the whole, Germans knew beforehand what was to be in the foreign press as it provided the *Mercedes Schreibdienst*, a free speedy typewriter service to foreign journalists: 'You dictate – we typewrite, without expenses'; see Organisationskomitee (1936, p. 164).
13. Also introduced for the first time 1920, see Coubertin (1920).

Chapter 3

1. In my list of the great nineteenth- and twentieth-century 'isms', I did not address nationalism. This is because it is not clear to me that we are about to enter a new period of post-nationalism; I am not sure that nationalist ideology is undergoing any great transformation in the twenty-first century.
2. See IOC website, Olympic.org, 2001 http://www.olympic.org, accessed 2001.

Chapter 5

1. Todorov defines the three traits of humanism thus:

    > the belonging of all men [sic], and of them alone, to the same biological species; their sociability, that is, not only their mutual dependence for purposes of nourishment and reproduction, but also for becoming conscious and speaking beings; finally their relative indeterminacy, therefore the possibility of engaging in different choices constitutive of their collective or biographical history, choices responsible for their cultural or individual identity. (Todorov, 2002, pp. 231–2)

2. de Coubertin's 'humanism' paralleled his support of paternal colonialism, with sport being a mechanism through which colonial administrators could both control, and over a period of time, educate the colonized into European civility. In 1902, de Coubertin noted that colonies 'are like children: it is relatively easy to bring them into the world; the difficult thing is to raise them properly. They do not grow up by themselves, but need to be taken care of, coddled, and pampered by the mother country; they need constant attention to incubate them, to understand their needs, to forsee their disappointments, to calm their fears' (cited in Hoberman, 1986, p. 39).
3. See Jean-Marie Brohm (1978) for a powerful if polemical critique of the 'Olympic opiate'.
4. David Goldberg (2002) makes an important analytical distinction between those forms of Enlightenment racial thought that were 'naturalist' and those that might be described as 'historicist'. In the former, exemplified in the writings of Hobbes, blacks were deemed to be inherently incapable of social, moral and cultural development and thus could never achieve full humanity. The latter (nominally liberal) tradition, found in the writings of Locke among others, believed blacks to be at a lower stage of maturation, thus holding out the possibility at least that black subjects might one day achieve white European levels of humanistic development, given appropriate colonial administration and education.
5. Slavery clearly posed a problem for Enlightenment thinkers, especially those such as Hegel who were concerned with the nature of human freedom. It was the assumed restricted maturation of blacks that allowed for a (partial) condonment of slavery

even when it contradicted central principles of human emancipation. For example see Hegel's comments that, 'Slavery is unjust in and for itself, for the essence of man is freedom; but he must first become mature before he can be free. Thus, it is more fitting and correct that slavery should be eliminated gradually than it should be done away with at once' (1975 [1830], p. 184).

6. On the construction of the 'African body' as an object of socio-medical discourse see Alexander Butchart's (1998) *The Anatomy of Power: European Constructions of the African Body*. See also John Bale's (2002) *Imagined Olympians: Body Culture and Colonial Imagination in Rwanda*.

7. The stereotype of the naturally athletic black body is of course an 'impossible object'. Hence, despite being unable to find the non-existent 'running/jumping gene(s)' that are believed (hoped?) to be lurking within the skins of Kenyan long distance runners, or 'West African descendant' sprinters, sport scientists still yearn for the magic piece of genetic machinery, always just around the corner, that will one day 'prove' their fantasies of biological racial difference.

8. See also Hardt and Negri (2000), when they note:

    > Only through opposition to the colonized does the metropolitan subject really become itself. What first appeared as a simple logic of exclusion, then, turns out to be a negative dialectic of recognition. The colonizer does produce the colonized as negation, but, through a dialectical twist, that negative colonized identity is negated in turn to found the positive colonizer Self . . . The gilded monuments not only of European cities but also of modern European thought itself are founded on the intimate dialectal struggle with its Others. (Hardt and Negri, 2000, p. 128)

9. Homi Bhabha, in locating ambivalence as central to the processes of stereotyping within colonial discourse, suggests 'in a very preliminary way . . . the stereotype is a complex, ambivalent, contradictory mode of representation, as anxious as it is assertive' (1994, p. 70).

10. I say *neo*-Kantian as Kant himself did not argue for the abolition of national republics. As Benhabib (2002) notes:

    > Kant envisaged a world in which all members of the human race would become participants in a civil order and enter into a condition of 'lawful association' with one another. Kant's cosmopolitan citizens still need their individual republics to be citizens at all. This is why he is so careful to distinguish a 'world government' from a 'world federation'. A world government, he argues, would be a 'soulless despotism', whereas a world federation would still permit the exercise of citizenship within bounded communities. (Benhabib, 2002, p. 183)

11. Interestingly, de Coubertin, as with most late-nineteenth-century European elites, was sceptical of cosmopolitanism preferring instead the 'true internationalism' within which nation-states and national allegiances are seen as central and even essential facets of human identity: 'Properly speaking, cosmopolitanism suits those people who have no country, while internationalism should be the state of mind of those who love their country above all, who seek to draw to it the friendship of foreigners by professing for the countries of those foreigners an intelligent and enlightened sympathy' (de Coubertin, 1898, pp. 429–34).

12. Indeed given the recent volume of work on cosmopolitanism there is a surprising lack of *empirical* research into its effects in changing people's actually existing identities and identifications towards a sense of the global cosmopolitan. For a rare example of such work see Szerszynski and Urry (2002).

13. Moussambani actually took 1 minute 52.72 seconds to complete the race. Most top level swimmers can complete the 100 metres in under 50 seconds.

14. Moussambani certainly made the most of his time in the Olympic limelight. He advertised various products, often in a self-mocking way, appeared on chat shows and a month after his Olympic 'success' found himself presenting, rather bizarrely, the National Television Awards for 'Britain's most popular entertainment presenter' at the Royal Albert Hall in London. For postmodern conspiracy theorists the award presented by the Olympic swimming star went to Michael Barrymore. Moussambani of course has his own website – http://moussambani.com.

15. Guttmann (2002, p. 192) incorrectly suggests that Kenteris was the first Greek winner since Louis but this overlooks Voula Patoulidou's victory in the women's 100 metres hurdles at the Barcelona Olympics in 1992 (Williams, 2000, p. 2).

16. Kenteris subsequently won the World (2001) and European (2002) Championships at 200 metres.

17. See for example the papers given at the First International Conference on Sports and Human Rights, 1–3 September 1999, Sydney, Australia. 'Sport and Human Rights' was also the theme of the 2003 North American Society for the Sociology of Sport annual conference, October 29–November 1, Montreal, Canada.

Chapter 6

1. Here, the emphasis of italics is pure literary affectation. The topic of *life history* and the idea of *fleshing-out* knowledge about sport and the body reflect the primary humanistic thrust that I am currently attempting to incorporate into my research and writing. The idea of *fleshing out* knowledge related to the body is a literal and figurative play on words. By italicizing the words, I hope to evoke reflection on the literal and figurative potential of the words, themselves, and the context in which I use them.

2. The idea of finding truth or new types of knowledge in the space between ideology and practice is evident in the work of a number of scholars. Certainly, Henri Lefebvre and Michel de Certeau have presented extensive meditations on the value of investigating the way people operate within the structure of everyday life. In a sporting and Olympic context (see MacAloon, 1995, pp. 32–53).

3. When Calgary's Oval was constructed, it was the first fully enclosed indoor speed skating facility in North America. When athletes competed at the XV Olympic Winter Games, it marked the first time this competition was held indoors. Until

2002, Calgary's Olympic Oval was celebrated for having the world's fastest ice. In 1998, the International Skating Union allowed new skate technology to be introduced. Skaters began using blades that articulated at the ball of the foot. The back of the blade was free and allowed for extra extension. This effectively lengthened the push phase of the skaters' movement. With this new type of skate, world records began to fall at every major competition at the Oval. This tradition continued until the Olympic Winter Games in 2002. In Salt Lake City, the combination of more sophisticated architecture and Utah's higher altitude brought an end (perhaps only temporarily) to Calgary's claim to the world's fastest ice.

4. While the Oval in Salt Lake City has taken most of the world records from Calgary's Oval, many insiders of the sport speculate about the longevity of the Salt Lake City Oval and its place in the world of international speed skating competitions and training. Certainly, two impressive indoor speed skating facilities constructed specifically for Olympic Winter Games have not had sustained or lasting impacts on the host communities. The Viking ship built for the 1994 Lillehammer Games and the M-Wave built for the 1998 Nagano Games have been referred to as beautiful white elephants.

5. 'Olympic-style' is a necessary qualifier when describing the sport of speed skating. At the Olympic Games, men compete in the 500m, 1,000m, 1,500m, 5,000m and 10,000m races. Women compete in 500m, 1,000m, 1500m, 3,000m and 5,000m races. Other forms of competition on speed skates do exist and are very popular. For example, canal racing remains a live cultural tradition in the Netherlands. There are also mass-start speed skating competitions. Both of these types of racing incorporate a number of different environmental and human factors that are less controllable. With 'Olympic-style' speed skating, athletes compete against the clock. While athletes skate two at a time, their bodies are separated by rules, judges and physical barriers.

6. Average recreational racers can achieve speeds of approximately 40 km/hour in the corners. Elite international skaters can reach speeds greater than 60 km/hour. The radius of the corner ranges from 25 metres on the inner lane to 29 metres on the outer lane.

7. The Olympic Oval Web Page.

8. Although the Oval administration uses the letters **A**, **B** and **C** to formally identify groups of skaters, use of the letter **P** is my own innovation. I have never heard the Oval staff refer to **P**s.

9. The idea of describing the social and cultural organization of people at the Oval as an imagined community was directly inspired by John Bale's recent investigation and analysis of colonial representations of Rwandan high jumpers. Bale discussed the European's need to make sense of these jumping performances by drawing on their own discourse of Olympism and modern competitive sport. The title of his book, *Imagined Olympians*, has provided me with a linguistic trigger that is especially helpful in terms of describing the complexities of identity and shared identity (see Bale, 2002).

Chapter 7

1. Although the Pacific region, often referred to as Oceania, is separate from Asia, the two regions share some common interests. Both share roughly similar time zones and their rise in prominence in the Olympic Games represents an alternative to European and North American dominance. There are also many synergies between the Sydney 2000 and the Beijing 2008 Olympic Games.

Chapter 9

1. This section on the Sydney opening ceremony is extracted from Tomlinson (2000a), elements of which are also included in Tomlinson (2004b).
2. This section draws upon an account published in the newsletter of the Australia and New Zealand Leisure Studies Association (see Tomlinson 2002).

Chapter 10

1. This is the 20 February 2001 stated intent of the listserv Forum for the Analysis of Sport Technology (FAST). See http://www.dmu.ac.uk/In/fast.
2.

> The viewer/subject in the CUBE enjoys a completely untethered visualization experience. A twenty-four sensor wireless Ascension MotionStar tracking system transmits 6DOF information from the subject. Active stereo is viewed through a Stereographics LCD shutter-glass system. Spatialized sonification is afforded each subject through head-related transfer function-generated sound, based on information from the Motionstar system. Additional data gathering/presenting devices, such as hand-held wireless computers, wireless microphones and wireless cameras can be incorporated in an individual experimenter's research. (http://elim.isl.uiuc.edu/; http://elim.isl.uiuc.edu/Labs/room_b650.htm)

3. See Walter Benjamin (1969b [1936]) for an earlier significant examination of questioning how technology impinges upon audience perception, aestheticisization and production of life activities.
4. A succinct definition of the coming community comes from Henry Chang:

> The basis of the coming community, the singular being, is *whatever being*—not in the sense of 'I don't care who you are,' but rather, 'I care for you *such as you are*.' As *such* you are freed from belonging either to the emptiness of the universal or to the ineffability of the individual . . . human identity is not mediated by its belonging to some set or class (being old, being American, being

gay). Nor does it consist in the simple negation of the 'negative community' . . . Such a singularly exposed being wants to belong—which is to say, it belongs to want, or for lack of a less semantically burdened and empty word, to love: The singularity exposed as such is whatever you *want* that is lovable . . . In [this] work, philosophy becomes once again, perhaps, a kind of homesickness, a longing to belong. To a permanent disorientation. To oscillation. To whatever. (Chang, 1994, pp. 48–50, 60, italics in original)

5. Interestingly, one of James's (1963) chapters contemplates Tolstoy's famous question, 'What is art?' in light of sport performance.

Chapter 11

1. On sportive nationalism as a psychological phenomenon, see Hoberman (1993).
2. On the persistence of (West) German sportive nationalism, see Hoberman (2000).
3. The first *gaijin* (foreign) sailing coaches hired to assist the Japanese with their Americas Cup project arrived in March 1987, or five years before the Nippon Challenge tried (and failed) to match the world's best 12-metre sailing teams: see Smith (1992).

Chapter 12

1. For the fundamental principles and the Olympic Charter, see http://www.olympic. org/uk/organisation/index_uk.asp
2. For information on viewer ratings, see http://www.olympic.org/uk/organisation/ facts/boradcasting/index_uk.asp
3. More precisely, strength refers to the force exerted by muscle groups during a single maximal muscular contraction; endurance refers to local muscular endurance and cardiovascular endurance; flexibility refers to suppleness of movement at a joint; speed refers to reaction time, frequency of movement per time unit, and speed of travel over a given distance; and coordination refers to the ability to rationally solve movement tasks which again in part depends upon coordination of the nervous processes in the central nervous system (Bompa, 1994, pp. 259ff.).
4. Sensation refers to experiences based on vision, hearing, smell, taste and various body senses; motivation refers to factors that energize behaviour and gives it direction and goals; emotion refers to strong mental states, usually involving high energy and excitement, that give rise to feelings and passions such as fear, anger and joy; cognition refers to perception, memory, reasoning, decision-making and

problem-solving; and personality characteristics refers to distinctive patterns of thought, emotions and behaviour that define an individual's interaction with the environment such as extraversion. The definitions are based on the glossary in Atkinson et al. (1996).

5. The distinction between basic abilities and skills is by no means unproblematic, and the role of genetic predispositions in their development is not clear. For example, rather little is known about the genetics of motor development (Bouchard, 1997, pp. 302–3). Are we genetically disposed to develop certain general skills such as basic locomotor movement patterns (walking, skipping, running), non-locomotor patterns (pushing, stretching, balancing) and manipulative patterns (kicking, throwing, striking)? Or should we view all skills as pure products of the environment in the sense that we must be stimulated in a particular way in order for them to be learned and developed? Is the erect gait really something all normal people learn without special stimulation? The discovery of children raised among animals (for instance wolves) indicates the opposite; these children, we are told, walk as if they had four legs. In this context, however, the simplistic ability and skill distinction can be justified as it helps define specialization and to formulate the vulnerability thesis.

Chapter 15

1. There has been concern raised that Olympic athletes do not know what Olympism is; consequently, the organizing committee for Athens 2004 is constructing interactive technical venues in the Olympic village to educate athletes on the values of Olympism (information provided by organizing committee members Kostas Georgiadis and Nikos Theodorou during discussions at the sessions of the International Olympic Academy, 2002).

Bibliography

ACLU (American Civil Liberties Union) (2001), ACLU of Utah sues Olympic Officials, www.aclu.org./news, 12 February.

Agamben, G. (1994), *The Coming Community*, trans. M. Hardt, Minneapolis: University of Minnesota Press.

Alkemeyer, T. (1996), *Körper, Kult und Politik. Von der 'Muskelreligion' Pierre de Coubertins zur Inszenierung von Macht in den Olympischen Spielen 1936*, Frankfurt/M.: Campus.

Allison, L. (2000), 'Event Comes Poor Second to the Myth', *Financial Times*, 15 September.

Anderson, A. (1998), 'Cosmopolitanism, Universalism, and the Divided Legacies of Modernity', in P. Cheah and B. Robbins (eds), *Cosmopolitics: Thinking and Feeling Beyond the Nation*, Minneapolis: University of Minnesota Press.

Anderson, B. (1983) *Imagined Communities: Reflections on the Origin and Spread of Nationalism*, New York: Verso.

Anderson, P. (1998), *The Origins of Postmodernity*, London: Verso.

Angell, N. (1910), *The Great Illusion: A Study of the Relation of Military Power to National Advantage*, London: Heinemann.

Anon. (1992), 'Olympic Games,' *The New Encyclopedia Britannica*, Chicago, 198.

—— (1997), 'Fetish', *Wired*, November, 80.

—— (2000), 'Stated intent of the listserv Forum for the Analysis of Sport Technology (FAST)', 20 February, see http://www.dmu.ac.uk/In/fast

—— (2001a), 'Hypothesis: Science Gap. Cause: Japan's Ways', *New York Times*, 7 August, 2.

—— (2001b), 'Best på livskvalitet', *Nytt fra Norge* (Oslo), 10 July.

—— (2001c), 'Konstanz im Wettbewerb der Nationen', *Neue Zürcher Zeitung*, 18 October.

—— (2001d), 'Seattle Entrepreneur more than a Backer of America's Cup Team', *New York Times*, 14 January.

—— (2002a), 'Mbeki Attacks West's "Survival of the Fittest"', *Times Online*, 27 August.

—— (2002b), 'Leveling the Playing Field', *International Herald Tribune*, 17 June.

—— (2002c) 'Playground of Billionaires', *New York Times*, 6 October.

—— (2002d), 'Skysurfing with Troy and Vic', http://viruszine.com/virus2/skysurfers/skysurfers.html

—— (2002e), 'SlamBall is Latest X Game', *New York Times News Service*, 23 August, http://extratv.warnerbros.com/dailynews/extra/04_02/04_23d.html

—— (2002f), 'Valgkamp i Yokohama', *Ekstra Bladet* (Copenhagen), 28 June.

—— (2003a) *News of Norway*, 12.

—— (2003b), 'Swiss Chairman Questions Need for a National Airline', *Neue Zürcher Zeitung*, 20 April.

Anti-Olympic People's Network (1999), Letter to IOC President Samaranch, 12 March.

Anti-Olympics Committee in Turin (2001), 'Shut Down the Olympics? Yes!' Posting to Utah Indymedia, 10 September, utah.indymedia.org

Archibugi, D. and Held, D. (eds) (1995), *Cosmopolitan Democracy: An Agenda for a New World Order*, Cambridge: Polity.

Arnaud, P. and Riordan, J. (eds) (1998) *Sport and International Politics: The Impact of Fascism and Communism on Sport*, London: Spon.

Asian Coalition for Housing Rights (1989), 'Evictions in Seoul, South Korea', *Environment and Urbanization*, 1: 89–94.

Atkinson, M. and Young, K. (2002), 'Terror Games: Media Treatment of Security Issues at the 2002 Winter Olympic Games', *Olympika*, 11: 53–78.

Atkinson, R. L., Atkinson, R. C., Smith, E. E., Bem, D. J. and Hoeksema, S. N. (1996), *Hilgard's Introduction to Psychology*, 12th edn, New York: Harcourt Brace.

Auf der Maur, N. (1976), *The Billion-Dollar Games*, Toronto: Lorimer.

Augustus-Ndu, O. (1994), 'Trouble, Confusion, Indecision', *African Concord* (Lagos), 28 March, 30.

AXN (1998), Fox Network, 'The Sky is my Canvas', 28 November.

Bairner, A. (2001), *Sport, Nationalism, and Globalization: European and North American Perspectives*, Albany, NY: State University of New York (SUNY) Press.

Baker, W. J. (1986), *Jesse Owens: An American Life*, New York: Free Press.

—— (2000), *If Christ Came to the Olympics*, Sydney: New South Wales University Press.

Bale, J. (1985), *Landscapes of Modern Sport*, London: Leicester University Press.

—— (2002), *Imagined Olympians: Body Culture and Colonial Representation in Rwanda*, Minneapolis: University of Minnesota Press.

—— and Maguire, J. (eds) (1994), *The Global Sports Arena: Athletic Talent Migration in an Interdependent World*, London: Frank Cass.

—— and Sang, J. (1996), *Kenyan Running: Movement Culture, Geography and Global Change*, London: Frank Cass.

Balibar, E. (2002), *Politics and the Other Scene*, London: Verso.

Bannister, R. (1997), 'Human Performance in Athletics: Scientific Aspects of Record Breaking', paper presented at the IAAF seminar 'Human Performance in Athletics: Limits and Possibilities', Budapest, 11–12 October.

Barney, R. K. (2000), 'Setting the Record Straight – Again: Dorando Pietri it is!', *Olympika*, 10: 129–30.

—— Wenn, S. R. and Martyn, S. G. (2002), *Selling the Five Rings: The International Olympic Committee and the Rise of Olympic Commercialism*, Salt Lake City: University of Utah Press.

Barreau, J-J. and Jaouen, G. (eds) (1998), *Eclipse et renaissance des jeux populaires*, 2nd edn, Karaez: FALSAB.

—— and Jaouen, G. (eds), (2001) *Les Jeux traditionnels en Europe: Education, culture et société au 21e siècle/Los juegos tradicionales en Europa. Educación, cultura y sociedad en el siglo 21*, Plonéour Ronarc'h: Confédération FALSAB.

Barthes, R. (1957), *Mythologies*, Paris: Le Seuil.

Bauman, Z. (1998), *Globalization: The Human Consequences*, Cambridge: Polity.

Beatty, J. (2002), 'Your ICBC Premiums Spent on Olympic Bid', *Vancouver Sun*, 7 November, www.canada.com.network

Beck, U. (2002), 'The Cosmopolitan Society and its Enemies', *Theory, Culture and Society*, 19: 17–44.

Behringer, W. and Ott-Koptschalijski, C. (1991), *Der Traum vom Fliegen: Zwischen Mythos und Technik*, Frankfurt/M.: S. Fischer.

Beinart, P. (1997), 'An Illusion for our Time', *New Republic*, 20 October.

Bell, D. (2000), 'International Games Resources at the AAF', http://www.aafla.org.

Benhabib, S. (2002), *The Claims of Culture: Equality and Diversity in the Global Era*, Princeton, NJ: Princeton University Press.

Benjamin, W. (1969a[1936]), 'On Some Motifs in Baudelaire', in H. Arendt and W. Benjamin, *Illuminations*, New York: Schocken.

—— (1969b[1936]), 'The Work of Art in the Age of Mechanical Reproduction', in H. Arendt and W. Benjamin, *Illuminations*, New York: Schocken.

Bennett, L. (2002), 'The Ugly Lack of Media Coverage of the "March for Our Lives,"', *JEDI for Women*, www.jedi4women.org, 8 February.

Berasconi, R. (1996), 'Casting the Slough: Fanon's New Humanism for a New Humanity', in L. Gordon, T. Sharpley-Whiting, and R. White (eds), *Fanon: A Critical Reader*, Oxford: Blackwell.

Bergson, H. (1991[1896]), *Matter and Memory*, trans. N. M. Paul and W. S. Palmer, New York: Zone Books.

Berkhofer, R. (1995), *Beyond the Great Story: History as Text and Discourse*, Cambridge, MA: Harvard University Press.

Bernett, H. (1980), 'Das Scheitern der Olympischen Spiele von 1940', *Stadion*, 6: 251–90.

—— (1985), 'Sportpublizistik im totalitären Staat, 1933–1945', *Stadion*, 11: 263–95.

—— (1986), 'Symbolik und Zeremoniell der XI. Olympischen Spiele in Berlin 1936', *Sportwissenschaft*, 16: 357–97.

Bernstein, A. (2002), 'Is it Time for a Victory Lap? Changes in the Media Coverage of Women in Sport', *International Review for the Sociology of Sport*, 37: 3–4, 415–28.

Bertels, U. (1993), *Das Fliegerspiel in Mexiko: Historische Entwicklung und gegenwärtige Erscheinungsformen*, Münster: Lit.

Bertine, K. (2002), 'Heavenly Bodies', *ESPN: The Magazine*, 22 July, 95–100.

Bhabha, H. K. (1994), *The Location of Culture*, London: Routledge.

Blake, A. (1996), *The Body Language: The Meaning of Modern Sport*, London: Lawrence and Wishart.

Blecking, D. (2001), *Polen, Türken, Sozialisten: Sport und soziale Bewegungen in Deutschland*, Münster: Lit.

Blinebury, F. (2000), 'Freeman Fulfills Hopes of her People in Sydney', *SportsLine*, 25 September, http://cbs.sportsline.com/

Bohrmann, H. (1993), *Presseanweisungen der Vorkriegszeit*, Munich: Saur.

Bompa, T.O. (1994), *Theory and Methodology of Training: The Key to Athletic Performance*, 3d edn, Dubuque, IA: Kendall/Hunt.

Booth, D. (1999), 'Gifts of Corruption: Ambiguities of Obligation in the Olympic Movement', *Olympika: The International Journal of Olympic Studies*, 8: 43–68.

—— and Tatz, C. (1994), 'Swimming with the Big Boys: The Politics of Sydney's 2000 Olympic Bid', *Sporting Traditions*, 11(1), 3–23.

—— and Tatz, C. (2000), *One-Eyed: A View of Australian Sport*, St Leonards, NSW: Allen and Unwin.

Borden, I. (2001), *Skateboarding, Space and the City: Architecture and the Body*, London: Berg.

Borghäll, J. and Copoeira, N. (1997), *Capoeira: Kampdans of livfilosifi fra Brasilien*, Odense: Odense Universitetsforlag.

Bouchard, C., Malina, R. M. and Pérusse, L. (1997), *Genetics of Fitness and Physical Performance*, Champaign, IL: Human Kinetics.

Boulongne, P-Y. (1975), *La Vie et l'oevre pédagogique de Pierre de Coubertin*, Ottawa: Leméac, 149–53.

—— (2000), 'Pierre de Coubertin and Women's Sport', *Olympic Review*, February–March, 23–6.

Bourdieu, P. (1986), 'The Struggle for Symbolic Order', *Theory, Culture, and Society*, 3(3): 35–51.

—— (1993), *The Field of Cultural Production*, New York: Columbia University Press.

Briggs, C. F. and Maverick, A. (1858) *The Story of the Telegraph . . .*, New York: Rudd and Carleton.

Brohm, J-M. (1978), *Sport: A Prison of Measured Time*, trans. I. Fraser, London: Ink Links.

—— (1986), 'Zum Verhältnis von Olympismus und Nationalsozialismus', in G. Gebauer (ed.), *Olympia-Berlin: Gewalt und Mythos in den Olympischen Spielen von Berlin 1936*, Berlin: Freie Universität Berlin.

Brown, D. (2001), 'Modern Sport, Modernism and the Cultural Manifesto: De Coubertin's *Revue Olympique*', *International Journal of the History of Sport*, 18(2), 78–109.

Brownell, S. (1995), *Training the Body for China: Sports in the Moral Order of the People's Republic*, Chicago: University of Chicago Press.

Bryman, A. (1995), *Disney and his Worlds*, London: Routledge.

—— (1999), 'The Disneyization of Society', *Sociological Review*, 47(1): 34–47.

Buck-Morss, S. (2002), 'A Global Public Sphere?', *Radical Philosophy*, 111: 2–10.

Burgin, V. (1996), *In/Different Space: Place and Memory in Visual Culture*, Berkeley, CA: University of California Press.

Burke, P. (1992), *History and Social Theory*, Cambridge: Polity.

Butchart, A. (1998), *The Anatomy of Power: European Constructions of the African Body*, London: Zed Books.

Butler, J., Laclau, E. and Zizek, S. (2000), *Contingency, Hegemony, Universality: Contemporary Dialogues on the Left*, London: Verso.

Byers, J. (2000), 'Beijing Marketing Advantage Overstated: Olympic Sponsors', *Toronto Star*, 28 November.

Cahn, S. (1995), *Coming on Strong: Gender and Sexuality in Twentieth-Century Women's Sport*, Cambridge, MA: Harvard University Press.

Caney, S. and Jones, P. (eds) (2001), *Human Rights and Global Diversity*, London: Frank Cass.

Carr, E. (1990[1961]), *What Is History?* Harmondsworth: Penguin.

Carrard, P. (1992), *Poetics of the New History: French Historical Discourse from Braudel to Chartier*, Baltimore, MD: Johns Hopkins University Press.

Cashman, R. (2002), *Sport in the National Imagination: Australian Sport in the Federation Decades*, Sydney: Walla Walla Press.

Cashmore, E. (2000), 'Modernity/Postmodernity', in E. Cashmore (ed.), *Sports Culture: An A–Z Guide*, London: Routledge.

Certeau, M. (1971), 'How is Christianity Thinkable Today?', *Theology Digest*, 19: 334–45.

Césaire, A. (2000[1955]), *Discourse on Colonialism*, New York: Monthly Review Press.

Chandler, J. (1991), 'TV Sport: Programmeming for Pleasure and Profit', unpublished paper, ASSH Conference, Canberra.

Chaney, D. (2002), *Cultural Change and Everyday Life*, London: Routledge.

Chang, H. (1994), 'Review of Giorgio Agamben, *The Coming Community*', *Postmodern Culture*, 4: 48–50, 60.

Chen, J. (1998), 'Snow Business', *Vogue*, March, 220–4.

China News Digest (1993), 'CND Survey Report on Readers' Attitude towards Beijing's Bid to Host 2000 Olympic Games,' Internet listserve, 12 May.

Citizen Activist Network – Olympic Education Project (2002), 'The Corporate Games: Why We are Protesting the Utah Winter Olympic Games', 7 January.

Class Action Lawsuit – Bid Corp and ICBC (2002), *Vancouver Independent Media Center*, www.vancouver.indymedia.org, 1 December.

Clifford, J. (1998), 'Mixed Feelings', in P. Cheah and B. Robbins (eds), *Cosmopolitics: Thinking and Feeling beyond the Nation*, Minneapolis: University of Minnesota Press.

Cole, C. (1998), 'Addiction, Exercise, and Cyborgs: Technologies of deviant bodies', in G. Rail (ed.), *Sport and Postmodern Times*, Albany, NY: SUNY.

Cordes, H. (1992), *Pencak Silat. Die Kampfkunst der Minangkabau und ihr kulturelles Umfeld*, Frankfurt/M.: Afra.

Coubertin, P. de (1898), 'Does Cosmopolitan Life Lead to International Friendliness?', *Review of Reviews*, 17: 429–34.

—— (1901), *Notes sur l'éducation publique*, Paris: Hachette.

—— (1902), 'La Charte de l'Amateurisme', *Revue Olympique*, 14–15.

—— (1908), 'Why I Revived the Olympic Games', in P. de Coubertin (2000), *Olympism: Selected Writings*, Lausanne: IOC.

—— (1911), 'Décoration, pyrotechnie, cortèges: Essai de Ruskianism sportif', *Revue Olympique*, 11.

—— (1913), *Essais de psychologie sportive*, Lausanne: Librairie Payot.

—— (1920), 'Autour de la VIIme Olympiade', in N. Müller (ed.), *Pierre de Coubertin: Textes Choisis*, vol. 2, Zurich: Weidmann.

—— (1931), 'La Valeur pédagogique du cérémonial olympique', *Bulletin du Bureau International de Pédagogie Sportive*, 7: 3–5.

—— (1966[1896]), *The Olympic Games of 1896*. Athens: Charles Beck.

—— (2000), *Pierre de Coubertin 1863–1937 – Olympism: Selected Writings*, editing director N. Müller, Lausanne: IOC.

Cox, G., Darcy, M. and Bounds, M. (1994), *The Olympics and Housing*, Sydney: Shelter NSW.

Culhane, J. (1983), *Walt Disney's Fantasia*, New York: Harry N. Abrams.

Culler, J. (1988), *Framing the Sign: Criticism and its Institutions*, Norman, OK: University of Oklahoma Press.

Cuvier, G. (1812), *Recherches sur les ossemens fossiles*, vol. 1, Paris: Detervill.

Darnton, R. (1999), 'The New Age of the Book', *New York Review of Books*, 18 March, http://www.nybooks.com/nyrev/index.html

Davies, T. (1997), *Humanism*, London: Routledge.

Dear, M. (2000), *The Postmodern Urban Condition*, Oxford: Blackwell.

De Certeau, M. (1974), *Culture in the Plural*, Minneapolis: University of Minnesota Press.

De Greiff, P. and Cronin, C. (eds) (2002), *Global Justice and Transnational Politics*, Cambridge, MA: MIT Press.

Deleuze, G. (1983), *L' Image-mouvement*, Paris: Les Editions de Minuit.

—— (1992), 'Mediators', in J. Crary and S. Kwinter (eds) *Incorporations*, New York: Urzone.

Denzin, N. (1989), *The Research Act*, 3rd edn, Englewood Cliffs, NJ: Prentice Hall.

Derrida, J. (2001), *On Cosmopolitanism and Forgiveness*, London: Routledge.

Dietrich, K. and Heinemann, K. (eds) (1989), *Der Nicht-sportliche Sport*, Schornorf: Karl Hofmann.

Donegan, L. (2002), 'Poor Pay the Price of Olympic Glory', *Observer*, www.observer.co.uk, 3 February.

Donnelly, P. (1996), 'Prolympism: Sport Monoculture as Crisis and Opportunity', *Quest*, 48: 25–42.

—— (1997), 'Young Athletes Need Child Law Protection', in P. Donnelly (ed.), *Taking Sport Seriously: Social Issues in Canadian Sport*, Toronto: Thompson.

—— (2000), 'Youth Sport in Canada: Problems and Resolutions,' in R. Jones and K. Armour (eds), *The Sociology of Sport in Practice*, London: Addison Wesley Longman.

Dorfman, A. and Mattelart, A. (1975), *How to Read Donald Duck – Imperialist Ideology in the Disney Comic*, New York: International General.

Dower, N. (2000), 'The Idea of Global Citizenship: A Sympathetic Assessment', *Global Society*, 14: 553–67.

Dreyfus, H. F. and Dreyfus, S. E. (1986), *Mind over Machine: The Power of Human Intuition and Expertise in the Age of the Computer*, Oxford: Blackwell.

Dyreson, M. (1998), *Making the American Team: Sport, Culture, and the Olympic Experience*, Urbana, IL: University of Illinois Press.

Eagleton, T. (2000), *The Idea of Culture*, Oxford: Blackwell.

Earthworker (2000), S11 Independent Media Center News, s11.indymedia.org

Eichberg, H. (1984), 'Olympic Sport – Neocolonization and Alternatives', *International Review for the Sociology of Sport*, 19: 97–106.

—— (1990), 'Forward Race and the Laughter of Pygmies: On Olympic Sport', in M. Teich and R. Porter (eds), *Fin de Siècle and its Legacy*, Cambridge: Cambridge University Press.

—— (1998), *Body Cultures: Essays on Sport, Space and Identity*, London: Routledge.

—— (2000), 'Life Cycle Sports: On Movement Culture and Ageing', in J. Hansen and N. K. Nielsen (eds), *Sports, Body and Health*, Odense: Odense University Press.

—— (2002), 'Three Dimensions of Playing the Game: About Mouth Pull and other Tug', in J. Nauright and V. Møller (eds), *The Essence of Sport*, Odense: University Press of Southern Denmark.

Elton, G. (1991), *Return to Essentials: Some Reflections on the Present State of Historical Study*, Cambridge: Cambridge University Press.

Emmendörfer-Brössler, C. (ed.) (1999), *Feste der Völker: Ein multikulturelles Lesebuch*, Amt für multikulturelle Angelegenheiten, Frankfurt/M.: VAS.

—— (2000), *Feste der Völker: Ein pädagogischer Leitfaden*, Amt für multikulturelle Angelegenheiten, Frankfurt/M.: VAS.

Entine, J. (2000), *Taboo: Why Black Athletes Dominate Sports and Why We're Afraid to Talk about it*, New York: Public Affairs.

Espy, R. (1979), *The Politics of the Olympic Games*, Berkeley, CA: University of California Press.

Eze, E. (ed.) (1997), *Race and the Enlightenment: A Reader*, Oxford: Blackwell.

—— (2001), *Achieving our Humanity: The Idea of a Postracial Future*, London: Routledge.

Fanon, F. (1961), *Les Damnés de la terre*, Paris: Maspero.

Fatès, Y. (1994), *Sport et Tiers-Monde*, Paris: PUF.

Favrholdt, D. (2000), *Æstetik og filosofi: Seks essays*, Copenhagen: Høst og søn.

Featherstone, M. (1995), *Undoing Culture: Globalization, Postmodernism and Identity*, London: Sage.

—— Patomämi, H., Tomlinson, J. and Venn, C. (eds) (2002), 'Special Issue on Cosmopolis', *Theory, Culture and Society*, 19 (1–2).

Fischer, D. H. (1970), *Historians' Fallacies: Toward a Logic of Historical Thought*, New York: Harper and Row.

Forsyth, J. (2002), 'Teepees and Tomahawks: Aboriginal Cultural Representation at the 1976 Olympic Games', in K. B. Wamsley, R. K. Barney and S. G. Martyn (eds), *The Global Nexus Engaged: Past, Present, Future Interdisciplinary Olympic Studies*, London: International Centre for Olympic Studies.

Foster, P. (2000), 'Olympian from the Equator Wins at a Crawl', *Daily Telegraph*, 20 September, 3.

Foster, S. (ed.) (1996), *Corporealities: Dancing Knowledge, Culture and Power*, London and New York: Routledge.

Foucault, M. (1972), *The Archaelogy of Knowledge*, trans. by A. Sheridan, London: Tavistock.

—— (1977), *Discipline and Punish: The Birth of the Prison*, trans. A. Sheridan, Harmondsworth: Penguin.

—— (1981a), 'The Order of Discourse', in R. Young (ed.), *Untying the Text: A Poststructuralist Reader*, London: Routledge.

—— (1981b), *The History of Sexuality: An Introduction*, trans. R. Hurley, Harmondsworth: Penguin.

Friedman, T. (2000), *The Lexus and the Olive Tree*, New York: Anchor.

Fröhlich, E. (ed.) (1987), *Die Tagebücher des Joseph Goebbels: Fragmente*, Munich: Saur.

Fukuyama, F. (1992), *The End of History*, London: Hamilton.

Galtung, J. (1982), 'Sport as Carrier of Deep Culture and Structure', *Current Research on Peace and Violence*, 2–3: 133–43.

—— (2002), 'September 11 2001: Diagnosis, Prognosis, Therapy', C. G. Jacobsen and K. F. Brand-Jacobsen, *Searching for Peace: The Road to TRANSCEND*, 2nd edn, London: Pluto. Also http://www.peace.ca/September11byjohangaltung.htm

Gay, P. (1974), *Style in History*, New York: Basic Books.

Gilroy, P. (2000), *Between Camps: Nations, Culture and the Allure of Race*, London: Allen Lane.

Giroux, H. A. (1999), *The Mouse that Roared – Disney and the End of Innocence*, Oxford: Rowman and Littlefield.

Givler, P. (1999), 'Books in Bytes? Not Yet', *Academe*, September–October, 61–2.

Gleick, J. (2000), *Faster: The Acceleration of Just About Everything*, New York: Vintage.

Goksøyr, M. (1990), '"One certainly expected a great deal more from the savages": The Anthropology Days in St. Louis, 1904, and their Aftermath', *International Journal of the History of Sport*, 7: 297–306.

Goldberg, D. (2002), *The Racial State*, Oxford: Blackwell.

Gordon, C. (ed.) (1980), *Michel Foucault: Power/Knowledge, Selected Interviews and Other Writings 1972–1977*, Brighton: Harvester Press.

Gordon, H. (1994), *Australia and the Olympic Games*, Brisbane: University of Queensland Press.

Gori, G. (2003), 'Italy: Mussolini's Boys at Hitler's Olympics', in A. Krüger and W. Murray (eds), *The Nazi Olympics: Sport, Politics, and Appeasement in the 1930s*, Urbana, IL: University of Illinois Press.

Gottschalk, L. (1969), *Understanding History: A Primer of Historical Method*, 2nd edn, New York: Alfred A. Knopf.

Gould, S. J. (1997), *The Mismeasure of Man*, 2nd edn, London: Penguin.

Graham, C. C. (1986), *Leni Riefenstahl and Olympia*, Metuchen, NJ: Scarecrow.

Greider, W. (1998), *One World, Ready or Not: The Manic Logic of Global Capitalism*, New York: Touchstone.

Gumbrect, H. (1998), Lecture on American Football, University of Copenhagen.

Guttmann, A. (1984), *The Games Must Go On: Avery Brundage and the Olympic Movement*, New York: Columbia University Press.

—— (1992), *The Olympics: A History of the Modern Games*, Urbana, IL: University of Illinois Press.

—— (1994), *Games and Empires: Modern Sports and Cultural Imperialism*, New York: Columbia University Press.

—— (2002), *The Olympics: A History of the Modern Games*, 2nd edn, Urbana, IL: University of Illinois Press.

Hambro, C. (2000), 'Toppidrett og topp forskning', *Dagbladet* (Oslo), 14 November, 3.

Hamrin, C. L. (1987), 'The Emergence of Humanism: Wang Ruoshui and the Critique of Socialist Alienation', in M. Goldman with T. Cheek and C. Hamrin (eds), *China's Intellectuals and the State: In Search of a New Relationship*, Cambridge, MA: Council on East Asian Studies/Harvard University.

Hansen, J. (1991), 'Fagenes Fest: Arbejderkultur og idræt', *Idrætshistorisk årbog*, 7: 113–34.

Hardt, M. and Negri, A. (2000), *Empire*, Cambridge, MA: Harvard University Press.

Hargreaves, J. (1994), *Sporting Females: Critical Issues in the History and Sociology of Women's Sports*, London: Routledge.

—— (2000), *Freedom for Catalonia? Catalan Nationalism, Spanish Identity and the Barcelona Olympic Games*, Cambridge: Cambridge University Press.

Hart-Davis, D. (1986), *Hitler's Games: The 1936 Olympics*, London: Hutchinson.

Harvey, D. (1989), *The Condition of Postmodernity*, Oxford: Blackwell.

Hegel, G. W. F. (1975[1830]), *Lectures on the Philosophy of World History*, Cambridge: Cambridge University Press.

Heinemann, K. (1998), 'The Cultural Secrets of Sport: Globalization or National Identity?', in J. Møller and J. S. Andersen (eds), *Society's Watchdog – or Showbiz' Pet? Inspiration for a Better Sports Journalism*, Vejle: DGI (Danish Gymnastics and Sports Associations).

—— and Schubert, M. (eds) (2001), *Sport und Gesellschaften*, Schorndorf: Hofmann 2001.

Heinilä, K. (1982), 'The Totalization Process in International Sport', *Sportwissenschaft*, 12: 235–54.

Held, D. (1995), *Democracy and the Global Order: From the Modern State to Cosmopolitan Governance*, Cambridge: Polity.

Hesse, B. (ed.) (2000), *Un/settled Multiculturalisms: Diasporas, Entanglements, Transruptions*, London: Zed Books.

Hill, C. R. (1996), *Olympic Politics: Athens to Atlanta 1896–1996*, 2nd edn, Manchester: Manchester University Press.

Hine, C. (2000), *Virtual Ethnography*, London: Sage.

Hoberman, J. (1986), *The Olympic Crisis: Sport, Politics and the Moral Order*, New Rochelle, NY: Caratzas.

—— (1991), 'Olympic Universalism and the Apartheid Issue', in F. Landry, M. Landry and M. Yerlès (eds), *Sport: The Third Millenium*, Sainte-Foi, Quebec: Les Presses de Université Laval.

—— (1992), *Mortal Engines: The Science of Performance and the Dehumanization of Sport*, New York: Free Press.

—— (1993), 'Sport and Ideology in the Post-Communist Age', in L. Allison (ed.), *The Changing Politics of Sport*, Manchester: Manchester University Press.

—— (1995), 'Toward a Theory of Olympic Internationalism', *Journal of Sport History*, 22: 1–37.

—— (1997), *Darwin's Athletes: How Sport has Damaged Black America and Preserved the Myth of Race*, Boston, MA: Mariner.

—— (2000), 'How Drug Testing Fails: The Politics of Doping Control,' in W. Wilson and E. Derse (eds), *Doping in Elite Sport: The Politics of Drugs in the Olympic Movement*, Champaign, IL: Human Kinetics.

Hobsbawm, E. and Ranger, T. (eds) (1983), *The Invention of Tradition*, Cambridge: Cambridge University Press.

Holmäng, P. O. (1992), 'International Sports Organizations 1919–25: Sweden and the German Question', *International Journal of the History of Sport*, 9: 455–66.

Howe, S. (1998) *Sick: A Cultural History of Snowboarding*, New York: St Martin's Press.

Howell, M. (1994), 'Comments on "Swimming with the Big Boys?"', *Sporting Traditions*, 11: 31–5.

Howell, R. and Howell, M. (1988), *Aussie Gold: The Story of Australia at the Olympics*, Melbourne: Brooks Waterloo.

Hughes, R. (2002), 'Koreans' Chests Swell with Pride', *International Herald Tribune*, 24 June.

Huizinga, J. (1955), *Homo Ludens: A Study of the Play Element in Culture*, London: Routledge and Kegan Paul.

Hulme, D. L. Jr (1990), *The Political Olympics: Moscow, Afghanistan, and the 1980 U.S. Boycott*, New York: Praeger.

Hunt, L. (ed.) (1989), *The New Cultural History*, Berkeley, CA: University of California Press.

Ignatieff, M. (2001), *Human Rights as Politics and Idolatry*, Princeton, NJ: Princeton University Press.

International Olympic Committee (1930), 'The Charter of Sport Reform', *Official Bulletin of the International Olympic Committee*, 3, 14.

—— (2003), *Olympic Charter*, http://www.olympic.org

James, C. L. R. (1963), *Beyond a Boundary*, New York: Pantheon.

James, H. (2001), *The End of Globalization: Lessons from the Great Depression*, Cambridge, MA: Harvard University Press.

Jameson, F. (1998), 'Notes on Globalization as a Philosophical Issue', in F. Jameson and M. Miyoshi (eds), *The Cultures of Globalization*, Durham, NC: Duke University Press.

Jardine, A. (1993), 'The Demise of Experience: Fiction as Stranger than Truth', in T. Docherty (ed.), *Postmodernism: A Reader*, New York: Columbia University Press.

Jarvie, G. (ed.) (1999), *Sport in the Making of Celtic Cultures*, London: Leicester University Press.

Jennings, A. (1996a), *The New Lords of the Rings*, London: Simon and Schuster.

—— (1996b), 'Sport, Kommerzialisierung und Postmoderne', in H. Sarkowicz (ed.), *Schneller, Höher, Weiter: Eine Geschichte des Sports*, Frankfurt/M: Insel.

—— and Sambrook, C. (2000), *The Great Olympic Swindle: When the World Wanted its Games Back*, London: Simon and Schuster.

Jokl, E., Karvonen, M., Kihlberg, J., Koskela, A. and Noro, L. (1956), *Sports in the Cultural Pattern of the World*, Helsinki: Institute of Occupational Health.

Joppke, C. and Lukes, S. (eds) (1999), *Multicultural Questions*, Oxford: Oxford University Press.

Kang, S-P., MacAloon, J. and Da Matta, R. (eds) (1987), *The Olympics and Cultural Exchange*, Seoul: Institute for Ethnological Studies, Hanyang University.

Katz, L. (1974), 'Power, Public Policy and the Environment: the Defeat of the 1976 Winter Olympics in Colorado', *Dissertation Abstracts International*, Part 1, 35: 12.

Kelly, D. (2000), 'So How Can the Punters Believe the CJ Hunters?', *Mirror*, 29 September, 57.

Kidd, B. (1984), 'The Myth of the Ancient Games', in A. Tomlinson and G. Whannel (eds), *Five Ring Circus: Money, Power and Politics at the Olympic Games*, London: Pluto.

—— (1992), 'The Toronto Olympic Commitment: Towards a Social Contract for the Olympic Games', *Olympika*, 1: 154–67.

—— (1996), 'Taking the Rhetoric Seriously: Proposals for Olympic Education', *Quest*, 58: 82–92.

King, F. (1991), *It's How You Play the Game: The Inside Story of the Calgary Olympics*, Calgary: Script.

Kister, T. and Weinreich, J. (eds) (2000), *Der olympische Sumpf: Die Machenschaften des IOC*, Munich: Piper.

Knudsen, K. A. (1895), *Om Sport: Indtryk fra en Rejse i England*, Copenhagen: Frimodt.

König, E. (1996), 'Kritik des Dopings: Der Nihilismus des technologischen Sports und die Antiquiertheit der Sportethik', in G. Gebauer (ed.), *Olympische Spiele: die andere Utopie der Moderne Olympia zwischen Kult und Droge*, Frankfurt/M.: Suhrkamp Verlag.

Kristof, N. D. (1999), 'At This Rate We'll Be Global in Another Hundred Years', *New York Times*, 23 May.

Krogshede, K. (1980), *Minder fra Ollerup og Gerlev*, Denmark: Delta.

Krüger, A. (1972), *Die Olympischen Spiele 1936 und die Weltmeinung*, Berlin: Bartels and Wernitz.

—— (1975a), *Sport und Politik: Vom Turnvater Jahn zum Staatsamateur*, Hannover: Fackelträger.

—— (1975b), *Dr. Theodor Lewald: Sportführer ins Dritte Reich*, Berlin: Bartels and Wernitz.

—— (1978), '"Fair Play for American Athletes". A Study in Anti-Semitism', *Canadian Journal of the History of Sport and Physical Education*, 9: 42–57.

—— (1982), 'Deutschland und die Olympische Bewegung (1918–1945)', in H. Ueberhorst (ed.), *Geschichte der Leibesübungen*, vol. 3, Berlin: Bartels and Wernitz.

—— (1994), '"Dann veranstalten wir eben rein deutsche Olympische Spiele": Die Olympischen Spiele 1936 als deutsches Nationalfest', in H. Breuer and R. Naul (eds), *Schwimmsport und Sportgeschichte: Zwischen Politik und Wissenschaft*, St Augustin: Academia.

—— (1996a), 'Sport, Kommerzialisierung und Postmoderne', in H. Sarkowicz (ed.), *Schneller, Höher, Weiter: Eine Geschichte des Sports*, Frankfurt/M.: Insel.

—— (1996b), '"The masses are much more sensitive to the perfection of the whole than to any separate details": The Influence of John Ruskin's Political Economy on Pierre de Coubertin', *Olympika*, 5: 25–44.

—— (1996c), 'Coubertin's Ruskianism', in R. K. Barney, S. G. Martyn, D. A. Brown and G. H. MacDonald (eds), *Olympic Perspectives: Third International Symposium for Olympic Research*, London, Ont.: University of Western Ontario.

—— (1997), 'Forgotten Decisions: The IOC on the Eve of World War I', *Olympika*, 6: 85–98.

—— (1999a), 'Strength through Joy: The Culture of Consent under Fascism, Nazism and Francoism', in J. Riordan and A. Krüger (eds), *The International Politics of Sport in the 20th Century*, London: Spon.

—— (1999b), 'The Unfinished Symphony: A History of the Olympic Games from Coubertin to Samaranch', in J. Riordan and A. Krüger (eds), *The International Politics of Sport in the 20th Century*, London: Spon.

—— (1999c), 'Ruskins politische Ökonomie als Basis für Coubertins moderne Olympischen Spiele?', in R. Naul and M. Lämmer (eds), *Willibald Gebhardt – Pionier der Olympischen Bewegung*, Aachen: Meyer and Meyer.

—— (1999d), '"Once the Olympics are through, We'll Beat up the Jew": German Jewish Sport 1898–1938 and the Anti-Semitic Discourse', *Journal of Sport History*, 26: 353–75.

—— (2000), 'Der Fahnenträger: Hans Fritsch (1911–1987)', in A. Krüger and B. Wedemeyer (eds), *Aus Biographien Sportgeschichte lernen: Festschrift zum 90. Geburtstag von Prof. Dr. Wilhelm Henze*, Hoya: NISH.

—— (2001), 'How "Goldhagen" was the German System of Physical Education, Turnen, and Sport', in A. Krüger, A. Teja and E. Trangbaek (eds), *Europäische Perspektiven zur Geschichte von Sport, Kultur und Politik*, Berlin: Tischler.

—— (2003), 'Germany: The Propaganda Machine', in A. Krüger and W. Murray (eds), *The Nazi Olympics: Sport, Politics, and Appeasement in the 1930s*, Urbana, IL: University of Illinois Press.

—— and Murray, W. (eds) (2003), *The Nazi Olympics: Sport, Politics, and Appeasement in the 1930s*, Urbana, IL: University of Illinois Press.

—— and Riordan, J. (eds) (1996), *The Story of Worker Sport*, Champaign, IL: Human Kinetics.

Kumar, K. (1995), *From Post-Industrial to Post-Modern Society: New Theories of the Contemporary World*, Oxford: Blackwell.

Kymlicka, W. (2001), *Politics in the Vernacular: Nationalism, Multiculturalism, and Citizenship*, Oxford: Oxford University Press.

Larsen, K. (2002), 'Effects of Professionalisation and Commercialisation of Elite Sport on Sport for All and Sports Consumption in Denmark', *Proceedings of the Ninth IOC 'Sport for All' Conference*, Arnhem, Netherlands, October 2002. Also in www.ifo-forsk.dk

—— (2003), *Idrætsdeltagelseog idrætsforbrug i Danmark*, Aarhus: Klim.

Larsen, N. and Gormsen, L. (1985), *Body Culture: A Monography of the Body Culture among the Sukuma in Tanzania*, Vejle: DDGU.

Larson, J. F., and Park, H. S. (1993), *Global Television and the Politics of the Seoul Olympics*, Boulder, CO: Westview Press.

Lenk, H. (1996), 'Auf der Suche nach dem verlorenen olympischen Geist', in G. Gebauer (ed.), *Olympische Spiele: die andere Utopie der Moderne Olympia zwischen Kult und Droge*, Frankfurt/M.: Suhrkamp Verlag.

Lennartz, K. (1994), 'Difficult Times: Baillet-Latour and Germany, 1931–1942', *Olympika*, 3: 99–106.

Lenskyj, H. (2000), *Inside the Olympic Industry: Power Polities, and Activism*, Albany, NY: SUNY Press.

—— (2002), *The Best Olympics Ever? Social Impacts of Sydney 2000*, Albany, NY: SUNY Press.

Levinson, D. and Christensen, K. (eds), (1996), *Encyclopedia of World Sport*, 3 vols, Santa Barbara, CA: ABC-CLIO.

Lévi-Strauss, C. (1966), *The Savage Mind*, Chicago: University of Chicago Press.

Liang L. J. (2000), *He Zhenliang yu Aolinpike (He Zhenliang and Olympism)*, Beijing: Olympic Publishing House.

Liu, L. H. (1995), *Translingual Practice: Literature, National Culture, and Translated Modernity, China, 1900–1937*, Stanford, CA: Stanford University Press.

Loland, S. (2001), 'Record Sports – An Ecological Critique and a Reconstruction', *Journal of the Philosophy of Sport*, 28: 127–39.

—— (2002), *Fair Play – A Moral Norm System*, London: Routledge.

Longman, J. (2002), 'How a Sport Galvanized South Korea', *New York Times*, 30 June.

Lord, C. and Watts, D. (2002), 'Equatorial Guinea Last to Embrace Eric the Eel', *The Times*, 20 September, 1–3.

Lucas, J. (1980), *The Modern Olympic Games*, South Brunswick, NJ: A. S. Barnes

—— (1982), 'Prelude to the Games of the Tenth Olympiad in Los Angeles 1932', *Southern California Quarterly*, 64: 313–7.

—— (1991), 'Ernest Lee Jahncke: The Expelling of an IOC Member', *Stadion*, 17: 53–78.

Ludwig, J. (1976), *Five Ring Circus*, Toronto: Doubleday.

Lukes, S. (1973), *Individualism*, Oxford: Blackwell.

Lyberg, W. S. (1996), *Fabulous One Hundred Years of the IOC: Facts, Figures and Much, Much More*, Lausanne: IOC.

Lyotard, J-F. (1984), *The Postmodern Condition: A Report on Knowledge*, Manchester: Manchester University Press.

Ma T. B. and Qin Y. Y. (2001), *Beijing 2008 – Shen Aode taiqian muhou (Beijing 2008 – Before and Behind the Scenes of the Olympic Bid)*, Beijing: Beijing University of Physical Culture Publishing House.

MacAloon, J. (1981), *This Great Symbol: Pierre de Coubertin and the Origins of the Modern Olympic Games*, Chicago: University of Chicago Press.

—— (1984), 'Olympic Games and the Theory of Spectacle in Modern Societies', in J. MacAloon (ed.), *Rite, Drama, Festival, Spectacle*, Philadelphia, PA: Institute of Human Issues.

—— (1988), 'Double Visions: Olympic Games and American Culture', in J. Segrave and D. Chu (eds), *The Olympic Games in Transition*, Champain, IL: Human Kinetics.

—— (1992), 'The Ethnographic Imperative in Comparative Olympic Research', *Sociology of Sport Journal*, 4: 103–15.

—— (1995), 'Interval Training', in S. Leigh Foster (ed.), *Choreographing History*, Bloomington, IN: Indiana University Press.

—— (1996), 'Olympic Ceremonies as a Setting for Intercultural Exchange', in M. de Moragas, J. MacAloon and M. Llines (eds), *Olympic Ceremonies: Historical Continuity and Cultural Exchange*, Barcelona: Centre d'Estudis Olimpics y de l'Esport..

—— (2000), 'Volunteers, Global Society and the Olympic Movement', in M. de Moragas, A. B. Moreno and N. Puig (eds), *Volunteers, Global Society and the Olympic Movement – International Symposium*, Lausanne: IOC.

McCorduck, P. (1996), 'Sex, Lies and Avatars', *Wired*, April, 106–10, 158–65.

McGrath, B. (2002), 'Gutter Mouth: Pete Weber Wants to Make Bowling the New Wrestling', *The New Yorker*, 23 September, 48–54.

Macintosh, D. and Whitson, D. (1990), *The Game Planners: Transforming Canada's Sport System*, Montreal and Kingston: McGill-Queen's University Press.

McKay, J., Hutchins, B. and Mikoza, J. (2000), '"Shame and Scandal in the Family": Australian Media Narratives of the IOC/SOCOG Scandal Spiral', *Olympika*, 9: 25–48.

Mackinnon, J. (2000), 'The Usual Suspects', *This Magazine*, July–August, 27–9.

Maffesoli, M. (1996), *The Time of the Tribes*, London: Sage.

Maguire, J. (1999), *Global Sport: Identities, Societies, Civilizations*, Cambridge: Polity.

Malkki, L. (1994), 'Citizens of Humanity: Internationalism and the Imagined Community of Nations', *Diaspora*, 3(1): 41–68.

Mandelbrot, B. (1982), *The Fractal Geometry of Nature*, San Francisco, CA: Freeman.

Mandell, R. (1971), *The Nazi Olympics*, New York: Macmillan.

Mangan, J. A. (ed.) (1996), *Tribal Identities: Nationalism, Europe, Sport*, London: Frank Cass.

Marriott, D. (2000), *On Black Men*, Edinburgh: Edinburgh University Press.

Martin, D. (ed.) (1991), *Handbuch Trainingslehre*, Schorndorf: Hofman.

—— and Gynn, R. (2000), *The Olympic Marathon: The History and Drama of Sport's Most Challenging Event*, Champaign, IL: Human Kinetics.

Marwick, A. (1998), *The Sixties: Cultural Revolution in Britain, France, Italy, and the United States, c.1958 – c.1974*, Oxford: Oxford University Press.

Matthews, G. R. (1980), 'The Controversial Olympic Games of 1908 as Viewed by the *New York Times* and the *Times* of London', *Journal of Sport History*, 7: 40–53.

Maurras, C. (1929), 'Les Nations dans le stade et la course de Marathon', *Le Voyage d'Athènes*, Paris: Flammarion.

Milbank, J. (1993), *Theology and Social Theory: Beyond Secular Reason*, Oxford: Blackwell.

—— and Pickstock, C. (2001), *Truth in Aquinas*, London and New York: Routledge.

—— Ward, G. and Pickstock, C. (eds) (1999), *Radical Orthodoxy*, London and New York: Routledge.

Millet, L. (1995), 'The Games of the City', in M. de Moragas and M. Botella (eds), *The Keys to Success – The Social, Sporting, Economic and Communications Impact of Barcelona '92*, Barcelona: Centre for Olympic Studies and Sport, Autonomous University of Barcelona.

Møller, V. (2003), 'What is Sport: Outline to a Redefinition', in V. Møller and J. Nauright (eds), *The Essence of Sport*, Odense: University Press of South Denmark.

Montalban, M. (1992), *Barcelonas*, trans. A. Robinson, London: Verso.

Moragas Spà, M. de, Rivenburgh, N. K. and Larson, J. F. (1995), *Television in the Olympics*, London: John Libbey.

Mouffe, C. (2000), *The Democratic Paradox*, London: Verso.

Muller, K. (1970), 'Land Diving with the Pentecost Islanders', *National Geographic Magazine*, December, 799–817.

Müller, N. (ed.) (2000), *Pierre de Coubertin 1863–1937 – Olympism: Selected Writings*, Lausanne: IOC.

Mulling, C. (1990), 'Dissidents' Perspective of the 1988 Seoul Olympics', in *Proceedings of Seoul Olympiad Anniversary Conference, Toward One World Beyond All Barriers*, 394–407.

Munslow, A. (1997), *Deconstructing History*, London: Routledge.

Munthe, C. (2000), 'Selected Champions: Making Winners in the Age of Genetic Technology', in T. Tännsjö and C. Tamburrini (eds), *Values in Sport*, London: Spon.

Nakamura, T. (2003), 'Japan: The Future in the Past', in A. Krüger and W. Murray (eds), *The Nazi Olympics: Sport, Politics, and Appeasement in the 1930s*, Urbana, IL: University of Illinois Press.

New York Herald Tribune (1933), 8 June,1: 6.

New York Times (1933a), 19 April, 21: 6.

—— (1933b), 20 April, 16: 5.

—— (1933c), 17 May, 21: 5.

—— (1933d), 9 May, 24: 5.

—— (1933e), 29 May,11: 6.

—— (1933f), 2 June, 24: 6.

—— (1933g), 5 June, 1: 3.

—— (1933h), 8 June, 1: 4.

—— (1933i), 9 June, 16: 4

Nielsen, N. K. (2002), 'Alting har sin tid – idrættens afsked med 1900–tallet', in C. Hauerberg (ed.), *Idrætshøjskolen i Sønderborg 50 år*, Sønderborg.

Nirre, R. (2001), 'The Genealogy of Dead Space', *Theory, Technology and Culture*, 24: 1–2.

Novak, M. (1976), *The Joy of Sports: End Zones, Bases, Baskets, Balls, and the Consecration of the American Spirit*, New York: Basic Books.

Novick, P. (1988), *That Noble Dream: The 'Objectivity Quest' and the American Historical Profession*, Cambridge: Cambridge University Press.

Nutrition (2001), Idea for February, posting to Utah Indymedia Website, www.utah. indymedia.org, 3 August.

Oates, J. C. (1987), *On Boxing*, London: Bloomsbury.

Official Report (1988), Edmonton, XV Olympic Winter Games and Calgary Olympic Development Corporation.

Olds, K. (1998), 'Urban Mega-events, Evictions and Housing Rights: the Canadian Case', unpublished paper, Department of Geography, University of Singapore, www.breadnotcircuses.org

Olympic Programme Commission (2002), *Review of the Olympic Programme and the Recommendations on the Programme of the Games of the XXIX Olympiad, Beijing 2008*, IOC Executive Board, August, www.olympic.org

Olympics officials keep eyes on protesters (2002), *Global Policy Forum*, www. globalpolicy.org

Omotunde, S. (1994), 'Editor's Note', *African Concord* (Lagos), 28 March, 6.

Organisationskomitee für die IV. Olympischen Winterspiele (ed.) (1936), *Amtlicher Bericht*, Berlin: Limpert.

Organisationskomitee für die XI. Olympischen Sommerspiele (ed.) (1937), *Amtlicher Bericht*, 2 vols, Berlin: Limpert.

Orwell, G. (1949), *Nineteen Eighty-four: A Novel*, New York: Harcourt, Brace.

Owens, J. (1970), *Blackthink: My Life as Black Man and White Man*, New York: William Morrow.

Packer, G. (2002), 'When Here Sees There', *New York Times Magazine*, 21 April.

Pan, P. P. (2001), 'Beijing's Olympic Dream-in-Progress: Social Issues, Facilities among Hurdles for 2008', *Washington Post Foreign Service*, 6 July, A01.

Parekh, B. (2000), *Rethinking Multiculturalism: Cultural Diversity and Political Theory*, Basingstoke: Palgrave.

Parks, B. (1998), 'Fetish: Transition', *Wired*, April, 51.

Parks, T. (2003), *A Season with Verona; Travels around Italy in Search of Illusion, National Character and . . . Goals!*, London: Vintage.

Parratt, C. (1998), 'Reflecting on Sport History in the 1990s', *Sport History Review*, 29: 4–17.

Parsons, T. (1966), *Societies: Evolutionary and Comparative Perspectives*, Englewood Cliffs, NJ: Prentice Hall.

Paton, G. and Barney, R. K. (2002), 'Adolf Hitler, Carl Diem, Werner Klingeberg, and the Thousand Year Reich: Nazi Germany and its Envisioned Post-War Olympic World,' in K. B. Wamsley, R. K. Barney and S. G. Martyn (eds), *The Global Nexus Engaged: Past, Present, Future Interdisciplinary Olympic Studies*, London: International Centre for Olympic Studies.

Pätzold, U. (2000), *Blüte, Frucht und Kern: Bewegungsformen und Musikstile im Bereich des Pencak Silat in West-Java und West-Sumatra*, Bonn: Holos.

Paz, O. (1972), *The Other Mexico: Critique of the Pyramid*, New York: Grove.

Pedersen, K. (1999), *'Det har bare vært naturlig.' Friluftsliv, kjønn og kulturelle brytninger*, Alta: Høgskolen i Finnmark.

Pesce, M. (2000), *The Playful World: How Technology is Transforming our Imagination*, New York: Ballantine.

Pfeiffer, R. and Krüger, A. (1995), 'Theodor Lewald: Eine Karriere im Dienste des Vaterlands oder die vergebliche Suche nach der jüdischen Identität eines "Halbjuden"', *Menora: Jahrbuch für deutsch-jüdische Geschichte*, Munich: Piper.

Pfister, G. (ed.) (1997), *Traditional Games*, special issue of *Journal of Comparative Physical Education and Sport*, 19.

—— Niewerth, T. and Steins, G. (eds) (1996), *Spiele der Welt im Spannungsfeld von Tradition und Moderne*, 2nd ISHPES Congress Games of the World, St Augustin: Academia.

Philips, D. (1999), 'Narrativised Spaces: The Functions of the Story in the Theme Park', in D. Crouch (ed.), *Leisure/Tourism Geographies: Practices and Geographical Knowledge*, London, Routledge, 91–108.

Phillips, D. (1992), *Australian Women at the Olympic Games 1912–92*, Sydney: Kangaroo Press.

Phillips, M. (2003), 'A Critical Appraisal of Narrative in Sport History: Reading the Lifesaving Debate', *Journal of Sport History*, 30.

Pickstock, C. (1998), *After Writing: On the Liturgical Consummation of Philosophy*, Malden, MA and Oxford: Blackwell.

Pieper, J. (1998[1952]), *Leisure: The Basis of Culture*, South Bend, IN: South Bend Press.

Pirie, G. (1961), *Running Wild*, London: W. H. Allen.

Pollock, S., Bhabha, H., Breckenridge, C. and Chakrabarty, D. (2002), 'Cosmopolitanisms', in C. Breckenridge, S. Pollock, H. Bhabha and D. Chakrabarty (eds), *Cosmopolitanism*, Durham, NC: Duke University Press.

Postan, M. (1971), *Facts and Relevance: Essays on Historical Method*, Cambridge: Cambridge University Press.

Preuss, H. (2000), *Economics of the Olympic Games: Hosting the Games 1972–2000*, Sydney: Walla Walla Press.

Rail, G. (1998), 'Seismography of the Postmodern Condition: Three Theses on the Implosion of Sport', in G. Rail (ed.), *Sport and Postmodern Times*, Albany, NY: SUNY Press.

Rashid, A. (2000), *Taliban: Islam, Oil and the New Great Game in Central Asia*, London: Tauris.

Rawls, J. (1971), *A Theory of Justice*, Cambridge: Cambridge University Press.

Rigauer, B. (1981), *Sport and Work*, New York: Columbia University Press.

Rinehart, R. E. (1998), *Players All: Performances in Contemporary Sport*, Bloomington, IN: Indiana University Press.

Riordan, J. (1993), 'The Rise and Fall of Soviet Olympic Champions', *Olympika*, 2: 25–44.

Ritzer, G. (2000), *The McDonaldization of Society – New Century Edition*, London: Pine Forge Press.

Robbins, B. (1998), 'Introduction Part 1: Actually Existing Cosmopolitanism', in P. Cheah and B. Robbins (eds), *Cosmopolitics: Thinking and Feeling beyond the Nation*, London: University of Minnesota Press.

Robbins, L. (2002), 'SlamBall is latest X Game', *New York Times News Service*, 23 August, http://extratv.warnerbros.com/dailynews/extra/04_02/04_23d.html

Roberts, J. M., Arth, M. J. and Bush, R. R. (1959), 'Games in Culture', *American Anthropologist*, 6: 597–605.

Roche, M. (2000), *Mega-events and Modernity: Olympics and Expos in the Growth of Global Culture*, London: Routledge.

Rodda, J. (1979), 'London 1908', in L. Killanin and J. Rodda (eds), *The Olympic Games*, London: MacDonald and Jane's.

Rogge, J. (1999), 'The Olympics in the Next Millennium', unpublished keynote address, Centre for Olympic Studies, University of New South Wales, Sydney.

Rosenberg, D. (2002), 'The Body, Technology and Record Breaking: Implications for Elite Record Sports', paper presented at the 2002 meeting of the International Association for the Philosophy of Sport, Penn State University, October.

Roughton, B. (2001), 'Two Major Decisions Top IOC's Agenda', Associated Press, 8 July.

Rürup, R. (1996), *Die Olympischen Spiele und der Nationalsozialismus*, Berlin: Stiftung Topographie des Terrors.

Rutheiser, D. (1996), *Imagineering Atlanta*, New York: Verso.

Ryan, J. (1995), *Little Girls in Pretty Boxes: The Making and Breaking of Elite Gymnasts and Figure Skaters*, New York: Warner.

Salt Lake Impact 2002 (2002), Report Card for the Salt Lake Organizing Committee and the City of Salt Lake, February.

Sansone, D. (1988), *Greek Athletics and the Genesis of Sport*, Berkeley, CA: University of California Press.

Sartre, J-P. (1967[1961]), 'Preface', in F. Fanon, *The Wretched of the Earth*, London: Penguin.

—— (1973), *Existentialism and Humanism*, London: Methuen.

—— (2001), *Colonialism and Neocolonialism*, London: Routledge.

Schmidt, R. A. (1991), *Motor Learning and Performance: From Principles to Practice*, Champaign, IL: Human Kinetics.

Schultz Jørgensen, S. (2002), *Industry or independence? Survey of the Scandinavian Sports Press*, Copenhagen: Monday Morning, special print.

Senn, A. (1999), *Power, Politics, and the Olympic Games*, Champaign, IL: Human Kinetics.

Shilling, C. (1993), *The Body and Social Theory*, London: Sage.

Sillitoe, A. (1975), *Mountains and Caverns*, London: W. H. Allen.

Simson, V. and Jennings, A. (1992), *The Lords of the Rings: Power, Money and Drugs in the Modern Olympics*, London: Simon and Schuster.

Slowikowski Sydnor, S. (1993), 'The Culture of Nintendo: Another Look', *Play Theory and Research*, 1: 1–16.

Smith, A. (2002), 'The Empire Strikes Back', Radio National [Australia], *The Sports Factor*, 26 July.

Smith, D. (1991), *The Rise of Historical Sociology*, Cambridge: Polity.

Smith, P. (1992), 'Letter from Japan', *The New Yorker*, 13 April, 89–99.

Sombart, W. (1929), 'Economic Theory and Economic History', *Economic History Review*, 2: 1–19.

Soper, K. (1986), *Humanism and Anti-Humanism*, London: Hutchinson.

Sparkes, A. (2002), *Telling Tales in Sport and Physical Activity*, Windsor: Human Kinetics.

Springwood, C. F. (1995), *From Cooperstown to Dyersville: A Geography of Baseball Nostalgia*, Boulder, CO: Westwood Press.

Standage, T. (1999), *The Victorian Internet*, New York: Berkley Books.

Stanford, M. (1994), *A Companion to the Study of History*, Oxford: Basil Blackwell.

Stevenson, N. (2002), 'Cosmopolitanism, Multiculturalism and Citizenship', *Sociological Research Online*, 17, http://www.socresonline.org.uk/7/1/stevenson.html

Stille, A. (2001), 'Globalization Now, a Sequel of Sorts', *New York Times*, 11 August.

Stinchcombe, A. (1978), *Theoretical Methods in Social History*, New York: Academic Press.

Stoler, A. L. and Cooper, F. (1997), 'Between Metropole and Colony: Rethinking a Research Agenda', in F. Cooper and A. L. Stoler (eds) *Tensions of Empire: Colonial Cultures in a Bourgeois World*, Berkeley, CA: University of California Press.

Strinati, D. (1994), 'Postmodernism and Popular Culture', in J. Storey (ed.), *Cultural Theory and Popular Culture*, Hemel Hempstead: Harvester Wheatsheaf.

Struna, N. (1986), 'E. P. Thompson's Notion of "Context" and the Writing of Physical Education and Sport History', *Quest*, 38: 22–32.

—— (1996), 'Historical Research in Physical Activity', in J. Thomas and J. Nelson (eds), *Research Methods in Physical Activity*, Champaign, IL: Human Kinetics.

Sudjic, D. (1992), *The 100 Mile City*, London: Deutsch.

Sugden, A., Tomlinson, A. and McCartan, E. (1990), 'The Making and Remaking of White Lightening in Cuba: Politics, Sport and Physical Education Thirty Years after the Revolution', *Arena Review*, 14: 101–9.

Sutton-Smith, B. (1986), *Toys as Culture*, New York: Gardner Press.

Sydnor Slowikowski, S. (1989), 'Ancient Sport Symbols and Postmodern Tradition', in R. Renson and M. Lämmer (eds), *The Olympic Games through the Ages: Greek Antiquity and its Impact on Modern Sport*, Athens: Hellenic Sports Research Institute.

Szerszynski, B. and Urry, J. (2002), 'Cultures of Cosmopolitanism', *Sociological Review*, 50: 461–81.

Tamburrini, C. (2000), *The 'Hand of God'? Essays in the Philosophy of Sports*, Gothenburg: University of Gothenburg Press.

Tännsjö, T. (2000), 'Is it Fascistoid to Admire Sports Heroes?', in T. Tännsjö and C. Tamburrini (eds), *Values in Sport: Elitism, Nationalism, Gender Equality, and the Scientific Manufacture of Winners*, London: Spon.

Tatz, C. (1995), *Obstacle Race: Aborigines in Sport*, Sydney: University of New South Wales Press.

Taylor, P. (1994), 'The State as a Leaking Container: Territoriality in the Modern World-System', *Progress in Human Geography*, 18: 151–62.

Teichler, H. (1976), 'Berlin 1936 – Ein Sieg der NS Propaganda?' *Stadion*, 2: 265–306.

Todorov, T. (2002), *Imperfect Garden: The Legacy of Humanism*, Princeton, NJ: Princeton University Press.

Tomlinson, A. (1984), 'De Coubertin and the Modern Olympic Games', in A. Tomlinson and G. Whannel (eds), *Five-Ring Circus: Money, Power and Politics at the Olympic Games*, London: Pluto.

—— (2000a), 'From the Field: Sydney 2000 and an Olympics Research Agenda', in M. Keech and G. McFee (eds), *Issues and Values in Sport and Leisure Cultures*, Aachen and Oxford: Meyer and Meyer.

—— (2000b), 'Carrying the Torch for Whom? Symbolic Power and Olympic Ceremony', in K. Schaffer and S. Smith (eds), *The Olympics at the Millennium: Power, Politics, and the Games*, New Brunswick, NJ: Rutgers University Press.

—— (2002), 'The Little Olympics', *Australia and New Zealand Association for Leisure Studies Newsletter*, 26 (April), 12–14.

—— (2004a), 'Olympic Survivals', in L. Allison (ed.), *The Global Politics of Sport*, London: Routledge.

—— (2004b), *Sport and Leisure Cultures: Global, National and Local Dimensions*, Minneapolis: University of Minnesota Press.

—— (2004c), 'The Making of the Global Sports Economy: ISL, Adidas and the Rise of the Corporate Player in World Sport', in D. Andrews and M. Silk (eds), *Corporate Nationalism*, Oxford: Berg.

—— and Whannel, G. (eds) (1984), *Five-Ring Circus: Money, Power and Politics at the Olympic Games*, London: Pluto.

Tosh, J. (1991), *The Pursuit of History: Aims, Methods and New Directions in the Study of Modern History*, 2nd edn, London: Longman.

Trangbæk, E. (1991), 'Kunsten "at svæve": Akrobatik, videnskab og drømme', *Idrætshistorisk Årbog*, 7: 48–60.

Truss, L. (2000), 'Eric is the Star of the New Olympic Movement', *The Times*, 20 September, 10.

Turkle, S. (1995), *Life on the Screen*, New York: Simon and Schuster.

United Nations (2000) http://www.un.org/news/press/docs/2002/sgsm8262.doc.htm

Urry, J. (2003), *Global Complexity*, Cambridge: Polity.

Van Bottenburg, M. (2001), *Global Games*, Urbana, IL: University of Illinois Press.

Vertinsky, P. (1994), *The Eternally Wounded Woman: Women, Doctors, and Exercise in the Late Nineteenth Century*, Urbana, IL: University of Illinois Press.

Vestergard, A. (2003), *The Elusive Quest: Gaining and Maintaining a Place on the Olympic Programme*, Sydney: Centre for Olympic Studies, University of New South Wales.

Vettenniemi, E. (2002), 'Kato neekeri hiihtää! Kiista modernen urheilun leviämisestä', *Finlands Idrottshistoriska Förenings årsbok, 2001/02*, Helsinki, 151–166 (with English summary).

Vinokur, M. B. (1988), *More than a Game: Sport and Politics*, Westport, CT: Greenwood.

Virilio, P. (1997), *Open Sky*, London and New York: Verso.

Voy, R. (1991), *Drugs, Sports and Politics*, Champaign, IL: Leisure Press.

Waddington, I. (2000), *Sport, Health and Drugs*, London: Spon.

Wagstaff, S. (1998), 'Street Cred: Smooth in the Crud', *Wired*, April, 129.

Walkom, T. (1999), 'The Olympic Myth of Calgary', *Star*, 8 February, 8.

Wallechinsky, D. (2000), *The Complete Book of the Olympics – 2000 Edition*, London: Aurum Press.

Walsh, W. (1974), 'Colligatory Concepts in History', in P. Gardiner (ed.), *The Philosophy of History*, Oxford: Oxford University Press.

Wamsley, K. B. and Heine, M. K. (1996), 'Tradition, Modernity, and the Construction of Civic Identity: The Calgary Olympics', *Olympika: The International Journal of Olympic Studies*, 5: 81–90.

—— and Schule, G. (2000), ' Rogues and Bedfellows: The IOC and the Incorporation of the FSFI', in K. B. Wamsley, S. G. Martyn, G. H. MacDonald and R. K. Barney (eds), *Bridging Three Centuries: Intellectual Crossroads and the Modern Olympic Movement*, London: International Centre for Olympic Studies.

Ward, G. (1997a), 'Introduction, or, A Guide to Theological Thinking in Cyberspace', in G. Ward (ed.), *The Postmodern God: A Theological Reader*, Oxford: Blackwell.

—— (ed.) (1997b), *The Postmodern God: A Theological Reader*, Oxford: Blackwell.

—— (2000), *Cities of God*, New York: Routledge.

—— (ed.) (2001), *The Blackwell Companion to Postmodern Theology*, Oxford: Blackwell.

Wasko, J. (2001), *Understanding Disney – The Manufacture of Fantasy*, Cambridge: Polity.

Waters, M. (1994), *Modern Sociological Theory*, London: Sage.

Watts, I. (2002), 'Selling Australia: Cathy Freeman and the Construction of an Australian Identity', in K. B. Wamsley, R. K. Barney and S. G. Martyn (eds), *The Global Nexus Engaged: Past, Present, Future Interdisciplinary Olympic Studies*, London: International Centre for Olympic Studies.

Wensing, E. H. and Bruce, T. (2003), 'Bending the Rules: Media Representations of Gender during an International Sporting Event', *International Review for the Sociology of Sport*, 38, 4, 387–96.

Werge, L. (2000), *Den olympiske bombe*, Aarhus: Klim.

White, H. (1973), *Metahistory: The Historical Imagination in Nineteenth-century Europe*, Baltimore, MD: Johns Hopkins University Press.

—— (1978), *Tropics of Discourse: Essays in Cultural Criticism*, Baltimore, MD: Johns Hopkins University Press.

Whitson, D. and Macintosh, D. (1996), 'The Global Circus: International Sport, Tourism, and the Marketing of Cities', *Journal of Sport and Social Issues*, 23: 278–95.

Williams, R. (2000), 'Athenian's Fast Ascent defies Campbell charge', *Guardian*, 29 September, 2.

Wise, T. (2002), 'The Invisible Whiteness of the Olympic Beer Riot', *AlterNet*, 25 February, www.AlterNet.org

Wright, G. (1978), 'The Political Economy of the Montreal Olympic Games', *Journal of Sport and Social Issues*, 2: 13–18.

Wuhrmann, S. (2002), 'Der Fall Swissair – ein Fall Schweiz', *Neue Zürcher Zeitung*, 11 April.

Wynsberghe, R. van and Ritchie, I. (1998), '(Ir),relevant Ring: The Symbolic Consumption of the Olympic Logo in Postmodern Media Culture', in G. Rail (ed.), *Sport and Postmodern Times*, Albany, NY: SUNY Press.

Wyschogrod, E. (1998), *An Ethics of Remembering: History, Heterology and the Nameless Others*, Chicago and London: Blackwell.

Young, D. (1984), *The Olympic Myth of Greek Amateur Athletics*, Chicago: Ares.

—— (1996), *The Modern Olympics: A Struggle for Revival*, Baltimore, MD: Johns Hopkins University Press.

Young, I. (2000), *Inclusion and Democracy*, Oxford: Oxford University Press.

Zukin, S. (1991), *Landscapes of Power – From Detroit to Disney World*, Berkeley, CA: University of California Press.

Index